Mexico

LATIN AMERICAN HISTORIES

JAMES R. SCOBIE, EDITOR

James R. Scobie: Argentina: A City and a Nation

Rollie E. Poppino: Brazil: The Land and People

Charles C. Cumberland: Mexico: The Struggle for Modernity

Mexico

THE STRUGGLE FOR MODERNITY

CHARLES C. CUMBERLAND

Oxford University Press
London Oxford New York

OXFORD UNIVERSITY PRESS

Oxford London New York
Glasgow Toronto Melbourne Wellington
Cape Town Salisbury Ibadan Nairobi Lusaka Addis Ababa
Bombay Calcutta Madras Karachi Lahore Dacca
Kuala Lumpur Hong Kong Tokyo

Library of Congress Catalogue Card Number: 68-15891
First published by Oxford University Press, New York, 1968
First issued as an Oxford University Press paperback, 1968
This reprint, 1971

Printed in the United States of America

Preface

Between 1940 and 1960 phenomenal change took place in Mexico, but it came only after an earlier revolution remarkable as much for its violence as for its program. The costs of that conflagration—in lives, in property, in trauma—cannot be calculated, nor can the stimuli for the destruction be fixed with precision. But revolutions of such ferocity are spawned by deep-seated ills, not passing fancies. This book is an attempt to clarify and to explain the social and economic issues which gave the Mexican Revolution such a distinctive stamp, and to account for the direction and the nature of the change. It is an attempt to view nearly half a millennium of Mexican history through the eyes of those who suffered from inequality and who finally exploded with incredible violence.

Two great themes may be discovered in this four-and-a-half-century Mexican experience. The first is that a people cannot be forever subjugated. Depending on a vast array of cultural factors, the "underdogs" will be either patient or impatient for change, but ultimately they will have it either peacefully or violently. The second is that no "race" or social class or segment of society has a monopoly on ability, and that the most precious natural resource for any nation is its people. Social attitudes by the dominant class create social institutions, and social institutions in turn determine whether the innate collective abilities are effectively or minimally used. Every nation in the world today has something to learn from the Mexican experience, and it boils down to this: attitudes, not mineral resources, are the key to economic development and social change.

The temptations to compare Mexican developments with those of other countries have been great, but for the most part they have been avoided; such comparisons would have been profitable, but they would have resulted in a different book. The criticisms levelled here at the mentality and the institutions which prevented healthy evolutionary change in Mexico should not be interpreted as implying that contemporary conditions in other regions were better, or that the leaders of other nations were endowed with greater imagination and foresight. But the fact that the seventeenth-century Englishman trafficked in human flesh does not mitigate the disastrous seventeenth-century Spanish treatment of the Mexican *indigene;* both were profitable, both were supported by the dominant leaders, and both were conducive to enormous problems for later generations.

To those graduate students who by adroit questioning helped me clarify my own thinking I owe a great and lasting debt. I am particularly grateful to Mrs. Robin Ulmer, David Bailey, Robert Hawthorne and Paul Kramer, all of whom aided me more than they know. And to those hundreds of unnamed Mexicans with whom I talked about conditions in their country, and who gave me much food for thought, I give my warmest thanks.

C.C.C.

Okemos, Michigan
January 1968

Contents

Maps

Tables

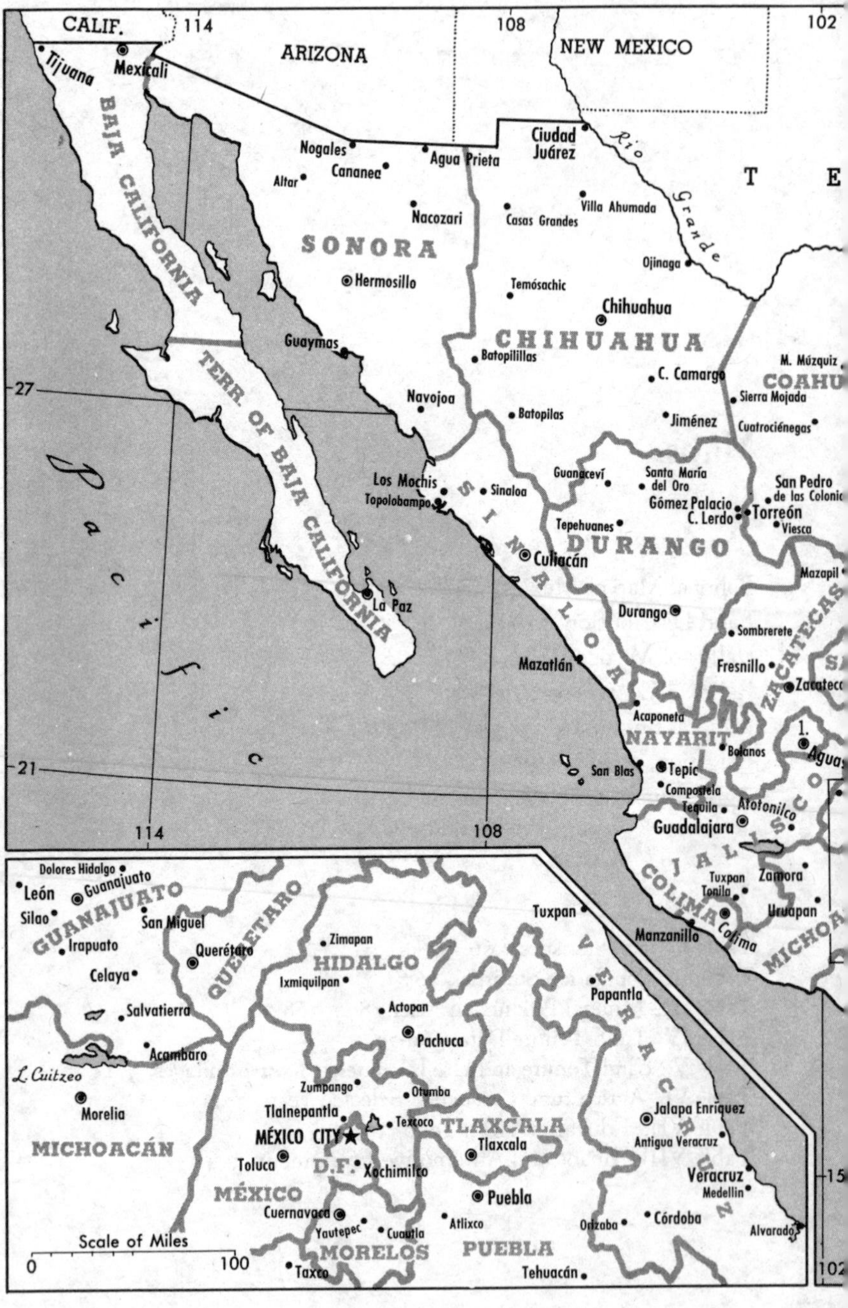
CALIF.
ARIZONA
NEW MEXICO
114
108
102
Tijuana
Mexicali
BAJA CALIFORNIA
Nogales
Cananea
Altar
Agua Prieta
Ciudad Juárez
Rio Grande
Villa Ahumada
Casas Grandes
Nacozari
SONORA
Hermosillo
Ojinaga
Temósachic
Chihuahua
CHIHUAHUA
Guaymas
Batopilillas
C. Camargo
M. Múzquiz
COAHU
Sierra Mojada
27
Navojoa
Batopilas
Jiménez
Cuatrociénegas
TERR. OF BAJA CALIFORNIA
Pacific
Los Mochis
Topolobampo
Sinaloa
Guanaceví
Santa María del Oro
Gómez Palacio
C. Lerdo
Torreón
San Pedro de las Colonia
Viesca
Tepehuanes
DURANGO
SINALOA
Culiacán
La Paz
Mazapil
Durango
Sombrerete
Mazatlán
Fresnillo
ZACATECAS
Zacateca
Acaponeta
NAYARIT
Bolanos
Aguas
21
San Blas
Tepic
Compostela
Tequila
Atotonilco
114
108
Guadalajara
JALISCO
Tuxpan
Tonila
Zamora
COLIMA
Colima
Uruapan
Manzanillo
MICHOA
Dolores Hidalgo
León
Guanajuato
GUANAJUATO
Silao
San Miguel
Irapuato
QUERETARO
Querétaro
Zimapan
HIDALGO
Tuxpan
Celaya
Ixmiquilpan
VERACRUZ
Papantla
Salvatierra
Actopan
Pachuca
Acambaro
L. Cuitzeo
Zumpango
Otumba
Morelia
Tlalnepantla
Texcoco
TLAXCALA
Jalapa Enríquez
MÉXICO CITY
Antigua Veracruz
MICHOACÁN
Tlaxcala
Toluca
D.F.
Xochimilco
Veracruz
Medellín
MÉXICO
Puebla
Cuernavaca
Córdoba
Orizaba
Yautepec
Cuautla
Atlixco
Alvarado
Scale of Miles
0
100
MORELOS
PUEBLA
Taxco
Tehuacán

POLITICAL MAP OF MEXICO
State boundaries
★ National capital
◉ Capital cities
Scale of Miles
0
100
200
300
96
90
27
21
15
X A S
STATE NAMES NOT SHOWN ON MAIN MAP
1. AGUASCALIENTES
2. GUANAJUATO
3. QUERÉTARO
4. HIDALGO
5. FEDERAL DISTRICT
6. MEXICO
7. MORELOS
8. TLAXCALA
9. PUEBLA
Gulf of Mexico
Ocean
Piedras Negras
(Porfirio Díaz)
Nuevo Laredo
Sabinas Hidalgo
Reynosa
Matamoros
Monterrey
Saltillo
NUEVO LEÓN
TAMAULIPAS
Matehuala
Soto la Marina
C. Victoria
Xicoténcatl
Antiguo Morelos
LUIS POTOSÍ
San Luis Potosí
Panuco
Tampico
Area shown in inset at left
MÉXICO CITY
VERACRUZ
Veracruz
San Andrés Tuxtla
Coatzacoalcos
Frontera
TABASCO
Villahermosa
Juárez
Tenosique
Progreso
Mérida
Tizimín
YUCATÁN
Ticul
Campeche
CAMPECHE
Xbonil
QUINTANA ROO
Chetumal
BR. HONDURAS
GUATEMALA
EL SALVADOR
Balsas
GUERRERO
Chilpancingo
Acapulco
Tuxtepec
Nochixtlán
Etla
Yalalag
Oaxaca
Tlacolula
Mitla
Juchitán
OAXACA
Salina Cruz
Punta Galera
Puerto Ángel
Tuxtla Gutiérrez
San Cristóbal de las Casas
CHIAPAS
Tonalá
Tapachula
Ayutla

Mexico

Chapter 1 • The Land

When Cortez crumpled a paper for Charles V to demonstrate the general configuration of the Mexican landscape, he was describing that portion of Central Mexico which he knew from personal experience. But the analogy, with modifications, might be used to characterize the physical appearance of most of the nation and to explain its patterns of settlement.

The Republic of Mexico is composed geographically of parts of two continents. Most of it consists of a long peninsular projection of the United States, running in a southeasterly direction and ending in a great sweeping curve to the east from the Isthmus of Tehuántepec. There it joins a peninsular projection of South America, embracing that part of Mexico lying to the east of the Isthmus. With its north-south limits at 32°43′ and 14°33′ respectively, and its east-west limits at 86°40′ and 117°08′, Mexico falls within a great rectangle nearly 1100 miles deep and 1900 miles wide. Its westernmost point lies directly south of San Diego, California, and its easternmost is almost due south of Montgomery, Alabama.

Its total area of 758,278 square miles is slightly larger than that of the combined states of Arizona, New Mexico, California, Utah,

Nevada, and Colorado, and slightly smaller than the combined midwestern states ranging from Ohio to the Dakotas and from Kansas to Minnesota. Mexico is roughly one-fourth the size of the United States, two-thirds as large as Argentina, and approximately four times as large as Spain. This area represents three-fifths of the Republic of Mexico's original national territory, the other two-fifths having been lost as a result of Texan secession, the U. S. War, and the Mesilla Valley sale. The Tropic of Cancer, that line marking the northernmost limits of the sun's vertical rays, crosses Mexico just south of Ciudad Victoria on the east and slightly north of Mazatlán on the west. Approximately one-half the national territory, then, lies in the geographic temperate zone, while the remainder is subjected twice a year to the sun's vertical rays, uncushioned by an oblique passage through the atmosphere. Mexico's latitudinal position therefore has an important bearing on general climatic conditions, which in turn have a marked effect on economic activity and social developments.

Mexico's geographic configuration is the result of millions of years of violent geologic action. Paleozoic seas covered most of the area, and the Mesozoic era brought convulsions of the earth's crust with periodic inundations over a major portion of the region. The Cenozoic brought new torments. Each sea laid down heavy sediments and each rise created widespread erosion; between inundations, volcanic action thrust to the surface a variety of minerals. The final convulsion pushed up the great mountain ranges, today the Mexican landscape's dominant characteristic; and it left a residue of volcanic action which is most dramatically shown by a violent eruption which, since 1943, has converted a Michoacán cornfield into a great hill of ash and lava.

Two major mountain ranges, geologically young and only slightly eroded, dominate the scene. The Sierra Madre Occidental, or the western range, rises in the states of Sonora and Chihuahua as an extension of the Rocky Mountains and moves southeastwardly in an ever-ascending and ever-widening path until it reaches the vicinity of Mexico City. It covers a major portion of eastern Sonora and western Chihuahua, virtually all of Durango, some eastern portions of the state of Sinaloa, and touches upon Zacatecas and the immediately contiguous states before it broadens to include most of the states of Querétaro, Jalisco, Michoacán, Morelos, and Mexico. The eastern range, the Sierra Madre Oriental, rises in the northeastern section not far from the Texas border and has some of the characteristics of the western range, becoming higher and wider in its movement to the south. The two ranges, then, beginning at the United States' border in the nation's extreme northwest and northeast corners at an altitude of some 6000 feet, join and mingle in Central Mexico in Puebla, Hidalgo, Mexico, and adjoining states. Here they reach the imposing heights of Orizaba, Popocateptl, and Iztaccihuatl, all of which soar more than half a mile higher than the tallest peaks in the United States, outside of Alaska, and here they form some of the world's highest valleys. Both ranges demonstrate a youthful ruggedness which leaves few practicable passes for communication purposes. So forbidding is the western range that in the 600 miles between Cananea on the north and Guadalajara in the south no lines of transportation were cut through until the middle of the twentieth century, when the Mexican government completed the Durango-Mazatlán highway. The eastern range is only slightly less hostile to man's efforts.

Between the two ranges nature's growing pains created a vast area of high country broken up by bold and wind-eroded tablelands. This great north-central interior bowl, made grim and forbidding by extensive wind erosion, enjoys sufficient water for welcome greenery in only a few spots. Isolated by imposing mountain ranges to the east and the west, the region is one into which man has entered reluctantly and then only to escape his enemies or to search for wealth. It is a region which early man passed through but did not occupy.

Two other major mountain chains bulk large in Mexican physiography. The Sierra Madre del Sur, covering nearly all the state of Guerrero and lapping well over into Oaxaca, is separated from the two northern chains by the deep depression which the Rio Balsas cut in its journey from Puebla to the Pacific. Of lesser loftiness than the other two, this southern chain bears a striking resemblance to them in its ruggedness; it is so devoid of convenient passes that in the entire 700 miles between Manzanillo and Salina Cruz only one road cuts through from the central highlands to the Pacific. Paralleling the coast, the range gradually descends in an easterly direction from a high point of 12,000 feet in central Guerrero until, beyond Oaxaca, it falls off rapidly and disappears into the lowlands of the Isthmus of Tehuántepec.

To the east of the Isthmus lie the great Chiapas Highlands, the northwestern portion of the chain which dominates Central America from Mexico to southern Nicaragua. A great rift depression known as the Valley of Chiapas, through which the Rio Grijalva flows, bisects the highlands. The portion south of the rift, the Sierra Madre de Chiapas, falls off from a maximum 12,000-foot elevation to the Pacific on one side and to the 1500-foot floor of the Valley of Chiapas on the other. Across the Valley the mountains again rise to 12,000 feet before dying out in the great limestone plain of the Yucatán Peninsula.

With very few exceptions the four great mountain chains rise precipitously from the sea coast and leave few coastal lowlands. There are lowlands on the coast of Sonora south of Hermosillo, but the band narrows as it proceeds southeast along the coast until it disappears near Tepic in Nayarit. Small and intermittent strips are located along the coasts of Guerrero and Oaxaca and farther to the southwest along the Chiapas littoral. The northeast is more fortunately endowed, but the lowland strip narrows, like that of the west, as it proceeds southward; it is finally squeezed into the sea near Veracruz. The major lowland areas are the Isthmus of Tehuántepec and the Yucatán Peninsula (the latter a flat limestone area undisturbed by contortions in recent geologic ages), but climate and soil prevent either from attaining great economic importance.

Interspersed among the mountains are a number of intermontane basins. These vary in altitude and size, but in all of them precipitous slopes tower above the flat valley floors with their remnants of lakes and marshes. Most such important basins are located within a section running from Veracruz on the east to Cabo Corrientes on the west, and from Aguascalientes on the north to Morelos on the south. Preston James lists seven major basins: the basins of Puebla, Mexico, Toluca, Guanajuato and Jalisco, and the valleys of Aguascalientes and Morelos. In this region almost half the Mexican population has concentrated, and within these basins five of the ten largest cities are located.

The basin of Toluca, with a minimum altitude on the floor of about 8600 feet and surrounded by mountains up to 15,000 feet, is the loftiest; the Morelos basin, with its floor at approximately 5000 feet, is the lowest. The same geologic conditions which created these major basins also contributed a less pleasant attribute; the basin line coincides with Mexico's line of major volcanic and seismic action. Most volcanic eruptions occur along the southern edge. The volcanoes include Orizaba (active until well after the arrival of the Spaniards) on the east and the Colima Volcano of Fire (which last erupted seriously in 1913) on the west; others, including Paricutín, lie between. Frequent tremors, sometimes of heavy and highly destructive intensity, plague the region. The geologic convulsions also produced the bed of Mexico's biggest river, the Lerma, which rises not far from Mexico City and flows westward into Lake Chapala and thence to the Pacific.

Intermontane basins exist in all Mexican mountain chains, but with the exception of the great Valley of Chiapas none of them compares in size and importance with those in the central region. The Chiapas basin, because of its tropical climate, is less heavily populated than the higher northern basins. The Oaxaca basin in the Sierra Madre del Sur, center of the great pre-Hispanic Zapotec civilization, is of sufficient size to be economically important, but those in the northern portions of the eastern and western ranges are isolated, small, and of little consequence.

The violent physical contortions which the earth's surface has undergone have had important economic consequences. The encroaching seas, each time the land mass submerged, laid down great masses of sedimentary materials; in the deeper waters teeming with animal life the most important deposits were limestone, but in the quieter marshy areas, particularly during the carboniferous period of the late Paleozoic, heavy deposits of decaying vegetable matter formed the raw material for modern Mexico's oil industry. Each period of submersion was followed by long ages of eruption and contortion during which the earth heaved its minerals to the surface as extrusions through great fissures in the crust. Subsequent inundations eroded the surface and bared the ores or, as was the case of gold in many areas, deteriorated the rocky material and left the metal free. Each great geologic age—

Paleozoic, Mesozoic, Cenozoic—left mineral deposits, but the most recent and the shortest, the Cenozoic, deposited the richest bounty in exploitable minerals.

Mexico's vast silver deposits, coming almost exclusively from the Cenozoic, have had profound and disadvantageous economic and social effects. With the arrival of the European who put high value on silver, the exposed ores tended to obscure the potential value of other minerals and to encourage the development of an economic and social system revolving around silver exploitation. During the Spanish colonial period Mexico provided the greatest single source of world silver and placed Spain in an enviable position in world economy, but the shining silver blinded Spain to many economic realities. Independent Mexico has created less stir in world circles with her silver production, but she has in fact increased production volume. During the two decades from 1920 to 1940 she produced more silver by weight than the Spanish extracted from the mines during the entire three-century colonial period.

But more important economically, both in terms of potential and in twentieth-century production, are the base metals which Cenozoic convulsions gave to the land. Lead and zinc, lowly metals seldom arousing cupidity, have each produced more income to the Mexicans than has silver since World War II, and copper is not far behind. Iron ore is sufficiently plentiful to support a budding iron and steel industry, partially powered by the coal beds nearby. In addition, a variety of commercially valuable metals, among which are antimony, cadmium, manganese, mercury, and tungsten, is of increasing industrial importance. Probably the single most important mineral resource is petroleum, found along the Gulf Coast from Matamoros to the Yucatán Peninsula. The geologic violence, then, which produced Mexico's extraordinarily rugged face and created a land difficult to exploit, has also brought forth valuable mineral products in partial compensation.

Three basic factors determine the rainfall in any given area: direction of prevailing winds, position and temperature of great bodies of water, and configuration of the land mass. The Pacific Ocean off Mexico's northwest coast, influenced by the Japanese Current, is relatively cool. Winds passing over the water gather slight moisture, and most of the vapor thus gathered remains in suspension until the western Sierra forces the winds upward into colder air. As a consequence rain is scarce along the coast, and both Baja California and the lower reaches of the mountain slopes remain deserts with less than ten inches of annual rainfall. The upper slopes enjoy slightly more water, but precipitation is insufficient for normal agricultural pursuits, except in those areas where the scarce water is impounded for irrigation. The lack of rainfall has also prevented water erosion and consequent alluvial deposits; even in the intermontane basins the soil is thin and poor.

South of Baja California the Japanese Current swings away from the coast, allowing the warming of the coastal waters to emit a high proportion of vapor; this is particularly marked below Cabo Corrientes. During the summer and fall, when southwest winds prevail and the air arrives over the continent heavily laden with moisture, torrential rains fall along the coasts of Jalisco, Michoacán, Guerrero, Oaxaca, and Chiapas. Most of this coastal region receives over 20 inches annually, while some sections average nearly 100. In the southern interior mountains the annual rainfall is sufficient; but some Chiapas regions are victimized by nearly 200 inches a year—an amount which leaches the soil, encourages profuse growth of noxious plants, and retards effective agricultural activity.

The waters of the Gulf of Mexico and the Caribbean Sea are among the warmest in the world and therefore give high moisture content to passing winds, but north of Tampico the prevailing winds pass over dry Texas plains or Mexican mountains instead of the Gulf. From Tampico south, easterly and northerly winds dump heavy summer rains along the coast as far as the Yucatán Peninsula, which itself receives more than 20 inches annually. Much of the coast, especially the northern portion of the Isthmus of Tehuántepec, counts on more than 80 inches.

The high eastern and western mountain chains effectively block the passage of moisture-laden winds into the interior. A great sweeping triangular-shaped area, with its three apexes at the Texas Big Bend country, Nogales, and Mexico City, is therefore deprived of water sufficient for normal agricultural endeavors. The two great interior depressions, the Bolsones of Mapimí and Mayrán in the center of the triangle, are for all practical purposes devoid of rain.

Annual average rainfall is not the determining factor in judging whether a land has sufficient water for agriculture. Twenty inches of rainfall, well distributed over the year in a temperate zone with good ground cover where rates of evaporation and run-off are low (Iowa is a good example), is sufficient for productive and regular cropping. But most of Mexico is not so blessed. On the contrary, the rains fall spasmodically and torrentially. Loss through run-off is high and the rate of evaporation extreme because of the low moisture content in the surrounding air. In most of northern and north-central Mexico the annual averages represent occasional torrential summer rains followed by long periods, sometimes years, of drought during which precipitation is not enough to settle the dust. In some mountain sections with an annual average of 25 inches, the water supply available for agricultural purposes limits cropping to one year out of every two or three. But the physiography of the interior bowl has one saving grace. Most of the rain which does fall remains within the confines of the region, since exterior drainage is limited to the northern Conchos and San Juan rivers, both of which flow into the Rio Grande and to the Gulf. This condition allows for greater ease in impounding water for irrigation and keeps the water table high enough to be tapped. The Laguna and Bajío regions especially have profited from the interior drainage.

In the regions east, west, and southeast of Mexico City the rain falls in sufficient amounts for steady agriculture, but the precipitation is concentrated in the summer months and is sometimes spotty in its distribution. Heavy summer rains occasionally cause floods in Mexico City while the contiguous basins of Puebla and Toluca remain powder-dry; at other times the pattern is reversed. Therefore, even in the great intermontane basins blessed with heavy rainfall, irrigation must be utilized to guarantee steady cropping. This is true even in the great Papaloapan district, covering parts of Oaxaca, Veracruz, and Puebla, where the annual rainfall is over 80 inches.

The Yucatán Peninsula is in a category of its own. There rainfall is well over 20 inches a year in all areas and more than 40 in the interior, but the basic characteristic of the region is aridity. During the geologic ages when the rest of Mexico was swept by convulsions, Yucatán remained placid though often submerged. The result has been a thick and relatively unbroken limestone cap through which the waters filter as soon as they fall, leaving the region virtually devoid of surface water during most of the year but with great amounts of groundwater, some of which can be tapped. Large-scale agriculture is impossible because of the lack of readily available surface water, and the basic economy revolves around plants which survive with a minimum of moisture.

Given the seasonal nature of the rains, the rates of evaporation and run-off, and the amount of rainfall, Mexico's potential for agriculture is not as favorable as the rainfall statistics alone might indicate. Jorge Tamayo has estimated that 50 per cent of the land suffers a continuous scarcity of water, 36 per cent lacks water during the winter, 1 per cent suffers during the summer, and only 13 per cent (as compared to the 47 in the United States) has sufficient rainfall in all seasons. Much of the well-watered area, of course, consists of mountains where agriculture is impossible.

Taking into consideration all these factors—availability of water, surface configuration, and erosion—the agricultural potential is limited. Of the total land surface about 10 per cent is potentially usable for agriculture, but in any given year less than 6 per cent is actually used for cropping; nearly 40 per cent of that cropped land is found in the central region, most of it concentrated in Guanajuato, Jalisco, Michoacán, Puebla, and Mexico. These states have the greatest concentration of intermontane basins as well as the greatest seismic and volcanic action. It is as if nature has ordained that the best lands shall also be the most dangerous.

Perhaps a comparison with the United States will indicate Mexico's limited agricultural potential. On a per capita basis, for every theoretically arable acre available to the Mexican agriculturalist, his northern neighbor has nearly six, and for every acre the Mexican farmer harvested in 1960 his counterpart in the United States harvested almost three. Illinois counts on more arable land than all Mexico, as do Kansas, Iowa, and Minnesota; in 1960 Iowa farmers harvested more land

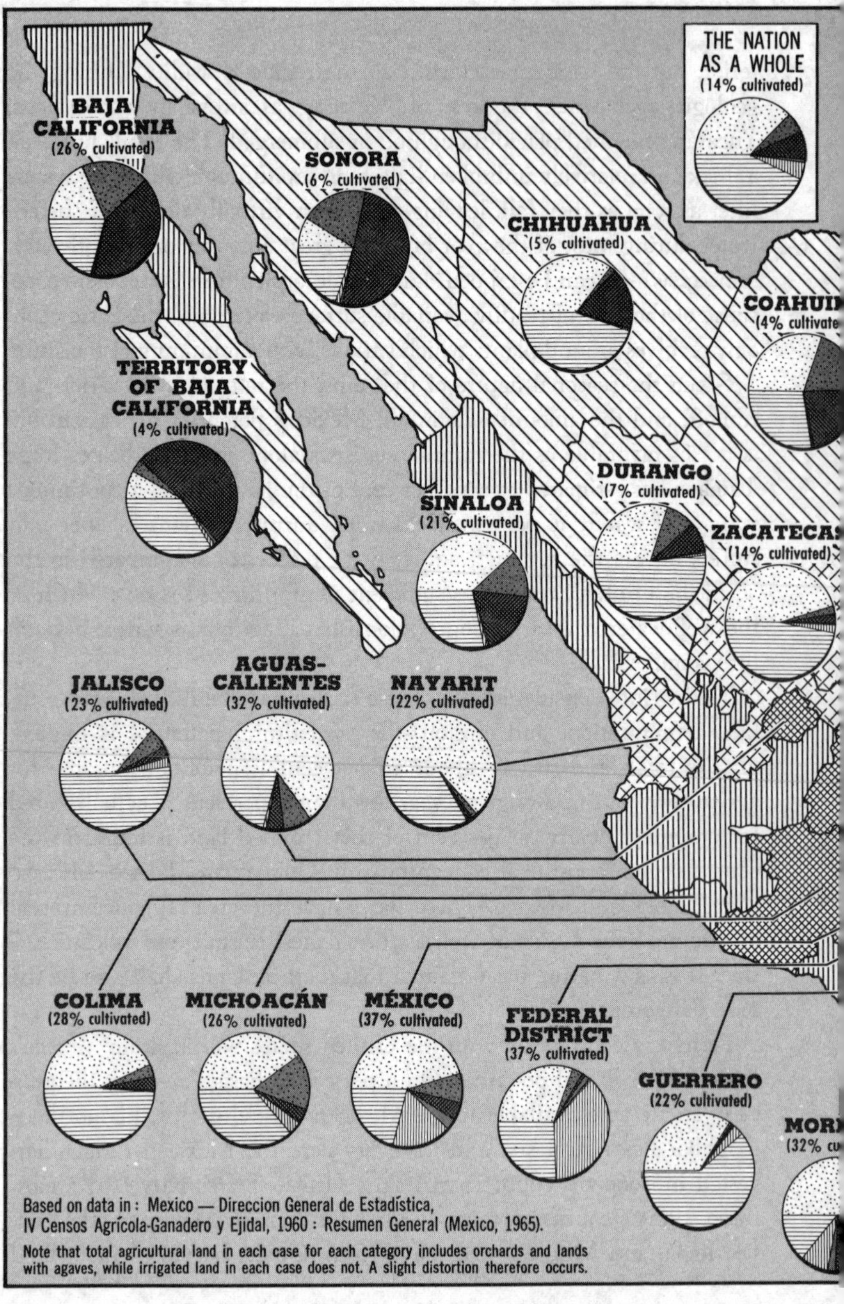

Based on data in: Mexico — Direccion General de Estadística, IV Censos Agrícola-Ganadero y Ejidal, 1960: Resumen General (Mexico, 1965).

Note that total agricultural land in each case for each category includes orchards and lands with agaves, while irrigated land in each case does not. A slight distortion therefore occurs.

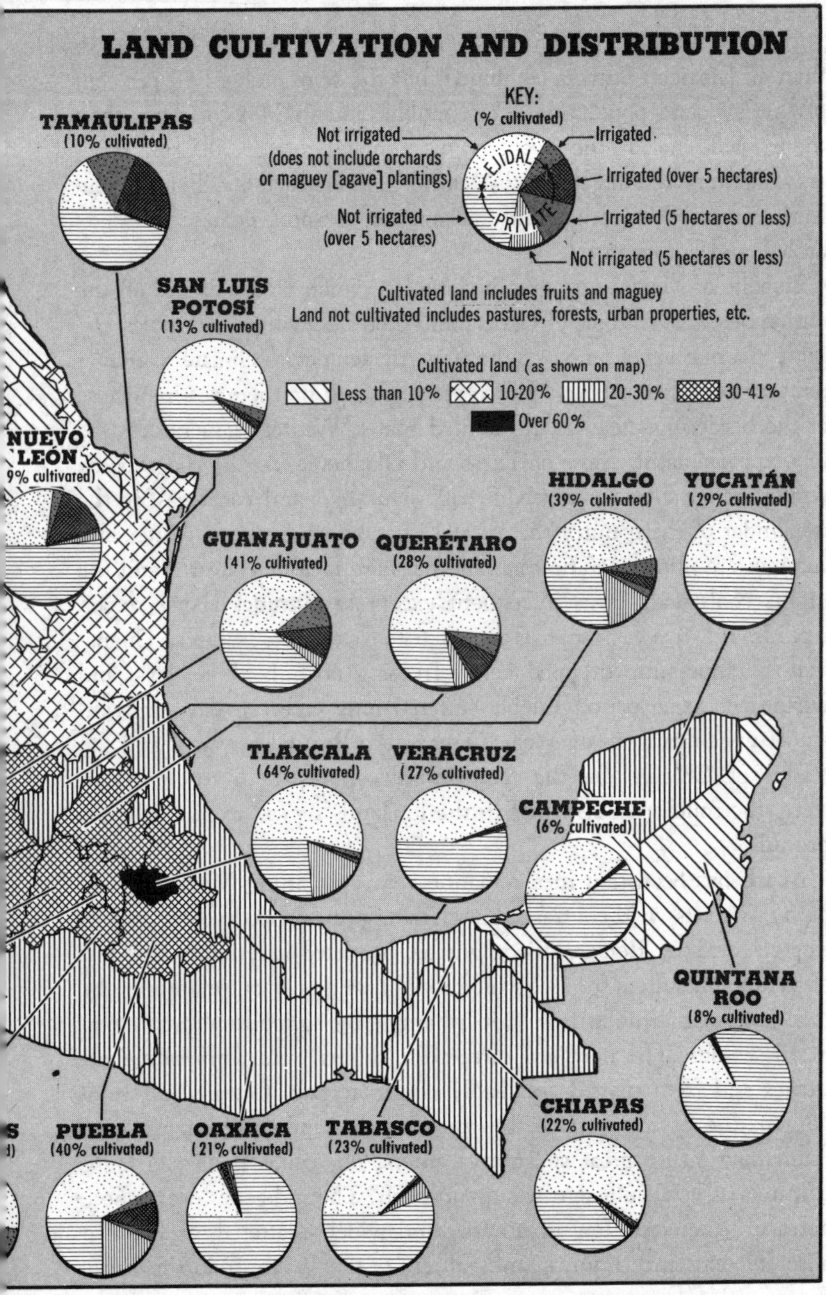
LAND CULTIVATION AND DISTRIBUTION
KEY:
(% cultivated)
Not irrigated
(does not include orchards or maguey [agave] plantings)
Irrigated
EJIDAL
PRIVATE
Irrigated (over 5 hectares)
Irrigated (5 hectares or less)
Not irrigated
(over 5 hectares)
Not irrigated (5 hectares or less)
Cultivated land includes fruits and maguey
Land not cultivated includes pastures, forests, urban properties, etc.
Cultivated land (as shown on map)
Less than 10%
10-20%
20-30%
30-41%
Over 60%
TAMAULIPAS
(10% cultivated)
SAN LUIS POTOSÍ
(13% cultivated)
NUEVO LEÓN
9% cultivated)
GUANAJUATO
(41% cultivated)
QUERÉTARO
(28% cultivated)
HIDALGO
(39% cultivated)
YUCATÁN
(29% cultivated)
TLAXCALA
(64% cultivated)
VERACRUZ
(27% cultivated)
CAMPECHE
(6% cultivated)
QUINTANA ROO
(8% cultivated)
PUEBLA
(40% cultivated)
OAXACA
(21% cultivated)
TABASCO
(23% cultivated)
CHIAPAS
(22% cultivated)

than all Mexican farmers combined, but the state had only 8 per cent of the Mexican population. Total arable land in Mexico is less than the irrigated land in the seventeen western states, and California farmers irrigate more land than all Mexican farmers together. Even herculean efforts at irrigation and reclamation cannot increase Mexico's arable land significantly.

In spite of Mexico's geographic latitude, which places about half the nation below the Tropic of Cancer and therefore within the tropics, the high mountains give most of the nation a temperate climate. Summer temperatures in northern Mexico are high, but no more so than those of the bordering states in the United States. Winter temperatures are low, approximating those of Texas and Oklahoma; during the 1966-67 winter, heavy snows paralyzed Saltillo, Durango, and Zacatecas. In the remainder of the country the annual fluctuations between winter and summer are minimal. The highland days are pleasantly warm and the nights cool, with frosts infrequent except at altitudes above 10,000 feet. In the five-year span from 1946 to 1951, for example, Guanajuato's temperature dropped below freezing on only three days, and during the same period Puebla suffered only eighteen days of frost, ten of which came in one year. Only in the Rio Balsas valley and the Valley of Chiapas are the temperatures oppressive in the interior; along the southern coasts and in the lowlands typical tropical climate prevails.

Much has been said in a romantic vein concerning Mexican geography, with its vivid contrasts, its towering snow-capped peaks, and its tropical verdure. Romantic it might be, but hard it certainly is. Most of the nation suffers from chronic drought, and only one-eighth of the total land mass benefits from rainfall ample for agricultural production in all seasons. The northern three-fifths suffers from temperature extremes and from rugged and badly eroded terrain. Given the forbidding nature of this section, the pre-Hispanic indigenous population could develop no great sedentary centers, nor could it develop agriculture to a level sufficient to support itself. The indigenes everywhere north of Querétaro, few in number and widely scattered, eked out a miserable existence hunting and gathering; they were, from the European point of view, a liability rather than an asset. In the remaining two-fifths, the topography and the climate combined to produce a land much more amenable to sedentary life and the development of higher civilizations. Rugged the land is, but the greater amounts of rainfall have formed lakes, deposited alluvial soils, and enhanced the growth of profuse vegetation which has softened mountainous contours. In this region almost all the pre-Hispanic population gathered, and in this region the modern Mexican has followed suit. A comparison of population density dramatizes the situation. In 1960 Tlaxcala supported 213 persons per square mile, Mexico state 201; Morelos 201, and Puebla 149. In contrast Chihuahua supported only 12, Coahuila 16, Sonora 9.5, and Baja California 2.7.

One might forecast that with the introduction of modern technology and the opening of new irrigated districts outside the central states, the population will become more widely dispersed over the nation. But irrigated land will always be only a small proportion of the arable land, and modern agricultural technology drives men off the land rather than concentrates them on it. Given this geography, the proportion of the population in Mexico's central region will not diminish significantly.

Chapter 2 • The People: The Native Population

Day and night the feast went on. Now a girl ran to the four parts of the city. Tassels of precious quetzal feathers hung from her head like the precious tasseled corn. Her sandals were scarlet like the chilli. The women sang to her and the warriors danced to her in a twisting course like a snake. . . . She walked in the daybreak, dark and lovely with scarlet sandals, up to the temple of the corn god. To the god of corn and the god of rain her heart was offered in a blue bowl.

FRANCES GILLMOR, *The King Danced in the Marketplace*

The times were bad; the winter had brought cold and frost and death to the young corn, and the spring and summer brought winds and clouds of dust. The gods were angry—or at least displeased—and unable to send the life-giving rain to the Mexican in the central valley. The girl whose heart was offered up in the blue bowl to Tlaloc by order of the Emperor Moctezuma had known from birth that in giving her life she would perform the noblest deed possible for a mortal being, and by so doing she would assure herself a special place reserved for her: time without end, strolling in a land of beauty and fertility where no one hungered and none felt pain. This was the essence of native Mexican religious belief.

The gods were everywhere, striving eternally to bestow upon mortals their sustenance and their happiness. But the forces of evil, too, were everywhere, and in the titanic never-ending struggle between the forces of good and the forces of evil, the deities demanded constant attention. When they tired, man soon knew, for his own fortunes waned; then man redoubled his efforts to support his gods. In pre-Hispanic Mexico, man's fate was inevitably and intimately linked to that of his gods.

Pre-conquest Mexico was a mixture of societies, the majority linked by conquest and tribute payments as well as by trade with the central highland Aztecs. Into the Valley of Mexico wandering tribes of Nahua-speaking people had migrated from the north and west, and when they saw the beauty and the richness of the land, with the lake in the floor of the Valley, they had conquered its inhabitants and remained. Early in the fourteenth century the final Nahua remnant arrived and, finding all the rich Valley land occupied, settled on the barren islands in the lake. There in the succeeding century the island people—the Tenocha or the Mexica of Tenochtitlán—established a strong civilization. Then, sometimes in concert with one or more of the lake-shore cities, they conquered most of the Nahua-speaking peoples and extended their power far beyond the area occupied by their linguistic kin. One major group they never conquered; the Tlaxcalans, who occupied a portion of the intermontane basin to the east, still maintained their precarious independence when Cortez and the Spaniards arrived.

But other sedentary people with highly developed skills and social organizations also tilled Mexico's soil. To the northeast of Mexico-Tenochtitlán, occupying much of the coast and a portion of the paralleling mountain range, lived the Huastecas, linguistically related to the Mayas of Yucatán but long separated from them. The Totonacs occupied the region south of the Huastecas, and in the present state of Oaxaca the Zapotecs built their mighty temples at Monte Albán and Mitla, while the Mixtecs carved and polished their magnificent jewelry. Immediately north of Mexico-Tenochtitlán, in the region of Ixmiquilpan, the Otomies wrested an existence from the arid soil but left little outstanding architecture. To the west the Tarascans, in the present state of Michoacán, tended their nets, grew their corn, and worshipped their gods. In short, the highlands regions with their intermontane basins teemed with people who depended upon the soil for their sustenance and upon a pantheon of gods for their protection. With the exception of the Tlaxcalans, by the year 1500 all these groups paid tribute to the island people of Tenochtitlán. Including the Tlaxcalans, the area's total population at that time undoubtedly reached between 20 and 30 million.

Beyond the northern boundary of the tributary groups lived the Chichimecs ("barbarians" in the Nahua tongue), occupying the forbidding northland, with their miserable existence dependent on what they could gather in the way of wild animal and plant life. Even farther north other gathering tribes (unrelated linguistically and culturally to those to the south and of whom the central Mexicans were ignorant) roamed the wilderness. Beyond the Isthmus of Tehuántepec, too, native people occupied the land; the most important of these were the incredibly talanted Maya of Yucatán, whose marvelous architectural and intellectual skills still confound the initiated. The Maya traded with the Tenocha and on occasion depended upon Mexican arms, but they never sent tribute.

Each civilization had its distinctive cultural pattern with its pantheon of gods, but by the early sixteenth century a degree of amalgamation had taken place and the most important gods had become common to all sedentary groups, although the gods' names and their hierarchy of importance varied. Within a broad spectrum Indian religious practices in Mexico demonstrated common traits; the Aztec, or Nahua, practices differed in detail from others but characterized them all.

Huitzilopochtli, whom the wandering Nahuas brought with them when they entered the Valley of Mexico and who had protected them in the centuries before they finally found the chosen land of Tenochtitlán, was, according to legend, born of fire and sacrifice. At a conclave of the gods Huitzilopochtli had sacrificed himself by fire to combat the forces of evil and thereby became himself a ball of fire, capable of destroying the demons who tormented both man and god. But the fire-ball remained stationary until other gods gave it mobility through their self-sacrifice. Huitzilopochtli then began his daily traverse of the heavens, giving light and warmth to mortals. The blood of the gods endowed the sun with mobility but not eternal movement; the movement continued only so long as mortal blood replenished the waning supply of the original sacrifice, and without blood the sun would stop in the sky. And should Huitzilopochtli's motion ever cease, the heavens would open and through the breach would stream all the fantastic demons of space. Only through the sun's daily travels and surveillance could the bulwarks against the demons be kept in repair. Should the demons descend in all their power, mankind would perish in an orgy of terror. Sometimes a few demons escaped to visit the earth; they could not be seen, but their presence was easily ascertained–disease spread, warriors met defeat, hunger prevailed. Huitzilopochtli protected a wandering people whose very existence depended upon their physical prowess and ability to defend themselves against outside attack. He had served his people well. He had brought them in safety to the haven of the Anahuac, and had made them prosper since their arrival some two or three centuries before the Spaniards'.

When the Nahuas arrived in Mexico's central valley they found it peopled with men who had long tilled the soil and who depended not upon their armies' military might but upon the produce of their armies of farmers. The rain god Tlaloc protected them, and upon him they depended for their existence. A god of bounty as well as rain, Tlaloc had served the Valley's sedentary people for centuries with the same effectivness with which Huitzilopochtli had served the nomadic Nahuas. When the Nahuas finally conquered the farmers and settled among them, they included Tlaloc in their pantheon.

But long before the coming of the Nahua people the Toltecs ("skilled workers") had occupied the mainland region to the north of Lake Texcoco. Builders of the architectural and decorative marvels of Teotihuacán and Tula, the Toltecs fell under the protective mantle of the god of learning Quetzalcoatl. The war god Tezcatlipoca (the Smoking Mirror), borrowed from the Toltecs and then incorporated along with Quetzalcoatl into the Aztec pantheon, determined the destiny of Texcoco.

When in the fifteenth century the Aztecs forced Oaxaca's Zapotecs into their tributary system, the chief protector of that civilization became another of the ever-growing group of gods for whom blood must flow into the sacrificial bowl. The Zapotecs worshipped Xipe Totec, the god of growth, the god of rebirth, the god of spring. Known as the "flayed one," his ritual included flaying the sacrificed human.

To these five, Huitzilopochtli, Quetzalcoatl, Tlaloc, Tezcatlipoca, and Xipe Totec, the people built temples in every community. Huitzilopochtli's magnificent temple in Tenochtitlán, begun by Moctezuma I and completed by his successor in the late fifteenth century, was so immense and imposing that even the Spaniards were awestricken. On a portion of its ruins and with some of its stones, the Spaniards constructed their own temple, the Cathedral of Mexico City. But in addition to the lofty temples to the major gods, in each community smaller temples honored a bewildering array of lesser gods, each a special protector to a small group.

In the same manner that each European invoked the intercession of his patron saint, so the individual Indian paid homage to his special god. Every misfortune or disaster which science has attributed to natural forces—earthquakes, disease, cold, drought, crop failure, flood—and every success which later ages have attributed to the mind of man, stemmed from the weakness, the anger, or the strength of the gods. The weak god must be fed, the angry propitiated, the strong kept powerful. Even the gentle Quetzalcoatl, who in his stay on earth as man renounced human sacrifice, had to be kept strong. The gods of other societies might be appeased with ambrosia and nectar, but the gods of the Aztecs depended upon the fire-singed flesh of the still-beating human heart and the gushing blood of mortal man.

Life, precious though it might be, was uncertain to the Mexican. Only through eternal struggle, a battle of cosmic order, could the gods ward off the destructive demons. Every man, as a price for his very existence, accepted a role in that eternal battle; the more important the part and the greater the personal sacrifice, the greater the ultimate reward. The gods rewarded with a special place in the everlasting him who died in the service of Huitzilopochtli either on the sacrificial stone or on the field of battle attempting to capture a sacrificial victim. Upon his death the vital part of his being was transmuted into the form of an eagle, and the eagle for a period of four years accompanied the sun each day in its orbit from the eastern horizon to the zenith. At the end of the four years' service as friend and guard, the eagle returned to earth as a hummingbird to live for eternity among the flowers and honey.

An equally pleasant fate lay in store for him who died in the service of Tlaloc: his life-essence wandered for a four-year span and then found entrance to an enchanted garden which eternally produced all the succulent foods necessary for eternal existence. Those who died in the service of other gods merited different futures, some being incorporated into the god himself. But for those who died in the service of no god, the future held great uncertainty, for the life-essence wandered for four years under fearsome conditions and then disappeared into the void.

Within this belief system, human sacrifice and war became inextricably interwoven as the dominant institutions sustaining Mexican society. The gods required mortal sacrifice, but their insatiable appetites could decimate a community. Huitzilopochtli did not discriminate; he could as well gain energy from the blood of those who did not serve him as from those who did. And other gods were no more discerning. Prisoners of war, then, became the most convenient source of sacrifice, and in the absence of real issues, communities agreed upon ritual war. In these ritual wars the object was not the conquest of territory, nor the forced payment of tribute, nor the defeat of armies, but simply the capturing of prisoners whose hearts and blood might be offered to the gods. In times of great crisis, as when the Spaniards were hammering at the gates of Tenochtitlán, those who went to the sacrifice numbered thousands.

But the priests found other sources for sacrifice as well. Under highly regulated conditions a *calpulli* (an urban ward) could purchase a slave for the honor; the inconsistency of giving life eternal to the lowest order of the society while denying it to members of the aristocracy bothered the Aztecs not at all. But for certain significant events a special person would be selected. Once every year, during the festival honoring Tezcatlipoca, the comeliest prisoner of war would go to sacrifice following a year of instruction and a month of cohabitation with four lovely maidens. And the dark and beautiful girl whose heart the high priest offered to Tlaloc in a blue bowl had been chosen for her beauty and grace.

The stone served most sacrificial purposes. Four priests held the victim over a concave stone, and a fifth, tearing open the cardial cavity with an obsidian knife, wrested from the body the beating heart and committed it to the flames of a brazier. On special occasions a greater number of priests officiated, and in affairs of great ritualistic import the "emperor" himself participated. For some gods the stone and the knife did not suffice. Xipe Totec demanded that the victim be tied to a grillwork and his body pierced with arrows, the dripping blood rejuvenating the earth and inducing the soil to bring forth again its bounty. But Xipe Totec, in addition to being the god of spring and rebirth, also served as the god of the goldsmith. A priest of the cult flayed the sacrificed body, tinted the skin to simulate the color of native gold, and donned the now-golden uniform to perform the ritual dance. Other gods demanded other forms of sacrifice, but all had the same end: the death of a mortal to strengthen the god.

Religion in Indian Mexico, whether among the Nahuas, the Totonacs, the Zapotecs, or the Mayas, was as harsh and demanding as the countryside. The priests constantly reminded all persons of their duties to society and of the strong possibility that they would be called upon to make the supreme sacrifice for the community. The mass of the population attended the ritual sacrifice, a public religious function which often terminated in ritualistic cannibalism symbolically investing the partaker of the flesh with the power of the divinity. This concept of transubstantiation revolted the Spaniards for they saw in the ritual the hand of the devil. The Mexican Indian in his simple faith believed that human blood was necessary to ward off evil; the European, more learned, knew that Jesus' blood purified the true believer.

Human sacrifice served a religious function only. Common criminals condemned to death for a wide variety of civil or religious crimes—drunkenness, for example, or sorcery, or laughter and idleness during times of solemn crisis—never saw the sacrificial stone; a public official simply garrotted them without ritual or public attendance.

A ritualistic and demanding religious structure induces, or is the product of, a rigid social structure. As long as the Nahua-speaking people (whether Aztec, Tlaxcalan, or other) wandered as nomadic food gatherers, both the religious and social structures were simple and uncomplicated. Religion revolved around the single important god Huitzilopochtli, whom they had found in a cave, and theirs was a simple unstratified democratic society. Each man acted as warrior, hunter, and food-gatherer, and many as priests as well. The tribe selected its leaders on the basis of prowess or other special attribute; the leaders possessed no absolute power of their own. But life in the Valley was more complex than life in the wilderness. By the middle of the fifteenth century, when Moctezuma I began the great campaigns to expand the sway of Tenochtitlán, most of the simple tribal religious and social practices had disappeared or had atrophied into vestigial forms. When the Spaniards arrived early in the next century they found all the people of Central Mexico (including not only the Aztecs and their Nahua kin but all tributary groups from Querétaro to Tehuantepec) in the midst of a great social transformation, which had largely destroyed the easy tribal democracy and had created a stratified society.

At the top of the social structure, that group having the greatest perquisites and advantages, presided a rapidly developing aristocratic group roughly analogous but not completely equivalent to the contemporary European aristocracy. The major difference, aside from that of culture and religion as well as function, was that the Mexican aristocracy had not yet congealed into a hereditary nobility. The nobility consisted of those to whom the term *tecuhtli* (Nahua for "lord" or "dignitary") was applied and, in a legalistic sense, designated the function rather than the person; all those of the upper administrative, judicial, and military hierarchy, wherever located, carried the title. Historically elective positions, by 1500 they had become appointive and virtually hereditary; in the conquered regions subject to tribute to Tenochtitlán the "emperor"* either designated local leaders as *tecuhtli*

* Inasmuch as the word *emperor* evokes a particular kind of ruler, quite different from that which existed in the Aztec world, the word is used with quotation marks. The Aztec "emperor," was both lay and religious leader.

or conferred the title upon his own trusted lieutenants. He in turn was chosen as the chief ruler by a group of *tecuhtli*. During the period of great Tenocha expansion, as new areas with their numerous villages and cities came into the fold, new positions of *tecuhtli* were constantly created and needed to be filled by competent men. But with the solidification of the tribute states the number of new *tecuhtli* waned, and the existing positions became titles of great honor and power. When a vacancy occurred by death or retirement, the "emperor" was free to appoint anyone he wished, but in the last years before the Spanish conquest the new noble, as well as the chief ruler, almost invariably came from his predecessor's family. It was to the *tecuhtli* that the Spaniards, borrowing a Jamaican term, applied the name "caciques."

A member of the aristocracy could be visibly identified by his dress, since to members of his class were reserved certain robes and jewelry. Originally the robes and jewels had been insignia of office, but when Cortez arrived they had become the adornments of a class, and anyone outside that class who dared affect aristocratic dress committed a crime punishable by death. Each member of the aristocracy had claim to land (the size of the holding depending on his importance) worked for him by commoners. Frequently such land lay far distant from his site of residence, a natural consequence of the growing population and the great conquests, and a form of absentee landlordship developed. Income from the land constituted the noble's basic salary, but each office had attached to it certain benefits which frequently amounted to more than the land's produce. A house and personal service for the family, both furnished by the local community, was standard, and in some exceptional cases all food and supplies were also furnished. In one recorded instance a great military chieftain of Tenochtitlán kept two thousand commoners busy in maintaining his household.

In theory any man in the society might become a member of the aristocracy through worthy and exceptional service to the community, and in fact the channels were open to allow men from the lower classes to ascend the social ladder. Military excellence provided the most common route, for promotion to officer rank brought the title with all its honors, and promotion depended largely upon the number of captives taken in battle; each captive meant a promotion, and the fourth captive gave a noble rank. But non-military meritorious service might also bring promotion to *tecuhtli* with its noble connotations. Once, according to a possibly apocryphal story, a commoner was elevated to the nobility because he told the "emperor" the truth.

Although the positions of *tecuhtli* were not hereditary, children of *tecuhtli* fell into a special category with a distinctive class designation, *pilili*. The *pilili* presumably had no special advantages, for they worked their own land or plied their craft, subject to the same method of taxation as the commoners, and in all respects save one their position was that of commoners. But the one exception was extremely important: the *pilili* were automatically eligible to attend the *calmecac*, the pre-Hispanic "university," and thus by virtue of education were in a position to enter the upper level of society. Not all *pilili* became *tecuhtli*, but virtually all *tecuhtli* had been *pilili*. But even those who did not become members of the nobility in the legal sense seldom sank to the lowest level of the commoner, since the wise *tecuhtli* gave to their sons the social insurance of an education and a craft, and most highly skilled craftsmen came from this segment of society.

By 1519 class lines had not yet frozen. Although in the natural course of events the nobility tended to maintain social relationships within their class, no taboos regarding such relationships outside the class existed. Frequently members of the aristocracy took commoners as wives or concubines, and occasionally the daughters of *tecuhtli* married commoners. Social mobility still existed but was on the wane.

Roughly equivalent to the civil-military aristocarcy was the priestly hierarchy, but inasmuch as the priests were celibate the question of heredity did not intrude. Perquisites attached to the priestly positions varied with the importance of the temple and the priest's position in the hierarchy; the high priests for Huitzilopochtli, Tlaloc, and Tezcatlipoca in Tenochtitlán enjoyed prerogatives equal to those of the highest military and administrative officials. The priests were all products of the *calmecac*, and since most students in that institution were *pilili*, the religious aristocracy was intimately related by family ties to the military and civil nobility.

One group, or class, occupied a curious position within the social hierarchy; this group carried on all trade with outlying areas, and since its members served as the eyes and ears for the central government they received special privileges, which were hereditary. These traders, the *pochteca,* enjoyed rights denied to other members of Tenocha society. The *pochteca* determined their own rules and regulations and enforced them in their own courts. They were not bound to community service as were others; they were not subject to military service; they had their own gods and their own priests—and they were enormously wealthy. According to Jacques Soustelle, the *pochteca* constituted a state-within-a-state, for within the *pochteca* a hierarchy existed. The reasons for their extraordinary position will be made clear when the economic function of the *pochteca* is discussed.

Skilled craftsmen occupied the next rung on the social ladder. The greatest prestige attached to silversmiths, goldsmiths, jewelers, and feather-workers—many of these were *pilili*—but all craftsmen, even the humblest pottery-maker or stone mason, were exempt from personal service and agricultural labor. Skilled craftsmen were looked upon with some degree of awe, since virtually all the truly skilled crafts were of "foreign" origin, the workmanship having been learned from conquered people.

The bulk of the population fell into a group known as the *macehuales,* whose position in society was so obvious that the Spaniards immediately labeled them "plebeians" and in so doing demonstrated both their own mentality and the realities of Aztec social classification. The *macehuales,* too, had their duties and their bonuses, with the bonuses more limited and the duties more onerous than those of the upper classes. Every *macehual* was allotted a plot of land large enough to sustain him and his family, from which he could not be dispossessed and to which he had the permanent right of usufruct. He was a citizen in every respect, with the theoretical right of participation in public affairs including religious rituals, commemoratve feasts, and the selection of municipal officials. Furthermore, he could send his children to the local school and possibly to the *calmecac,* and if he were a *macehual* of Tenochtitlán he shared in the tribute from conquered regions.

And he could, by luck or hard work or both, move into the rarefied atmosphere of the aristocracy.

In return for these rather limited, often nebulous, advantages he assumed grave duties, for the whole society depended on him. He was always held for military duty, though the army after 1500 was largely professional. He paid taxes, and it was these taxes from the tributary areas which in fact made up the tribute. The *macehuales,* without payment of any kind, worked the aristocrats' lands, built the aristocrats' homes, maintained the noble families, constructed temples, swept the streets, and built the roads, the causeways, and aqueducts. The *macehual* was the beast of burden, the farm laborer, the unskilled worker—with many responsibilities and almost no privileges. The *macehual* of Tenochtitlán lived a hard but not impossible life, since to his meager farm income could be added his share of the tribute from distant lands. But the *macehual* in those distant lands was the member in society upon whom the heaviest burden fell, and who probably found life under the Spaniards no more exploitative than that which he had endured before.

Slightly below the *macehual* in social status but about equal in economic well-being was the *tlalmatl,* the landless peasant who had no rights and few duties. According to Indian philosophy common to all Central Mexico, there should have been no category of *tlalmatl,* since a basic precept was that every man should as a matter of right have access to the land. But in the great wars of expansion the victors divided the spoils, and among the spoils land was a prime treasure. The losers, frequently finding themselves without land of their own, were forced to seek a lord to whom they could attach themselves. But the position of *tlalmatl* was not always the result of war. Late fifteenth- and early sixteenth-century religious responsibilities were exacting; and every citizen was expected to fulfill his obligations to the fullest by contributing produce, work, and, if need be, life itself. In some communities many citizens objected to the growing demands imposed by the priesthood, and in many areas the custom grew of giving every man an opportunity, immediately prior to the greatest of commemorative festivals, to eschew his obligations. This he could do, but in the act he also gave up all rights of citizenship, including those of access to land, and was forced to leave the community. As a non-citizen the only road open to the *tlalmatl* was to find a lord who would allow him to work a small plot of land in return for labor in the fields. To the land he had no right; he could be displaced at the will of the lord. But as a non-citizen he paid no taxes, assumed no religious responsibilities, and owed nothing to the community in the form of personal service. His only duty to society was that of military service in case of need. This curious class which should not have existed was in fact growing rapidly in the last years before the Spanish conquest. Had native Mexican society continued undisturbed for another hundred years it is probable that the *tlalmatl* would have become a great submerged class more numerous than the *macehuales*.

Last in the hierarchy were the slaves, mostly concentrated in the Tenochtitlán area, where they were dispatched as tribute from the Tarascans and others who specialized in slave traffic. Some slaves became so by virtue of a criminal act, and a large proportion through voluntarily selling themselves or their children to interested buyers. A complex set of regulations surrounded the institution, limiting strictly the conditions of servitude and the rights of the slaves as individuals. They had none of the rights—or duties—of citizenship, but they could marry free persons, all children were born free, and any slave could become free by paying to his master the price paid for his original condition of enslavement or by having another substitute for him. A slave could be bought for sacrificial purposes—the one source of victims for those who wished to make a special gift to their gods but who could not capture a prisoner—only if the slave were recalcitrant and had been warned by the master three different times before witnesses. The most interestingly unique aspect of the regulations gave a slave in the market a right to escape if he could, and no man save the master himself could do anything to prevent the escape.

The number of slaves cannot be ascertained, nor can the proportion, but the records indicate that there may have been as many as half a million and that the proportion had not significantly changed in the two generations prior to the conquest.

The Mexican native economic system, as could be adduced from the description of the social structure, was agriculturally based but highly complex. A full understanding of Central Mexico's truly remarkable economy must begin with an awareness of the absence of any beast of burden and a total lack of any concept of the wheel as a machine. The absence of the draft animals common to Eurasia is easily understood as an evolutionary accident, but the failure to use even rudimentary wheels—logs, for example—by a people who demonstrated some remarkable intellectual heights and technical skills is indeed baffling. That minds could conceive the instruments for astronomical observation and the mathematics to convert those observations into a calendar more accurate than that of the contemporary Europeans, or discover the secret of fusing gold and silver, or develop intricate irrigation systems, but could not recognize the utility of a log as an instrument for moving heavy stone pillars bewilders us. But the unadorned fact is that all energy was human energy, and all transportation was movement on the backs of man. This makes the construction of great public works and the transportation of masses of material even more remarkable.

The single most important agricultural product, universally cultivated by sedentary groups long before the arrival of either Nahuas or Spaniards in Anahuac, was maize. In its various forms of preparation—the tamale, the tortilla, and *atole,* for example—it was the staple food without which the people, rich and poor alike, could not have survived. The importance of the grain is attested to by the existence, in each culture group, of a goddess of maize to whom human sacrifice was frequently made. Peppers and beans followed maize in importance. Not only could all three products be used in a variety of ways, but they could be dried and preserved almost indefinitely, enhancing their value in an area of uncertain agricultural production. Farmers cultivated a great variety of squash which served not only as a food but, when dried, as containers and utensils. Tomatoes, too, grew on almost every plot of land. In addition to the foods common to all regions, many areas produced special foods which could be grown successfully only in limited sections; of these the most important was chocolate, which became noted as tribute and as money.

Aside from foodstuffs, the soil also produced cotton in some regions, and in all areas a fiber plant in one form or another. Cotton, because of its finer quality, was in the greatest demand and became important as tribute and also as a medium of exchange. The central valley itself produced no cotton, nor did the immediately contiguous areas, but the far outlying tributary sections on both the Gulf and the Pacific coasts devoted much energy to growing the coveted fiber, and that was probably a strong element in Tenochtitlán's decision to make war on them.

In the immediate vicinity of Tenochtitlán most agricultural activity originally took place along the margins of Lake Texcoco but spread into the nearby valleys as the population grew. In 1519 the lake complex, consisting of Lake Texcoco, Lake Chalco, and a number of smaller connected lakes, was much larger than it is today. At that date Tepeyac (the site of the Shrine of the Virgin of Guadalupe), Tacuba, Coyoacán, Ixtapalapa, and Texcoco were all situated on the shores of Lake Texcoco or Lake Chalco. The inhabitants exploited nearly 200 miles of lake-shore, as well as a roughly equal amount of feeder-stream valleys, for agricultural purposes. But as the population of the lake and shore cities grew (the Spaniards estimated Tenochtitlán alone to have nearly a third of a million inhabitants), the natural soils became insufficient to produce food for the citizenry. As a consequence, farmers created *chinampas,* or floating gardens, in the shallow waters along the shores, particularly on Lake Chalco. Of these remarkable essays into productive agriculture only the dreary "floating gardens" of modern Xochimilco remain as doleful reminders.

Both in the intermontane basin of Mexico and in the other sedentary regions the inhabitants put their faith in irrigation systems as well as in Tlaloc, whose largess was always seasonal. But in their irrigation the native Americans seldom showed the imagination and the perseverance demonstrated in their city water systems, which frequently were well-constructed and well-sealed double aqueducts of stone. In spite of their primitiveness, the irrigation systems were effective and only in extremely dry years failed to serve their purpose.

Even though the economic base was agriculture, non-agricultural technology was well advanced and claimed the productive efforts of a

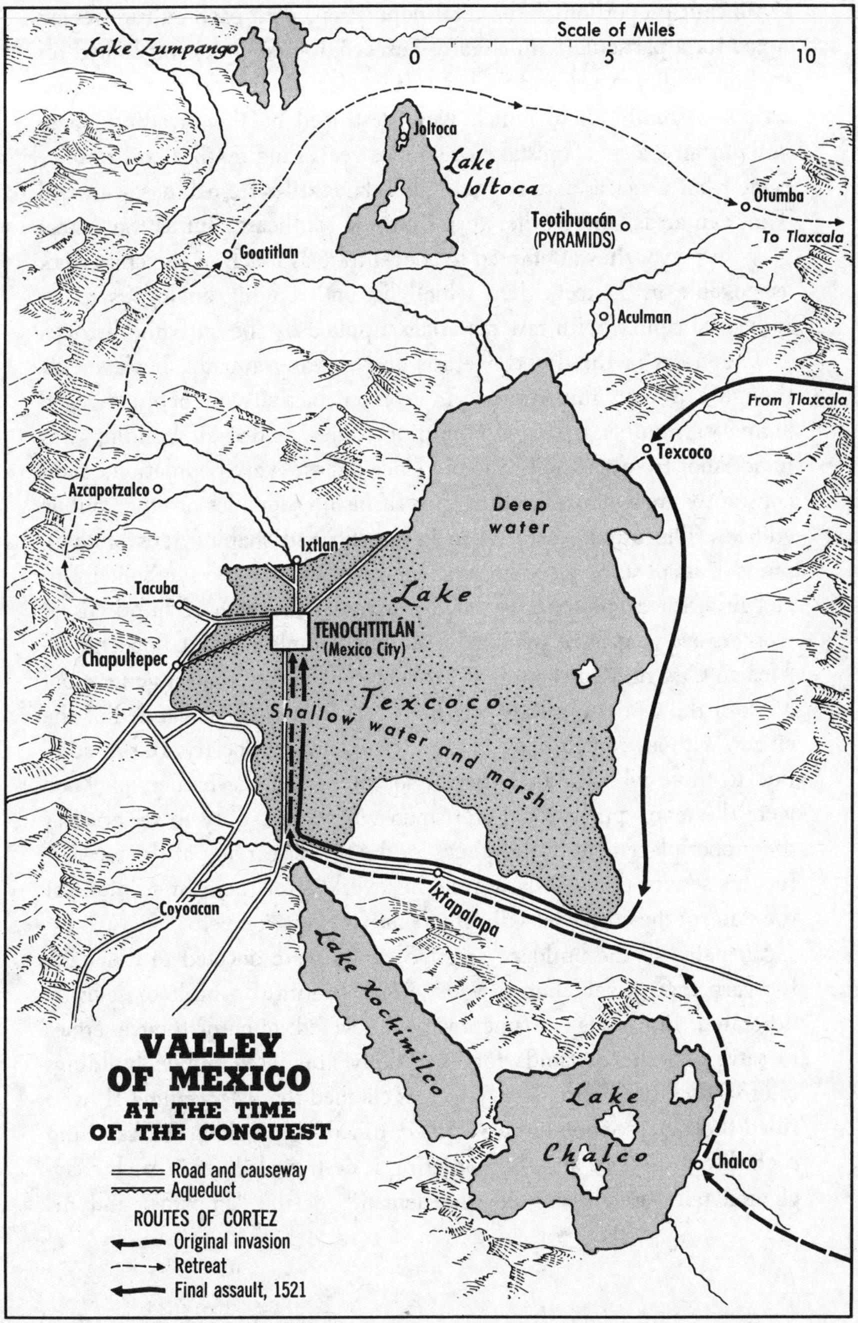
Scale of Miles
0
5
10
Lake Zumpango
Joltoca
Lake Joltoca
Otumba
Teotihuacán (PYRAMIDS)
To Tlaxcala
Goatitlan
Aculman
From Tlaxcala
Texcoco
Azcapotzalco
Deep water
Ixtlan
Lake Texcoco
Tacuba
TENOCHTITLÁN (Mexico City)
Chapultepec
Shallow water and marsh
Ixtapalapa
Coyoacan
Lake Xochimilco
Lake Chalco
Chalco
VALLEY OF MEXICO AT THE TIME OF THE CONQUEST
Road and causeway
Aqueduct
ROUTES OF CORTEZ
Original invasion
Retreat
Final assault, 1521

significant proportion of the total population, with each culture region noted for a particularly fine craft. Texcoco, for example, was famed for its fine quality paper and its beautifully decorated hieroglyphic manuscripts—virtually all of which were destroyed by the invading Spaniards in an excess of mistaken religious zeal. Fine textiles and jewelry came from Oaxaca, pottery from Cholula, textiles from Huastecan and Tarascan areas, and featherwork from the southeast. But as the Aztecs grew in power they attempted to concentrate as much of the craft work as possible in Tenochtitlán, which became roughly analogous to an industrial center, with raw materials supplied by the outlying districts.

The crafts in the decorative arts and wearing apparel, however, although extremely important as an economic activity, probably engaged a smaller number than the "building trades," since all building was hand labor from start to finish and since almost every population center constantly engaged in building or refurbishing temples or other public edifices. The infinite care taken in cutting and shaping tens of thousands of small stone pieces to produce the geometric and symbolic forms at Mitla, for example, must have demanded the time of hundreds of workers over a span of years. The glorious temple to Huitzilopochtli in Mexico City needed thousands of workers for more than a generation. Most of the work on public buildings was free work, demanded of the citizen without compensation as part of his duty to society. But in addition to those who were the hewers of stone and the haulers of wood were the many professional craftsmen whose only duty to society was the proper placement of the stones, or the proper carving of the facades; for this service their lands were either worked for them by minions of the state, or they received a direct income from the "emperor."

Virtually all the builders' creative efforts were devoted to the state, for very few private homes were either beautifully built or lavishly decorated. But other craftsmen as well devoted much of their energies to satisfying the demands for exquisitely appointed public buildings or ornately attired public officials. It is claimed that Moctezuma II, who ruled the Aztecs when Cortez arrived, dined from golden dishes, using each dish only once and then ordering it destroyed. Even if such exaggerated tales are discounted, the demands of the "emperor" and his household must have kept an army of goldsmiths occupied at their forges and worktables. Other artisans and craftsmen working with silver, copper, feathers, jade, jadeite, obsidian, and a great variety of other materials toiled constantly to produce all the insignia of office and the adornments necessary for the stratified and complex society. But not all the products of the artisans' efforts were reserved for the emblems of office; some found their way into the market, where they were bought by those who could afford the price and whose position allowed them to own and display articles of wealth.

Every center of population had its market for the exchange of goods of all kinds. Marketing was essentially a bartering operation, but by the early sixteenth century most regions had standard media of exchange which served as the base for transactions. The most valuable of these was a *quatchli* of cotton cloth, a measure of stipulated quantity and quality used as a base for tribute. A man could live on 20 *quatchli* a year; therefore in modern terms one *quatchli* approximated a day laborer's wage for about twelve working days—scarcely a medium of exchange for the purchase of a small piece of pottery or a handful of peppers. For minor purchases the more common medium was a small copper hatchet, a small transparent turkey quill filled with gold dust, or a bag of cacao beans; these items were subject to stringent regulations by a market official whose duty was to maintain a par value for each. All transactions were negotiated in terms of these exchange items, even though the physical exchange might well be in different products.

Each city had its market square and its market days well regulated and operated under the watchful eye of a galaxy of officials. In general the "markets" occurred every five days fitting the calendrical system, but larger centers such as Tenochtitlán, Tlaltelolco, Texcoco, and Cholula saw daily trading in the normal market and every fifth day special market with greater variety and quantity of articles. Shops as we know them did not exist; all buying and selling took place in a market square generally open to the weather but with porticoes for the most desirable and delicate items. Not unlike contemporary European markets, or many modern Latin American markets, each section was devoted to a particular product. The shopper, wandering from section to section, chose from a bewildering array of goods. In one area he found all the fruits and vegetables, locally and seasonally available, along with sweets—natural honey or a sirup made from maize stalks—which added zest to the meal. Hard by in the meat section the householder had the option of rabbit, deer, turkey, a variety of wild fowl including ducks in season, or, if he felt in particularly affluent mood and wished to celebrate, the little hairless dogs. In the fish section his choice included a number of different kinds of fish and crustaceans from nearby lakes; coastal markets sold fish from the seas. But the average householder probably bought little in the meat section, for his diet was largely vegetarian. Nearby, the market visitor might purchase all the standard and exotic herbs and nostrums for maintaining or regaining health, virility, or fertility, including beauty aids. When Cortez first visited the market at Tlaltelolco and saw the vendors of herbs and medicinal plants, he was reminded of the Spanish apothecary's shop. Only approved and sound health aids could be bought openly; law forbade the sale of witches' brews and fetishes under pain of death.

Not too distant from the sections devoted to comestibles was that of the more mundane household items. Here a purchaser selected from an assortment of pottery, including small delicately molded and beautifully decorated cups for drinking chocolate, large and crude cooking vessels, and everything in between. Here, too, he found dried gourds of all sizes and shapes for use in food storage. He could buy wood or charcoal for cooking, resinous torches to light his way at night or to illuminate his house, or any of a vast array of materials to furnish or build a home. Passing on, he encountered a section devoted exclusively to clothing—some of it beautifully embroidered—and to the materials from which clothing could be fashioned; here lay heaps of cotton textiles brought from the hot lands, the coarser textiles made from the fibers of various maguey-like plants, the tanned and untanned skins of animals, and occasionally a rare piece of textile made from animal hair. Those who enjoyed warm luxury and who had the price bought beautifully worked blankets of rabbit skins.

The metalsmiths, the jewelers, and the feather-workers, as the aristocrats of the craftsmen, normally displayed their wares under the porticoes. Only high officials bought the colorful feather mosaics fashioned into robes, shields, or headdresses; both price and law prohibited their possession by the *macehual*. Beautiful adornments in gold, silver, and copper, generally cast by the *cire perdue* method and then delicately engraved, could be bought, as could a vast variety of worked stones.

Finally, the market visitor refreshed himself after his day of haggling by patronizing the vendors of prepared foods and drinks. Food-vending establishments varied from those which sold complete meals to the peripatetic dispenser of boiled corn on the cob, or tortillas, or tamales.

Reputedly the greatest of all markets was that of Tlaltelolco, Tenochtitlán's neighbor and often bitter rival on the lake islands. Cortez and his companions reported with awe that the marketplace was greater in size than any in Spain; Cortez himself estimated it to be twice as large as that of Salamanca, and the variety of wares reminded Bernal Díaz del Castillo of Medina del Campo. According to European sources, the average daily attendance at the Tlaltelolco market exceeded 20,000, and on "market day" the number doubled or trebled. Men and women from all walks of life attended, the aristocrats followed by porters carrying both purchases and the necessary media of exchange, and the lower classes clutching their bags of chocolate beans and haggling over each meager transaction. Magistrates were conveniently located to settle any dispute concerning quality or measurement of goods; these officials rendered all judgments on the spot and there meted out penalties and collected fines.

The markets owed their size and excellence to a specialized group of "foreign" traders known as the *pochteca* as well as to the people in the immediate vicinity who flocked to the cities to buy and sell. Trading between Indian linguistic and culture groups was a phenomenon well before the emergence of the Aztec empire; yet George Vaillant believes that Mexican knowledge of metallurgy came, by way of stages through Central America from Ecuador, no earlier than the eleventh century. Certainly trading among all groups was active, but it was just as certainly unorganized, until the Nahuas in the exercise of their one true genius—organization—took a hand. As Aztec power grew, the conquerors withdrew the trading privilege from the conquered and left all inter-cultural trading in the hands of Mexican Valley residents who came to concentrate in Tenochtitlán and Tlaltelolco in specially designated boroughs. The traders, the *pochteca,* enjoyed an absolute monopoly of such trade, but in return they rendered an enormous service to their cities by acting as the advance intelligence service upon which later conquest could be based. In their journeys to regions beyond Aztec sway, they gathered information concerning the nature of the social structure, the forms of religion, the wealth, the population, and the military organization. Such an expedition dispatched to Oaxaca with carefully detailed instructions from Moctezuma I paved the way for the incorporation of that rich province into the tribute system. Before the Aztec collapse under Spanish guns, the *pochteca* ranged into the Chichimec region to the north, the Tarascan to the west, and the Mayan to the southeast, while maintaining their regular expeditions into the regions already incorporated into the empire.

A trading expedition was a veritable human caravan, organized and carried out with military discipline and dispatch. On an expedition only *pochteca* members and their porters, generally slaves, were allowed, and each member of the group bore the responsibility for his own goods; but the caravan functioned as a unit, with every man prepared at any moment to fight. In battle their object was to protect themselves and their goods, not to take captives. This was a rugged and determined group involved in a dangerous but lucrative enterprise.

Since the *pochteca* functioned in part to help establish Tenochtitlán as the empire's "industrial" hub, most of the goods they carried from Tenochtitlán to the hinterland consisted of finished products, while they brought back raw materials. Embroidered cloth, rabbit-fur blankets, medicinal herbs, dyes, obsidian knives, and jewelry figured prominently in the outgoing bundles, while semi-precious stones in their natural state, feathers of the quetzal and other birds, pearls, tortoise shells, amber, untanned animal skins, and copper nodules made up the bulk of the items brought back to the city. The *pochteca* were forbidden to trade in cotton, cotton cloth (except that which had been reworked in Tenochtitlán), gold, and chocolate beans; these were rigidly controlled tribute items, transported to the metropolis by special imperial messengers. Tribute products certainly contributed an important part of the goods displayed in the Tlaltelolco and Tenochtitlán markets, but the *pochteca,* trading throughout Mexico, gave to those markets an air of the exotic and a quality of richness.

The member of the *pochteca* more closely approached the prototype of "economic man" than any other in Mexican society. For all others wealth was an attribute and a result of position. The Mexican aristocrat who wore his rich and colorful robes proudly, who decorated himself with all the finery available to him from his world, did so because they constituted his emblems of office; he carried those emblems in exactly the same way that a modern Guatemalan village official carries his staff of authority. Through these manifestations of wealth his fellow citizens identified him as an official; that they also recognized him as a man of wealth was completely incidental. The *pochteca,* on the other hand, occupied no official position in the hierarchy of control; a member of the trading group had no badge of office save the distinctive but serviceable and inexpensive—even grubby—clothing he wore on the road. His activities brought no public praise nor did they give him religious solace. The trader sought wealth for itself, and he gained it. Reputedly the wealthiest of men, excepting only the "emperor," he never flaunted his wealth in public; his dress differed little from the poorest *macehual.* But the interior of his home, closed to all citizens other than members of his own trading class, was lavishly furnished and beautifully appointed, while the exterior appeared as humble as the poor man's hut. The traders constituted a potential power threat, but the aristocracy appeared to agree tacitly with the traders' drive for wealth as long as they made no public display of that wealth. Whether in the long run, had the orderly evolutionary process not been upset by the conquering Spaniards, the traders' wealth would also have brought them power is an interesting speculation.

Mexican economy operated under a pall of unproductive workers whose labors were necessary to the maintenance of an accepted pattern of life but which gave no help to the production of consumable goods. Although the annalists have left us no records by which to estimate the size of this non-productive group, the entire social and economic fabric suggests a top-heavy structure. In the larger population centers the governmental bureaucracy—tax collectors, accountants, tribute distributors, magistrates, and the like—constituted a large segment of the labor force. To be sure, they all had land allotted to them, and in the lower echelons they probably performed some of the work on the land, but most of the actual farming fell to the lot of *macehuales*. The bureaucrats were a highly trained professional group, dedicated and hard-working but essentially parasitic.

The army made up the second great class of non-productive workers. The citizen-warrior had, by the sixteenth century, all but disappeared; now the security of the home front and the extension of the frontier (as well as the supply for the sacrificial stone) lay in the competent hands of professionals, except during times of extraordinary crisis, when the "emperor" called upon all able-bodied men to protect their civilization. To be sure, every man served his tour of military duty when he reached the age of maturity, but those who failed to distinguish themselves mustered out as soon as possible, while those to whom military life appealed remained as a part of the standing army. The size of this professional army we cannot know with precision, but the nature of the society, the extent of the empire, and the number of captives sacrificed to various gods each year suggest an army proportionately larger than those of modern nations, even militaristic ones.

The priesthood comprised the third significantly large group which depended upon the productive capacity of the other members of the society. The chroniclers have left us no estimate of their numbers, but the priestly function and the number of gods indicate that they were many. A principal priest attended each temple, and eight to ten priests of second rank along with a number of aspiring neophytes aided him in his demanding tasks, but attending temples made up only a small part of religious work. With religious ritual so intimately interrelated with all other aspects of life, and with such a multitude of gods to succor (Vaillant names 63 "principal" gods), the society demanded and received much from its priests. They kept both the ritual calendar of 260 days and the solar of 365, and their astronomical observations and mathematical calculations determined the course of events. Political leaders constantly consulted them as to the auguries for crops or temple construction, water supply or health; military leaders called upon them for priestly help in divining the need for godly intercession in campaigns of expansion or entrenchment, or the simple maintenance of peace in potentially rebellious regions. The priests determined the time, the number, and the nature of the sacrifices, and then officiated at the gory rituals. They worked out in detail the religious demands to be made upon the citizenry, and created the ambient within which the public participated in them; since the average citizen devoted more time to religious observances than to any other single endeavor, all within a precise but highly variable pattern, this task alone consumed vast amounts of priestly energy. The priestly class was responsible, in short, for the orderly rhythm of life. In a very real sense it governed daily activity to a greater degree than did the civil bureaucracy, and it was probably as large.

And so the native Mexican society was functioning when the Spaniards arrived on the Gulf Coast and began their march inland. To European eyes the empire of the Mexica presented a baffling picture, at once highly sophisticated but barbaric. The beauty of the public buildings, the cleanliness of the city and the people, the generosity of the "emperor," and the wealth of the nation all strongly attracted the emissaries from the Old World, but all these things stood in sharp contrast to the repulsive filth of the sacrificial priests with gore-matted hair, the rapacious cruelties of the tribute collectors, and the obvious destitution of the half-naked *macehuales*. Civilization and barbarism, intellectual sophistication and technological primitiveness showed the two faces of native American society. These contradictions were obvious to all who would look, but not so clear were the rapid changes then taking place in the social and economic structures. The fast-growing aristocracy demanded more than ever before from the citizenry at large, but the mass of the population enjoyed none of the advantages of a well-endowed society in spite of the greater complexity of Mexican life in 1519 than in 1450 and despite the great wealth concentrated in the capital. Perhaps the central Mexican *macehual* received some psychic income from his frequent participation in the great religious festivals and from his being a part of a conquering people, but of material wealth he knew no more than had his forefathers as members of a wandering tribe. But even he suffered less than the *macehual* of the surrounding and tributary cultures who had seen his income, cut into by the demands of the tribute system, dwindle away to mere subsistence. Furthermore, religious obligations for all men had become ever more extensive and ever more onerous; the average man devoted some 30 per cent of his waking hours to some aspect of religious observance, to which he gave not only his time but his goods. The gods, once the benevolent protectors of struggling men, had grown cruel and oppressive as the priests translated their demands; the thousands of skulls adorning the top platform of the great temple to Huitzilopochtli mutely testified to the changed character of those gods and to the barbaric cruelties perpetrated in their behalf. To the mass of native Mexicans, the Spanish victory may well have been as much a deliverance as a conquest.

Chapter 3 • Society under the Spaniards

They do nothing but make demands, and no matter how much is done for them they are never satisfied. Wherever they are they spoil and corrupt everything, emitting a stench like spoiled meat. They make no effort to do anything but command. They are the drones which consume the honey which is worked by the poor bees, the Indians. What the poor people are able to give them does not satisfy them. They are unreasonable. . . . I do not know whence our Spaniards acquire possessions. They come from Spain very poor and carrying a sword. After a year they have more trunks and clothes than a drove of beasts could carry while their houses have to be like those of gentlemen.

TORIBIO DE MOTOLINÍA, *c.* 1540

When he wrote these bitter lines less than a generation following the Spanish conquest of Mexico, the pious Franciscan did not include all Spaniards in his denunciation—he castigated particularly the overseers and tribute collectors—but he came unfortunately close to characterizing all new arrivals. The long violent struggle against the Moors, which reached its crescendo in the thirty years just prior to the discovery of America and, by unhappy coincidence, its victorious conclusion the year Columbus set sail, formed the sixteenth-century Spaniard. First and foremost a fighter, the adventurer who set off to conquer the new world was restless, symbolically a nobleman, quarrelsome and proud to the point of arrogance; he dreamed of the time when he would in fact become the lord of all he surveyed. This attitude he brought with him to Mexico, and this frame of mind imposed its will on the native population.

Furthermore, the fifteenth-century Spanish struggle revolved in part around a contest between Christianity and Islam, leaving its residue of bias. Sixteenth-century clerics in Mexico, men like Motolinía or Bernardino de Sahagún or Pedro de Gante, might rail against the newcomers because they failed to fulfill their religious obligations, yet the man who came from Spain—be he regular communicant or occasional church visitor—did show a fanatical Christian zeal. Even Nuño de Guzmán, who dragged a priest from the pulpit during Mass because the clergyman dared criticize Guzmán's policies, considered himself a devoted defender of the true faith. To men of this mentality non-Christians were heathens, by definition workers for Satan, deserving extermination. The devil showed his works everywhere in Indian religious life: idolatry, polytheism, human sacrifice, perverted rituals. But Satan and his minions worked not only in the New World; in the Old the zealous fires ignited by the titanic struggle with Islam had been replenished when Martin Luther posted his Ninety-five Theses. Spain became the center and defender of the true faith, beset on all sides by dangers, and the conscience of every loyal Spaniard demanded that he defend his religion. When he arrived in Mexico and confronted the incredible task of bringing his own true values to the alien culture, he came with religious as well as social convictions.

In a curious way the Aztecs and Spaniards shared the same genius and the same weaknesses. The Aztecs built their imposing empire by sheer organizational and administrative genius, bolstered by awesome military power. The Spanish too achieved in the colonial regions a political and administrative system little short of miraculous, though the system proved not as effective in practice as it appeared in theory; and Spanish armies swept all before them. But both Spanish and Aztecs created social and economic systems based upon false assumptions, and neither Spaniards nor Aztec could envisage a society with any underlying precept other than rigidly drawn and legally enforced class lines.

The Spaniards never constituted more than a mere fraction of Mexico's total population throughout the three centuries of their dominion. When Cortez first sighted the wonders of Tenochtitlán, Spain's people numbered less than 8 million, and only a tiny minority was free by law and circumstance to leave her boundaries. A fantastic choice confronted those who might leave, for the New World opened to them was forty times the size of Spain and supported a population seven to ten times as large. Small wonder, then, that at the end of a century and a quarter of occupation, Mexico's European population had grown by only slightly more than 1000 a year. During these five generations the total number of arriving Spaniards was smaller than the number of Indians who died *every sixty days* during the occupation's first generation.

Official Spanish emigration policy was clear-cut and restrictive. In contrast to the English, who encouraged or even forced their religious and political dissidents to quit the mother country and establish colonies, the Spanish demanded the utmost in civic and religious conformity. A slavish loyalty to Spanish institutions prohibited any originality in the creation of new institutions, or the adaptation of old ones to meet the challenge of the Mexican ambient. To be sure, some dissidents found their way to Mexico—Spain has always been much better at creating law than enforcing it—but these few soon disappeared into the general population and left no indelible mark on institutional development.

The foregoing statements do not imply that the Spaniards in Mexico constituted one cohesive and co-operative group. Far from it. The squabbling, quarreling, and backbiting, notorious in the first generations, did not occur over the creation of new and experimental institutions; they concerned the selection of old institutions and the exercise of power—economic, political, social. Even among those whose very creeds and oaths bound them to gentility and brotherhood—the clerics—the din of quarrel resounded symbolically throughout Europe. Franciscan suspected Dominican, both feared Jesuit, and all three engendered jealousy among secular clergy. But all the clergy agreed on one thing: catastrophe lurked in a grant of power to lay authority.

The Spanish crown required that its emigrants be solid citizens, respected in their home communities, free from debt, and practiced in a profession or a skill advantageous to the budding colony. The crown did not deny single men passage, but it preferred family men accompanied by wives and children, since family responsibilities gave social stability. Furthermore, each traveler to the New World was required to prove his *limpieza de sangre,* freedom from taint of heresy or Islam or Judaism for three generations. Since all its colonists thus represented the virtues of solid Spanish Catholic respectability, the crown expected the development of idyllic and profitable colonies, untroubled by sedition and rebellion. And in fact, for nearly three hundred years Spain was untroubled by insurrection, even though the majority of the Spaniards who came did not quite fit the mold designed by crown advisors. Solid citizens practising a respectable trade they might have been in Spain, but once they arrived in New Spain they forgot their trades and sought more lucrative and gentlemanly outlets. Energetic they were, but the rudest peasant whose only previous economic activity had been tilling the soil refused to sully his hands by planting or reaping. And regardless of their good intentions with respect to their families, only a distinct minority either brought their wives with them or sent for them later. The pattern, developed early, varied little during the three-century span of colonialism: the colonists were male, vigorous, lusty, ambitious, and zealous—and far from home. They were confronted with the very real problem of bringing some kind of political, social, and economic order out of an essentially chaotic condition. The results might have been foretold.

News of Cortez's victory over the Aztecs created a sensation in Spain, and every telling of the event embellished the tale. Young men hurried to the ports, avid to search for the mountains of gold and silver in the New World to be had for the asking. Debarking in Veracruz, founded by Cortez before he marched on Tenochtitlán, they quickly made their way to the new Spanish capital of Mexico City, built on the ruins of Tenochtitlán-Tlaltelolco. From that point they sought the key to a fortune. The new arrivals joined forces with the original conquerors fanning out in all directions to complete the occupation, for the fall of Tenochtitlán had simply heralded the fall of the Aztec empire and left much work to be done. In late 1521 the settled areas of the Gulf Coast to the north and south of Veracruz were occupied, and in the following year an expedition to the south convinced the Zapotecs and the Mixtecs to submit to the new power. The western Tarascans, who from afar and with mixed feelings watched the Aztecs struggle with the Spanish, decided after the fall of Tenochtitlán that the Spaniards were worth courting and therefore despatched to Mexico City a delegation in 1522, submitting themselves to the European nation without a struggle. The conquerors magnanimously sent a small expedition into the Tarascan country to establish Zacatula as a center of Spanish power. During the next few years the Otomies to the north and the Huastecans to the northeast were brought under Spanish dominion, and control over the latter group became assured with the establishment of the city of Pánuco. Nuño de Guzmán drove the Huastecans to despair and rebellion by his enslaving activities as their first governor, but they were helpless against the rapidly increasing Spanish power. Before the end of the first decade the Spanish occupied the present state of Jalisco, all southeastern Mexico along the Gulf Coast to Yucatán, and all of the hinterland. By 1540 the sedentary groups, with the exception of pockets of Mayas in Yucatán, were effectively controlled and the potential profits from the occupation parceled out among those who had had a hand in the conquests. To this point the fabled wealth of the Aztecs had proved a chimera; no great treasure hoard had been found in either Aztec or outlying centers, and an earthquake had permanently destroyed the only producing silver mine yet discovered.

Those who somehow missed out on the distribution of the spoils, and those who arrived too late for a share in the largess of Indian labor and tribute, began casting further afield for wealth. Rumors of great treasure impelled Francisco de Coronado to undertake his hazardous trek to Gran Quivira which, like the end of the rainbow, could never be found. Even though his search was fruitless, those who entered the Chichimec country in the forbidding area to the north between the mountain ranges were more fortunate. In 1546 a small group of adventurers discovered, well within the "barbarians'" stronghold, an imposing hill of silver ore; La Bufa became a great mining center, with the city of Zacatecas sprawling at its feet. The Chichimecs, quite understandably, resented this intrusion and, egged on by their warrior-priests who feared a loss of their own power, undertook to drive the invaders from their land. Fifty years and thousands of Indian lives later, the region and the long road connecting it with Mexico City were secured. In the meantime the ore, low in quality but vast in quantity, poured out its cascade of silver. While the war with the Chichimecs flared, the Spaniards uncovered even richer deposits of silver between Zacatecas and Mexico City in Guanajuato and then, a little later, other veins to the east of Guanajuato at San Luis Potosí. But while some men probed the great unknown land beyond the Chichimec country in search of mineral wealth, others dug into promising outcroppings nearer the center of population, and they came upon enormous riches of the Pachuca region as well as the important but less valuable mines near Taxco.

By the end of the sixteenth century the bolder souls among the Spanish had moved into and occupied—tenuously, perhaps, but permanently—most of the area now encompassed in the Republic of Mexico. Only in that area comprising the extreme northern parts of the states of Sonora, Chihuahua, Coahuila, Nuevo León, and Tamaulipas did the *indios broncos* retain sway. These areas, with their forbidding land and climate, wandering and savage Indians, and no mineral sources of any note, the Spaniards adjudged unworthy of their efforts. Not until many generations later, pushed by the stimulus of international politics rather than the search for wealth, did Spain bestir herself to extend the northern frontier into the limits of the present United States.

Two economic factors determined the settlement patterns. The first was the presence of large numbers of sedentary Indians whose labor could be used for the enrichment of the intruding Spaniards. Since the intermontane basin of Mexico had constituted the center of the Aztec empire and contained, with the immediately contiguous basins of Puebla on the east and Toluca on the west, millions of indigenes now thoroughly cowed and ready to hand, this region attracted the heaviest Spanish settlement; the Spaniards always focused on Mexico

City. But some more distant areas also held the great attraction of numerous Indians whose energies might be exploited directly through forced labor or indirectly through tribute; these groups acted as magnets to draw the Spaniards into Oaxaca, Chiapas, Tabasco, Michoacán, Jalisco, and Yucatán.

Silver mining also created settlement clusters. The very geologic and climatic circumstances which produced exploitable mineral deposits also produced an ambience unattractive to human habitation. Millennia of water erosion, so necessary for fertile soil and mass vegetation, obscured rather than laid bare the ore; wind erosion left ore outcroppings visible to the prying eye. The Indian civilizations, dependent upon agriculture and unsophisticated regarding metallic ores, left the barren hills of Zacatecas and other potentially rich mineral areas unoccupied, and so mining regions demanded that a population be imported. Forced labor, to be described subsequently, met one problem quite nicely, but mining settlements required food-producers as well as ore-diggers, and each mining region therefore attracted new agricultural and pastoral entrepreneurs. Zacatecas, Guanajuato, San Luis Potosí, Parral, Sombrerete, Batopilas, Ramos, and other mining towns within the forbidding central bowl certainly never rivalled Mexico City as metropolitan centers but they gathered a significant population which with the passage of time took on the trappings of high European civilization; Guanajuato even sported an opera house.

A discussion of population in New Spain during the colonial period, whether of the European, the indigenous, or the mixed groups, must be approached somewhat timorously, since all data are highly speculative. In the twilight of the empire, in 1793, colonial officials gathered the data for the first census, incomplete and inaccurate. The viceroy undertook the survey at this time only because a momentarily reform-minded Spanish government finally determined that intelligent policy could be formulated only on the basis of data rather than intuition. In the intervening two and three-quarters centuries a number of observers had made intelligent guesses, and since that time scholars have put their talents to a determination of the population. But at best the following data are indicative rather than finite.

European population in New Spain increased in a gradually ascending curve until late in the colonial period, when the rate of increase showed a marked decline. By 1570, half a century after the initial occupation of Tenochtitlán, the Europeans numbered 63,000, of whom 12,000 lived in the city of Mexico and 24,000 in the larger diocese of Mexico, which included those areas most intimately connected to the defunct Aztec empire. One of every 25 Spaniards was a cleric, engaged in convincing the Indians of the great advantages accruing from European standards. By 1646 the European population had doubled through natural increase as well as immigration which brought a trickle of women: about one of every ten. Of the 125,000 Europeans, 48,000 found the capital more attractive than the hinterlands, and another 10,000 remained within the diocese although not in the city. The clergy increased more rapidly than the general population, largely by natural expansion since seminaries boomed, and now one of every nineteen was a man of the cloth.

By 1770 the European population had grown to slightly more than three-quarters of a million, over 10 per cent of whom resided in Mexico City and about 46 per cent of whom remained within hailing distance. The rest had scattered, with the present states of Michoacán and Puebla each attracting well over 100,000. The clerical proportion had declined enormously during the intervening century and a quarter, and now only one in each 78 had taken the vows. The first official census, in 1793, indicated a European population of slightly more than a million, one-eighth of whom still sought the joys of metropolitan living in the capital and the vast majority of whom lived within the central highland complex.

Immigration played but a small role in population increase after the first fifty years, for from that time forward the American-born Europeans outnumbered the Spanish-born in ever-increasing proportions. Alexander von Humboldt estimated that in 1803 only 70,000 European-born resided in Mexico, constituting slightly more than 6 per cent of the total. The relatively low rate of population increase—between 1 and 2 per cent annually in the late colonial period—can probably be accounted for by the distinctly smaller numbers of women than men except in the great urban centers. Women did not immigrate to Mexico, and those born in the colony left the pioneering to others. Von Humboldt estimated that only ten Spanish-born women for every 100 Spanish-born men resided in Mexico City, while among the *criollos* (Mexican-born of European heritage) 136 women had to vie for the attentions of 100 men. The greater proportion of women in the cities, of course, meant a dearth in the countryside, and a young rancher in Oaxaca or Durango or Jalisco frequently found it impossible to select a suitable European wife. The *criollo* male was at a particular disadvantage, since the Mexican woman, *peninsular* or *criolla*, preferred the peninsular man with his Old World airs. Competition for women created an animosity between the *criollo* and the peninsular men.

From the beginning miscegenation, either in the form of concubinage or legal marriage, created a new population constituent. Both Church and crown originally encouraged it, but by the end of the sixteenth century society's most prestigious members attached a social stigma to intermarriage and thereby discouraged its legality but left concubinage and casual liaison untouched. While society frowned, Spanish men and Indian women produced a new group, the *mestizo*. Transportation of African slaves introduced another racial strain, and new mixtures soon appeared. Before the end of the colonial period the European applied the term *castas* to all combinations of European, African, and Indian genetics, and he considered all inferior to him. Regardless of social status, the *castas* expanded rapidly; by 1650 they accounted for 160,000, and by 1800 they exceeded the Europeans by two to one.

While the white and mixed populations steadily increased, the Indian declined catastrophically for the first hundred and twenty-five years and then began a slow increase. During the first twenty-five years the indigenes disappeared at such an unbelievable rate that it constitutes one of civilization's major calamities. Beset by devastating new diseases, the 20 million native population of 1520 declined to six and one-half million by 1540. During the next generation their group lost another two million, by 1607 the total had declined to two million, and by 1650, only slightly more than a million natives could be found.

From that low point the Indians gradually increased during the remainder of the colonial period and grew to approximately two and one-half million by 1800, slightly less than one-half the total population.

The Spaniard brought with him not only social attitudes and a political system; he brought diseases to which the native population had no natural immunity and which, sweeping through the Indian centers, frequently turned back upon the European with terrifying force. Smallpox epidemics followed a cyclical pattern, descending with lesser or greater violence every seven or eight years. Smallpox destroyed entire indigenous communities while Motolinía worked among them, and it killed nearly 20 per cent of the population of Mexico City as late as 1779. Only with the introduction of an inoculation-vaccination procedure in the late colonial period did the ravages of the disease assume less serious proportions. Measles, too, took a heavy toll, particularly among the native population during the first hundred years. But the Indian population was hardest hit by a mysterious disease, as yet unidentified but believed to have been either a form of influenza or of typhus, called by the natives *matlazahuatl*. Torquemada estimated that an epidemic in 1545 took the lives of 800,000, and that a more serious and widespread epidemic in 1576 decreased the population by two million. As late as 1780 the disease took a heavy toll throughout the central area, with the Bajío region especially hard hit. The malady intrigued many minds during the colonial period inasmuch as it had some peculiar characteristics. The native population seemed particularly susceptible to it, even though it existed prior to the Spanish arrival; cases among the Europeans were so rare that some accounts erroneously insist that Europeans were completely immune. Furthermore, the disease struck only the highlands, with no cases reported below the 3000-foot level and with the greatest virulence at the 6000-foot elevation and above.

Danger to the Europeans from coastal diseases, especially yellow fever, forced the Spaniards to move to higher grounds as soon as possible after arrival; Veracruz remained the most important port, but the city never attracted a European population sufficient to give it the flavor of a great urban center, and it remained as little more than an entrepôt.

Disease had effective allies in crop failure and malnutrition. Increasing demands by Europeans for Indian labor during the sixteenth and seventeenth centuries, just when the Indian population went into a disastrous decline, siphoned off so large a proportion of the able-bodied that many Indian communities could no longer produce enough food. Endemic malnutrition became near-starvation during years of unfavorable weather; the weakened bodies then became easy prey for disease, and epidemic disease usually accompanied widespread crop failure. The last of these allied scourges occurred in 1784 and the two following years, during which an estimated 300,000 lost their lives to respiratory infections which struck in areas already hard hit by drought. In all these epidemics accompanying malnutrition the Indians and *castas* suffered most, since the Europeans used the power of their governmental control to guarantee food for their own kind.

The net population result of three hundred years of Spanish control was little short of catastrophic. Even if we accept the earlier and more modest figure of 11 million instead of the most recent of over 20 million as the pre-conquest population, the total population in 1800 was only slightly more than one half that of 1519, and not for another hundred years did the Mexican population equal its pre-conquest level. The same held true for the great urban centers. The conquerors estimated the population of Tenochtitlán at 300,000 or more, rather a moderate number if we accept a market attendance of 60,000. But in 1800 the city numbered only about 125,000, and it was not until well into the nineteenth century that the residents came up to the earlier figure. The populations of Tlaxcala and Cholula have never grown to pre-conquest size, and recent investigations indicate the same to be true of the major population centers of the Zapotecs. Population decline was not the result of a deliberate policy of extermination; it came from a compound of ignorance, cupidity, and Indian susceptibility to European diseases. But regardless of cause, a population shift and decline left behind grave social and economic problems.

When the first Spaniards arrived in Mexico they found a major problem of social control, since they were a tiny minority surrounded by a potentially hostile group. Coming as they did, too, with preconceived notions concerning their own world position, they were terribly concerned with the development of institutions which would allow them both to control and to exploit the natives. The resulting *encomienda-repartimiento* system, to be examined in the next chapter, reflected social attitudes which became an immutable attribute of colonial society.

As the proportions and the character of the population changed through immigration and miscegenation, the dominant European developed his control techniques to a fine point. Toward the end of the colonial period, Bishop Antonio de San Miguel of Valladolid (now Morelia) wrote to Charles IV in righteous indignation:

> The population of New Spain is composed of three classes of men; to wit, whites or Spanish, Indians, and castes. . . . Almost all property and wealth is in their [Spanish] hands. The Indians and the castes till the soil; they serve the upper class, and live only by the work of their arms. From this grows, between the Indians and the whites, an opposition of interests, a reciprocal hate, which so easily springs up between those who have everything and those who have nothing, between masters and slaves.

Fra Antonio was as much concerned with practical and dangerous realities as he was with man's inhumanity to man; he saw in the class system the germ of future disasters, and unfortunately he assessed the situation correctly.

The Spanish dominated the power structure immediately after the conquest, and even though circumstance and policy divided them into two antagonistic groups, they never relinquished that control. The numerically inferior but politically superior colonials were those born in Spain who were favored by the Spanish government; they called themselves *peninsulares* but the American-born Spaniard, the creole, referred to them as *gachupines,* a contemptuous term. Spanish law treated the two groups as equals, giving them the same advantages and demanding of them the same duties; but Spanish action made a clear distinction between them. The European Spaniard then, as now, simply assumed that the atmosphere in the New World produced an inferior product, one which could not be trusted with the responsibilities of important civil, military, or clerical office and one whose loyalty was ever in question. The crown therefore quite naturally reserved all high offices—to be sure, a diligent search can unearth some glaring exceptions—to the *peninsulares,* and the crown officials in turn extended what favors they could to their European-born compatriots. The recent arrival, his ego fed by the "official" view in Spain and often bolstered by fawning creoles, treated the American-born with a contempt equaled only by the contempt which all of European parentage felt for Indians. He demanded, and frequently received, special treatment by a viceregal government which would allow him to live in comfort; to him fell lucrative governmental positions, special concessions and social acceptance. But *gachupines* exceeded sinecures, and every urban center had its share of *peninsulares* who, like Lazarillo's noble gentleman, had more pride than food. Economic failure merely exacerbated the feelings, and before the end of the colonial period a dangerous animosity existed between the 70,000 *peninsulares* and the million or more creoles whose mines and cattle ranches formed the base of colonial economy.

At the opposite end of the social continuum rested the largest population group, the lowly Indian. Every vestige of the pre-conquest hierarchy had disappeared under European domination. Destruction of the Indian aristocracy resulted from deliberate policy, not accident. Soon after the conquest many Spanish, particularly some dedicated and able clerics, envisaged a society in which the Indian aristocracy, educated into European standards and values, might lead the mass of the population to religious and social salvation. With this in mind Fra Pedro de Gante established a school for *pilili* immediately after the conquest, and the great Viceroy Antonio de Mendoza gave it his blessing and support shortly after his arrival in 1535. The school was an undoubted success; in fact its success was so patent as to give pause to the majority of Spaniards who feared social uplift for the native population. Jerónimo López, one of Mendoza's counsellors, took violent exception to his superior's support of the school; in a letter written directly to Charles V in 1541 he complained about the clerics and their Indian education program:

> Not satisfied with having the Indians know how to read and write, illustrate books . . . or be musicians, they have put them to learning grammar. They give them so much, and with such care, that there

> were boys, and every day there are more, who speak as elegant Latin as Tullius. . . . Concerning this, when it began, many times . . . I spoke before the Oidores of the error involved and the harm which would come from the Indians studying sciences. . . . It seems to me that the only remedy now is to bring it to an immediate end.

López was not alone in his fears, and his views prevailed; by the end of the sixteenth century no Indian was to receive a formal education. Descendants of the proud *tecuhtli* sank to the level of the *macehuales*.

The Spaniard placed the Indians socially and legally into a class apart. He considered them wards of the state, potentially able to assimilate the merits of civilization but in fact remaining immature and childlike, and he consequently designed a legal system applicable to the Indians alone. Law excused the Indian from payment of the onerous *alcabala,* a heavy transaction tax, but it forced him to pay tribute and in so doing denied him citizenship while leaving him for twelve generations a conquered man in his own land. Financially the tribute exacted less than the *alcabala;* psychologically it produced trauma. Law also prevented the Indian from contracting a debt greater than 5 *pesos,* thus effectively eliminating him as a possible competitor in every major capital-demanding economic activity and forcing him to depend upon rudimentary farming. Law isolated him into ghettos in the urban areas and denied to him the use of firearms, or cattle branding iron, or European dress. But law also gave him some dubious advantages. He was seldom subject to fine, rarely sent to prison, and almost never executed. Nor was he subject to slavery except for rebellion. But this legal protection frequently did not save him from the slave branding-iron. The Indian guilty of a breach of law learned Spanish virtue through lashes across his bared back; if his offense were grave he might be maimed. The Spanish could justly point out that after three hundred years of European domination the Indian had changed little from his primitive ways and, further, that the primitive nature of the Indian demanded a separate legal code. He would vehemently deny that the code itself prevented change.

But in one major outward respect the Indian had indeed changed. Early arrivals in Mexico, including the conquerors, universally commented on the gaiety of Indian life; certainly the Indian's keen sense of humor and his wit impressed the dour Spaniard. In contrast, by the end of the colonial period observers spoke of the Indian as lugubrious, withdrawn, sad, and serious even in his songs and dances:

> The indigenes of Mexico who have experienced ages of slavery, both under their own rulers and under the first conquerors [said Alexander von Humboldt], suffer with patience the vexations to which they are still frequently exposed on the part of the whites; their defense against them is a cunning covered by a veil of most deceptive appearances of apathy and stupidity.

A sad phlegmatic people seething with resentment, ready to wreak vengeance on those who had so mistreated them but without the instruments at hand for that vengeance: this was the native. Few Spaniards in 1800 recognized the resentment, and those who denied its existence had the weight of history on their side; save for an inconsequential rebellion by a group of Tlaxcalans in the seventeenth century, not a single Indian movement menaced Central Mexico between the Mixton War of the early 1540's and the revolution for independence in 1810.

Between the Indian pariah and the dominant European stood the social component destined to become Mexico's controlling force, a population segment stemming from the others but not fully accepted by anyone. The Spanish, with their often obscured but extreme sensitivity to "race," distinguished sixteen different racial classifications, each with its distinctive generic name depending upon the racial strains of the parents. One, the product of the Spanish-Indian union, was the *mestizo*. The Spanish-Negro union produced the mulatto, and a Negro-Indian union the *zambo*. With classical lack of logic the Spaniard identified some strains to the fourth generation, but with others he stopped at the first or second, still others he did not list at all. For example, a *mestizo*-Spanish union gave *castizo,* but *castizo*-Spanish returned to Spanish, while Spanish-*mulata* gave *morisco,* Spanish-*morisca* gave *albino,* and Spanish-*albina* produced *torna atrás* according to one classification and *salta atrás* according to another—but in neither case Spanish. Children of Negro-*castiza* and Indian-*mulata* had no niche in the official designations, perhaps on the assumption that such uinons did not exist. Confronted with the task of inventing hundreds of new, descriptive, and disdainful names if the classification were carried through logically to the third or fourth generation, the Spanish solved the problem by calling all mixtures *castas* and by lumping them together in a legal condition between the Spanish and the Indian, with the advantages of neither and many of the duties of both.

Since many *mestizos* resulted from casual liaisons between the Spanish male and the Indian female, neither the Spanish parent nor the Indian grandparent demonstrated any particular desire to accept the social responsibilities for the newly born. Shut off from European society and cut off from the Indian as soon as he could fend for himself, the young *mestizo* found himself in a most difficult social situation. Like the Spaniard, he paid the *alcabala,* he could be called for military duty, and he faced fine, imprisonment, or death for infractions of the law. But unlike the European he could occupy no political post, he could not practice certain professions—law, for example—and he received from the government no special privileges. Like the Indian he could not use a cattle branding-iron, he could not have "in his possession a lance or hocking knife of any kind whatsoever," and he could not reside in certain urban residential areas. But regardless of the social and economic restrictions to which the class was subjected, it prospered in numbers. Possibly the *mestizo* inherited from his Spanish forebears a degree of immunity from the most virulent European communicable diseases, for the hardy *castas* proved to be the fastest growing population segment throughout the colonial period. By 1800 the *mestizo* and Indian populations were roughly equal in number.

Before Mexican independence, the Negro as a constituent part of the population had almost disappeared. Early in the colonial period the Spanish began importing African slaves to perform tasks considered too arduous even for the Indian, but by the early eighteenth century the Spaniards had discovered that the Indians could, and would if properly paid, perform any task which a Negro could, and the market for slaves withered away; by 1800 less than a hundred slaves a year arrived. Spanish law gave easier access to freedom for the slave than did English law, and as a consequence a large proportion of the Negroes at any date were free rather than slave. The free Negro through intermarriage merged with the general caste population, and before independence only a minute proportion of the total population could be identified as Negro. Those so identified were subject to the same general restrictions as *mestizos*.

Restrictions on economic activity and the dead-end street which confronted the rejected *castas* created urban slums, which in turn spawned an indigent population always ready for any situation which might bring profit. Contemptuously referred to as *léperos* but occasionally toadied to by the *gachupines* or *criollos,* who found them an effective weapon against viceregal authority, this human flotsam—products of social prejudice—posed a constant and serious problem. In their normal and calmer moments they begged, robbed, and occasionally murdered, making the dimly lit streets full of nightly peril. In their more vicious moods, generally stirred up by Europeans who had their own political ends in view, and attracted by the prospect of loot, the mobs engaged in *tumultos,* destroying property and lives with wanton abandon. In two such riots of 1624 and again in 1692 the mobs battled the local police and army, invaded government offices, and finally destroyed the viceregal palace by fire. In each case a rebellion seemed in the offing. But without leadership from their own class, and sated after a night of riotous looting, the *léperos* crept back to their hovels each with the hope in his heart that his participation had gone undetected. The *tumultos* always brought official investigations, the execution of *léperos* who had been recognized, a few unimportant changes—but left unchanged the conditions that produced the riots.

But the *léperos* did not restrict their activities to the urban centers. Banditry between Veracruz and Mexico City was endemic, and foolhardy indeed was the man who journeyed from any city to another without escort. Indians seldom took part in banditry—to be sure they sometimes actively resented intrusion by outsiders—and the *criollos* involved normally occupied the positions of leadership. *Léperos,* whether urban thieves or rural bandits, were almost always *castas*. The European interpreted these unwholesome activities as manifestations of a blood taint, about which he could do little, instead of the harvest of a degrading system, about which he could have done much.

The most characteristic Mexican colonial social institution, the bulwark of the entire social framework and the principal molder of social attitudes, was the *hacienda*. Ostensibly an economic institution, since it was the basic pattern of land tenure for Europeans, the *hacienda* was more fruitful for social control than economic production. To the Spaniard recently arrived in Mexico, land constituted the symbol of aristocracy, and he dreamed of a great estate which he could entail to be passed on intact to his heir. Frequently the immigrant received his grant prior to his departure from Spain, sometimes he received it from the viceregal government in return for a service rendered, and often he received it not at all—but he lusted after land as some men do after women. Small estates grew large through purchase, additional grants, seizure, or simple occupation which the passage of time legalized, and frequently they grew into small kingdoms far removed from the great urban centers.

The typical *hacendado* put little emphasis on high land productivity; his contentment came from ownership of the land itself, and any income over that necessary to satisfy his immediate—and expensive—needs he looked upon as fortunate but not necessary. Frequently the *hacienda* owner resided in a nearby city during most of the year, and sometimes he stayed in Spain or France for lengthy periods while an overseer managed his property. But regardless of where he lived, his domain was his own, and he laid down the rules for social and economic intercourse. On the *hacienda, hacienda* law rather than royal law prevailed, and *hacienda* minions rather than crown officers enforced it. Each *hacienda* constituted a self-contained unit with its poorly paid settled laborers, its administration, and often its own priest performing his clerical functions in a church constructed by the *hacendado*. The priest, supported by the *hacendado,* considered it his spiritual duty to discourage any overt manifestation of discontent on the part of the laborers. Land use and treatment of laborers were so notoriously bad in the late colonial period that the Bishop of Michoacán urged the Spanish crown to institute a thoroughgoing land reform program which would bring about better distribution of land and more effective cultivation. Any serious land reform would of course have undermined the basic assumptions upon which the Europeans constructed their social system, and neither the court of Charles IV nor the aristocracy of colonial Mexico could view the result with anything but fear and distaste. And even though the economically unproductive *hacienda* occupied most of the good arable lands, leaving only precipitous mountain slopes for the *mestizo* who sought a small plot for himself, any suggestions that the landholding abuses be curbed caused amusement rather than concern.

The Church as a social institution almost defies adequate and acceptable description because of the complex interrelationships which existed, and in view of the confusion between the Church as an institution and the clergy as members of society. Late in the fifteenth century the Papacy, as a reward for Spain's determined and successful effort to evict Islam from Western Europe, conferred upon the newly consolidated Spanish crown a participation in Church affairs denied to other lay princes in Europe. The relationship between Church and state became so intimate, not only in Mexico but throughout the Spanish world, that the functions of one could scarcely be divorced from those of the other. Churchmen filled many political and administrative positions both in Spain and in Mexico; Mexico's second *audiencia* president was a bishop, and a number of the viceroys moved from chief of see to chief of state and back again. On the other hand, prominent laymen sometimes received high Church positions directly—albeit not technically—from the king's hand. Church vows could be enforced by crown officials and Church tithes collected by crown fiscal officers. The Church, therefore, occupied a position as intimately connected with colonial policy as did any other Spanish agency or institution; the Church acted for the state, the state for the Church, and both for Spain.

The Church has been frequently maligned for its wanton destruction of priceless pre-Hispanic artifacts and documents, with Bishop Zumárraga bearing the brunt of the castigation for his burning of the great collection of codices at Texcoco. The limited educational opportunities open to the public have brought additional opprobrium to the Church, as has the Church's obvious support of Spanish social policy. These are all certainly justified criticisms, but the critics have selected the wrong target, which should be the Spanish system; the Church was not and could not be separated from that system. Furthermore, condemnation of clerical immorality fills many pages, quite justifiably; too many clerics were too worldly, too many took concubines with the same freedom as laymen, too many charged outrageous prices for the administration of the Sacraments, and too many were little more than simpering sycophants to arrogant aristocrats.

But what little social consciousness was to be found rested with the Church and the clergy. The fealty and devotion to a task demonstrated by the missionaries Eusebio Kino and Junípero Serra have few parallels in history, and they were merely the most successful and outstanding of a great army of men who sought their glory in service to God and mankind rather than in the ownership of landed estates. Sahagún, Gante, Motolinía, and Torquemada not only fought for the Indians—unavailingly, to be sure—but they bitterly assailed those who, laymen and clerics alike, made a mockery of Christian brotherhood. And it was another cleric, Antonio de San Miguel, who pointed out the dangerous and insupportable injustices meted out to the Indians and *castas* in the late colonial period. Furthermore the clergymen, from the sixteenth-century Franciscan Motolinía to the eighteenth-century Jesuit Francisco Clavigero and a host in between, kept alive historical scholarship. At the same time the clerical system supported others who gave tone to the entire intellectual dvelopment.

Regardless of accolades or recriminations, the Church clearly functioned as an important social institution, and within the crown policy it functioned effectively. The reports of vast and spontaneous conversions, numbering up to 30,000 in a mass ritual, may well be doubted, but that the vast majority of those living in Mexico—Europeans, *castas*, or Indians—at the end of the colonial period claimed to be Catholic cannot be questioned. Many lacked theological and dogmatic sophistication and many more slighted their religious obligations, but they supported the Church, sought the parish priest's counsel, celebrated their saint's day, and rejected all other religious beliefs. To be sure, some isolated pockets of Indians continued to worship in the old tradition, and others mixed pre-Hispanic and Catholic ritual, but when Mexico achieved her independence she did so as a Catholic nation.

In addition the Church through its clerics served an important function in disseminating the use of Spanish as the common tongue. Late colonial population statistics do not show the proportion of those who spoke Spanish, but it would be safe to assume that the majority of Indians spoke some and that all *castas* did. Inculcating the use of a foreign tongue among the native population was no mean task, one which of course the Church did not perform alone but one to which it probably made the most important contribution.

In assessing the importance of the Church as a social institution the modern student must be constantly aware that the clerics did not constitute a great cohesive group. In general, the Church as an institution tended to work for the conservation of those aspects of the society which had brought grandeur to it; in this respect it assumed a conservative position. Religious philosophy, indeed any well-established religious philosophy, could hardly decree otherwise. But among those clerics who worked in the areas far from the great urban centers with their European communicants, a genuine concern for human dignity and justice manifested itself in myriad ways. Father Hidalgo and Father Morelos are only the most famous of the clerics who in the absence of other means sought through military action to bring significant change in the relations among social groups, but they represented a great many other religious men who desired change. Some clerics did strip Hidalgo of his priestly robes and surrender him to the civil power for execution, but other clerics execrated those responsible for the deed.

On balance it would be folly to point to the colonial Church or the colonial cleric as a paragon of social justice and social equality. The Church and the clergymen were no better and no worse than the society which produced them.

In summary, the Spanish designed their colonial social institutions—or let them develop—in such a fashion that the worst aspects of early modern European life, without the recompense of its best, held sway. Social stratification was not merely an attribute of social customs; it was indelibly stamped into the social fabric by law as well. There were, to be sure, some cases in which colonial administrators gave a legal designation of *mestizo* to ethnically pure Indians, and others in which *mestizos* became elevated into the *criollo* class by law. These unusual actions in no sense illustrate a breakdown of class rigidity; on the contrary, they forcibly demonstrate the virtual impossibility of class mobility. The European found the social system highly satisfactory, and he wanted no change. It guaranteed him, regardless of his economic condition, a kind of status—a comfort closely akin to that enjoyed by the Georgia "red neck" surrounded by the segregated Negro. He could endure the disadvantages of colonial life, among which the miserable educational system stood out, as long as he could bask in the glow of social position. The creole might quarrel with the *peninsular* over access to public office and fruitful monopoly, but on the issue of the proper place for the *casta* and indigene he differed not. Whether the European recognized the keg of social dynamite—one which did not explode completely for nearly a hundred years after Spain lost control—is doubtful; certainly very few expressed any real concern over the potential dangers.

Subsequent events and contemporary observations, generally but not always from foreigners, prove conclusively that resentment did exist in a virulent, albeit quiescent, form. Indian resentment, inchoate and submerged, expressed itself almost exclusively in withdrawal, except in those short and bloody early days of the movement for independence. But *casta* resentment, fanned by those of their class who had managed enough education to recognize the stupidity of the system, emerged in a thousand forms in the late colonial period and became a dominant factor in the first century of national development. The Spanish, judged by many criteria, governed well during their three hundred years; but they left, alas, a bitter social legacy.

Chapter 4 • Controlled Labor

Because it is just, it is my wish that, since the Indians must work and occupy themselves with all the things necessary for the Republic and that they must live and sustain themselves from their labor, that they be well and satisfactorily paid, and that they be given good treatment.

CHARLES I, KING OF SPAIN

American natives, so the Spanish insisted, would not work unless forced. Colonial and crown officials agreed that the Indian, ignorant of the value of money and indolent by nature, could be depended upon to produce only under the prod of a firm and disciplined hand; and, they argued, only through productive labor could the native become a part of the civilized world. This simple economic axiom the Spanish settlers in Santo Domingo developed and transmitted to Spain, whence the conquerors brought it to Mexico along with the other trappings of their cultural baggage.

All official colonial Mexican labor policy derived from that axiom, tempered by the crown's deep concern for order and elementary justice as defined in sixteenth-century Spain. A great contest between the crown and the settlers ensued, one which seldom broke into the open but which always lay at the root of colonial quarrels with the home government. From the metropolis the crown attempted to protect the new wards of the state, for Spanish theological and anthropological theoreticians had concluded that the native Americans were in fact members of the human race, though many of their practices smacked of the bestial. As humans, they deserved treatment equivalent to that of Europeans, but as primitives their cultural immaturity demanded treatment as children with all the power and majesty of law marshaled for their protection. The settlers, on the ground and confronted with what they called cultural and economic reality, strove to force the indigenous population to labor in their behalf, unrestricted by laws drawn in Toledo and Madrid by men who had never seen a native American. Law therefore gave a protection which practice often denied; theory proclaimed freedom while actuality demanded servitude. The institutions developed to create a balance between the needs of the settlers and the concern of the crown with respect to the utilization of Indian labor were a compromise, arrived at after long and acrimonious debate, and were in part based upon experiences outside Mexico.

For a full generation prior to the Mexican conquest the Spanish sought El Dorado which rumor described. Columbus always insisted that great riches were to be found soon; he and those who followed him scurried through the islands and along the coasts seeking the mythical land of jewel-encrusted diadems and gold-embellished buildings. But everywhere they went they found the same dreary conditions: primitive people living in ease gathering tropical fruits with a minimum of effort, unorganized, untutored, indifferent to Spanish wealth and submissive to Spanish power. The island and coastal indigenes, with few exceptions, held the Spanish in awe and reverence, and they gave of their goods freely to the first arrivals; but their social organization and their value systems could not easily meet the demands imposed by large numbers of newly arrived Europeans. Unable to encourage the natives to labor for profit (the Spanish had nothing which the Indians really needed except weapons, and these the Spanish were loath to furnish to potential rebels), the Spaniard sought to instill labor discipline by power. He forced the island Indians to work by demanding, under pain of the lash, a given quantity of gold dust, the scrapings of unproductive placer mines, at stipulated intervals. But at best the islands produced no great riches and the bitterly disappointed European drove the Indian with unreasonable fury; as he grew gaunt from malnutrition and cruel from frustration, the native sank into incredible misery. Overwork and European diseases took an appalling toll of Indian lives; the native fled from mine and field to the questionable haven of the jungle, from which the Spaniard dragged him back to his slave-like labors. These conditions, particularly in Española, stimulated Bartolomé de Las Casas to a scathing denunciation of Spanish cupidity, but neither his strictures nor his experiments in communal living solved the basic problem of establishing a system under which the European could come to the New World with some assurance of economic success. But the island experiences had two great influences: they convinced the newly crowned Charles I that these conditions *must not* be repeated on the mainland, but they also convinced the colonial that no native American would work except under the lash.

When the Spaniards arrived in Mexico they were again disappointed. First reports indicated untold wealth, and when Moctezuma II in his uncertainty heaped valuable gifts on Cortez, the Indian generosity merely sharpened Spanish thirst. But by the time Cortez, as victor, could on that August day in 1521 survey the ruined city of Tenochtitlán, the vaunted wealth of the Aztecs had disappeared (if it ever existed), and the Spanish again found themselves with heavy hearts and empty hands despite the hardships they had endured. Harking back to the experiences in the islands, where many of them had long resided, and confronting a civilization with a highly developed and disciplined social system, the conquerors determined to build upon their knowledge to create a stable economic system. From this combination came the Mexican version of the *encomienda* and *repartimiento,* the two great institutions which early regularized the basic economic relations between European and native.

The *encomienda,* in its simplest form, constituted a geographic region "commended" to one or more individuals. These *encomenderos* had the right to demand stipulated services from the inhabitants and the duty to give protection and other services in return; the *encomienda* grant did not include land itself. The *repartimiento,* on the other hand, forced individual members of the society to render service for the public weal. Both *encomienda* and *repartimiento* long antedated Columbus in European life, and both had counterparts in pre-Hispanic Mexico. Castillian sovereigns granted *encomiendas* to military commanders especially successful against the Moors, and all European nations demanded public service from their citizens. Compulsory military service differs not one whit from the *repartimiento* in theory, although in practice the differences are great. As the two institutions developed in Mexico they reinforced each other. They both grew out of a set of experiences and a series of assumptions; that the experiences came from a different milieu and the assumptions proved to have little validity apparently never particularly bothered either Spanish colonial or Spanish crown.

In view of the disaster which had accompanied the *encomienda* in Española, Charles I in 1520 prohibited grants of *encomiendas* in any region to be conquered thereafter. The crown sought to control, and to protect through its own royal officials, all newly conquered people and thereby to prevent the debacle of the islands. Charles sent orders to this effect to Cortez, but when the latter completed his razing of Tenochtitlán and discovered nothing but dust to compensate him for his trouble, he faced a serious problem for, as Bernal Díaz wrote with such charming candor, the conquerors "came to serve God and the King and also to get rich." Glory Cortez's men gained when they served God by proving the Aztec's gods false, and now the fifteen hundred survivors demanded wealth; but this wealth could come only in the form of Indian labor. In spite of the king's orders and much against his will (so he reported to his sovereign), Cortez was forced by circumstance and growling subordinates to grant *encomiendas* to those who had endured the greatest hardships and demonstrated the greatest fidelity and courage. Exactly how many of these grants he made remains a mystery, but in his acts of distribution he certainly showed no great personal reticence. As the leader of the expedition and the driving force behind the conquest he had served his king and his God well, and in his subsequent policies of stabilizing the government and extending Spanish sway he earned the gratitude of all his people. At least so he assumed, and he granted to himself *encomiendas* befitting his station: a series of villages to the north of Tenochtitlán, another and slightly more populous group near the present city of Cuernavaca, and vast numbers from the Zapotec Valley of Oaxaca. By his own account his charges numbered 115,000, but recent scholarship places the number at more than twice that estimate. No other *encomienda* grant even approached them in size and potential wealth.

Charles I, in keeping with his stated policy, ordered the immediate extirpation of the *encomiendas,* but under urging from Cortez and others, reversed his earlier decision by validating all the grants made by the Conqueror. As granted by Cortez and agreed to by the crown, the *encomienda* grant gave to the recipient a temporary right to demand from the Indians commended to him any service desired and any tribute he could collect. An open invitation to exploitation, these terms brought to Mexico the very conditions which the vacillating Charles hoped to prevent, and events soon proved the king's fear well-grounded. Eager tribute collectors, whom Motolinía scourged as "drones" taking the "honey which is worked by the poor bees, the Indians," demanded more and ever more at a time when each decade saw death overtake nearly half the native population. At the same time *encomienda* overseers solicited and received labor services in the form of field hands, herdsmen, personal servants, and housebuilders. The appalling exploitation in Mexico and in other parts of the empire stimulated the crown to re-examine the entire *encomienda* question, and the "final" word came out in the form of a group of decrees known as the New Laws of 1542. These decrees closely circumscribed and regulated the rights of the *encomenderos* as to the amount of tribute and the nature of labor which could be demanded, and further stipulated that the *encomienda* would revert to the crown upon the death of the recipient of the original grant. News of the provisions created an uproar in New Spain where the *encomenderos,* now numbering more than five hundred, had enjoyed nearly a generation as men of wealth and looked forward to passing on their *encomiendas* to their heirs. Public demonstrations, widespread talk of a possible rebellion, and clerical coolness to the new decrees led Viceroy Antonio de Mendoza to urge reconsideration. Constant bleating by the *encomenderos* and their friends finally convinced Francisco Tello de Sandoval, whom Charles I sent to Mexico to supervise rigid enforcement, that any attempt at full enforcement would bring disaster. Even Toribio de Motolinía, one of the severest critics of

Spanish exploitation and cupidity, decided in favor of the *encomienda* as a permanent institution and counseled a closer definition of responsibilities along with greater penalties for evasion, rather than complete abolition.

The arguments that the critics of the New Laws used were hoary with age by 1545 when the quarrel reached its crescendo; they had been used for thirty years by men urging the conversion from temporary to perpetual grants. The Indians were, in the words of one bishop, "a beastly, ungrateful, lying set, audacious and insolent," over whom the Europeans must exercise rigid control in order to preserve the economy and bring about its further development. Furthermore, the temporary *encomienda* worked to the disadvantage, not the advantage, of the commended Indians. The cure for any existing evils lay not in suppressing the *encomienda,* but in making it a grant in perpetuity. The *encomendero* who had only a limited time to extract a fortune from his Indians, so the argument ran, would be much more inclined to exploit his charges to the limit than he would if his grant were permanent. In the latter case his concern for his heirs and their well-being would lead him to take great care lest his tributaries die from mistreatment; the perpetual *encomienda* guaranteed Indian welfare. A short-term *encomienda* would lead to vicious exploitation, and abolition of the system would place the Spanish in such severe economic straits that they would be forced to return to Spain, abandoning the colony and leaving the benighted natives to barbaric ways and Satanic worship.

These two arguments—and all others were merely variations on the theme—are not without their fascination, indicating as they do the realities of the colonists' values. The crown might look upon the native population as wards of the state, potential members of a civilized society worshipping the True God, men with souls endowed with all the attributes of humanity and therefore deserving of special concern and protection; but the colonists saw the Indians as a commodity, a resource not differing in kind from the soil, or the forests, or the water. One policy would encourage the husbanding of the resource, while the other would stimulate its rapid and profligate exploitation. Colonial argument divested the indigenes of any vestige of humanity, for the colonists spoke of the multiplication of their cattle in equivalent terms. At the same time the colonists could not envisage themselves as laborers or as tillers of the soil. The question was not merely one of guaranteeing an adequate labor supply for healthy economic growth; it was one of survival. Without the Indians to produce the food and to perform personal services the Spanish would starve.

Charles I was no great visionary, and in spite of his German birth he knew his subjects' ways. Hounded by the arguments presented by a delegation of colonials and confronted with inevitability, he succumbed; he and his successors thereafter contented themselves with regulating the practice rather than attempting to abolish it by law. Time, people dying without heirs, and changing conditions—not Madrid-drafted law—finally brought the practice to an end before the termination of the colonial period.

The modified regulations prohibited any personal service to the *encomendero* by the Indians without just compensation, and limited the rights of the *encomenderos* to the collection of tribute from the heads of families. But the crown reserved for itself the collection of tribute from the Indians not on privately held *encomiendas,* and required the private *encomenderos* to conform to royal practice in both the nature and the amount of tribute collected. The crown enjoined the *encomendero,* in return for income derived from tribute, to maintain his Indians in peace, to protect them against European or native interlopers, to educate them in Christian ways, and to incorporate them into a civilized society. The first and second mandates the *encomendero* accepted with a good will, for his own fortunes depended upon their observance. Rebellious Indians paid no tribute, and the wise *encomendero* did all in his power to encourage his charges to follow peaceful pursuits; in general he was extraordinarily successful in this endeavor, for Indian rebellions were few and far between, scarcely disturbing the orderly relations between master and vassal. Furthermore, any attack from the outside on the economic and social stability of an Indian community would lessen the community's ability to deliver its regular tribute; the *encomendero* particularly resented any attempt to divest his Indians of their land—unless, of course, it was he who did the divesting.

Occasionally the sovereign or one of his officials, either in ignorance or by design, granted land within an existing *encomienda* even though royal decrees forbade such grants; in the vast majority of the cases the *encomenderos* successfully appealed to the courts against such action and forced the revocation of the grants. But only rarely did the *encomendero* accept his other duties—Christianization and education—with equal fervor, for he and his heirs stood to gain little or nothing from such activities. In principle the *encomendero* had nothing against the conversion of his charges to Catholicism, but this he considered to be the function of the clergy; most clergymen he distrusted until they proved that their Christian education would not undermine Indian docility. But to incorporation of the Indian into civilized society he had grave objections. Such incorporation would mean, ultimately, the disappearance of distinctions between Indian and European, the complete destruction of the *raison d'être* for the *encomienda* system. Few men work, anywhere at any time, for the destruction of those very social institutions which give them status and economic well-being, and few indeed were the *encomenderos* who worked assiduously for the incorporation of their Indians into the basic pattern of European life. The *encomienda* Indian received no greater benefits of European civilization than did the Indian who remained a direct charge of the crown. He received no formal education, he was introduced to no aspect of contemporary European technology, he was not taught the precepts of Spanish law, and he certainly learned little of the basic philosophy or dogma of Christianity; he merely transferred his fealty from his own pantheon of gods to what he assumed to be the conquerors' pantheon. But all other things aside, the *encomienda* Indian did have one great advantage over his non-*encomienda* kin: as long as he remained on an *encomienda* granted to a vigorous and forthright man, he had his own land to work.

In theory and practice the crown "commended" every populated place to someone, either to a private individual or to itself; therefore every native had a patron to whom he could look for protection and to whom he certainly paid tribute. The exact number of private *encomiendas* granted by the crown is virtually impossible to ascertain from known records. Viceroy Mendoza reported that of the 1385 heads-of-family living in Mexico at the time of the great debate over the New Laws, 577 enjoyed *encomienda* grants. This means that 40 per cent of the Spaniards lived directly from *encomienda* income and that a large percentage of the remainder subsisted indirectly from the same source. The proportion of the Europeans whose income came from the *encomienda* did not, of course, remain constant. By 1550 the Spanish had conquered and cowed all sedentary Indians (save a few in the Yucatán backlands) from whom tribute could reasonably be expected; after that date additional *encomiendas* for new arrivals could not be found. Crown representatives did break up a number of the larger *encomiendas* in order to make new grants during the first century, but the original grantees always objected to such actions, and the heavy death rate among the native population tended to discourage widespread application of the policy. Furthermore, crown policy always worked for the eventual elimination of the institution, and as a consequence the proportion of Spaniards whose sole or primary source of income derived from the *encomienda* gradually dwindled into nothingness by the close of the colonial period. As the number of private *encomiendas* decreased, the number of native communities directly dependent upon the crown increased. In the middle of the sixteenth century, by which time crown policy had become fairly well stabilized, more natives paid tribute to *encomenderos* than to the crown, but before the end of the century the majority paid directly to crown agents. By the end of the seventeenth century probably eight of every ten tributaries delivered their goods to royal officials.

Even though the original *encomenderos* had been granted the right to collect tribute in any form they saw fit, royal policy and changing conditions regularized the collection system. In the beginning both royal government and private *encomendero* tended to assess tribute in a manner not significantly different from that of the Aztecs. First and foremost, tribute was a community, not an individual, responsibility; ultimately, of course, the individual in the community gave his goods and time to meet tribute demands, but upon the community elders the Spanish imposed the onus of collecting and delivering the assessed goods. This practice conformed to traditional native usage and, in theory, had the distinct advantage of placing indigenous community leaders between the tribute collector and the individual in the society. But from the Indian point of view it had one great disadvantage: it was relatively inflexible. A light tribute assessed in 1526, based upon the number of adult males, had become an unbearable burden by 1550 when the population was only one-third of the original number. Revision in the tribute schedule presumably balanced population decline, but the high death rate made each revised assessment obsolescent as soon as made. A general revision in 1551 led Motolinía to characterize the tribute burden on the Indians as less onerous than the tax burden on the peasant in Spain, but within a few years many villages, again stricken by epidemics, bore too heavy a load. This particular problem plagued royal officials and private *encomenderos* alike—as well as the "poor bees, the Indians"—until the middle of the seventeenth century, when the native population ended its long decline and began to increase.

Until 1551, tribute generally consisted of a combination of produce and labor, the nature of the produce varying from district to district, depending upon traditional agricultural pursuits and the success with which the Spanish introduced new pursuits. The crown, in line with its policy that all work deserved payment, forbade the collection of a labor tribute after 1551 and thenceforward for half a century assessed its tribute almost exclusively in produce. Private *encomenderos* presumably followed suit, for the prohibition extended to them, but half a century later some villages still furnished a steady work force as well as a wide variety of products. As Indians came to earn more specie by daily-wage labor, both crown and private *encomendero* began to "commute" produce tribute into money tribute; by the middle of the eighteenth century almost all tribute came in the form of specie. As the Indian population stabilized and then began to grow after the middle of the seventeenth century, tribute payments became less and less burdensome; toward the end of the colonial period the average payment consisted of considerably less than one *peso* per year per person or, on the average, roughly 2 per cent of the annual earning capacity of the head of a household.

An Indian village near Mexico City typifies the process of change in the *encomienda* system. Granted by Cortez to one of his men soon after the conquest, the village of some 6000 souls contributed a daily work force of fifty men and four women plus a few items of food during the years immediately after the grant. In the early 'fifties the *encomendero* commuted a portion of the work force into additional produce. For the next generation the village contributed roughly 30 tons of corn and half that amount of beans annually, twenty-five petticoats, and the same number of shirts every eighty days (an Aztec unit of time for tribute), and a steady work force of thirty herdsmen. In addition, the villagers furnished the *encomendero's* overseer a daily ration of one chicken, a few eggs, sufficient forage for his animals, wood for his fires, and tortillas for his table. The village also delivered to the *encomendero* in Mexico City a weekly tribute of thirteen hens, thirteen quail, an unspecified number of eggs, fish for his fast days, wood and charcoal for the daily fires, hay for the animals, household pottery items as needed, and two women servants. These weekly tribute items allowed the *encomendero* to maintain a household of some fifteen or twenty people—his immediate family, relatives, and friends—in some comfort while the other tribute items gave him a good outside income. The record is mute on his contribution to the village. Inasmuch as the village population had declined at the same general rate which had stricken other communities, the above tribute constituted an extremely heavy burden by 1570, and the Indians needed relief. The *encomendero* first abandoned the labor tribute—no doubt at the insistence of royal officials—and then, toward the end of the sixteenth century, brought his other tribute assessments into line with the reduced population. Further reductions followed in the succeeding century and, as Indian produce and Indian labor brought cash to the community from a growing Mexico City, money gradually replaced produce as tribute. By the time the *encomienda* finally lapsed in the latter part of the eighteenth century, the not-too-heavy tribute consisted almost exclusively of specie.

As has been stated, every community was "commended" either to a private individual or individuals, or to the crown itself; but some villages were jointly held. As a consequence, Indian villages fell into one of three categories of supervision: the private *encomienda,* dependent upon an individual; the crown *encomienda* under the direct control of the sovereign and his agents, frequently clerics; and the joint *encomienda,* in which both private individual and crown had a direct interest. Population studies raise some interesting questions regarding the relationship between type of control and population decrease. The evidence suggests that the population declined at a significantly lower rate on those supervised by the crown than on the *encomiendas* under private control, and therefore that the Indian found the crown a less brutal master than the private individual; but the data here are inconclusive. On the other hand the data leave no room for doubt regarding the jointly held *encomienda;* here the population declined at a rate only one-third—and possibly as low as one-sixth—of that of the privately held. The important question of whether the lower rate of decline reflects a lower death rate or a higher in-migration cannot be answered, but the data make it perfectly obvious that the Indian found life on the joint *encomienda*—for whatever reason—more attractive than on that privately held. Lesley Byrd Simpson, who in discussing sixteenth-century royal concern with the catastrophic population decline pointed out this differential, sums up:

> The phenomenon suggests one final observation; that is, it seems remarkable that in the century-old controversy over the proper disposition of the Indians it occurred to no one that their preservation would have been more probable if they had all been placed in joint encomiendas [sic].

The *encomienda*-tribute system constituted a form of taxation which assured to the Spaniards a steady flow of goods indigenous to the area, but it could not be depended upon as a mechanism for the introduction of new processes or for the maintenance of public facilities. For these purposes the conquerors needed a constant labor force under close supervision. Correctly or incorrectly, the Spanish had concluded from their island experiences that American natives could not be induced to work steadily for wages; the indigene's simple economic demands had not prepared him to comprehend the personal advantages coming from a market economy, and his few wants made money in the European sense worthless. It followed then to the Spaniard—and probably with some justification immediately after the conquest—that no native would work for the conquerors except under duress. But the crown, looking forward to the time when all natives would be loyal, Christian, and civilized subjects, abhorred Indian slavery as even a temporary answer to the labor problem. Caught between an apparent reality—Indian reluctance to work for wages—and a deep conviction regarding the necessity to pay for work performed, the Spanish kings fostered the development and regulation of a forced labor system with a guaranteed wage.

The native population found no cause to object to the concept of forced labor as it developed under the *repartimiento* system; the indigenous societies had long demanded uncompensated forced labor from their members, and the original regulations concerning the use of Indian labor were neither onerous nor ruthless. Even though one could quarrel seriously with the basic assumptions behind the laws, or question the validity of a system which put and maintained the native population in an inferior position, none could seriously sustain the position that the laws deliberately enslaved the indigenes. The original provisions, stipulating that no individual could be called upon for more than one week's forced labor per year, for which he would receive a wage set by the crown, constituted no excessive demand upon the native population but did serve to supply ample labor for work vested with a public interest. Even when the law was changed to allow as much as two or three weeks of such labor, the Indian communities fared not too badly because of the vast numbers of men available. In the middle of the sixteenth century, when the crown designed the basic ordinances, the few Spanish colonials, surrounded by teeming millions of natives, could make only limited demands upon the total work force under any conditions. But the laws allowed forced labor under the *repartimiento* for projects in the public interest only. Had the laws, and the principles behind the laws, been adhered to, the average *macehual* would have found his situation regarding forced labor considerably less onerous than it had been under his own rulers.

But law is one thing, and practice quite another, particularly in New

Spain. When the crown enunciated its basic policy, the ratio between Spanish colonial and indigenous populations was roughly one to 4000 or 5000; with this proportion the law could be adhered to without problem. But devastating epidemics among the Indians, contemporaneous with a rapid increase in the Spanish population, reduced the ratio to one to 65 by 1570 and one to 20 in the opening years of the seventeenth century; by this date the colony suffered a serious labor shortage. Inefficient administration coupled with this disastrous shortage led to breaches of the law; by 1600 the obvious and almost inhuman exploitation of Indian labor so scandalized the Spanish government that it ordered a complete investigation and revision of existing practices. After 1609, when the new code went into effect, more rigid enforcement and stiffer penalties for infractions removed the most vicious practices, even though many injustices continued throughout the colonial period.

The two basic provisions of the legal code surrounding the *repartimiento*—forced labor for work in the public interest only, at an adequate wage—almost invited exploitation in a frontier society because the terms could not be defined with precision. "Public interest" is a well-accepted concept, but any attempt to make a clear distinction between public interest on the one hand and private gain on the other reaches a point of fuzziness. Obviously the construction of a church, a fort on the frontier, or a public office building is in the public interest; so too is the construction of a public thoroughfare, a bridge, or a road between two cities, even though in many cases these public facilities were built by private individuals who hoped to make a profit through the collection of tolls. Just as obviously, personal service in a private household, the construction of a private dwelling, the construction of a boundary fence, or the harvesting of a tomato crop is not normally vested with a public interest. Between these two extremes lies a great gray area always open to interpretation. Silver mining certainly brought enormous personal gain to the lucky concessionaires, but crown interest in the extraction and coinage of silver gave the activity a mantle of public interest. Wheat harvesting brought the *hacendado* private income, and during bountiful years the public was little concerned with the harvest on a particular estate; but generally the public had a vital interest in the availability and price of this staple product, and this interest became acute during years of short harvest. These issues and similar ones were always a matter of interpretation by crown officails, some of whom were rigid, some lax, some honest, some greedy—and all intensely human with a greater concern for the welfare of the Spaniards than of the Indians. Wages, too, were subject to interpretation. The crown insisted, in the words of Charles I, that the Indians "be well and satisfactorily paid," but any attempt to translate this general philosophy into specific and generally applicable monetary sums was well-nigh useless since economic conditions fluctuated violently from region to region and month to month. An adequate wage in Chalco in 1536, for example, would scarcely suffice that year in Coyuca, where poor crops had doubled the price of corn. A satisfactory wage in a village near Cuernavaca in early 1568 would have been insufficient five months later, when the price of maize had doubled, but would have been adequate in 1569, when the grain price had returned to the level of the previous year. Prior to 1609 these variables forced the royal government to depend upon local officials, usually the town councils, to set the wage for the *repartimiento* laborers and to allow or disallow payment in a medium other than coin of the realm. The adequacy of the wage, therefore, depended upon the concepts of social justice held by local officials, who frequently had a personal financial stake in the wage set. After the reforms of 1609, the viceroy had the authority and the responsibility for setting the wage. The change probably assured the Indians that the set wage would be determined with greater objectivity than in the past, but with no greater efficiency in meeting the fluctuating needs. In general, those who used *repartimiento* labor probably paid a wage sufficient to meet the basic needs of the laborer, but frequent Indian protests pointed out many cases in which the employers paid far below the minimum standards.

The colonials designed a relatively simple system for gathering the forced labor contingent and for assigning the workers to their tasks. The government designated a crown official (usually called the *corregidor de indios*) for each administrative entity in the colony, and to this official the colonials applied for a work force each week; each prospective employer, in his application, had to justify his claim to *repartimiento* labor in terms of public weal. The crown officer then set the number to be assigned to each applicant, and further assigned to each populated place in his jurisdiction a quota of men to be selected for the *repartimiento*. Local Indian officials had the responsibility for designating the individual men and for gathering the recruits at the municipal center normally on Sunday afternoon, where the workers either volunteered or were assigned to work for the various applicants. The employer, or his agent, then instructed the work crew as to the place of work, collected from each laborer a material possession—a blanket, a tool, or a utensil—as an earnest of his appearance at the work site, and left the laborers to their own devices to appear at the proper place and time to begin work. On the following Saturday afternoon all gathered again at the same locale, where the employer paid his laborers the stipulated wage under the watchful eye of the crown official. In the hands of competent officials and humane colonials the system worked well with little cause for criticism, but the very simplicity of the method opened it to all manner of abuses in the hands of incompetent or greedy men.

Indians complained frequently and bitterly that the number of workers demanded often far exceeded the maximum set by law, for the regulations specifically stipulated a stated proportion—varying from 2 to 14 per cent depending upon the period and the season—as the maximum subject to the *repartimiento* at any given time. Insatiable demands, often the result of collusion between the *corregidor de indios* and the local Indian leaders who received bribes from the employers, removed so many men from the communities that the crops suffered. Furthermore, as many Indians insisted, some individuals found themselves subject to repeated calls while others seldom worked. Some natives accused the colonials of paying less than the designated wage or of paying them in goods for which they had little or no use. Others cried out against frequent and unjustified lashings by the colonials, their overseers, or the magistrates who would "indulge their appetites for gratuitous floggings and tortures." Some employers, fearful lest their laborers might flee during the night, locked the Indians in corrals like so many cattle, even though the work site stood hard by the native village. Complaints before the *juzgado de indios,* a special court established to protect the Indians, accused the *corregidores* of graft, corruption, extortion, and cruelties ranging from exorbitant prices for required purchases (salt, for example) to vicious floggings and exposure in stocks. Law and courts to the contrary, these abuses remained an integral characteristic of the *repartimiento* system.

But the most pernicious attributes of the system came not from cupidity or collusion or even incompetence; they were a function of the economy and geography. Silver mines demanded labor, enormous amounts of hard, back-breaking labor. With few exceptions—the Real del Monte near Pachuca the most notable—ore deposits were far from centers of population. Between the great silver hill at Zacatecas and the available Indian labor supply in modern Michoacán stood 200 hard and dangerous miles; according to late sixteenth- and early seventeenth-century travelers, skeletal remains of *repartimiento* laborers who did not quite make their destination outlined the road north to the mines. Tarascan village officials complained to crown officials that in order to keep ten men working the Zacatecas mines in 1600, thirty men had to be absent from the community: ten going, ten working, ten returning. Agricultural labor suffered less in this respect than did the miners, but in peak seasons of planting and harvesting many *repartimiento* natives had to travel as many as three or four days to reach the work site at the very time that their own lands needed attention. During the sixteenth century under the law, and in the seventeenth often in spite of the law, employers paid their *repartimiento* laborers only for the days actually worked; they made no provision for transportation to the place of work or for subsistence while on the road. Confronted with a week's journey in unfamiliar terrain, the inexperienced native frequently carried insufficient food and arrived exhausted and undernourished, if he arrived at all. This profligate waste of human resources may have been economically justified in 1546, when Juan de Tolosa and his companions discovered the Zacatecas ore deposits, but by 1600 the dwindling labor supply made it impossible to sustain. It was this consideration as much as any other which brought forth the early seventeenth-century reforms.

The new code, although not universally obeyed, corrected most of the obvious abuses. The employer, who could require his workers to travel no more than one day's journey, paid the men from the time they left their village until they returned, and made adequate provision for their sustenance while en route. The workers received cash, not commodities, for their labor, with the wage established by the viceroy instead of by local officials. Employers could no longer mete out corporal punishment, and laborers had the right to return to their abodes at night when distance made such return feasible. *Repartimiento* labor could not be used in certain kinds of hazardous work, such as sugar mills, or in the notoriously noxious textile sweatshops, even though such activities might be vested with the public interest. And finally, no employer could claim the use of *repartimiento* labor as porters or carriers regardless of the nature of the goods. A generation after these reforms went into effect the Marquis of Cerralvo abolished the *repartimiento* for agricultural labor. The regulations, none rigidly adhered to, continued in force during the remainder of the colonial period and brought some relief to the stricken native population. From that time forward the *repartimiento* tended to occupy a less prominent position as a labor institution than it did during the first hundred years, but the shift came not because of a changed assessment on the part of the colonials but because the Indian population took advantage of two economic realities to gain a modicum of labor freedom.

With the catastrophic decline of the Indian population, labor became a scarce and precious commodity; the inefficient *repartimiento* system, with its hit-or-miss assignment of inexperienced men to sometimes technical tasks, could no longer meet the needs. Forced or slave labor, as John C. Calhoun discovered much later in South Carolina, never reaches the peak of efficiency demonstrated by free labor, and the Mexican native soon learned that he could sell his technical skill at a rate higher than that paid for *repartimiento* labor. Mining most clearly demonstrated the shift from forced to free labor, for even in its most rudimentary form the extraction of silver ore demanded a skill which only experience could teach. The constant flow of mining neophytes coming through the *repartimiento* into the ore deposits meant highly inefficient and oftentimes unprofitable operations; mine owners therefore welcomed the development of a group of professional miners who commanded a higher rate of pay than forced labor, but whose higher rate of production more than compensated for the wage differential. Even before the end of the sixteenth century the operators depended to some degree on free labor; the existence of this group in fact allowed the crown to limit the distance to be traveled by forced labor gangs. After the mine operator found himself obligated, under the 1609 reform, to pay for travel time as well as work time, he could no longer afford to pay the *repartimiento* wage for work performed at a great distance from sedentary centers. Additionally, the change had a built-in accelerator. As labor became more and more scarce toward the middle of the seventeenth century (a function of declining population), while mining operations expanded enormously, free miners demanded and received higher wages; by the end of the century free miners received a daily income roughly eight times that of forced labor. *Repartimiento* laborers quite understandably resented the extraordinary differential and sometimes showed their irritation by sabotage, riots, and other acts of violence. The prudent mine owner, basking in a rising silver market, could better afford to dispense with cheap and inefficient forced labor, and depend entirely upon free labor. When Baron von Humboldt studied Mexican mining toward the close of the eighteenth century, he found not a single *repartimiento* worker in the mines he visited, even though every mine operator had a perfect right to claim such labor.

Urban labor went through an analogous process. As urban centers developed and grew, Indian laborers in the environs discovered that the private Spanish colonials had need of their skills as artisans and craftsmen. As free laborers they moved into the cities, draining the surrounding regions of the *repartimiento* labor force and thus requiring the colonial agriculturalists to shift from forced to free labor, and even making it mandatory for public officials to hire free laborers for the construction of public works. By the end of the colonial period *repartimiento* labor had all but disappeared, except for a limited application to public works and to agricultural activities—forbidden but practiced—in areas distant from the urban centers.

But the faltering of the *repartimiento* did not constitute a net gain for Indian labor. The development of a new institution of "free labor" all too often became uncompensated labor rather than freedom of choice in selecting employers. Exactly when debt peonage began, how it developed, and how many it affected during the colonial period must remain unanswered, but as early as the second half of the sixteenth century some *hacendados* made money advances to indigenes to attract them to live on the *hacienda* rather than in the village. The practice had become so widespread before the end of the century that the royal government felt constrained, in 1601 and again in 1609, to forbid any technique to attach natives to privately held land, or to retain them on the *haciendas* against their will. Like so much of the legislation decreed to protect the native from European avarice, the prohibition remained on paper but had little effect in practice, and instances are recorded wherein these "*hacienda* Indians" performed tasks for their masters under the *repartimiento*. Occasionally the crown attempted to hinder the practice by limiting the amount of money which could be advanced to a native, but the decrees merely prevented the Indian from borrowing sufficient funds for land purchase or capital improvement while they protected him not from debt peonage. As late as 1783 a mining ordinance limited deductions to one-fourth of the daily wage as repayment for loans, proving quite conclusively that debt peonage had existed in the mines, and von Humboldt a few years later noted that a major proportion of those toiling in the textile sweatshops did so under debt bondage. Sixteenth- and early seventeenth-century village leaders, objecting to debt peonage not on moral grounds but taking the eminently sensible position that the practice removed potential tribute contributors and *repartimiento* workers, complained repeatedly to the royal government with little discernible effect. The eighteenth-century Bourbon monarchs, more concerned with increased productivity and tax collection (and they did increase tax income sixfold) than with the niceties of economic freedom for the indigenes, politely turned their heads when confronted with evidence of increasing debt peonage. At any rate, by the end of the eighteenth century the practice was pervasive and pernicious. Using a variety of techniques, some ethical and some not, employers maneuvered laborers into contracting debts which could be repaid by work; land-owners particularly used this device for assuring themselves a steady work force. Once in debt, the laborer found it next to impossible to free himself or his heirs, for the debts were passed from father to son regardless of the law to the contrary. The *encomienda* and the *repartimiento* died with the colonial period, but debt peonage continued into the early twentieth century, exacerbating relations between labor and capital.

From the vantage point of the mid-twentieth century it seems remarkable that the Spanish colonial so tenaciously adhered to and passed on a set of assumptions which experience proved unfounded. The original assumptions that the native would not work for personal profit, that he was childlike and could not learn the skills necessary in a complex economic system, and that he could never achieve an intellectual sophistication equivalent to the European gave birth to the *encomienda,* the *repartimiento,* and to debt peonage. Even the great reforms of 1609, ostensibly eliminating the most vicious and exploitative aspects of the *repartimiento,* clearly sprang from the same assumptions; the provision prohibiting forced labor in certain dangerous occupations, for example, may have reflected a genuine humanitarianism and a deep concern for the native population, but it certainly assumed an incapacity on the part of the Indian. And yet the experiences in the mines and in the urban centers proved conclusively that the Indian would, under proper economic stimulus, work steadily and efficiently at tasks demanding great technical skill and imagination.

Aztec life demanded from the mass of the population as much as, and probably more than, the Spanish system in terms of hard labor and contributions to central authority, but the pre-conquest native at least had the psychic salve of laboring for his own civilization. The Spanish system denied him even this. In the early sixteenth century he found himself a conquered man in his own land, working for an alien civilization, and so he remained until the early nineteenth century when Spain passed him on, his condition unchanged, to the independent Mexican government.

Chapter 5 • Colonial Economy

One finds nearly a thousand mines in the short distance of six leagues; some abandoned, some presently working and others held in reserve. . . . I went to a mine called the Trinity because it has three openings, . . . all giving access to the same vein or lode. Respecting its wealth, persons worthy of belief who know the region told me that in ten years this mine has produced forty million pesos, with nine hundred to a thousand men working it daily.

GEMILLI CARRERI, C. 1700

Gold and silver have ever been twin sirens, luring men to false values and blinding them to reality. The silver cascade pouring from the land of the conquered American natives made Mexico the gem of the Spanish crown, but it diverted energies from potentially more solid achievements and created an economic and social order revolving around extractive and exploitative enterprises which took much and gave little. At no time during the colonial period did the Spaniards use their massive silver deposits as a base for general economic development in Mexico or in Spain, but rather focused on precious mineral production to the degree that any economic benefits which accrued from nature's bounty came incidentally rather than deliberately.

Mexican mineral wealth the Spanish accepted as an article of faith from the moment Cortez set foot on Mexican soil. Aztec gold and silver ornamentation, seized by the Spanish but lost in Lake Texcoco during a mad dash for safety a year before the final conquest of Tenochtitlán, convinced the invaders that gold and silver lay in great deposits under the soil. This conviction they transmitted to the crown and, though the intensity of the belief certainly waned in the years immediately following the razing of the Aztec capital, events ultimately proved them right. Native miners in pre-conquest Mexico may or may not have extracted the ores and smelted the metals; the sparse evidence leads to serious question now, but it convinced the Spanish then. Every explorer became a prospector, and every prospector a potential nabob in his own imagination. Small deposits discovered near modern Taxco and in the present state of Michoacán whetted appetites only a few years after the triumph in Lake Texcoco; the disappearance of the Michoacán mine under rocks shaken loose in an earthquake before the operator had been able to extract any significant amounts of ore was a bitter blow, but it did not discourage others from seeking the ore wherever fate and imagination sent them. The Spaniard *knew* that mines would be discovered, and abortive expeditions such as that of Coronado's, whose fabulous Seven Cities of Cibola proved to be little more than poverty-stricken people in mud huts, did little to dampen ardor. Finally, a full generation after the conquest, faith and persistence found their reward in the barren lands of the Chichimecs.

Juan de Tolosa, leading a small band of missionaries and explorers far into the hostile country nearly 400 miles north and west of the capital, discovered with native help a vast deposit of low grade ores in 1546. At the foot of the imposing hill of La Bufa, where the veins reached the surface, the subsequent swarming miners and mining operators built the city of Zacatecas and fought off the resentful natives of the region. A few years later a convoy on the road to the Zacatecas mines discovered the richer and ultimately more productive lode at Guanajuato, well within the Chichimec country but 150 miles nearer to Mexico City. Not long thereafter another expedition uncovered veins in the present state of San Luis Potosí (misnamed for the fabulous mines in the viceroyalty of Peru, discovered in 1545); then, in rapid succession, concessionaires opened mines in the Real del Monte near Pachuca (the mines which so impressed Carreri in the late seventeenth century), at Taxco, and at other sites in the Sierra Madre del Sur and the Sierra Madre Occidental. By the end of the colonial period silver had poured from mines located in eleven of the present Mexican states, running from Guerrero in the south to Sonora and Chihuahua in the north. Alexander von Humboldt set the number of mining districts in the late eighteenth century at five hundred, within which concessionaires worked 5000 individual mines. The most highly productive of those districts, and responsible for over 90 per cent of the production, were, in order:

Mining District	*Location*
Guanajuato	Guanajuato
Catorce	Northern San Luis Potosí
Zacatecas	Zacatecas
Real del Monte	Near Pachuca, Hidalgo
Bolaños	Northern Jalisco
Guarisamey	Western Durango
Sombrerete	Northwest Zacatecas
Taxco	Northern Guerrero
Batopilas	Southwestern Chihuahua
Zimapán	Northwestern Hidalgo
Fresnillo	Central Zacatecas
Ramos	Western San Luis Potosí
Parral	Southern Chihuahua

From these and other mining districts the Spanish reaped a harvest of about two and a quarter billion dollars in gold and silver in the two hundred seventy-five years of mining activity; gold, only a small proportion of the total, came almost completely as a by-product of silver mining.

According to Spanish law and custom, all mineral wealth belonged to the crown, but the government worked no mines in its own name save those for mercury in Almadén, Spain, and in Huancavelica, Peru. Private individuals worked all other mines under concession from the crown, and in this legal sense there were no mine "owners" during the colonial period; they were operators and concessionaires. The crown took care to reward the enterprising soul who braved the unknown to seek metallic ores, for the royal government guaranteed to the discoverer of an outcropping the first option on the concession to work that particular vein. But latecomers also had rights under Spanish practice; the crown granted the original discoverer only the concession to work one mine, not all the potential mines in a district or, in Spanish terminology, a *real*. Mining codes allowed the concessionaire either to work his mine or to sell his rights to others, but they did not allow him to hold a concession for future development without any attempt at exploitation. Law required each concessionaire to work his mine a minimum of four months a year, using the labor of a minimum of four men; most of von Humboldt's 5000 mines, in fact, fell within this minimum legal category and were little more than holding operations. Traditional Spanish law required each mine operator to surrender to the crown, as the cost for the concession, a stipulated proportion of the extracted metal; at one time, in 1504, as high as two-thirds, the royal government reduced it to one-fifth—the famous *quinto*.

Practice in Peru adhered to this proportion, but to operators in New Spain, the royal authorities made a special concession to meet the high cost of mercury, an essential in the extractive process. Prior to the discovery of America, Spain had the greatest known deposits of mercury ore, from which the crown extracted a high proportion of the mercury then available to the world; the fluid metal was widely used wherever silver or gold ores needed treatment to surrender their wealth. Since mercury constituted an essential element in the extraction of silver from the ores, and inasmuch as a ratio of mercury used to silver produced could be established, the royal government used the purchase of mercury by mining concessionaires as a fairly accurate index of the amount of silver produced. Because mercury could be used as a control device, and also because its sale could bring great profit, the crown maintained a strict monopoly over the production and marketing of the metal. But soon after the discovery of silver in Peru, prospectors discovered rich mercury mines not too distant from the silver areas; Peruvian concessionaires, consequently, could obtain mercury at a rate which did not include the prohibitively high transportation costs from Spain. In order to allow Mexican mining to develop concurrently with that in Peru, the royal government conceded to the concessionaires in New Spain a reduction to one-tenth; the *diezmo*, rather than the *quinto,* remained the basic cost of the concession for silver mining during most of the colonial period.

In addition to the costs involved in paying to the crown one-tenth of his produce and the purchase of artificially expensive mercury, the mine operator found it necessary to pay a number of other fees and taxes. The crown maintained a legal monopoly over blasting powder, so critical to hard-rock mining, and then charged the operator fees for refining, minting, assaying, and stamping the metals. Not content with collecting these charges, the royal government added a stiff export duty. When he added all his taxes, fees, *diezmos,* duties, and monopoly costs, the operator found that the law required him to pay roughly 20 per cent of the value of his production. Since ores in general were poor and production costs high, the entire system invited cheating, and it occurred. Surreptitious mining, black market mercury sales, bootleg blasting powder, and bar silver smuggling became the order of the day. Between 10 and 20 per cent (von Humboldt drew the figure 14 out of his hat) of all silver coming from Mexican mines during the colonial period was illegally produced.

Judged by modern standards, or even contemporary European practices, Mexican colonials used primitive methods for extracting and processing the ores, and the methods used in 1800 differed little from those in 1550. The process depended upon a minimum of machinery and a maximum of human labor. Most mines operated on the "rat hole" method (an English corruption of the Spanish *de rato*), in which the miners followed the outcroppings of the ore from the surface through its twistings and turnings until the vein became exhausted or unprofitable. The dimensions of the tunnelings and galleries depended upon the size of the lode, some of those in the Veta Grande of Guanajuato measuring more than a hundred feet in depth and width but most of them so small that work was difficult. Only on rare occasions did an operator sink a vertical shaft or construct a horizontal drift, except to remove water. The system did not necessitate any substantial shoring, and as a consequence any work stoppage which allowed water to rise virtually assured heavy damage.

With few exceptions, even in mines as deep as 1500 feet, workmen carried ore to the surface in leather buckets which held from 150 to 300 pounds; much of the journey from the workings was up primitive "chicken ladders" with the miner carrying a torch in one hand and maintaining a precarious balance with the other. The mere experience of negotiating the route to the closest workings, accompanied by mine officials and guided by miners who carried torches, so terrified Gemilli Carreri that he vowed never to repeat the experience. Frequent accidents befell the ore carriers—almost without exception Indians—but until accident or ill-health took them out of the mines they performed prodigious feats: a third of a mile descent into the bowels of the earth and a return trip carrying 200 pounds of ore every hour during a twelve-hour work day took enormous stamina and will to work. These expenditures did not placate the concessionaires, who constantly complained of their workmen's inefficiency and malingering.

Miners removed virtually all water, and on rare occasions some of the ores, by the use of mule- or horse-driven whims (*malacates*) which lifted leather buckets—filled by hand in the mine—to the surface; tens of thousands of animals strained at the traces throughout the mining regions in a sometimes vain effort to keep the water under control. The perfection of the steam engine in the second half of the eighteenth century had no perceptible effect on mining technology; a combination of scarce fuel, ignorance, traditionalism, poor transportation, and indolence limited the use of the new power plant for either the pumping of water or the lifting of ores.

Once the ores reached the surface, a great number of workers, frequently women and children, hammered them into smaller pieces and hand-selected them into two categories. Extraordinarily rich ores went directly to the smelting ovens, but such concentrations were scarce; the great proportion of the ores contained a low concentrate of silver compound which necessitated a beneficiating process involving amalgamation, and it was this process which demanded the use of mercury. Mexican mining operators, almost without exception, used the *patio* method, a technique devised by the colonials and first used within ten years after the first major silver strike; peculiarly fitted for the climate and ores, it remained the common method well beyond the colonial period. The process began when the owner of the *hacienda de beneficio* (the processing or reducing plant) ran the ores through a series of *arrastres,* or great basalt grinding mills not greatly different in operating action from the old-fashioned stone grain mill, which reduced the mineral to a fine powder. Washing removed some of the gangue, leaving a heavy sludge which was then dumped in an open-air flagstoned patio in sufficient quantity to form a huge cake, or *torta,* roughly 100 feet in diameter and two feet thick. Once the menials had placed and formed the *torta,* the *azoguero* (mercury man) showed his skill or lack of it. The autocrat of the mining process, to whom even the mine operator and the *hacienda* owner spoke with respect, the *azoguero* played a role of prime importance. The success or failure of the *patio* process depended upon him, his leather flagon of mercury, and his testing gourd. By adding salts, lime, or copper pyrites (magistral), depending upon the chemical characteristics of the *torta* as determined by sight, touch, and smell rather than analysis, he allowed his cake to "cook" for a few days. At the moment he judged proper he sprinkled mercury from his flagon, a few drops at a time, over the surface; he then retired to allow tromping men and beasts to mix the mass thoroughly under his watchful eye. For the next month, or five, depending upon the ores and the weather, he hovered over his cake as faithfully as a bird over a clutch of eggs. Now he added lime or pyrites to heat it, or salt to cool it; then he added mercury to speed the amalgamation process or to assure full amalgamation. Frequently he scooped up an ounce or two of the mixture in his gourd, washed it in water, and observed the results; often he ordered the men with their animals onto the cake to give it a thorough mixing. Finally the moment arrived; he hailed the amalgamation process as completed and his work as finished. Other workers then washed and agitated the mixture in a series of connected vats, allowing the wastes to run away and the heavier amalgam to settle. After squeezing the amalgam in cloth sacks to separate the excess mercury, refiners then sublimed the remaining mercury through a heating process, recovered the mercury in liquid form, and, hopefully, produced a bar of silver which probably contained bits of gold, lead, and zinc.

The *hacienda de beneficio* owner expected the *azoguero* to produce an ounce of silver for every six ounces of mercury put into the cake, and to leave the mixture in a form which would allow the recovery of most of the mercury and silver. Too much mercury put into the cake meant an expensive waste, for even under the most careful operation some mercury escaped in the washing and subliming process; too little mercury meant improper amalgamation and a residue of silver compound in the tailings. A truly skilled *azoguero* could extract 95 per cent of the silver from low-grade ores (15 ounces to the ton) with a minimal mercury loss; mining men generally demanded less. In spite of the crudity of the process, which had as its greatest defects the enormous amount of labor required and the long passage of time from beginning to end, it seemed almost perfectly fitted for the Mexican ambient. A mining mission sent by Charles III in 1788 discovered, after years of experimentation, the method to be more effective in Mexico than the semi-mechanized and modernized Born process used throughout Europe.

Mercury constituted the key to Mexican mining, and over mercury the royal government exercised a tight and sometimes unreasonable control. Working as it did for its own profit the great mines at Almadén and Huancavelica, the crown forbade the utilization of the cinnabar ore found in Mexico in the justified belief that its exploitation would be too difficult to regulate. From 1590 to 1750, the crown fixed the price of 187 *pesos* a *quintal* (approximately 100 pounds); in the latter year a more realistic Bourbon government attempting to increase Mexican silver production reduced the price to 82. Such immediate and beneficial results came that in 1767 and 1778 Charles III brought the price down to 62 and then 41, where it ostensibly remained to the end of the colonial period. But after 1778 the Peruvian mines at Huancavelica dwindled away and Almadén could no longer meet the demand, whereupon the government purchased mercury from Germans and fixed its price at 63. From that time forward the Mexican mining concessionaires battled among themselves for the privilege of buying the cheaper Spanish product.

The crying demand for mercury, its price always held high by monopolistic control, poor administration, and inadequate transportation, materially affected silver production. Every European war was reflected in mining statistics; war upset commerce, infrequent ships created a mercury shortage, and the dearth of mercury reduced the mining output. The long Seven Years' War made mercury in such short supply that many operators were forced to close mines, many of which flooded badly and suffered such interior damage that they never reopened. But the mercury monopoly had other drawbacks as well, for it enticed crown agents to play favorites, to use the metal as a political weapon, and to take advantage of shortages to fill their own pockets. Mine operators in the Pachuca district in 1697 reported to Carreri that the viceroy forced them to pay 300 *pesos* a *quintal* rather than the official price of 187; the viceroy, Carreri assumed, kept the difference. A hundred years later Alexander von Humboldt insisted that thc biggest mine operators could always buy Spanish mercury, while the small operators could find only the German product at the higher price. The great silver barons needed the cheap product less critically than did those of second rank, but they had the social and political influence which allowed them to make a claim to it. Guanajuato and Zacatecas concessionaires frequently complained that mercury sales were both inefficiently and corruptly handled. Whether these and equivalent accusations were based on fact, or whether they were characteristic, remains in doubt, but certainly control over mercury put a powerful weapon in the hands of the viceroy, whom the mine operators could ill afford to cross.

In spite of the Spanish propensity for paper-work, royal officials in Mexico left no accurate records regarding total silver production during the first century and a half of intensive mining activity. Until 1690 the royal government collected its share when the bullion arrived in Spain, and officials there made no distinction regarding place of origin. Estimates, based upon the amount of mercury imported, yield a total of over 400 million *pesos* in a combination of gold and silver from the conquest to 1690, when the Mexican mints began to keep complete records. Using the estimate in conjunction with mint records, and adding one-seventh for fraud, von Humboldt estimated a total production of slightly more than two billion up to 1803. Adding another estimated quarter billion for the 1803-20 period gives a total of about two and a quarter billion, over 70 per cent of which poured forth in the last hundred years. Data compiled by the national Mexican government place the total a little less, but other estimates place it somewhat more. In the present century of astronomical government and business budgets, a sum of two and a quarter billion dollars (the *peso* had a silver content roughly equal to that of the dollar) creates scarcely a ripple. But in an age and a place where a *peso* was an excellent daily wage which would buy 200 pounds of beans, or two or three turkeys, or five dozen eggs, or 100 pounds of corn, the amount represents a truly magnificent income. But lest we be blinded by the reflection of gold and silver, we must be aware that the annual value of corn production in Mexico came close to that of the precious metals, and that in some years the retail value on European markets of cacao shipped from Ecuador surpassed it.

The impact of gold and silver production on Mexican colonial society and economy is difficult to assess, for some of its material effects may be easily discerned, while the psychological results are impossible to measure. Certainly the existence of great stores of silver ore discouraged the development of other known metallic resources. Spanish royal policy, in its concern over collecting the tenth and in maintaining its monopoly over mercury, forbade the exploitation of known cinnabar deposits which would have been capable of rendering a supply sufficient to meet most annual needs for the greater part of the colonial period. Copper, lead, zinc, and other base metals the colonials left in the natural state unless forced to exploit them along with the silver ores. At a time when other Western European nations began their industrial drive with base metals, Spain concentrated on the production of the precious—but unfortunately could not even use the flow of those metals to improve her own domestic economy, which after 1600 steadily fell behind that of the neighboring countries. Furthermore, both the internal and external trade and communication systems of Mexico were designed to meet the needs of the mines rather than the general economy. The early viceregal governments marked out ill-kept but well-guarded roads, over which wagons and carriages could pass in safety but not in comfort, to all seats of mining activity. Over these "highways" the silver, high in value in proportion to bulk, could pass at relatively small cost from the mines to the mints and thence to the ports. But roads in general were so miserable and so scarce that most materials moved by pack train rather than by wagon. The transportation system was so ineffectual that in some regions corn would go begging from overproduction, while less than 100 miles away the poor could not afford to buy it. Potentially rich agricultural regions, with potentially marketable products, remained even more isolated than they had been before the Spaniards arrived. But in justice to Spanish colonial policy, it should be pointed out that seventeenth-century roads in Spain were no better than those in Mexico.

On the other hand the mines stimulated the founding of cities and the development of the frontier. Every mining *real* had its city or cities, and every road leading to the mines had its towns surrounded by agricultural or pastoral activities. The rich Bajío Valley, from Querétaro north, owed its development as a major agricultural region to the discovery of mines north and east of the ancient lake bed. Much of the income from mining, too, went into *haciendas* far from the mining region, for the Spaniard prized land above all else and used his wealth from other sources to acquire that which gave him prestige.

While mining occupied the pre-eminent position in men's minds, agriculture dominated the economy both in its demands on the labor force and in total value. But it came far from reaching its potential. Alexander von Humboldt, mild-mannered though he usually was, registered deep disgust at what he saw:

> Mexican agriculture is held up for the same set of political causes that prevent the progress of industry in the peninsula. All of the vices of feudal government have been passed from one to the other hemisphere, and in Mexico the abuses have been much more dangerous in its effect. The soil of New Spain, as it is in the old, in great part is found in the possession of powerful families who have slowly absorbed the small private holdings. In America as well as in Europe there are great stretches condemned to serve as animal pasture and to a perpetual sterility.

The scientist's judgment found an echo in the observations of others, particularly of some churchmen, who saw in the high land concentration not only economic stagnation but social degradation. Spain's colonial economic policy, heavily influenced by mercantilist doctrines to the last, tended to regulate, restrict, and prohibit rather than encourage. Spain's concern was always Spain, and her economic policies were designed to give to Spain that economic power she craved. If the colonies too, benefited, well and good; but if the royal government decided that its own position might be enhanced by putting the economic squeeze on a colony, the colonials suffered. In this respect Spain differed not at all from its contemporary colonial powers, and if her policy-makers recognized the economic factors in the British North American colonial revolt they gave no sign. To be sure the eighteenth-century Bourbon governments conceded a number of economic "reforms" which benefited the colonies—limitations on some monopolies, reduction of some commercial fees, permission for ships to sail to Spain direct from additional ports and the like—but all these changes presupposed additional income for the royal government and for the residents of the peninsula. Within this mercantilist concept only a few agricultural products would play any dominant and positive role, and these the royal government encouraged or monopolized as conditions warranted.

One example of Spanish neglect of Mexican agricultural potential should suffice to make clear the *peninsular* approach to economic development. Pre-conquest Mexico produced sufficient chocolate to make that commodity a regular item of trade, exchange, and consumption. The cacao-producing regions far to the south and east of the colonial capital could easily have been tapped by the construction of decent roads either to the capital or to the nearest potential port. But the government did nothing to alleviate the region's isolation, population declined drastically, and within fifty years Mexican chocolate disappeared as an item of trade. In the meantime cacao seeds dispatched to Venezuel and Ecuador took root and flourished; in these regions geography and population combined to make chocolate production profitable. Venezuelan chocolate fell into the hands of the Dutch through their genius for smuggling, but that of Ecuador entered into Spanish trade and found its way to Spanish tables. A late colonial estimate placed the value of Ecuadorian chocolate on the Guayaquil wharves at about 3 million *pesos*. Expensive transportation costs over the Isthmus of Panama and profits to a number of monopolistic middlemen swelled the retail value to about 12 million *pesos* in Havana. Additional transportation costs and more intervening profits elevated the retail value in Spain to a staggering 20 million; from Spain, and at these prices, merchants re-exported the bean to Mexico. This colony, her own production having declined to zero, annually imported chocolate valued at a million *pesos* (about one and one-half times the value of mercury imports) when it reached Veracruz and probably twice that figure when the colonial purchased it in the Mexico City markets. At these prices only the well-to-do could afford the luxury of a cup of chocolate. The rapid rise in the price of chocolate, in fact, took place early in the colonial period and was a function of declining production. In 1548 a skilled Indian laborer in Mexico City, at prevailing wages, could still enjoy his chocolate-flavored *atole;* twenty years later the cost was prohibitive. Thus an agricultural production which sufficed for twenty million in 1520 declined so disastrously that it could not meet the needs of one-fifth that number two generations later; a product which a little social capital could have elevated into an important export item became in fact a drain on capital formation. It must be noted that the decline in Mexican chocolate production worked a hardship on those living in Mexico, not those living in Spain; it was immaterial to the Spanish crown or to the Spanish consumer whether the bean came from Mexico or Ecuador.

In numerous ways, however, the Spanish government did encourage the colonials to establish an agricultural economy which would at least meet their basic needs; this was especially true in the early years, and more often than not revolved around the introduction of non-American products. Under the prodding of royal officials, sugar cane moved from the Canaries via Española to Mexico. At one time the crown required every ship departing for the New World to carry grape vines and seeds or shoots of olive trees. In 1531 the royal government made a special effort to introduce both grape and olive to New Spain. The crown gave prizes for the most successful efforts to acclimatize wheat, dispatched cattle of all sorts, sent chickens, furnished farm implements, and even required the *encomendero* to invest at least 10 per cent of his tribute income in the construction of permanent buildings or in the cultivation of land. Most of the efforts were sporadic and many of the requirements poorly enforced.

But agriculture did develop into an economic activity which surpassed in market value the product of the mines and, occasionally, constituted as much as 20 per cent of the export value. Corn, the staple food of the vast majority, reigned supreme in production statistics. In 1802 the Intendancy of Guadalajara, not a heavy grain producer, harvested nearly 100,000 tons at a retail value of 2 to 4 million *pesos*. Total annual production in the late colonial period sometimes surpassed a million tons, with a retail value exceeding that of silver; it always reached at least three-quarters of a million tons, and its value was never significantly below that of the precious metal. Since European palates never found the Indian maize savory, corn entered into the export trade not at all.

Sugar cane, the colonials found, grew well in some of the interior valleys. By the middle of the sixteenth century, Mexican sugar producers refined more than enough for the local market and began exporting to both Spain and Peru. Before 1600 the industry had achieved sufficient importance to warrant crown regulation, and by the middle of the century sugar was second in value among agricultural products. Toward the end of the eighteenth century its value averaged something more than 7 million *pesos* annually, of which about one-fifth reached non-Mexican markets. Wheat, consumed only by the European colonials and a small portion of the *mestizos,* was grown in sufficient quantities to meet all local demands and to provide a sizable export surplus for over two centuries. In the late years production failed to keep pace with local demands, and this, coupled with vastly increased production in other parts of the world, virtually eliminated Mexico as an important exporter of the grain and its flour.

Cotton, indigenous to Mexico and the common clothing fiber for the pre-conquest population, fell off in importance during the colonial period. Potentially a valuable product but one which demanded a great deal of hand-labor to separate the fiber from the seed, it deteriorated in culture with the population decline. Few Europeans devoted their energies to its cultivation. The natives continued to grow enough for their own use in those regions where climate and social systems allowed it, but the colony as a whole did not produce enough cotton even to maintain a stumbling textile industry which never met local demands. Mexican cotton followed somewhat the same path as that of chocolate, but in a degree not so exaggerated; in this case it was Venezuela which supplied the Spanish market. Venezuelan soil and topography made cotton culture there more attractive and profitable than in Mexico, where the mountainous terrain and the dearth of roads were prohibitive for transportation, and it was the Venezuelan rather than the Mexican colony which received encouragement from the home government. Again it was the Mexican resident, not the Spanish empire, which suffered.

At one time Mexican silk bade fair to become one of the viceroyalty's most profitable non-mining economic enterprises. With the blessing of Charles I, Dominican friars in 1530 began planting mulberry trees and soon thereafter imported the worms. Within ten years, partly because of the special interest which Cortez's son gave to the project, silk culture covered a great area running from Puebla to central Oaxaca; Motolinía reported the crop of 1541 to be bountiful and of such excellent quality that it surpassed Spanish silk. For the next generation or so, production increased and encouraged the establishment of mills in Mexico City to fabricate satins, velvets, and taffetas; the boom lasted until near the end of the century. The Spanish conquest of the Philippines after 1565 and the founding of Manila in 1571 gave Spanish merchants access to higher quality, cheaper Chinese silk at roughly the same time that disease struck both tree and worm in Mexico; the combination doomed the industry even before the royal government began in 1596 to discourage Mexican silk production. A few Indians continued planting trees and tending worms, maintaining a steady but small production of inferior silk, and on this base Charles III attempted to reinvigorate sericulture. But two centuries of neglect had doomed silk production, and the crown's efforts could not revive it.

Vanilla followed a course somewhat analogous to that of chocolate.

Like the cacao tree it was indigenous to the Aztec-Maya world, where the native population had harvested the bean from both wild and cultivated vines for centuries before the conquest; the Spanish introduced it to European markets. Despite European demands and the high price the product could command, neither crown nor local officials gave special encouragement to vanilla cultivation. Still, Mexican vines furnished almost all vanilla reaching European markets in the sixteenth and seventeenth centuries. By the early part of the eighteenth all attempts at formal cultivation had been abandoned and the harvest consisted of spare-time pickings from wild trees by natives who sold their meager gleanings to local merchants. By the end of the colonial period vanilla constituted slightly more than 1 per cent of Mexican agricultural exports, and less than three-tenths of 1 per cent of total exports. Unlike chocolate however, Spain itself lost income as production of vanilla declined in Mexico; non-Spanish lands supplanted Mexico as the world's supplier.

As was true in the case of so many potentially valuable products, Spain neglected the cultivation of tobacco until it was too late. Columbus brought some of the leaves to Spain, where one medical man extolled the marvelous virtues of the new American plant, but no one made any serious attempt to capitalize on the product. Cortez found native Mexicans using tobacco, and Indians continued to grow it for their own use; Spaniards who took up the habit in the islands and on the mainland made little attempt to market the cured leaves in Europe. Not until the English had settled in Virginia did tobacco become popular in Europe; the English were better salesmen. During most of the colonial period anyone who wished could plant tobacco, but as a part of the general scheme of the Bourbons to obtain greater crown revenues, the Spanish government established tobacco monopolies in Spain and in the colonies. After 1764, when the monopoly was instituted in Mexico, royal officials allowed tobacco cultivation only in a few restricted districts near Orizaba, Córdoba, and Veracruz. The restrictions kept the harvest low and the prices high, while they allowed no production for export. In most years, in fact, the royal tobacco factories imported some of the leaf from Cuba in order to meet local demand.

The government price paid to the cultivators reached scarcely half a million *pesos* a year, but the finished cigars and cigarettes retailed for about 8 million *pesos*—over half of which was clear profit.

Rounding out agricultural production for national and foreign markets were indigo and cochineal. Indigo farmers in the coastal areas produced enough of the dye to satisfy the domestic textile needs and to furnish over a quarter of a million *pesos'* worth for the foreign markets. Cochineal, not strictly an agricultural product since the red dye comes from a little scarlet bug, may be considered an agricultural process inasmuch as the culture of the insect depends upon the cultivation of a particular species of cactus plant. Native to Mexico and widely used by the indigenous population prior to the arrival of the conquerors, it flourished particularly in the Oaxaca Valley, where climate, topography, and soil combine to make almost ideal growing conditions for both insect and cactus. By the last two decades of the eighteenth century cochineal production, like vanilla gathering, had been left entirely to the Indian population by default; thousands of Indians tending their *nopaleros* shook off and dried a sufficient quantity of the mature insects to produce all the red dye needed in Mexico and to send abroad an amount valued at about 2.5 million *pesos* in Veracruz—by far the greatest export other than precious metals.

The average annual value of total agricultural production entering the market (excluding a vast array of items grown for home consumption) must remain a mystery in view of the sparse satistics, but some estimates may be made. Alexander von Humboldt, using tithes as his basis for computation, arrived at a figure of 29 million *pesos* in the late colonial period. A generation later Lucas Alamán, a distinguished historian-statesman of conservative bent, used the same method to calculate the average at 30 million. Both these estimates appear too low in view of the known prices demanded for some products and the estimated production of those goods. In 1802, for example, estimates of wheat production reached 150,000 tons, with an estimated value of 18 million *pesos*. In that same year corn came to 850,000 tons, and sold at a price of from 20 to 100 *pesos* per ton in various parts of the colony. Even at the lowest price the corn was worth 17 million *pesos*, and this added to the 18 million for wheat gives a total of 35 million for these two items alone. The total value of agricultural production, as marketed by the producer, therefore probably came closer to the 50 million than 30 million mark. But even if we take the lowest of the estimates, von Humboldt's at 29 million, the figure is 80 per cent more than the average value of precious metals. Had the Spanish regime devoted as much energy and social capital to the stimulation of agriculture as it did to mining, and had it been concerned with Mexican economic development as such, the total agricultural output could have been doubled in value.

Any attempt to array alongside agricultural production the value of its allied pastoral activity leads only to frustration and confusion. If we are to give credence to observers, the countryside teemed with horses, mules, cattle, sheep, and goats, frequently untended and sometimes highly destructive to crops. Carreri, during his visit in 1697, reported that a Jesuit-run *hacienda* near Pachuca could count over 100,000 sheep and goats, 10,000 cattle, and 5000 horses. Reports from the mid-eighteenth century and later suggest that the average large *hacienda* ran 30,000 head of cattle alongside thousands of horses and mules. But of these millions of animals very few entered the marketplace. The mines needed mules and horses by the thousand–the Guanajauto district alone used 14,000 at all times–and the Veracruz overland transport used 20,000, but the population simply could not absorb the fantastic number of animals. Meat destined for markets normally came from local ranchers, but occasionally the Bajío *hacendado* supplied the Mexico City market by driving his cattle the intervening 200 miles; other major markets also frequently found their most economical sources at some distance. Mexican cattle furnished the colony's few leather needs (the mines, needing leather buckets, probably made the greatest demand), but hides seldom constituted an important export item. Beef tallow emerged as a poor grade of soap from the factories of Guadalajara, Puebla, and Mexico City. And despite the hordes of sheep and goats, Mexican wool production never equaled that of Spain in quality or quantity. The royal government made no serious effort to encourage wool production, with the consequence that New Spain never produced sufficient wool to clothe her people; textiles, fabrics, and clothing consistently outweighed in value all other imports combined.

But in spite of these conditions, and perhaps responsible for them, the Spanish government through the mechanism of the *mesta,* or cattlemen's power group, hemmed in the pastoral *hacendado* with a maze of regulations. Perhaps in no economic endeavor is the quality of the Spanish administrative mind so clearly, so brutally shown in its weakness. In the late sixteenth century, at a time when the governor of Nueva Viscaya owned 33,000 calves and sold 6000 mature animals to one man at a *peso* and a half each, colonial officials became distraught over the problem of cattle conservation. New regulations went on the statute books. The law thenceforward prohibited any owner of cattle from killing any animal even for his own use without a special license, and stipulated that only old animals, past the age of fecundity, could be sent to the slaughterhouse or killed for hides and tallow. Furthermore, Indian towns could build no public slaughterhouses, and every Spanish town had its meat monopolist who had the sole right to sell meat in the market. Two hundred years later, with at least one ranchman claiming ownership of 150,000 head and with wild cattle roaming the hinterlands, these regulations still held. The market places still sold only tough and stringy meat, and the rancher still applied for permission to kill for his own table one of his 40,000 animals. Royal officials still prohibited public slaughterhouses in Indian towns, and an Indian still received 100 lashes for killing a cow, even one incontestably his own, without a license. Small wonder, then, that pastoral activities contributed so little to the total economy.

Colonial industry, discouraged by the same frame of mind which prevented full-blown agricultural and pastoral development, scarcely got off the ground; the merchants to whom the crown gave trading monopolies consistently fought any local manufacturing development. In the late colonial years the total annual value of fabricated products reached nearly 16 million *pesos,* but half this amount came from the elevated prices which the crown received from the cigars and cigarettes rolling from its monopolistic tobacco factories. The royal tobacco factories paid on the average no more than half a million *pesos* for the leaf tobacco and expended another 3 million on wages for the 10,000 workers and administrators, but sold the product for approximately 8 million and thus garnered a profit of some 4.5 million.

The only privately owned industry even approaching cigar and cigarette retail value was that of textiles. Soon after arrival, the Spanish grafted their own techniques on the native population's well-developed weaving process and established small shops using both cotton and wool. In the course of time the Spanish themselves left the looms, surrendering the actual labor to Indians and *mestizos* but keeping control of most of the factories. Climate and raw materials tended to concentrate the major activities in Guadalajara, Puebla, and Querétaro, each producing textiles of about 600,000 *pesos'* value. These three centers used some 5000 laborers in small sweatshops known as *obrajes* or *trapiches*. The very word "sweatshop" conjures a vision of misery and filth and degradation; the colonial *obraje* epitomized the term at its worst, and even the crown recognized the sordid conditions when it prohibited the use of *repartimiento* labor in such factories. The late sixteenth-century *obraje,* with its crying need for cheap labor, set the pattern of bringing within its confines those who could not otherwise work—the cripples, the drunks, the ill, and the destitute—and conditions grew worse in succeeding centuries. By the late eighteenth century the inspection of an *obraje* almost made von Humboldt physically ill. A small, poorly illuminated and airless room filled with a miasmic stench and occupied by 15 or 20 incredibly dirty and half-naked laborers bending over work tables from dawn to dusk behind locked double doors—that was the typical weaving establishment. Many workers were prisoners consigned to the *obraje* owner for a small fee; at the close of day they marched back to their squalid prison cells and the day following trudged to the equally squalid shop, both trips closely guarded by a prison official. The remainder, held by a debt peonage as strong as the chains and bars which held the prisoners, stayed on the premises during the week and then, clutching the pittance which passed for the week's wage, spent Sunday at home. They were miserable but skilled, some of their exquisite work finding buyers in the best markets throughout the empire. Their labor produced wealth for the *obraje* owners, some of whom owned dozens of the shops, but it did not produce enough clothing to meet Mexican market demands even when supplemented by the cheaper textiles coming from the thousands of native looms far from the urban centers.

Other industries played a small part in the general economy. Mexican factories produced enough cheap soap to supply most needs, the total product reaching a value of nearly a million *pesos* a year. A flourishing pottery and china industry centered in Puebla in the late seventeenth century had dwindled by the late eighteenth to a trickle because it could not meet central European competition. Higher quality goods coming from the great fur-trading companies drove Mexican felt hats from the European markets at about the same time. A wide variety of other fabricated products—leather goods, furniture, cooking utensils, shoes, boots, blankets, and the like—fall more into the category of artisanry than industry and in any event probably made little economic impact.

All in all, Mexican colonial manufacturing output presents a dismal picture, but in this respect Mexico differed not at all from other Spanish colonies, or the colonies of the other European nations of the same era. Spanish dedication to mercantilist principles led to a bewildering welter of regulatory legislation, most of which was restrictive and little of which stimulated sound economic development. Of all regulations, those controlling shipping probably had the most deleterious effect upon potential manufacturing and agricultural achievement.

The archaic fleet system, instituted in the sixteenth century to protect Spanish treasure ships from the rapacious English Sea Dogs and tenaciously retained long past its usefulness, somehow never worked as well in practice as it did in theory. Designed to be annual convoys bringing European goods to Veracruz and transporting Mexican produce to Spain, the fleets in fact were more nearly quadrennial sailings. Goods waited for years in the seacoast warehouses, moldering and piling up storage costs. The 1778 fleet, the last arriving in Mexico before Spain abandoned the system completely, picked up agricultural cargos which had accumulated over a four-year period. With transport to the outside so uncertain, colonial Mexico could not develop an economy depending upon markets abroad, and her small European population could not sustain any significant manufacturing development regardless of the availability of raw materials. Furthermore, since Spain insisted upon using income from Mexico to sustain the administrative costs in the other colonies and in Spain, the royal government left almost no funds in viceregal hands for the kinds of social investment which lead to economic development.

In spite of these restrictions and weaknesses, Mexico occupied the premier trading position among the Spanish colonies during most of the colonial period, and the gap widened enormously after 1789. With the abolition of the fleet system, mercantile activity in Veracruz took an amazing leap. Within a decade agricultural exports quintupled and general imports more than doubled; the port handled an average of a new ship arrival every day, and in exceptional years 500 ships arrived and departed. In the twenty-year span from 1790 to 1810, Veracruz accounted for nearly half the total trade value between Spain and her American colonies.

Annual trade between Mexico and the remainder of the empire usually ranged between 25 and 40 million *pesos* after 1790, the total tonnage reflecting the intensity of the European conflict then raging spasmodically. Between 10 and 15 per cent of the total trade in these waning years of the great empire was with the other Spanish American colonies and the remainder with Spain itself; the crown forbade trade outside the Spanish world. Exports always exceeded imports, the ratio in the late years being roughly three to two. Precious metals accounted for about three-quarters of the total export value, nearly half of the gold and silver in either minted or bullion form going to the treasury in Madrid or to one of the viceregal governments in the Western Hemisphere. The other half went into private accounts in Spain. A combination of cochineal and sugar made up over 80 per cent of the remaining exports, with some flour, indigo, salt meat, dried vegetables, rawhides, and vanilla usually completing the list. Occasionally pottery, china, and textiles found a market in the other colonies, but at best all three combined totaled less than 1 per cent.

Among the imports almost two-thirds came in the form of various textiles, either in finished clothing or bolts of material, and a major proportion originated in non-Spanish mills. Paper, cacao, and distilled alcoholic beverages of various kinds, all of which could easily have been produced in Mexico at less cost, each contributed about 7 per cent to the import value; wine, mercury, iron, wax, and steel, in that order of importance, completed the bulk of the imports. From the above it will be noted that trade revolved around two products—precious metals and textiles—which accounted for over 70 per cent of the value of goods shipped in or out in the last years before the end of the colonial regime; in earlier times the relative importance of these items was even greater.

During most of the colonial period a small group of favored monopolists controlled all legal import trade; these merchants, under a charter granted to them in the sixteenth century, effectively limited the amount of goods coming to the colony and jacked up the prices to outlandish figures. The commercial system not only limited the volume of goods; it also closed the doors of profitable trade to the creoles because the merchants, through a tortured interpretation of their charter, retained trading privileges for the *peninsulares* alone. As a part of the general relaxation of trade restrictions late in Charles III's reign, new commercial regulations broke the monopolists' power. Many of the great Spanish merchants in Veracruz and Mexico City, faced with the prospect of falling profits because of stiff competition, diverted their finances from commerce to mining; to this shift in investment patterns Lucas Alamán credits the remarkable increase in silver production after 1790. But breaking the monopoly did not mean an immediate benefit to the colonial consumer; twenty years later a Spanish general in Mexico could say, with justified bitterness, that "the scarcity and high price of goods is in fact a result of mercantile speculation and the passage of goods through many hands." The entire mercantile system, with its emphasis on the economic advantages accruing to the *gachupín* almost to the exclusion of the *criollo,* probably did more to push the creole toward independence than did any other single royal policy.

In contrast to the English colonial system, which put little emphasis on colonial tax collection as a source of crown revenues, Spain looked to her colonies to give fiscal support to the royal government as well as economic comfort to her people; she expected her colonies to give her necessary funds to carry on her European enterprises. During the first century the viceroyalty of Peru, with its great silver mountain of Potosí, served as the crown's major income producer; in that hundred-year period Mexico returned a net profit to the royal coffers, but in some years costs exceeded revenues and either Spain or Peru made up the difference. As the Potosí mine began to peter out and as Mexican mining expanded in the seventeenth century, Mexico replaced Peru as the prime income producer. After 1790, of all funds flowing into colonial treasuries 55 per cent were collected in Mexico, and on a per capita basis tax collections there outstripped those in Spain by a good margin in spite of the colony's 40 per cent Indian population.

Prior to the introduction of the tobacco monopoly the crown enjoyed three major sources of revenue in Mexico: Indian tribute, the *alcabala* (a transaction tax), and a combination of various taxes and fees in connection with mining. Indian tribute, usually averaging from 5 to 8 *pesos* for male heads of families, often brought in the greatest amount from a single source. As *encomiendas* escheated to the crown the proportion of total Indian tribute coming to the crown increased, but until 1650 the declining population meant a generally declining total tribute collection. After that date the total amount steadily grew; in 1746 the sum of 650,000 *pesos* (about 17 per cent of all revenue) came from tribute, and by the end of the century the total take had almost doubled. By this latter date, however, other sources had increased so significantly that tribute accounted for only 6 per cent of the total. The *alcabala*, a characteristic Castillian tax which generally amounted to about 10 per cent of the value of all commercial transactions in the old country, first came to Mexico in 1575 as a tax of 2 per cent. About fifty years later a special assessment of 2 per cent additional was tacked on for what was announced as a fifteen-year period but proved to be permanent, and after a few more years the crown added another 2 per cent. Occasionally for short periods the tax was higher, but the rate of 6 per cent held with a fair degree of uniformity during most of the time after 1636. A maze of regulations revolved around the collection, each type of enterprise subject to a different mode and time of collection. Itinerant merchants, for example, were required to pay every day, wine sellers every week, and wholesalers every four months. In each case the seller reported the value of his sales and paid his taxes accordingly; a system of checking and reporting presumably kept the declarations fairly accurate and honest. Mexico City paid a fixed sum for all such transactions during the last two centuries, with tax farmers handling the actual collections from the individuals. Since the tax applied to every transaction (except for those exempt, the most important being that of the sale by an Indian of his own produce) and not merely that which put the goods into the hands of the consumer, it had a multiplier effect which not only hindered economic activity but helped push up the price of goods to the ultimate user. But it produced revenue. Until well into the eighteenth century the tax consistently produced more than the *quinto* and the direct taxes on mining.

Royal income from mining activities came from three general sources —those directly concerned with mining itself, including the *quinto;* those connected with the activities of the mints, including assaying, refining, and coining; and those involving the monopolies on mercury and blasting powder. From the beginning of the eighteenth century onward a combination of these fees and taxes gave the crown roughly one-quarter of its collected revenues each year; of these the concession fee amounted to something less than half. The minting and coining process usually produced about half as much as the direct taxes on mining, but the profit was considerably less since the actual costs to the royal government of maintaining the mints ate up a good portion of the income. The monopolies brought only a small proportion of the total income derived from mining activities.

The tobacco monopoly, after its introduction in 1765, proved to be the greatest single source of income, both in terms of total revenues and in net profit to the treasury. In 1803, for example, all taxes on mining, including the minting fees and the monopolies, brought in something under 6 million *pesos;* of this amount about 3.5 million came from the concession fee and other direct taxes on mining. In that same year the total tobacco income reached about 8 million, of which 4.5 million was clear profit to the crown.

Customs duties on goods moving between Spain and Mexico were generally collected in Spain and do not figure in the colonial financial structure, but goods moving between New Spain and the other colonies were valued and taxed in Veracruz. Although the system and the rates changed frequently, the duties seldom went over 10 per cent and frequently descended as low as 1 or 2 per cent, with many goods exempt from such duties. Customs duties added little to colonial royal income and seldom constituted a real deterrent to trade. A wide variety of other taxes, licenses and fees (half annates, cock-fighting licenses, postal fees, stamped paper, for example), and a number of monopolies (playing cards, ice, salt, pepper) produced dribbling bits for the exchequer, and in the late colonial period a new source of profitable taxation was discovered: a tax on pulque. During the first century after the conquest the crown attempted to prohibit the fabrication of alcoholic beverages, but the prohibition did not prevent the fermentation, or sale, of the native maguey juice. By the middle of the seventeenth century the royal government officially permitted sale, but only under closely guarded circumstances. Sales could take place only during daylight hours, the sexes were not allowed to mingle, none could partake of food while seated, and none could "remain after having drunk, or have a harp, guitar or other instrument, or dance or play music, under pain of" 50 lashes for the first offense and 200 plus banishment for the second. Some local officials imposed small taxes on the liquor, but these funds did not find their way into the royal coffers. The Bourbons, always searching for new sources and more efficient than the Hapsburgs, regularized the pulque impost by farming the tax, a system by which the crown sold to individuals a concession on tax collections. In 1764 the crown abolished the farming system and immediately doubled the royal income from this source, without increasing the tax paid by consumers or producers, and income increased during the remainder of the colonial period. At times it reached nearly a million *pesos* net after collection costs, and it averaged 800,000—an amount not significantly lower than that coming from Indian tribute.

If tax income is a reliable indicator, the eighteenth century was one of rapid economic growth. In 1746, with a population of roughly 3 million, tax collection amounted to little more than 4 million *pesos;* fifty-four years later, with a population of about 6 million, total collections reached 20 million. During that span of little more than two generations the per capita revenue increased from one and a third *pesos* to three and a third, without any significant change in the value of the *peso*. Revenue receipts grew steadily in the last half century, and in the final twenty years they increased spectacularly. How much of the growth came from greater Bourbon efficiency, and how much represented real economic advance, could be the subject of lively debate; but at least a third of the increase came from the new tax sources on tobacco and pulque.

Throughout the colonial period the crown used the excess of collections over the carefully guarded expenditures to subsidize other colonial governments or the home administration; as early as the middle of the sixteenth century Mexican revenues helped finance Caribbean island government. As tax revenue increased faster than expenditures (a rather remarkable development in view of the proliferation of offices and duties), the proportion of total collections supplied to Spain or the other colonies expanded. In a typical late colonial year total fiscal collections came to about 20 million *pesos*. Of this sum 30 per cent (6 million *pesos*) went directly to the Madrid government and another 17 per cent (3.5 million) helped finance other colonial governments. Almost half the total collections, then, helped subsidize non-Mexican endeavors—and this was in addition to the sums collected in Spain on Mexican commerce. Of the 10.5 million expended in Mexico, 3.5 went to pay the direct administrative costs in collecting the tax, 4 (nearly 40 per cent of the budget, it will be noted) to the maintenance of the military force, a little more than a half to jails and hospitals, and the remainder to pay the salaries of the viceroy and other royal officials. The royal government allocated no revenues for the construction of port facilities, roads, bridges, or other items of social investment; private individuals or groups, operating under monopolies, constructed such facilities and charged tolls for their use.

These data on tax collections and expenditures point out some facets of colonial life which other data do not clarify. In the last thirty years before the movement for independence began, for example, gross collections under the *alcabala* averaged about three and a quarter million a year; during ten of those years the rate held at 8 per cent, while in the other twenty it remained at the normal 6. Even if we assume that the numerous exceptions to the tax left half the transactions free, the rate of collections shows an incredibly low rate of commercial activity. Computing tax collections at the rate of 6 per cent, even though the rate was at times higher, gives a total of commercial transactions of about 100 million a year—a per capita average of roughly 18 *pesos*. This suggests that the vast majority of the Mexican people were self-sustaining and hardly entered at all into the market economy. Even if we eliminate the Indians completely from the computation and include only the Europeans and the *castas*, the per capita transaction amounts to a minute 30 *pesos*.

Furthermore, a perusal of the tax sources quickly dispels two major myths concerning the colonial economy; that the mining income, particularly the *quinto*, was crucial, and that customs duties hindered trade. Royal concern with mining activity, and the special perquisites and legal advantages granted those engaged in mining, leave the impression that the colonial financial administration would have collapsed without revenue from the mines. But the data show clearly, particularly for the eighteenth century when mining reached its apex, that income from other sources more than met the needs for local expenditures and, conversely, that income from mining alone never reached a level sufficient to maintain colonial administration. In addition, the famous King's Fifth in Mexico never accounted for more than half the revenue collected from the total mining operation. After 1770 the tobacco monopoly probably put more net proceeds into the royal coffers than did the mines.

The average rate of collections on imports and exports not only made a tiny contribution to the total tax revenue (about 2 per cent) but was low enough to make trade profitable. Compared to the import duties of 60 per cent *ad valorem* imposed by the Mexican national government in the nineteenth century, or to the U.S. tariffs ranging from 25 per cent upward during the same century, the colonial duties were low indeed, since they seldom exceeded 10 per cent and often descended to 2 per cent. Colonial trade undoubtedly limped along at a low rate, but duties on such trade were not responsible.

The fiscal data further point up general administrative inefficiency.

Costs in collecting the *alcabala* averaged close to 13 per cent, in spite of the collection methods which made each seller responsible for reporting his sales and paying his tax; the proportion of costs to collections was not only incredibly high, but varied little from year to year although the total amount collected varied greatly. Costs of collecting the tax on pulque ran at a significantly lower rate—about 7 per cent—but still at a proportion completely at variance with sound fiscal policy. And in maintaining its tobacco monopoly the crown expended more on administration than on raw materials and labor combined.

But perhaps the most interesting aspect of the data is the low rate of per capita tax collection. The colonials frequently objected to the tax structure, which certainly could have profited from a general overhaul, and complaints concerning high taxes fill the records. But to say that "excessive taxation galled and irritated," in the words of one scholar, is to put the emphasis in the wrong place. Even in the late colonial period, when the per capita collection reached its highest point and exceeded by a good margin that of Spain, annual tax collections amounted to little more than 3 *pesos* a person, or somewhat less than the cost of two pairs of shoes or the income for less than a week's unskilled labor. Tax stupidities and inequities, not general rates of collection, "galled and irritated."

By 1800 Spain had ample cause to feel a degree of self-satisfaction regarding the economy of her colonial jewel. In retrospect many of the glaring injustices, inconsistencies, and inefficiencies stand out for all to see, but from the Spanish point of view conditions were excellent. Silver production steadily increased, funds remitted to Spain grew from year to year, the devastating epidemics of earlier times had all but disappeared, the total population had approached that of Spain herself, and—perhaps most important of all—the colony remained loyal and at peace. Any threat to the viceroyalty appeared to come from the outside, from the rambunctious young nation to the north or the older and still jealous England, not from inside New Spain itself.

Chapter 6 • An Attempt at Revolution

The color, the ignorance and the misery of the Indians put them at an infinite distance from the Spaniards.

MANUEL ABAD Y QUEIPO TO CHARLES IV

Death to the *gachupines!*

MOB RESPONSE TO HIDALGO, SEPTEMBER 16, 1810

The persecutions of the Spaniards were uniform and general in all the provinces in which the fire of revolution was lighted; in all they were imprisoned and despoiled of their goods. . . .

LUCAS ALAMÁN, 1850

When the native and caste populations finally saw an opportunity to emerge from servile docility, they exploded. The first few months of the movement for independence, begun on that memorable early Sunday morning in September 1810 when creole Father Miguel Hidalgo y Costilla tolled his church bells to summon his parishioners, turned into a nightmare of horror for the peninsulars of Central Mexico. In concluding his impassioned exhortation that the crowd strike immediately for independence, Hidalgo incited his impoverished listeners to thoughtless and vicious devastation: his *viva* for the Virgin of Guadalupe gave the populace a Mexican—a native—symbol rather than one with Spanish heritage; and his obviously approving gesture when the crowd responded with its *muera* for the peninsulars invited his followers to destroy all things Spanish. This parish priest of Dolores certainly did not desire a caste war, but the Indian and *mestizo* hordes soon made it so in their wild rampage through central Mexico.

Hidalgo's revolution followed a long chain of events and came as the natural conclusion to the Spanish colonial system with its blind spots and its inequities. Creole animosities against the peninsulars, endemic for two centuries and reaching the critical stage during the reign of Charles III, grew acute after the beginning of the French Revolution. French revolutionary philosophy left no room for a distinction between men born in Spain and men born in America of Spanish parentage, and many creoles saw the entire revolutionary pattern in France as a rationale and a justification for their own demands for real equality with the peninsulars. The 1808 French invasion of Spain and Napoleon's sequestration of Ferdinand VII, leaving the Spanish government in a shambles, reverberated throughout Spanish America. In Mexico, as in other Spanish dependencies, the creoles insisted that the disappearance of the Bourbon crown gave to the people of Mexico their sovereignty—and the "people of Mexico" included the creoles, who outnumbered the peninsulars by ten or fifteen to one. But the peninsulars, jealous of their prerogatives and as contemptuous as ever of those not born in Spain, held firmly to the belief that government could come only from Spain and therefore took the perfectly consistent position that a *junta* in Sevilla, fighting for and governing in the name of Ferdinand VII, still maintained complete jurisdiction over Mexico. The corrupt, inefficient, and indecisive viceroy, José de Iturrigaray, fiddle-faddled for a couple of months after he received, in June 1808, notice of Ferdinand's fall; but by September the peninsulars became convinced that the viceroy would succumb to the creole demands and so, in the small hours of September 16, removed him from office and appointed in his stead a pathetic old man whom they cast in the role of figurehead and tool. The coup, of questionable legality but quite clear as to motive, did little to assuage exacerbated creole feelings, and creoles who earlier had merely wanted a hand in government now began to talk unguardedly about the advantages of independence. The newly imposed viceroy, Pedro de Garibay, had neither the energy nor the inclination to stamp out overt manifestations of creole discontent; his residence in Mexico for forty of his eighty years had made him somewhat sympathetic to creole aspirations. The *gachupines,* now thoroughly frightened, convinced the Spanish *junta* to remove the old gentleman and to replace him with another of their group. Archbishop Francisco Javier de Lizana y Beaumont, who had supported the original coup against Iturrigaray, proved to be—from the peninsular point of view—a worse choice than Garibay. As infirm as his predecessor and even less inclined to harsh and forceful action, he pursued a policy of sweet reason in treating plotting creoles that infuriated the peninsulars who, true to form, then effected another change in administration. In May 1810, on orders from Spain, Lizana turned the government over to the *audiencia* and happily retired to his episcopal residence, heartily sick of peninsular demands and creole plots. But the clumsy *audiencia* could neither raise money for the fight against the French (every ship brought demands for money and more money) nor bring an end to the obvious intrigues among the creoles. Peninsular merchants became insistent that the badly straitened government in Spain dispatch a vigorous and able viceroy to bring some order to a deteriorating situation. This time the Cádiz Regency, established in early 1810 as the last vestige of Bourbon control and generally thought to be the dying gasp of a defeated nation, appointed Francisco Xavier de Venegas, a military officer exprienced in the war against the French. A stern man and hard, with a "glance angry and threatening," he landed in Veracruz on August 25, dallied a number of days on the road, and finally reached Mexico City on September 14, a scant thirty-six hours before Hidalgo rang his church bells.

In the meantime creoles and *peninsulares* plotted and counterplotted. In Valladolid an 1809 attempt at revolution, presumably to put the creoles in control rather than to effect independence, came to an inglorious end, but the failure did not deter other groups from meeting in secret to discuss a major change in government. By mid-1810, creoles in every major urban center had committed themselves to some form of action against the existing government. In more or less constant communication one group with another, they formed a kind of Mexican "Committee of Correspondence" working for independence. One of these groups, including members from Querétaro and Guanajuato as well as the nearby villages of San Miguel and Dolores, recruited creole officers in the military establishment, fabricated arms and ammunition, suborned some municipal officials, and aimed at December 8, 1810, as the day of action. A plot of such ramifications could scarcely escape detection; too many men in too many places had word of it. Intimations of the plan reached the ears of royal officials as early as August 11, and Venegas learned a few details while he made his leisurely way to the capital. But most peninsulars apparently agreed with the minor official who assured the viceroy the creoles were so timorous that at the sight of "an official piece of parchment at the end of a stick they would be frightened like asses."

Among those in the Querétaro-Guanajuato region dabbling in this dangerous game, but certainly no major leader, was Miguel Hidalgo y Costilla, the parish priest at Dolores; his role prior to September 15 had been to convert other clerics to the cause, while army men of the stamp of Ignacio Allende and Juan Aldama perfected the operation's more practical side. Overwhelming evidence concerning the magnitude of the revolutionary plan finally overcame the royal officials' comfortable torpidity, and on the night of September 13 the authorities in Querétaro ordered a general round-up of the local conspirators. Despite the secrecy and the rapidity with which the royal troops swooped down on the first plotter selected for apprehension, the wife of an official sympathetic to the cause managed to warn one of the local adherents. He rode posthaste the 40 miles to San Miguel, where he gave the warning to Aldama on the morning of the 15th. Aldama, in turn, rode immediately the additional 20 miles to Dolores, arriving there at two in the morning to discover that Allende, warned in some still unknown fashion, had arrived a few hours earlier; along with Hidalgo they decided upon quick action. Before sun-up on that Sunday morning, September 16, Hidalgo called his Indian and *mestizo* parishioners to his church, but instead of officiating at a sacramental service he preached the political doctrine of independence. To this point all maneuvering toward independence had been handled by creoles, whose one aim was to replace *peninsular* with creole and to leave the social and economic structure unchanged. But the Indians and the *mestizos* had other ideas.

The men of Dolores held their parish priest in high esteem, and by mutual consent Hidalgo became the leader of the little band which left that day for San Miguel to seize military supplies. Leadership may have been imposed upon him by accident, but it was a leadership which, unfortunately, he did not relinquish until just before his capture six months later. After taking San Miguel, Hidalgo backtracked and moved on Guanajuato, where he arrived a week later. By now the neat and disciplined creole army which Allende and Aldama had envisaged as the spearhead of the revolutionary movement had died aborning; the army which confronted the royalist forces in Guanajuato was a tremendous, unruly, and undisciplined mob of Indians and *mestizos,* armed with anything ready to hand capable of inflicting wounds—guns, swords, lances, machetes, miners' picks, bows and arrows, slings and stones—and bent on destruction. The crown officials, outnumbered and fearful, gathered all the *gachupín* population into the great public granary, the Alhóndiga de Granaditas, for safety. There Hidalgo's mob, joined now by the suppressed classes of the city, found them and their wealth when the furious *castas* breached the massive wooden door on September 28, and there they died. When the bloodbath was finished, between 400 and 600 men, women, and children had been hacked to death in a fearful demonstration of insane fury which Hidalgo and his officers could not contain; but the attackers paid an awesome price, for the Spaniards with their bullets and their grenades left 2000 men slaughtered in the streets. For two days the mobs sacked the city, destroying buildings and appropriating for themselves anything of value which they could carry. The Guanajuato orgy did not bring surcease to tormented souls. The great horde, for now it would be inappropriate to call it an army, increased its ranks from the lower classes of the city and split into two waves, one flowing north toward Zacatecas and the other west to Valladolid.

The Zacatecas peninsulars scattered before the furious revolutionists and thus saved their lives and their portable wealth, but the relentless *castas* destroyed or confiscated the remaining properties. A few weeks later San Luis Potosí suffered a like fate. The western wing of the flowing mob, 60,000 men under the direct leadership of Hidalgo, seized Valladolid without opposition and so had no excuse for pillage; it sacked only a few houses. A few days later Hidalgo led his motley army, now grown to 80,000, a small proportion of whom were trained and disciplined militiamen, toward Mexico City. In the high mountains separating the basins of Toluca and Mexico the revolutionists defeated a much smaller peninsular army, but again the better-armed and disciplined royal forces exacted an awful toll; between 2000 and 4000 (no one counted the dead so who can say with exactitude the number?) died in the six-hour battle. Appalled by his losses, distraught over the condition of his troops, and probably fearful of a repetition of the Guanajuato hecatomb, Hidalgo chose not to attack the capital. After lingering three days he turned west toward Guadalajara over Allende's objections.

In early November the revolutionists took Guadalajara without a fight. Long before Hidalgo appeared on the road to the city, the bishop with great fanfaronade organized the Crusade, composed of "young men of commerce and university students" who swore to defend the city against the "plebes" and the "rabble"; but as the insurgents drew near the Crusade fled with the bishop in the van and most of the peninsular population straggling in the rear. But here, unlike Zacatecas, the *gachupines* went neither fast enough nor far enough; the revolutionaries rounded them up and returned them to the city. During the course of the next month the insurgent leaders, including many priests, "took them out quietly at night in groups of forty or more and put them to death in barrancas and other hidden areas close to the city," according to one contemporary. Uncertainty concerning the number so disposed of indicates the incredible confusion of the times. Hidalgo believed the number to be about 350. Carlos Bustamante, a participant in the revolution but not present at Guadalajara, put the figure at 700 which agreed with the estimate made by General Félix Calleja who recaptured the city in January 1811. Lucas Alamán, who had lived through the horror of Guanajuato, said "it was generally agreed it was about a thousand." Perhaps the most accurate estimate came from Hidalgo's brother Mariano, who testified that it was "a multitude." Whether 300 or 1000, the executions were a savage reprisal for generations of arrogant maltreatment. And one of the most enthusiastic executioners was the *mestizo* Agustín Marroquín, who only shortly before Hidalgo's arrival had suffered the pain and indignity of 200 lashes for a petty crime.

The flaming destruction and wanton murder—no other term can be applied to the blind killing of individuals guilty of no crime—on the part of the insurrectionists brought like reprisals from the royal forces. When Calleja recaptured Guanajuato from Allende in late November he gave orders no less barbarous than those of Hidalgo and his aides; the traitorous creoles, he thought, needed a lesson they would not forget. Perhaps he had some justification, for the afternoon before he entered the city a mob had perpetrated a new massacre at the Alhóndiga, hacking to bits over 200 of the 250 *peninsular* and creole prisoners the insurgents had placed there. Calleja's first reaction was one of blind fury, and he ordered the complete destruction of the city and its population; squads of his soldiers shot down and left lying where they fell anyone on the streets, and many of those slain had even less sympathy for the revolution than Calleja. Within a few hours, and after how many deaths no one knows, Calleja regained a degree of sanity; he revoked the decree of fire and sword "for reasons of humanity," he said in his report to the viceroy, but then embarked on a course of deliberate terror. In the next five days he hauled 56 men, many of them selected by a macabre casting of lots, to gibbets and firing squads. Some he hanged in public squares by the light of flickering torches. One group of 23 he had shot, one after the other, at the Alhóndiga; the bestiality of the proceedings, which had to be halted midway to remove the blood and gore from the pavement, sickened even his own officers. Finally, tired of the savage game, he issued a general pardon; two men with nooses around their necks were thus saved by one of Calleja's rare acts of mercy.

But even Calleja seemed mild in comparison to some of his subordinates. One of them, General José Cruz, reported to his superior that he had given "the strictest orders to the commanding officer of the patrol to put to the sword any town, hacienda or settlement where rebels are found or where they have received succor, rendering them all to ashes." Another royal officer tempted a small group of insurgents to parley under a flag of truce, and then treacherously shot down 60 of them; this was justified, he felt, because they were "contemptible mulattoes."

Thus went the early days of the independence movement, the Indians and *castas* vicious in their persecution of the peninsulars, and the royalists equally vicious in their turn. Lucas Alamán, forty years later, summed it up:

> As the revolution became more extensive and general, the war came to be more cruel and sanguinary on both sides: the insurgents put to death all Spaniards whom they could catch, all the members of the corps raised to guard the towns, and on many occasions the people in the countryside who refused to make common cause with them; the commanders of the royal troops treated in the same manner all the captured chieftains of the insurgent forces, many of the prisoners, many of the town residents who were adherents of the cause or who were understood to have given them aid. All executions were performed without any attempt at judicial procedure, . . . the commanders arbitrarily disposing of the lives and fortunes of all.

When he began flirting with the idea of independence in 1810, Hidalgo never dreamed that the movement would take the nasty tack it followed. He believed, in fact, the righteousness of the cause to be so apparent that all creoles would join gladly and by sheer weight of numbers so overwhelm the peninsulars that fighting would be unnecessary. This parish creole priest, half-legendary now, whose ultimate recantation is a touching monument to human frailty, saw peninsular control as stultifying and destructive to human dignity. Personally resentful of an attitude which would prevent him, as a creole, from advancing as fast or as far as a peninsular, and philosophically opposed to the rigidity of the class system then maintained, he believed that independence would bring social and economic change along with the political. To his rather romantic mind the *gachupín* appeared as the evil; rid the country of his baneful and avaricious influence, so Hidalgo steadily contended, and all men would live in sweet reasonableness. He held, as an article of faith, that under a creole government the authorities would "govern with the sweetness of parents, treat us as brothers,

[and] banish poverty." He wanted to create a government, he said on one occasion, which had as its "basis the liberty of the nation and the enjoyment of those rights which the God of Nature has given all men." But no Deist he—regardless of the charges of heresy hurled at him by the episcopate—this parish priest of orthodox Catholicism insisted that the principal functions of a proper creole government would be to "maintain our sainted religion and dictate gentle laws, beneficent and accommodated to the needs of each people." A dreamer with nebulous ideas, a gentle man forced by realities he did not comprehend to be party to a savagery he deplored, Hidalgo was no revolutionary. But he was a humanist and a humanitarian. His entire ecclesiastical career demonstrated his concern for the unfortunate; most of his income as a parish priest went to various kinds of aids—some of them pregnant for economic development—to his low-income parishioners. His approach to social justice was paternalistic, and his decree of December 1810, abolishing slavery and suspending the collection of tribute, must be viewed as paternalism and not jacobinism.

Hidalgo neither wanted nor foresaw the independence movement as a struggle between Indian and *casta* on the one hand and the European on the other; independence to him meant merely the eviction of the peninsular. But a major portion of those who took the field against the royalist forces in those tempestuous early days thought of independence —if they thought of it at all—as a condition in which the social injustices they had suffered would disappear. Hidalgo's ideas may have been nebulous, but the average Indian or *casta* hacking away with a machete at a *peninsular* in Guanajuato or Guadalajara knew at least a portion of what he wanted. With scarcely a thought for the abstract principle, he wanted independence in fact: independence from oppression by the European, independence from the mesh of customs and legalities which kept him in thrall, independence from the indignities of the lash, independence which land and material possessions could give. And so he took the land vacated by the fleeing European, be he *gachupín* or creole, and he took for his own the property left behind. He tore the iron grills from windows in Guanajuato, Zacatecas, and San Luis Potosí so that he might fashion tools or weapons. He broke down doors and carried off silver plate. He raided municipal treasuries and walked away with silver bars or silver money. He helped himself to the food and drink he found in the markets—and sometimes became violently ill from his gorging. He drove the cattle from the *haciendas* and satisfied his raging hunger with the meat which he craved but had seldom tasted. And he worked the land: "The Indians maintained possession of the lands which they seized in the various areas to which the revolution extended, and they defended themselves when they were attacked," Lucas Alamán complained.

To Hidalgo, Allende, Aldama, and the other creole leaders who dreamed of independence and plotted for it, the difference between a despised *gachupín* and a suffering creole was easy to discern; attitude, bearing, and sometimes speech set them apart. To the Indians and *castas* all Europeans looked alike; the creole exacted no less tribute, the creole ordered no fewer lashes, he paid no better wages and he occupied no less land. Bands razed creole properties, pillaged creole stores, and butchered creole men; the war for independence, willy-nilly, took on all the trappings of a caste war. The creoles, most of whom wanted only the elimination of the *gachupín* and cared not one whit for social or economic improvement for the masses of Indians and *mestizos*, soon lost their appetite for what they had begun and, appalled, drew back. Creole insurgent commanders in Tepic, San Blas, Zacatecas, San Luis, Monclova, San Antonio, and many other places switched sides and took prisoner many creoles who had not returned to the fold. By mid-1811 most of the responsible creole leaders had either accepted a pardon and retired or had been, like Allende and Hidalgo, captured, shot and put on public display; Hidalgo's head graced one corner of the Alhóndiga in Guanajuato for the next ten years. With the disappearance of these men the northern and central areas were bereft of leadership and what had started as a political revolution degenerated into a mixture of banditry and anarchy.

Félix Calleja, a hard-nosed, tough, and efficient military man, saw the issue between creole and peninsular with extraordinary clarity. Soon after he recaptured Guadalajara in early 1811, and with Spain occupied completely by the French, he wrote Viceroy Venegas a confidential report remarkable for its frankness:

> This vast kingdom weighs too heavily on a metropolis whose fortunes waver; its own sons [the creoles], and even the Europeans themselves, are convinced of the advantages which would result from an independent government, and if Hidalgo's absurd insurrection had been built upon this base, it seems to me as I now look at it, that it would have met with little opposition. No one is ignorant of the fact that the peninsula is responsible for the lack of specie; that the scarcity and high prices of goods is in fact a result of mercantile speculation and the passage of goods through many hands, and that the premiums and recompenses [in the army] which are so scarce in the colony are widespread in the metropolis.

Hidalgo's "absurd insurrection" died with him but another, and more profound, followed in slow stages. José María Morelos y Pavón a parish priest born a *mestizo* but generally dubbed a creole, possessed all those qualities which Hidalgo lacked. One of Hidalgo's students from an earlier day, and deeply devoted to the older man, Morelos sought out Hidalgo in October 1810, and accepted a commission from him to operate in the south. Humble, steadfast, disciplined, and statesmanlike, without his mentor's intellectual breadth but also without his quixotic qualities, the southern priest-commander knew what he wanted for his country, and he set out to get it. Disdaining great mobs of undisciplined and ill-armed men, he always operated with a relatively small force over whom he had firm control. Seize properties and confiscate wealth he did, but always deliberately and always with a purpose; looting and pillaging in his territory were rare. One of the great tragedies of Mexico is that Hidalgo, not Morelos, assumed leadership at the beginning, for by the time Morelos established his name as a distinguished leader in the south, most of the creoles were thoroughly frightened and willing to co-operate with the peninsulars. But perhaps this is mere speculation without foundation. The creoles were terrified by Hidalgo's undisciplined mobs; they probably would have been equally terrified by Morelos's disciplined ideas.

During the years of his ascendancy—the royalists executed him, proud to the last and without recantations, in late 1815—Morelos left no doubt about his own ideas of an ordered society. As a *mestizo* and a laborer for many years before he entered the priesthood, he well knew from firsthand the miseries attached to social stratification based upon the Spanish concept of "race." Legal and social distinctions depending upon such a base were anathema to him, and in the areas of his command he forbade—with what success is not clear—the very use of the words "Indian" and "caste" to describe men. Outraged by the inefficient land use he saw everywhere, he had long since come to view the great *haciendas* as economic and social anomalies, suited better for the perpetuation of stultifying class distinction than for agricultural production; land, he insisted, should be available for those who could work it, even at the cost of confiscating *hacendados'* lands. A clergyman himself, and a devout and orthodox Catholic—though certainly no sophisticated theologian—despite the charges made against him by members of the episcopate, he nevertheless favored the abolition of the special privileges accorded to the clergy in the *fuero* granted to the Church. He furthermore opposed, and this particularly struck home to some of the upper clergy, the compulsory collection of Church tithes by royal officials; tithing, he thought, should be a voluntary manifestation of love and affection for the true Church by devout parishioners who could afford it, and not a money-grubbing operation undertaken by cynical men to support the opulence of *gachupín* bishops. He even went so far as to advocate the distribution of Church lands among the poor, and in so doing increased episcopal wrath. On one occasion, as a military measure, he recommended the confiscation of all properties belonging to "all rich persons, nobles and officials of the highest ranks, whether creoles or *gachupines*," and their equal distribution to the poor and to the army. More than once he expressed his faith in popular sovereignty and representative government, neither of which is an expression of social revolution but both of which stem from a deep conviction of the equality of man—and both in violent opposition to dominant creole and peninsular thought. Morelos was certainly no wild-eyed social reformer anxious to destroy the fabric of existing society, and in the twentieth century, his proposals, except for those to meet military exigencies, seem mild indeed. But in the Mexican milieu of the early nineteenth century they were so radical that they led Lucas Alamán, nearly forty years later, to accuse him of socialistic and communistic thinking.

To the heart of the smug creoles, secure in their social station and enjoying a code of law which separated them from the mass, Morelos's address to a representative assembly, gathered in Chilpancingo to draft a constitution, struck terror:

> Spirits of Moctezuma, Cacamatzín, Cauhtemoc, Xicotencatl, and Calzontzín! Take pride in this august assembly, and celebrate this happy moment in which your sons have congregated to avenge your insults! After August 12, 1521, comes September 8, 1813! The first date tightened the chains of our slavery in Mexico-Tenochtitlán; the second broke them forever in the town of Chilpancingo. . . . We are therefore going to restore the Mexican Empire!

Rhetoric, perhaps, but calling on pride in Mexican, not Spanish, ancestry. Morelos fought for more than political independence from Spain; he wanted no less than the creation of a Mexican nation, unique, in which all its peoples would coalesce to form an integrated whole.

But significant social change was doomed almost before it started. The senseless violence of the early days, quarrelling among the insurrectionists themselves, the deep conservatism ingrained into the creoles as a class, and Calleja's ruthlessly efficient military campaigns all combined to defeat not only the independence movement but reform as well. Morelos's capture and execution in late 1815 almost brought an end to any organized insurrectionary movement. Calleja, appointed viceory in 1813 by a revivified Spanish government, stalked and destroyed with feral persistence rebel groups until 1816, when the situation was so well in hand that the crown, reinstalled in Madrid after Napoleon's defeat, could afford to change its tactics through the appointment of a more moderate viceroy. One after another the patriot forces, broken up and isolated and wooed by offers of amnesty, surrendered to the royalists or simply disbanded. Some pockets of resistance continued to give trouble to the central government, but with few exceptions these resembled out-and-out bandit bands rather than guerrilla armies fighting for an honourable cause; of these quasi-revolutionaries the most persistent—and the least admirable—was Padre Antonio Torres operating in the Guanajuato region.

By 1819, only two of those leaders who had accepted the basic Morelos point of view still survived steadfast and free: Guadalupe Victoria and Vicente Guerrero, one a creole and the other a *mestizo*. Victoria, born Miguel Fernández y Félix, but generally known as Félix Fernández before he adopted the pseudonym by which he is presently called, was from the north country but made his mark in the center. Magnificently successful during the heyday of the insurrection, he fell on evil days after 1816 and met defeat after defeat. But he refused to accept defeat even when he had neither men nor arms with which to fight, and he refused to accept a pardon; instead, he moved into the mountain forests between Puebla and Veracruz, where he wandered for two years, sleeping in caves and subsisting on what he could catch and gather with his own hands, absolutely alone but completely convinced that he would one day help Mexico achieve her independence. In the Sierra Madre del Sur, Vicente Guerrero and his 2000 ragged and poorly supplied men managed to continue the fight. With arms and ammunition captured from the royalist forces, they fought on despite hardship and cajolery; in 1818 the viceroy even used Guerrero's elderly father as a missionary of peace, but the southern warrior refused to disband, to surrender, or to accept a pardon. He believed in that for which he fought, and he fought for the principles he had learned from Morelos. But he fought alone.

And then, in one of the greatest frauds ever perpetrated against a suffering people, Mexico almost overnight received her independence. Early in 1820, in Spain a liberal movement led by Colonel Rafael de Riego forced the autocratic and tyrannical Ferdinand VII to install a constitutional government. The new government, dominated by men influenced by the Enlightenment and by some of the ideas emanating from the French Revolution, undertook to eliminate at least some of the social, economic, and political injustices which so marked Spanish life. The new government soon lifted the rigid censorship imposed on the press and actually allowed men to speak their minds in public on issues of public interest; to the traditional Spanish conservative, home resident or colonial, such libertinism meant utter anarchy. Not satisfied with giving affront to established customs regarding personal freedom, the new government furthermore released a great number of political prisoners, including some who had engaged in the Mexican independence movement. To make matters worse, the constitutionalists confiscated some Church properties and gave other evidence of accepting anti-clericalism as a basic tenet of governmental reform; justified or not, the Spanish anti-clerical occasionally demonstrated a peculiarly venomous attitude toward the Church hierarchy, and the government which Riego spawned showed such symptoms. The thought of a liberal, anti-clerical government in Spain, and the spectre of such a government spreading its doctrines and its powers into Mexico, appalled those peninsulars and creoles alike who had been most adamant in their pursuit and persecution of patriot forces. The bishops who had enveighed against the egalitarianism of Morelos, and who had held those ideas to be heretical, were not likely to accept similar ideas as orthodox merely because they came from a government in Madrid. The higher clergy had earlier excommunicated Hidalgo, Morelos, Guerrero, and virtually all those involved in the independence movements for expressions not significantly different from those arriving daily from Spain; Spanish liberalism was, in their eyes, particularly offensive and godless because of Spain's historical role as the Protector of the Faith. In an abrupt about-face the creole and peninsular conservatives, aided spiritually and financially by the episcopate, decided that their own fortunes would best be served by an independent rather than a colonial Mexico, and they set about securing independence through underhanded methods. One twentieth-century priest-historian, holding steadfastly to the values of the early nineteenth-century Mexican conservative clerics, has justified the hierarchy's position:

> To repress these licentious [anti-clerical] laws and the evil spirit of irreligion—which a Spanish officialdom already largely in the hands of Masonry propagated—was the motive of the group which initiated a new movement for independence, the one which, in the end, came to be effective and did in fact achieve our necessary and highly desirable separation from corrupt Spain.

A cabal of those who dreaded new policies which would come from a "corrupt" Spain chose as their instrument Agustín de Iturbide, a creole royalist officer then in malodor with the viceroy because of making a personal fortune by gouging the inhabitants in the regions of his military commands, but a man of undoubted imagination, verve, military merits, and chicanery—a perfect man for the job to be done. In order to set the stage, they arranged that Iturbide be given command of an army, late in 1820, for the ostensible purpose of destroying Viceroy Apodaca's one remaining *bête noir,* Vicente Guerrero. In a magnificent demonstration of effective duplicity, Iturbide marched and counter-marched, engaged in a few inconclusive skirmishes which he reported as fantastic victories, and demanded more men and money from viceroy and episcopate alike to conclude what Apodaca assumed to be Guerrero's destruction and the episcopate hoped to be Mexico's independence. When money from official sources failed to flow in the desired quantities, Iturbide managed to convince the merchants in Mexico City that they would be safe in dispatching to Acapulco a consignment of silver destined for Manila; when the half million-*peso* shipment reached Iguala, Iturbide's headquarters, the general simply appropriated it for his own use. To carry out his schemes he wanted to eliminate Guerrero, but he discovered that he could neither defeat him in battle nor induce him to surrender, whereupon he invited the southern general to join him. Guerrero, wily and suspicious, finally agreed to support Iturbide's gambit when the pseudo-royalist announced that "All its [Mexico's] inhabitants, without distinction other than merit and virtue, are fit citizens to follow any line of employment." With Guerrero on his side, and with the pilfered Manila money in his treasury, on February 24, 1821, Iturbide "pronounced" for independence in the Plan de Iguala and invited all "Americans, under whose name are comprehended not only those born in America, but the Europeans, the Africans and the Asiatics who live here," to join together . . .

> to carry forward an enterprise which in all aspects (though I have played only a small role in it) must be called heroic. . . . Amaze the nations of European culture: let them see that Northern America has emancipated herself without shedding a single drop of blood. In the ecstasy of our jubilation shout out: Long live the sainted religion which we profess!

Iturbide was unable to bring independence without shedding a drop of blood, but he came close to it. When Guerrero agreed to support the plan, all *bona fide* patriots who heard the news hastened to join. Carlos María Bustamante, one of the first to join the original revolution and one of the last to surrender to the overwhelming power of the royalist armies, hurried to give aid to the new crusade. Messengers soon found Guadalupe Victoria in his mountain fastness, and he reorganized his army. Leader after leader of the old Morelos breed hauled their arms from hiding places, reformed their bands, and marched in that "ecstasy of jubilation" toward independence. Creoles, too, joined the parade. Anastasio Bustamante, one of the most diligent in persecuting insurgent bands from 1810 to 1820, and in command of a large army in the Bajío, declared in favor of independence in mid-March and joined Iturbide in a triumphal march to Guanajuato; he set an example for other royalist officers, both creole and peninsular. Viceroy Apodaca did what he could to stem the tide, but the odds were too great and independence came with only a slight tremor. On September 27, 1821—touchingly, his thirty-eighth birthday—Iturbide marched into Mexico City, flanked on either side by Vicente Guerrero and Guadalupe Victoria.

The independence which Iturbide and his cohorts handed to Mexico bore only a faint resemblance to the independence sought by Morelos and envisioned by Guerrero, but it differed only slightly from that desired by those creoles who plotted in 1809 and 1810. It was, in essence, a minor change at the top, a substitution of the conservative creole for the conservative peninsular and a continuation of the social system created by the class-conscious Spaniard during three hundred years of rule; it was to be, according to Iturbide's plan, a monarchy under a Bourbon prince, and the provision that the Spanish constitution would prevail until Mexico cast one of her own was little more than a fraudulent bait tossed to the liberal creoles. Of the Morelos brand of social consciousness there was little among the newly installed political leaders; the government was in the hands of a group whose every intent was to re-create, in all respects save that of political personalities, the dominant colonial patterns. The great creole landowner, the successful creole merchant, the member of the episcopate, the army commander: all were imbued with a sense of class and of special privilege, and they wanted no change. Carlos María Bustamante soon discovered this disturbing fact, for within a matter of a few months he was in jail for publishing an article offensive to the governing clique. But change, slow to come and far from the dominant plutocracy's mind, had in fact been injected into Mexican society. Whether the Iturbides and the Anastasio Bustamantes recognized it, that change was symbolized by Vicente Guerrero and Guadalupe Victoria, both liberals from differing castes and both unswerving in their convictions, who rode with the conquering hero to the viceregal palace on that September morning.

Eleven years of bitter internecine struggle exaggerated old and created new animosities and made the perfection of any system of government highly dubious. Those residents of Guadalajara who had been forced, by decree, to witness the execution in 1812 of the aged Antonio Torres, another insurgent priest, were not likely to forget the scene or forgive the mentality of the creole officer responsible for it: hanged on a specially constructed gallows giving a maximum view, beheaded and the head paraded on a long pole, quartered with the four parts of the body suspended in public view in the city and surrounding villages. Nor were the followers of Morelos or Guerrero likely to forget the crude epithets (monsters, cowardly assassins, wretches, canaille) used by creole royalist commanders to describe the insurgents. The creoles who perceived the insurgents of 1815 as "worthless rabble" still believed that class to be beneath contempt after independence, and the *mestizos* who looked upon creole royalist commanders as bloody tyrants in 1815 still distrusted that class in 1822.

But marching armies, roving bands, and fleeing citizenry did something more as well; they devastated the colonial economy upon which the new nation was to be founded. The entire economy, correctly or incorrectly, appeared to revolve around mining activities, and the military struggle had almost ruined that industry. The revolution began only a few miles from the richest of the mining districts, Guanajuato, and that great mining center not only witnessed the horror of the early days of fighting but became the object and the pawn of every insurgent and royalist commander in the region from 1810 to 1819 when the incredible Padre Antonio Torres was finally cut down by one of his own men. In the carnage of the Alhóndiga in 1810, insurgent slaughtered *gachupín* mine operators, mining engineers, and mining administrators from the nearby works, along with those who had no connections with the mines. Calleja sent creole mining administrators and *mestizo* mining foremen to firing squads and gallows when he recaptured the city. Most peninsular and some creole mine operators who had escaped the wrath of the insurgents fled their properties in fear of their lives, and miners left the shafts in droves to join the insurrection. Pípila, that probably legendary hero whose audacity under fire is credited with breaching the Alhóndiga defenses, is popularly identified as a miner from a nearby *real*. Mines abandoned by operators and miners soon filled with water which rotted away timbers and collapsed tunnels, making work within the mines impossible without extensive rehabilitation. *Arrastres, malacates,* and other machinery left unused and unrepaired in the open air fell into a state of veritable junk; tools left by workmen were gathered by both sides for use as weapons or as materials to make armaments. Unprincipled and ignorant insurgents and loyalists alike wreaked such havoc to the Guanajuato mines that of the 2000 *arrastres* which worked from daylight to dark six days a week in 1810 pulverizing the ores for amalgamation, only 168 could be found in working condition in 1821—a 92 per cent reduction. All of the mines working the famous Veta Madre were, in 1825, "nearly filled with water, and . . . but partially worked." By the end of the revolution the Valenciana mine, the single most productive mine in Mexico, was in such ruinous condition that workers were "employed in picking out the best pieces from the heaps of refuse, which, in more prosperous times, had been thrown away as rubbish."

The city of Guanajuato and the surrounding towns suffered along with the mines. The town of Valenciana, which had a population of 22,000 in 1810, was in ruins and had a poverty-stricken 4000 people living in the rubble after independence. Prior to the revolution the city of Guanajuato rivaled Mexico City for size, beauty, and opulence. Prosperous shops displayed European and Mexican wares, a magnificent opera house graced one of the squares, and 80,000 people from the city and the surrounding villages bustled through the streets. By

1822 the few shops remaining open sold only local goods, the public buildings stood in decrepit silence, and the 35,000 destitute and bitter people wandered wretchedly with little visible means of support. Joel Poinsett, traveling through the region a few years after independence, was struck by the "abject poverty" of the men "who, when the mines were in successful operation, were all wealthy and lived extravagantly."

Other mining districts did not suffer the wrack which Guanajuato experienced, but none emerged unscathed. The insurgents early captured Zacatecas, but the royalists held the territory most of the time and mining activities suffered only from a shortage of labor and the absence of operators who abandoned their properties in the fear that future rebel successes would put their lives in jeopardy. San Luis Potosí and most of the mining districts of that area fell to the insurgents at one time or another, as did those in Durango and even in Hidalgo and Jalisco. The great Bolaños mine virtually ceased operations, and the Real del Monte mines filled with water. Even when the mines themselves were not threatened, and the mine operators felt secure in their especially protected status, production suffered. Travel and transport between the major cities sometimes came to a standstill, and the insurgents always threatened—and sometimes captured—silver bullion on the way from the mines to the mint or silver coin on the return trip. Long before the revolution began, Mexican mining suffered from an endemic labor shortage; the chaotic conditions between 1810 and 1818 exaggerated the existing weakness and left scarcely enough labor, in some areas, to keep the water under control and take out a minimum amount of ore.

Under these conditions mining obviously fell off, and badly. Exactly how much production declined cannot be determined with any precision since an unrecorded amount was taken over by insurgents and since some mine operators took advantage of the parlous times to engage in illicit mining activities. Data on coinage do exist, and they tell a doleful story. In 1809 bullion to the value of nearly 25 million *pesos* reached the mints; only twice before, in 1804 and 1805, had total production reached such a figure. In 1810, with the last four months of the year filled with military conflict and with the Guanajuato mines almost completely closed, the figure fell to 18 million. In 1811 about 8 million reached the mints. In 1812 it declined to the lowest level since 1702 and amounted to a mere 15 per cent of the average in the decade preceding the revolution. From 1813 to 1820 coinage slowly increased as the royalist forces gradually cleared the principal mineral areas and beat down the insurrection, but at its highest the value of the metals coming to the mints scarcely reached 40 per cent of the earlier level. Iturbide's "ecstasy of jubilation" again called men out of the mines, independence caused some peninsular mine owners to leave Mexico, and in 1822 coinage had descended to the level of 1740. Not for another generation, and until millions in foreign investment had poured into the industry, did the production of silver and gold again compare with that of the first decade of the century.

The serious curtailment of mining undermined the economy not only because it made coin scarce and deprived both government and operators of an important source of income, but also because closed mines meant men out of work. During the fighting many of those ordinarily drawing wages from mining activities found a living in either royalist or insurgent armies and were not therefore unemployed, but when mustering-out time came they found no work to which to return. Including the men in the militia who drew pay from local governments, the royalists forces employed some 85,000 thousand soldiers and probably an equal number in activities intimately related to the military operations. The insurgents certainly used over 100,000 at the height of their activities, and probably more. When the battles ended, these nearly 300,000 men—between 15 and 20 per cent of the adult males—found themselves without jobs or income and constituted not only an economic problem but a ready source of social and political upheaval.

But the economic losses sustained by the mining interests, with all the waste and loss of employment, made up only a minor part of the total loss which brought a kind of economic paralysis. The loss cannot be measured with any statistical accuracy since adequate records do not exist, but some accounts have left a vivid impression of the widespread economic doldrums which plagued the new nation. The scorched-earth practice followed by insurgents and royalists alike brought desolation to great parts of the most productive regions. Royal forces burned villages, seized crops, and took or killed animals which might give sustenance to the rebel cause. Insurgents burned *haciendas,* looted towns, and drove off cattle in regions giving strong support to the crown. The result near Mexico City, as seen by the wife of the Spanish minister to Mexico twenty years after independence, was:

> . . . ruins everywhere—here a viceroy's country palace serving as a tavern, where the mules stop to rest, and the drivers to drink pulque—there, a whole village crumbling to pieces; roofless houses, broken down walls and arches, an old church—the remains of a convent.

Or, a bit further on,

> We stopped at San Miguel, a country-house belonging to the Count de Regla, the former proprietor of the mines which we were about to visit; the most picturesque and lovely place imaginable, but entirely abandoned; the house comfortless and out of repair. We wandered through paths cut in the beautiful woods, and by the side of a rivulet that seems to fertilize everything through which it winds. . . . But all these beautiful solitudes are abandoned to the deer that wander fearlessly amongst the woods, and the birds that sing in their branches.

Far to the north, on the road between San Luis Potosí and Zacatecas, an English mining official, a few years after the revolution,

> saw the houses roofless and in ruins blackened by fire, and had ridden over plains still bearing faint traces of the plow; but the Rancheros who had tilled the ground had been murdered with their whole families during the war. In the space of forty miles we passed no fewer than fifteen crosses set up at the roadside, to mark the spot where an assassination had been committed.

Not far from Valladolid (now Morelia), the same traveler visited the small village of Ozumatlán:

> The church, which was once good, is large; the walls not having suffered when the Spaniards burnt it and a great part of the village,

> in revenge for not having found the natives so rich as a vicinage to Ozumatlán might be supposed to have made them.

The first United States minister to Mexico stopped overnight between Salamanca and Irapuato; among the debris of a once-imposing building ragged women and children huddled in misery.

> This hacienda was burnt in the first war of the revolution; and not far off, we saw another in ruins. In our progress from San Juan del Rio, we have seen a great many ruins. These haciendas are generally spacious buildings with two court yards [and a number of buildings used as stables, granaries and the like]. . . The loss of such buildings is ruinous to the farmer, and no attempt has yet been made to repair them.

Everywhere he went this controversial diplomat, but perceptive observer, saw the ravages of ten wartorn years; one village, about 35 miles north of Guanajuato and well outside the mining district, epitomized the devastation:

> San Felipe presented another melancholy example of the horrors of civil war. Scarcely a house was entire; and, except for one church lately rebuilt, the town appeared to be in ruins. We stopped in the principal square, and passed through arches built of porphyry into the courtyard of a building which had once been magnificent; nothing but the porticoes and ground floor remain.

Not all *haciendas* went up in flames, not all *ranchero* families met death at the hands of passing military forces, and not all agricultural villages had their public and private buildings destroyed by fire or cannon. But too many did for the new nation to come through with a healthy rural economy; the countryside certainly presented a bleak picture.

But most of those who commented on the state of the new nation agreed that men in the countryside, compared to those in most urban sections, lived well and comfortably. Urban miseries came not from physical destruction; with few notable exceptions, the contending parties did little damage to public or private buildings in the major cities.

Insurgent armies destroyed great sections of Guanajuato in the first few days, and the rebels who took Zacatecas and San Luis Potosí enjoyed tearing apart buildings belonging to the government or to peninsulars, but the rebel forces which occupied Valladolid, Guadalajara, Puebla, and other such major centers left little physical evidence of their victories. The shock to the urban dwellers, a majority of whom always found day-to-day living a precarious adventure even in prosperous times, came from the roving bands of insurgents and bandits who isolated the cities from the rest of the nation and from the surrounding rural economy, preventing the movement of goods in or out. As late as 1816, Valladolid had to be abandoned by the royalists as a military command center because of transport difficulties over roads under constant attack. The thriving textile industry in Querétaro and in Guadalajara could no longer be sustained in the absence of raw cotton shipments, and in 1820 these centers produced less than half their accustomed output; the thousands of *obraje* laborers sank even lower in the economic scale and so returned to the beggary which spawned them. Puebla fared little better, and other cities which depended upon regular commerce to maintain a viable economy came through the revolution in bad shape.

National economy also received a hard jolt from capital flight. Most of the peninsulars in the interior cities—whether merchants, miners, or *hacendados*—maintained much of their capital, and almost all their liquid capital, in the form of silver coin or plate. When they fled before the rampaging insurgents, or from the threat of such rebels, they took as much of their capital as they could. Oftentimes they could not save their treasure; one *hacendado* buried nearly 200,000 *pesos* in coin and plate, but a roving band of insurgents "liberated" it. Frequently the peninsulars could move their treasures when they left the cities, and they left in droves, leaving little to be used as a circulating medium. The loss paralyzed the economy. And then, when independence did finally arrive, the great majority of the peninsulars left for Spain and took their liquid capital with them.

With the general decline in the economy, and insurgent control over large sections of the country, the viceregal government sought extraordinary sources of revenue to support the heavy expenditures of pacification. Falling back on an old expedient, the government early increased the *alcabala* to 16 per cent in the confident expectation that the tax would bring in more funds, but the very conditions which made the tax necessary also voided it as a realistic mechanism. Dwindling commerce, ineffectual collection brought on by the widespread insurgent activities, and the size of the tax itself combined to lessen the net income year by year. Even in 1820, by which time the royalists controlled most of the territory and all of the cities, and the *alcabala* could be lowered to a less stultifying level, total collections amounted to a mere 800,000 *pesos*—one-fifth the pre-revolutionary level of a 4 million annual average. Indian tribute all but disappeared. Income from mining fell to a trickle. Under these circumstances the government begged all loyal citizens to make substantial gifts to help finance the war, and with great fanfare some citizens did indeed contribute. But the financial officials found, when they added it all up, that the contributors gave more words of advice and patriotism than they did money; the total collection in hard coin turned out to be a pittance. A request for voluntary loans to the viceroy, at high interest rates to be paid at the conclusion of the war, brought in little since few men wished to risk their capital voluntarily in such a dubious adventure. Forced loans of cash then followed, and field commanders simply requisitioned goods at the local level, giving notes for future payments. The viceregal government also continued the tobacco monopoly, but failed to pay the growers for the raw product; this in turn hindered tobacco culture and reduced the revenue from that source. The local governments, charged by the viceroy with the responsibility of maintaining military units to protect themselves, had the same fiscal problems and met them in the same capricious fashion. These fiscal policies in both central and municipal governments, justified though they may have been under the emergency circumstances, drove money into hiding, stifled healthy economic activity, and left a heavy debt for the new nation to pay.

The insurgents, too, had to contend with a financial problem, and each commander met it his own way. Some issued paper money, some depended upon confiscations of property belonging to presumed enemies, some resorted to forced loans from friend and foe alike, some merely gave chits for goods seized. Many of these became debts for the Mexican nation. When added to the debts of the viceregal government which the independent nation assumed, and when these debts were further bloated by usurious interest rates, the new nation found itself saddled with an internal debt of over 75 million *pesos*—and no income.

Even under the best of circumstances, given the fiscal needs and the nature of the conflict, the economy would have been jeopardized seriously; but graft, fraud, and profiteering added to the economic miseries. Royalist commanders frequently found the confused conditions highly profitable, for they used the excuse of military need to get control of goods and markets. Commanders responsible for the safe passage of merchandise, military and civilian, between Puebla and the distant Oaxaca were left unsupervised by the viceregal government; distance and the nature of the terrain demanded that the local commanders be left to their own devices to guard the roads against insurgent raids. Taking advantage of the situation, and operating under a broad band of authority granted by the government, one military chief along the route not only collected more-or-less legitimate special convoy taxes, but also used his position to monopolize certain popular consumer goods to reap a fortune. Citizens in Oaxaca complained that he boosted the price of sugar, one of his favorite monopolies, to an unreasonable level. Another commander in the same region, operating under the same authority, confiscated all cotton belonging to men with rebel sympathies—and by a strange coincidence he found all major cotton producers to be insurgents at heart. Other commanders in other regions monopolized or confiscated other goods, but it all added up to the same answer: too many of the royalist commanders engaged with more zeal in mulcting the local populations for all they were worth than they did in prosecuting the war.

Among the military men engaged in such profitable ventures Agustín de Iturbide holds a special place for ruthlessness and greed; from every district, and in every time, in which he held a military command, he reaped a handsome personal profit. Most profiteering military men depended upon one technique—monopoly, confiscation, seizure, forced loans—to line their own pockets, but to Iturbide goes the palm for his imagination in using them all. As Commandant of the Army of the North, embracing the agriculturally rich Bajío district from Querétaro to Guanajuato, Iturbide experimented with all methods, but he found the most effective was monopolizing grain. Through a small army of agents and on the plausible grounds that insurgent activity threatened crops, he forced the grain producers to sell at a low fixed price and in turn sold the cereals in the local markets at a price which guaranteed him a fat profit. His arrogance and greed pushed his unethical activities to such scandalous proportions that the viceroy felt compelled to remove him from his command—but the hero of independence retained his fortune. These shady dealings by the royalist commanders, which may have included Calleja himself, were so widespread that Lucas Alamán felt justified in charging that "the commanders did not push very hard to bring an end to the revolution [since they were] obtaining such great advantages from the existing state of things."

On the other hand, many of the "patriots" used the military situation for their own self-aggrandizement. No hint of personal profiteering can be found in the careers of Hidalgo, Morelos, Guerrero, or Victoria; but the quarreling and backbiting among many of the lesser leaders—and some of the major as well—suggest that a large number of those who paraded as great patriot leaders fought for reasons other than pure loyalty to the principles of independence. Certainly Father Antonio Torres achieved notoriety not only for his barbaric cruelty, his ineptness, and his profligacy, but also for his confiscations of properties belonging to both royalists and insurgents, for his refusal to co-operate with other insurgent bands, and for his passion for his own self-importance. Torres was simply the most outstanding of hundreds of leaders whose activities in looting, killing, and destruction suggest banditry rather than patriotism. They masqueraded as patriots, but they operated for private pleasure and profit. These groups probably did more to undermine the economy than did the purely patriot armies, for all the true insurgents' deliberate destruction of commerce and seizure of property.

The battle for political independence came to an end in 1821, but the struggle for social justice and economic viability had just begun. The long war destroyed the Spanish economic base, but it did not create a Mexican economic system or a Mexican mentality. The old animosities and the old economic precepts remained. Most of the peninsulars left Mexico within a decade after independence, to be sure, and whatever influence the Spanish-born had had over the development of social and economic systems soon disappeared; yet the majority of the creoles had been thoroughly imbued with the economic thought of the Spanish and sought to recreate in the Mexican nation the general pattern of the economy which had prevailed in the Spanish colony of New Spain. The creoles, as a class, were no more anxious to bring about a radical change in social and economic interplay than have the white Africans in more recent times been willing to surrender to the native populations the fruits of independence in the broadest sense. Their prime concern was reinstitution, not change. Nearly twenty years after independence a Mexican priest-politician, distraught at the sorry political and economic conditions which existed, summed up the weaknesses:

> The meddling spirit of the Spanish government, still strong in the authorities of the States and the Federation, is the worst of the country's politics, and for many years will retard progress in all branches of public prosperity.

José Luis Mora, who wrote those words in 1838, proved to be more accurate in his prediction than he feared. Most of the history of the first hundred years of the Mexican nation is the bitter story of attempts by one segment of the population to bring to that country some of the benefits of independence as Morelos and others of his age saw them, and the efforts of others to retain in the new nation those values so ingrained in the Spanish colonial system.

Chapter 7 • Marking Time

If there is anything true in the science of political economy . . . it is that the productive resources of Mexico are inadequate to the maintenance of such an army, civil list, and church establishment. And with the Mexican people the only panacea for evils of all sorts is a new revolution.

WADDY THOMPSON, 1846

During independent Mexico's first fifty hectic and catastrophic years, over thirty different individuals served as president, heading more than fifty governments. One person occupied the presidential chair on nine different occasions, and three others sat on that rickety pinnacle of power three times each. In one short span (1837-51 inclusive) sixteen different men served twenty-two governments as president. Cabinet ministers changed more often than presidents, and those fifteen years saw forty-eight foreign ministers, sixty-one ministers of government, fifty-seven secretaries of finance, and forty-one secretaries of war. Frequently two groups claimed control of the government at the same time, and sometimes three. The pendulum swung from empire to federal republic to centralistic government to dictatorship and back again. Rebellions, *cuartelazos, coups d'état* happened with dreary regularity, interspersed with an occasional rigged election. In that half century of chaos the first and last elected presidents served their complete terms, and one other president completed the truncated term for which he was elected. Aside from these three, no president occupid the chair for longer than two consecutive years, and some served only a few weeks. One year saw five changes in government, another four, and still others three. Incessant internal struggles, coupled with a short war against the French in 1838, a greater war with the United States in 1846-48, and the titanic struggle against the French and their imposed Emperor Maximilian from 1862 to 1867, sacrificed thousands of lives. Disturbed conditions discouraged any potential immigration and kept the local death rate high. So the population grew slowly; in those fifty years it increased at a rate considerably less than that of the late colonial period and only one-tenth of that of the United States. Under these traumatic conditions little economic growth could be expected, and little developed.

The new nation confronted two major and closely related economic problems: the creation of a fiscal system which would bring sufficient funds for the government, and the re-establishment of a viable national economy. But in attacking these critical issues the Mexican creole—and for many years to come the creole dominated governmental affairs—was a victim of his own propaganda. With increasing vehemence he had preached for years before independence that all the ills accruing to the Mexican economy came from *gachupín* dominance; with independence he could now eliminate the *gachupín* and, according to the theory, all economic problems would be solved automatically. Furthermore, the incredible wealth from the mines would now be Mexico's, not Spain's, and with the flow of precious metals Mexico could become a major power. Firm in these convictions, the creole set about re-ordering the economy, the first step of which was the establishment of a system of public finance.

From the very beginning the leaders of the new independent government went about their business of government finance with an almost childlike simplicity. During the first three months of independent existence (the last three months of 1821), government revenues exceeded expenditures by a little more than 2000 *pesos,* allowing the treasury officials to trumpet with pride that the government had managed its finances so well that it showed a surplus. But a closer look at the figures reveals an appalling condition, one which plagued fiscal and political policies for generations to come. Of the nearly one and a third million collected, almost 40 per cent came from direct and indirect loans and from other sources which could not be considered as normal revenues. Worse yet, almost 80 per cent of the expenditures went to the maintenance of the military establishment. And, to put the final touch to the dreary picture, most of the local tax-collecting agencies spent more on the task of collecting than they received as revenue.

In spite of these circumstances, the provisional government abolished in late 1821 all special war taxes imposed by the royal government, lifted the special tax on pulque and mescal as a gesture of largess to the lower classes, and reduced the *alcabala* to 6 per cent. At roughly the same time a government decree wiped out all the old taxes connected with mining and substituted for them a flat 3 per cent tax on gold and silver production. Two months later the government abandoned the tobacco monopoly and now depended for most of its income on "spontaneous and general contributions," since it was the "obligation of every citizen to help according to his means." The provisional government apparently felt that the Mexicans also owed a heavy obligation to Iturbide, for it voted him—as a token of appreciation for his services to the cause of independence—a gift of a million *pesos;* this sum amounted to one-fifth of the ordinary revenues expected for the following year.

A modicum of reality finally struck the government in the spring of 1822 when, with Iturbide on the new throne as Emperor Agustín I, it discovered that the *gachupines* fleeing to Spain took their gold and silver with them and left little in Mexico in the way of a circulating medium. To counteract this drain and its drastic economic consequences, the government forbade the export of gold and silver, authorized the minting of half a million *pesos* in copper coin, set up a loan of a million and a half—and voted pensions to the widows, mothers, and fathers of military personnel. With income down and expenditures up—Iturbide kept increasing the size and splendor of the army as well as creating a sycophantic nobility and a royal court to rival those of Europe—the imperial government authorized new loans up to 30 million and the printing of 4 million in paper. Fortunately for Mexico, Iturbide's attempts to borrow money abroad were as ill-conceived and ineffectual as most of his financial schemes, and his agents could find no takers. But the great hero of independence continued on his disastrous course by borrowing locally at ruinous interest rates, issuing paper money, and, on one occasion, simply confiscating 1.3 million *pesos* in gold and silver belonging to private individuals. When a military movement forced him to vacate his high post in March 1823, he left the treasury in a shambles and the government overloaded with debts.

The new republican government, perhaps more responsible but only slightly more adept, had little more fortune in coping with the basic ills but considerably more success in negotiating loans; an English translation of von Humboldt's panegyric on Mexican mineral wealth whetted British appetites. Within fifteen months of Iturbide's hasty departure, and even before His Britannic Majesty had recognized Mexican sovereignty, the government had negotiated a loan in England; this was the first of a long series which kept the new nation strapped and scrambling for funds for the next fifty years. The Mexican agent who negotiated the loan got a "tremendous satisfaction" from his success since, as he claimed, the mere fact of the loan indicated that Mexico had arrived at a place of respect in the world community. Politically the loan may have been advantageous, but economically it approached disaster. For assuming an indebtedness of 16 million *pesos* at 5 per cent, the treasury actually received a little more than 5.5 million in disposable money. Most of this money was quickly dissipated in a variety of petty ways, only one of which (the purchase of tobacco for the re-established monopoly) aided economic development or produced future revenue. At about the time the bonds went on sale in England, the new government validated revolutionary internal debts to the amount of 45 million *pesos* and authorized a new foreign loan of an additional 16 million. The new loan, also negotiated in England, set aside 4 million to reduce the first, and consisted in part of military supplies of questionable quality and need. Thus within two years the republic saddled itself with a debt of some 73 million *pesos*, and had little to show for its efforts.

The size of the debt itself was not so staggering, since it amounted to little more than 11 *pesos* a person; but juxtaposed with government income it was formidable. According to a budget estimate prepared for the first seven months of 1825, the government could count on about 9 million *pesos* of ordinary revenue, but faced an expenditure of over 21 million. Sixteen million of the 21 was assigned to the army, and an additional 3 to the navy; thus over 90 per cent of the budget went to current military expenses. The foreign debt obviously could not be serviced when such a deficit stared the treasury in the face, and so from the very beginning the fiscal structure was unsound—and it improved little with time.

A comparison between public finance as shown in the budget of 1825 and that of the late colonial period shows some interesting facets. To be sure, the conditions had changed drastically in the intervening years, for the last decade of the colonial period had been profitable in spite of the Napoleonic wars. Furthermore, an independent nation has many expenditures not necessary to a colony. In addition, too, uncertainty concerning the future course of Spain, which not only insisted that Mexico remain a colony but still retained possession of the island fortress in Veracruz harbor to prove it, justified some concern regarding national security. Fighting continued in some portions of South America, Spain appeared to have the backing of the French who had only recently re-established Ferdinand VII in his autocratic power, and, the Monroe Doctrine to the contrary, many Mexicans feared a Spanish attempt to reconquer the nation. But given all these concerns and differences, the national budget compares ill with that of the late colony.

First and foremost, the size of the military establishment and the amount of the military budget stand in strong contrast to that of the colonial period. In the late colonial years the maximum annual expenditure on the military reached no more than 4 million *pesos,* and in most years it scarcely reached 3. Even in 1819, the one year during the revolutionary period for which financial statements exist, the total viceregal expenditures reached only 10 million, about half of which fell into non-military categories. At the very height of the revolutionary wars, before Morelos's capture and execution, the military expenditures probably amounted to less than 10 million. In view of these data, a seven-month budget of 19 million for the military—a rate giving over 31 million for the year—seems exorbitant, and a standing army of 50,000 fully equipped men seems excessive. They may be better explained as incidents of national politics—jealousies, fears of insurrections, sources of lucrative positions—than as reflections of genuine concern over national security. This is particularly true in view of British investments and the well-publicized English foreign policy which served as a counterpoise to any possible French aid to Spain.

Secondly, the budget shows the same disregard for social capital as those of the colonial period. In spite of the critical need for economic rehabilitation, especially in transport and in the mines, the government allocated not one *peso* for such work. To be sure, the low tax on mining may have acted as a stimulus, but roads, wharves, bridges, and public buildings were left in the state of disrepair to which eleven years of insurrection had reduced them.

Third, the sources of expected revenue bore only a faint resemblance to those of the colony and emit an aura of unreality which even a cursory study of public finance in other countries could have underscored. Import and export duties became the mainstay of the government; this in spite of Spanish interference with trade through their control of the fortress in Veracruz harbor. But this budget set the pattern, and for the next fifty years duties of 50 to 60 per cent produced 80 to 90 per cent of normal revenues. The federal government imposed no taxes on mining, since the national government authorized the states to collect taxes on this enterprise. But in return for this authorization, which the states quickly put to use, the units of the federal system committed themselves to pay a "contingent" which the treasury officials counted on to yield more than 2.25 million; in fact, in subsequent years the "contingent" yielded more acrimony between the national and state governments than it did income to the federation. The budget-makers expected the tobacco monopoly to produce about one-quarter of that normally collected by the colonial government, and hoped that the *alcabala,* under another name, would give about half that collected in the average pre-revolutionary year. Obviously, in view of the low expectations from tobacco and the *alcabala,* economic activity suffered from greater doldrums than it had at an earlier time.

Finally, by way of comparison, the expected income was significantly lower than that of the normal pre-revolutionary year and expenditures soared enormously. Even assuming the collection of every *peso* expected—an unwarranted assumption—the total collections would have been at a rate of about three-quarters of that of the viceregal government and the expenditures at a rate about three and a half times. The financial situation was indeed desperate.

It would be feckless to pursue in detail the dreary course of public finance for the next fifty years; it would be merely a variation on a theme. Racked by an internal dissension which became a constant in Mexican politics, robbed by a hungry horde of public officials whose capacity for graft far outweighed their ability to govern, pushed into a financial morass by long-term foreign loans at ruinous rates and short-term domestic loans at rates sometimes as high as 50 per cent for ninety days, the government stumbled from one financial crisis to the next. Normal revenues never met the needs, and every tactic known to desperate public financiers was resorted to: forced loans, special taxes, advances on taxes, confiscations, hypothecations, refundings, paper money, debasement. By 1850 the foreign debt had grown to over 56 million, and the domestic debt reached 61; by 1867, after thirteen years of intermittent war and revolution, of which the French Intervention and Maximilian empire was a part, the foreign debt had climbed to a staggering 375 million and the domestic to nearly 79. By that time almost 95 per cent of the customs revenues had been hypothecated to the payment of various debts. This was, obviously, an impossible situation.

The sorry state of public finance merely reflected general economic conditions which, save for a few faintly bright spots, floundered deeper into a quagmire of inefficiency, poor productivity, and regional isolation. Any attempt at systematic and rational analysis of economic conditions and economic growth from the close of the colonial period to the conclusion of the Maximilian empire in 1867 is doomed for lack of hard data; on this point all who have studied the period agree. José

Luis Mora, an active participant in domestic affairs until he left his country in disgust with Antonio López de Santa Anna's reactionary policies in 1834, attempted to give the Europeans the clearest picture possible of the Mexican economy. His tortuous computations demonstrate the lack of information:

> It is not possible to evaluate with exactitude and precision the value [of foreign trade] in the Republic, and all calculations concerning it must be risky; nevertheless, having no other data which give any security, it is necessary to make use of those giving the collections from the maritime and frontier custom houses. According to the latest tariff, forty percent of the appraised values must be paid as an import duty. . . . The latest memorial of the Ministry of Hacienda, presented to Congress on May 20, 1833 . . . [says that] the maritime and frontier custom houses produced 9,133,337 pesos in the previous fiscal year, which would assume an importation of 22,833,842 pesos [*sic*]. Everything makes one believe that exportation should be the same, . . . which added to the first gives a total of 45,667,684 *pesos*. But a greater difficulty is in knowing how much this is raised through smuggling; nevertheless the three percent internal tax on consumption [indicates] . . . an additional two-thirds over that registered in the customs houses, and thus fraudulent importation should be valued at 16,445,126, to which when we add an equal amount for exportation, we have as a result the sum of 32,980,252 *pesos,* which added to the legal imports and exports give a total of 78,557,936 *pesos*.

Using somewhat the same kinds of calculations, Mora gave the total value of internal trade as 58 millions a year. His arithmetic may be open to question, and his assumptions certainly are, but he highlights the problem. Sixty years later Matías Romero, again attempting to impress the foreigner with Mexican realities, was confronted with the same lack of data, but his answer was much simpler:

> I could not give even a tentative statement, which I could vouchsafe, of our total imports and exports from 1821 to 1867, but the statement of our cusom houses from 1823 to 1875 . . . gives an approximate idea of our imports, considering that the receipts amount to about from 50 to 60 percent of the value of our imports.

But when he discussed revenues, the same author stated:

> It is very difficult to give a correct statement of the receipts of the Mexican custom houses before the year 1875.

Romero's estimates concerning exports suffer from the same lack of hard data. A reasonable export figure, he said, would be the total of silver and gold coined, with an addition of 30 to 40 per cent to account for smuggled bullion. Romero's calculations lead to an import total of about 14 million for 1832, whereas Mora gave a figure of over 39 million for that year. Mora gave an equal figure, 39 million, for exports, but Romero's method results in an export value of scarcely 10 million. Romero's estimates for total trade, then, are less than one-third of those for Mora. Other contemporary statements concerning the magnitude of foreign trade vary greatly one from another in other years, even though one could assume that if any statistics on early national Mexican economy approach accuracy it should be those dealing with foreign trade. The dearth of data and the widely varying "guesstimates" indicate the impossibility of finite analysis and emphasize that the following descriptions of economic conditions are impressionistic only.

The one evidence of healthy economic growth, and that relative only to other parts of the economy, can be found in the re-establishment and reinvigoration of mineral production. By 1841 gold and silver production showed a marked increase over the low point immediately after independence; in 1855 production roughly equaled that of the late eighteenth century; and by 1868 the total was only slightly less than that of 1808. In that nearly half-century of slowly increasing production a number of significant changes occurred, and not all of these changes were beneficial to ultimate Mexican economic development.

The most noticeable change, clearly indicated by reasonably accurate coinage statistics, came in the shift away from Guanajuato as the center of silver production. The independence struggle so thoroughly ravaged many of the mines in the district that they could never be rehabilitated. The colonial system of "rat-hole" mining, with its labyrinthine tunneling and casual cribbing, complicated the problem of renewed working in some potentially productive mines and made their exploitation economically prohibitive. Zacatecas, with its mines less subject to disrepair and abandonment during the revolutionary period

—most of the mine owners at least kept the water under control—and less intensively worked during the colonial period, emerged as the leading silver producer. Hidalgo, with its mines centered in the Pachuca region hard-hit but not ruined by the revolution, ran the more northern district a close second, and forced Guanajuato into third place. In the far northern states of Chihuahua and Sonora silver mining quickened in spite of poor communications and Indian depredations, and by 1870 produced over 10 per cent of the national total. Miners in Sinaloa, taking advantage of isolation, managed to develop some mines profitably only because they evaded tax payments and smuggled their product to the outside; tighter enforcement of customs laws beginning in 1867 all but killed the industry there. In spite of its loss of status as the premier silver producer, Guanajuato continued to occupy the first place as producer of gold and clung to a tenuous second place for the total value of minerals mined. This queen of the colonial mining districts brought copper, copper pyrites, tin, and mercury—for which the government paid a bounty—in addition to the gold and silver from her 343 operating mines in 1870.

At least the beginnings were made in changing mining technology. The *patio* method still occupied first place as an amalgamation process, but foreign mine operators introduced a more highly mechanized practice which was less wasteful of mercury, less dependent upon the highly skilled touch of the *azoguero,* and less dangerous to the health of men and animals alike. But the incredibly poor roads and the original heavy investment for the machinery, plus a manifest inertia on the part of Mexican owner and worker alike, prevented more widespread use of the process in spite of its clear advantages. Some foreign owners equipped their mines with steam power to remove both water and ore, but the same factors which inhibited change in amalgamation slowed the introduction of European technology. The entire mining process, then, was in the throes of change from the waste and inefficiency of the colonial period, but the shift would have to wait for the development of new political, social, and economic institutions. In the meantime costs in Mexican mining far outstripped those in Western Europe and the United States. State-imposed taxes, costly transport, scarcity of mercury and fuel, and antiquated methods all added heavy burdens to the cost of production; one Mexican economist has calculated that the complete processing of a given quantity of his country's ore cost nearly eight times that of the same quantity in Germany or England. English and German use of a number of by-products which the Mexican ignored increased the differential.

Furthermore, once the metal had been extracted from the ore the mine owner had to pay a series of additional taxes and meet additional expenses. Laws passed in 1831, and remaining in force until after 1870, required the miner to present all his gold and silver at the mints for the purposes of refinement and coinage, even though the silver coins so minted were destined to be remelted for ultimate use in the fabrication of various kinds of silverware. At one time or another fifteen such mints operated, but at any given time a maximum number of eleven refined the silver and minted coins. While the additional mints certainly made the process easier than during the colonial period, when all coin passed through the mint at Mexico City, the necessity for transporting the metal sometimes hundreds of miles over bandit-infested trails added materially to the costs of production. In the early national period the government owned and operated all the mints, but a liberal-*laissez faire* government in the 1850's surrendered control of all but one to private contractors. The mints not only charged fees for assaying and refining, and collected a variety of state, municipal and federal taxes, but also tacked on to the costs of minting a considerable profit for themselves—5 per cent of the total value, according to some critics. An estimated 90 per cent of the minted coin went to the export market, on which the federal government collected a charge of 7.5 per cent. Adding up all the charges and taxes, some of the latter collected twice through a loophole in the laws, the mine operator paid about 25 per cent of the value of the metal; these payments slightly exceeded those collected by the viceregal governments. Internal fiscal policy, then, magnified the basic problem of high costs. High costs in turn engendered additional waste, since mine owners cast aside or passed by ores of low assay. Production of the precious minerals did increase—at a rate, in fact, higher than at any time during

Spanish domination—but considering the heavy investment coming from foreign sources, and the special encouragement given to foreigners, the increase was agonizingly low.

And the foreigner did come with his money, seeking the bonanza in Mexico. Early in the national period the government, recognizing the futility of attempting to refurbish the industry using only national resources, modified the old Spanish mining codes to allow foreigners to obtain possession of, and to work, existing mines; the new codes gave virtual ownership as opposed to a mere concession. With this as an encouragement, and with the republication of von Humboldt's work in English as an added stimulus, a mild Mexican mining fever broke out in Europe. Widespread and not too accurate propaganda activities by developers—even young Benjamin Disraeli tried his hand at publicity blurbs—increased the virulence of the fever until all semblance of common sense succumbed. The mania grew to such proportions, according to Mora, that

> In London the illusions over the products of Mexican mining enterprise reached such a point that it was seriously feared, and was the subject of hot debate, that the price of wheat and other article of popular consumption would triple, as had happened in the sixteenth centurn as a result of the new silver discoveries.

Within the next few years the British organized seven mining companies, bought concessions, sent out experts, and poured upwards of 25 million *pesos* into the works. The French and the Germans came next, both in time and amount, and then the prospector and speculator from the United States. No accurate figure can be given for the amount of money the foreigners invested in Mexican mining in the two generations following independence, but it probably fell between 50 and 100 million, and it may have exceeded the value of the metal taken out by the foreign concerns.

Much of the investment was neither wisely nor profitably spent. Most of the foreign concerns, perfectly aware of the antiquated technology characteristic of Mexican mining, came as emissaries of the new technology and brought with them often heavy and cumbrous machines. With transport facilities in such a decrepit state it frequently proved impossible to move the equipment to the isolated mines; much of the expensive European machinery ultimately rusted away, abandoned far from any mine. Furthermore, most of the managers or agents sent out from Europe knew little of the country and less of silver mining; from this condition the home companies suffered, for

> The result [according to Mora] was that finding themselves confronted with the necessity of making use of subaltern agents hundreds of leagues from home, they have frequently been ill-used or cheated. Sometimes they have made use of the miners of the country, who, though having the advantage of the knowledge of the [Mexican] process, are naturally addicted to their routines and are enemies of any new method.

Too frequently the managers on the site were inefficient and profligate; probably the conviction of the great bonanza always only a few yards away led to a kind of abandon in pursuing operations. In any event, the loss of money in some concerns created a scandal.

But even under proper conditions the re-establishment of mining production entailed high risks, as is clearly shown by an English experience in the Pachuca region. One of the most productive of the eighteenth-century mines, producing a net profit of 15 million *pesos* in thirty years, was located near Pachuca in the Real del Monte. Charles III, in gratitude for a magnificent gift of silver and a ship, had given to the mine operator the title of Conde de Regla. The count, on his death, bequeathed both title and mine to his son, who continued to reap a great silver harvest. Excessively high costs of drainage cut the profits, but the second Conde de Regla continued to operate the mine until, in 1810, the revolution forced him to abandon the works. In 1818, with Pachuca and the surrounding territory firmly in government hands, the Conde attempted to resume production but to his distress found that one of the main tunnels had caved in, that the water had risen to cover all the old workings, and that the cost of rehabilitating the mine was beyond his resources. Living in England at the time of the great mining fever there, he leased the mine to a group of stockholders who formed the Real Del Monte Company in 1824, after an English mining engineer had submitted a favorable report. The company appointed a retired captain of the Royal Engineers as manager of the Mexican operations, and he in turn assembled an exceptionally able group of technicians to accompany him to Mexico. He needed two years to transport the 1000 tons of machinery to Pachuca from Veracruz, a distance of about 250 miles; at places the company built its own roads as the machinery progressed, but the time and expense seemed to have been worth it in view of the enormous jump—from 500 to 8000 *pesos*—in the market value of the shares in England. The manager needed three additional years to install the machines, drain the mine, install new cribbing, and begin ore extraction. The ores proved to be poor and unprofitable, so the manager elected to sink a new shaft to a lower level; additional water problems necessitated new equipment with all the attendant delays and expenses. The company found and extracted ores; by 1846 10 million *pesos* in silver had been coined—but at a net loss of over 5 million. The constant drain on the home office soured the investors, whose general disgust with the venture forced the shares down to about 12 *pesos*. In 1848 the bankrupt company disposed of its assets for a nominal sum. Ironically enough, within twenty-five years the same mine became one of Mexico's heaviest, and most profitable, producers.

Not all foreign investments, of course, followed the pattern of the Real del Monte. Another group of English financiers took over part of the Zacatecas and all of the Bolaños operations, both of which returned profits after many years. Before mid-century the government allowed foreigners to open new concessions as well as exploit old, and in the hectic 'fifties, the foreigners flooded into the country. The net result, according to the historian Francisco R. Calderón, was that by 1870,

> It could be said that the major part of the mineral exploitation was in the hands of foreigners, above all the English, the French and North Americans. Almost all the foreign investments in mining were made . . . before the War of Reform, the Intervention, or the Empire.

Mexican mining benefited from an infusion of foreign capital and technology. The expelled Spaniards took with them most of their liquid capital and left little in Mexico for the heavy investments necessary. Not a single private banking institution existed in Mexico prior to 1864; the merchants and commercial houses who served as moneylenders did so at such fantastic rates of interest that they could not be used as sources for the heavy and long-term investments necessary for mining. Foreign money, then, constituted the only ready source of capital for development, and the government early set a pattern of encouraging such investment; the late nineteenth-century Díaz policies merely amplified an existing concept. But foreign investments, in spite of their value as a spur to development, had some distinct drawbacks, particularly when those investments were made under conditions which allowed the foreigner special benefits. As Mexican nationalism grew toward the latter part of the nineteenth century and became rampant in the twentieth, foreign control of many of the basic economic activities created acrimony and resulted in international tensions. The foreigner with his money certainly played a dominant role in mining development, but just as certainly established a base for future troubles.

The Mexican economy in areas other than mining presented a dismal spectacle in the fifty years following independence. If, as it is sometimes said, the lines of transportation form the veins through which flows the blood of commerce, Mexican economic growth suffered from a form of pernicious anemia until well after 1870. At the conclusion of the independence movement the nation could claim only three highways worthy of the name, and all three had fallen into a lamentable state during the struggle. The Spanish crown in its three hundred years of control did almost nothing for road construction. A rough road, over which wagons could pass with difficulty, connected Zacatecas and the intervening points with Mexico City, and until late in the eighteenth century an equally rough road, little more than a trail wandering through the mountains, served as the sole connection between the capital and Veracruz. Toward the end of the colonial period the Consulado of Mexico City, a merchant group enjoying a virtual commercial monopoly in the area surrounding the capital, undertook to construct a decent road connecting the center with the port; at approximately the same time the Consulado of Veracruz thought of building a road from Veracruz to Mexico City. The two groups agreed to co-operate in building the section between Mexico City and Puebla, but in characteristic fashion they disagreed so violently on the route between Puebla and the coast that they could reach no agreement. One group then paid for the construction of a paved road from Puebla through Orizaba and Córdoba to Veracruz, while the other built its road from Veracruz through Jalapa (the traditional site for the exchange of goods, and dear to the Veracruz merchants' hearts) and Perote to Puebla. In the meantime the Mexico City group, hoping to profit from trade with the interior, constructed a road through the mountains to Toluca, 40 miles to the west. All three roads proved to be highly successful in cutting transportation costs. Users of all three paid tolls to give a return on the investment and to form a fund to keep the roads in repair. But, says Mora,

> These roads from 1810 to 1829 were in total abandonment and their funds during all this time were distracted from their destined application, first because of the war of independence, and then because of the abolition of the Consulados.

In the rest of the country there was nothing resembling a real road. All transport to the Pacific Coast moved on pack saddles, and most of it to the interior used the same system. Straggling wagon trails connected some of the interior cities, but seasonal rains made them all but impassable for wagons or coaches and kept transport rates prohibitively high. After three centuries of occupation and settlement, Mexico was still one vast frontier. The first generation of national life saw little change. Mora complained in 1838 that the Mexican wagon-makers confused mass with strength and efficiency; their products were "so heavy by virtue of their mass as weak by their structure" that they could carry little cargo. And Mexicans were not particularly disposed to follow the example of European and North American wagon-makers, since the Mexicans approached any new idea "with a certain timidity and lack of confidence" because their errors had been "nursed, nurtured and fortified by their education." Slow-moving oxen pulling inefficient wagons over miserable trails could scarcely give a strong pulse to economic life.

The delightful Frances Calderón de la Barca, with her marvelously perceptive eye and facile pen, frequently commented on the poor state of the roads during her sojourn there as the Scottish-born wife of the Spanish minister from late 1839 to 1842. On a trip to Pachuca in 1841 her carriage traveled "over rocks and walls, torrents and fields of maguey; . . . arriving in sight of walls, the mozos gallop on and tear them down." The reaction of the walls' owners, if there were any, she did not record. In the Pachuca region (the fourth greatest silver producer in the eighteenth century and the center of a heavy sedentary population), she saw "no roads worthy of the name" until she arrived at the Real del Monte properties. "The carriage ascended slowly the road cut through the mountains by the English company; . . . [it was] the first broad and smooth road I have seen as yet in the Republic." A few years later Waddy Thompson, who had just completed a tour as U.S. Minister to Mexico, commented that most of the commerce between Veracruz and Mexico City still depended upon the pack animal. Carl Sartorius, that enthusiastic German transplanted to Mexico in 1824, could scarcely contain his optimism about Mexico in general when he wrote in 1850, but even he commented on the

> hopeless condition of the roads leading from the coast to the interior. Nothing is done in the way of constructing roads, or very little indeed, whilst tolls are called for, without the money being applied to keeping the roads in repair, although the vehicles may be every moment in danger of turning over, or of sticking fast in the mud. This is the case on the sole practicable high-road from Vera Cruz to Mexico; we may therefore easily conceive the state of the other roads through dense forests and ravines. This circumstance renders the transport of goods singularly expensive . . .

Madame Calderón confined her observations not just to the discomforts of travel over rough trails; she too became fully aware of the economic implications of inadequate transport. At the *hacienda* of Tepenacasco, between San Juan Teotihuacán and Real del Monte, she and her husband fell into conversation with the *hacendado;* Calderón asked the proprietor why he did not use the available lake water for irrigation to grow wheat.

> [The] proprietor of the lake and of a ruined house standing near, which is the very picture of loneliness and desolation, remarked in reply, that from this estate to Mexico, the distance is thirty-six leagues; that a load of wheat costs one real a league . . . so that it would bring no profit if sent there.

The thirty-six leagues represented the sinuosity of the route; the straight-line distance is less than half that.

Foreign travelers and residents did not stand alone in their concern over the status of transportation. State governments, the central government, and municipalities filled the air with their wailings—but did little about the situation except to charge a fee, or toll, for the use of any road. The various governmental units did construct some roads, after a fashion, but they devoted more of their energies to marking out roadsites and rudimentary passages than to constructing good roads for heavy traffic. And they confronted all manner of human as well as geographic difficulty. The nature of the terrain itself, it should be made clear, posed problems of no mean order, but these problems could have been overcome with the technical knowledge then available. The major problem was the eternal scarcity of funds, "which neither enthusiasm, nor tenacity, nor work could resolve," according to one Mexican scholar. Money allocated for the payment of wages seldom reached the hands of the men who did the labor on the road-building gangs before 1860. Contracting companies used surplus agricultural labor in the off seasons and, with authorizations from government officials, offered as pay an exemption from military service; the practice was little more than a variation on the colonial *repartimiento,* for foolhardy indeed would be the young man who refused the offer. He would soon find himself in uniform.

Government agents complained that the people themselves, in spite of the constant clamor for better communications, not only refused to give aid but often did much to prevent the construction and the maintenance of highroads. Landowners, they said, asked exorbitant prices for the land used for the right-of-ways, frequently refused builders access to rock deposits, or charged outrageous prices for the rock, thus in countless little ways hindering operations. Furthermore, *hacienda* owners frequently allowed their stock to roam over roads under construction, and the animal herds sometimes destroyed in one day all the work done in the preceding week. Those who used the roads left stones in the middle or failed to replace displaced stones or left big holes when they dug their vehicles from the mud. But in spite of financial shortages, peculation, public nonco-operation, and the difficult terrain, by 1865 a network of roads in more or less good repair connected Mexico City with Veracruz, Oaxaca, Guanajuato, San Blas (through Guadalajara), Toluca, and Apam. All roads led to Mexico City. Over these roads, one publicist crowed,

> . . . a passenger can cross the Republic from one sea to the other, a distance of 350 leagues, from the Port of Veracruz on the Gulf to San Blas on the Pacific Ocean, visiting the principal cities, including the capital, in only 11 days.

For this trip the brave traveler paid something over 100 dollars, and during it

> . . . the passengers formed a mass in the interior of that closed box, suffering bruising blows and when they were free to alight they sometimes had suffered a broken arm, a crushed rib or a cut cheek.

The experience of the stagecoach passenger in Mexico, however, was not distinctly different from that of one anywhere, except that the roads were rougher than most and he was in greater danger of losing his effects to road agents.

Stagecoaches, under proper conditions, could average nine or ten miles an hour and travel as far as 110 miles a day, but the cargo carriers trudged along at two or three miles an hour and rarely covered more than 15 miles in a day. The Mexican *arriero,* with his cart or his pack-train, was the cultural brother of every drover in the world. He developed the same colorful—and often obscene—language with which he presumably communicated with his beasts. He was dirty and he was uncouth, but he was trustworthy—and he was needed. Hardworking, frequently foolhardy, surrounded by a romantic aura which obscured the danger and the loneliness of his work, the *arriero* served as the instrument for the small commercial interchange then going on. His charges varied with the commodity, the season, the terrain, and the demand; normally on the main lines of traffic he charged between two and three cents per mile per 100 pounds. He carried anything anyone wanted transported, but the conditions under which he worked, and the charges he demanded, virtually prohibited the transport of material other than that of high value compared to bulk, and that which could stand the rough journey without damage. At the average rates, wheat would have cost 5 or 6 dollars a bushel to transport from Querétaro to Mexico City.

The inadequate road system and the great costs of transport even where roads existed left the country cut up into thousands of little enclaves, each self-sufficient and content to stay that way. These villages had little interest in developing a road system, but this very lack of interest, said one economist,

> . . . made the necessity of communications more imperious from two points of view. On the one hand, without such communication it would never be possible to build a national economy, for the roads would make the nation one in all its aspects and all its attributes; on the other hand, without roads the rudimentary life of these small isolated and self-sufficient communities would never be improved.

To the poor material condition of the roads as a hindrance to cargo and passenger movement must be added widespread and endemic brigandage. Highwaymen began their work early in colonial history, but their activities increased enormously in the last twenty-five years —a herald of social disintegration—in spite of more rigid law enforcement through a special court and police force established in the eighteenth century. From 1782 to 1808 this force meted out summary justice, frequently crucifixion, to unrecorded thousands; it also brought nearly 48,000 offenders before the court. Of these, 10,000 received sentences to prison or to military camps (each probably receiving the customary one or two hundred lashes) and almost 1400 dangled from public gallows. Nine hundred forty-five died in prison "with all spiritual and temporal aids," according to the officials. But even though nearly 2000 prisoners appeared before the court each year, and in spite of the heavy penalties, brigandage appeared to be increasing rather than declining in the late years of the colonial period. The eleven-year independence movement, of course, merely added stimulation and experience. In the new nation the road agents almost dominated the countryside. Captain G. F. Lyon, sent out by an English mining company in 1826, described one of his numerous meetings with highwaymen:

> Here in a close defile we met three poor fellows, who informed us of their having been stopped and robbed two days before, by thirteen men completely armed. These rogues had plundered them of three mules with valuable cargoes, . . . completing the business by stripping them naked and leaving them bound hand and foot on the road all night. At sunset we . . . [encountered] a party of seventeen armed merchants with valuable cargoes from Guadalaxara [*sic*]. On the preceding day these people had met the robbers, fifteen in number. . . . I was informed that almost every man, and the captain in particular, in this formidable gang was known to the people of Guadalaxara. They always fearlessly spent their money which they gained on the road, in the city; and then as openly assembled their forces and sallied out to plunder again.

Fanny Calderón passed hard by a robbers' roost not far from Mexico City fifteen years later:

> Several men, with guns, were walking up and down before the house —sporting looking characters but rather dirty—apparently either waiting for some expected *game*, or going in search of it. Women with rebosos [*sic*] were carrying water, and walking amongst them. There were also a number of dogs. The well-armed men who accompanied us . . . precluded all danger of an attack; but woe to the solitary horsemen or the escorted [*sic*; unescorted?] carriage that should pass thereby.

Further on her journey, Madame Calderón had an opportunity to talk with an *hacienda* administrator who doubled as the captain of a troop of guards dedicated to pursuing brigands:

> He gave us a terrible account of these night attacks, of the ineffectual protection afforded him by the government, and of the nearly insuperable difficulties thrown in the way of any attempt to bring these men to justice. He lately told the president he has some thought of joining the robbers himself, as they were the only persons in the republic protected by the government.

In one short span during 1843, brigands robbed seven consecutive stages from Veracruz to Mexico City. As late as 1863, three consecutive shipments of bar silver and gold from one mine in Sinaloa fell to highwaymen. Robberies on the road were so common that all shipments of valuables of any kind were heavily escorted—frequently by hired gunmen, some of whom acted as scouts for the road agents—and every stage stop maintained an emergency supply of blankets and clothing to cover passengers denuded by the brigands. On one occasion a group of passengers arrived in Mexico City covered only by old newspapers. Mexican transport may not have served the economy particularly well, but it certainly had zest.

Railroad construction, of course, should have been the answer to most of the nation's transportation problems; but the virtual bankruptcy of the government eliminated that source of financing, and the political turmoil discouraged foreign investment. In 1837, amid great enthusiasm and glowing oratory, the government let the first concession for a railroad, to connect Veracruz and Mexico City; but three years later the president canceled the contract, since nothing had been done. In 1842 Santa Anna granted another concession for the same route, and the contractors actually began construction of the right-of-way; seven years later the Herrera government canceled that concession, inasmuch as the company had built only three miles of right-of-way. The state of Veracruz then took over the project and opened the first line—all eight miles of it—in 1850. By 1854, additions to that line and a new line between Mexico City and Guadalupe—three miles—

gave the nation about fifteen miles of serviceable track and passenger equipment. New revolutions and wars interrupted construction again and in 1860, after twenty-three years of work and planning, the total mileage remained the same. By contrast, in 1860, the United States had over 30,000 miles of track.

Poor transportation had a deleterious effect not only on commerce, for

> . . . the lack of communication facilities powerfully influenced the development of national agriculture. . . . Agriculture would never be able to arrive at a high rate . . . while its transport had to be made over the rough roads of the period and [to depend upon] the antiquated system of ox carts or pack trains.

With the gradual increase of the population, which reached an estimated 9 million in 1870, farm products grew as well. But the basics of Mexican agriculture, in both technology and in crops, changed little in the fifty-year span. Corn still occupied first place in quantity and value, the price having changed little but production having almost doubled to a million and a half tons. Cotton, encouraged by the government through import restrictions which sometimes drove the price up to 50 cents a pound (compared to 15 in the United States), never met the domestic demand; an estimate at mid-century indicated that the nation produced only a third of the 100,000 bales it needed. Planters experimented with the crops in widely separated regions, including the Laguna district, which has since become the major producing section, but poor transportation facilities restricted the economic feasibility of cotton planting to *haciendas* near the textile mills in Puebla and Guadalajara.

With the exception of indigo and cochineal, both of which declined disastrously, other colonial agricultural products expanded at a rate roughly proportional to the population growth. Sugar received a major impetus when the first Cuban movement for independence (1868-78) resulted in heavy damage to plantations and mills, but military movements in Mexico itself largely voided the potential growth. In spite of the small change in agricultural production, however, those agricultural and pastoral products figuring in the export trade changed markedly. By 1870, hides, both raw and tanned, occupied first place in exports. Sisal and *ixtle* together occupied second place, followed by lumber and dye woods in third and coffee in fourth. The other export items—vanilla, cochineal, live cattle driven into the United States, tobacco—were unimportant. The big change came in the first three items; between 1825 and 1870 hide exports increased twentyfold, fibers twelvefold, and lumber six times.

The Mexican agriculturist, beset by a climate, a transportation system, a disturbed political condition, and a mentality that militated against any real progress, continued to apply the rudimentary technology which characterized the colonial period. The primitive digging stick, the ineffectual ox-drawn wooden plow, and all the other wasteful and inefficient practices he retained; the agricultural revolution then in process in Western Europe and in the United States passed him by completely. And such inefficiency takes its toll. In spite of the low wages paid to agricultural workers—in some regions as low as 25 cents a day, and in the highest less than a *peso*—the costs of production were prohibitively high. At a time when cotton sold for 15 cents a pound in U.S. markets, the Veracruz producer spent 13 cents a pound to get his fiber from the field to the buyer. Prices of products varied enormously from place to place, depending upon the abundance of the local crop. Sugar which cost a penny a pound to produce sometimes sold for less than that in the immediate vicinity but for 25 cents a pound in regions distant from the cane fields. Wheat which cost five and a half *pesos* to produce sometimes sold for three and a half *pesos*. As a consequence, the planter perceived a bountiful harvest to be an unalloyed disaster; if he sold locally he could do so at a loss, and if he moved his crop to another region the transportations costs, the taxes, and the middleman's share would eat up any profit. Government fiscal policy did not help. The *alcabala*, sometimes collected twice under different names, and a variety of other national and local taxes averaged about 20 per cent of the market value; the internal custom houses caused expensive delays, and the mountains of paper-work added to the costs. Confronted with these conditions and heir to a cultural inertia which made him reluctant to accept new processes or equipment, the poor farmer saw little need to change his mode of production.

At the same time, the small profit per acre and the social values inherited from colonial times encouraged an increased concentration of land ownership. As an incident of the bitter Church-state fight, the government forced the Church to divest itself of rural properties, and these lands in the main became the core of great private estates. In addition, under the mistaken belief that both the society and the economy would benefit from the division of community holdings into small private plots, the liberal governments after 1856 forced the villages to distribute their common lands or *ejidos* among the heads of family; by 1870 the estate owners had managed to acquire most of these lands. But the greatest single process of concentration (other than the colonial heritage) came from an ill-advised attempt by Juárez to raise funds in 1863 to combat the French invaders. His government offered to sell "vacant lands" for cash, and within the next four years the peripatetic "Constitutional President" issued titles to nearly 4.5 million acres of such lands to individuals and companies in plots averaging over 14,000 acres. For this vast amount of land, much of it prime, the government received the kingly sum of 100,000 dollars—about two and a half cents an acre.

Land concentration in itself portended problems for the future, but the sale of "vacant lands" set an evil precedent and helped create another situation which posed a greater danger. No one knew exactly what "vacant lands" were. Common terminology applied *terrenos baldíos* to all those lands which had belonged to the Spanish crown and had come to be the property of the Mexican nation at independence, but the crown had never undertaken by survey or title investigation to determine with any exactitude what it still owned in 1810. As a consequence, many of the Indian villages which had occupied lands since pre-conquest times, but whose titles had never been authenticated nor registered, found themselves legally dispossessed by the sales. To add to the confusion, some of the state governments took advantage of their "sovereign" constitutional status and sold *terrenos baldíos* to favored citizens. The lack of land for Indians had long been a source of irritation, particularly on the central plateau; in the late 'sixties the indigenes of Hidalgo showed their dissatisfaction by overt action. Under the leadership of Julio López ("the John Brown of the Indians") they simply dispossessed the legal owners and began working the land for themselves. López's capture and execution ended his leadership but did not disperse his partisans nor solve the basic problem.

But any suggestion of an attempt to meet the agrarian problem head-on by reform legislation engendered violent antagonism. Such projected legislation was, according to one editorial writer, a "project of social dissolution." A deputy in the national Congress characterized a proposed bill as one which would whet appetites and invite a caste war, a synonym for "sack, fire, assassination, extermination." Agrarian reform involving land distribution, insisted one contemporary, would be useless and dangerous:

> Any such revolutionary project would either be suffocated in blood or would send us back to a state of savagery.

A Mexican economist has summed up the situation, with either conscious or unconscious irony:

> The indigenes rose up on other occasions for agrarian reasons; but without attending to the demand for lands, they were pacified by violent means.

By 1870, then, Mexican agricultural land-tenure patterns presented a dismal picture. The few changes which did occur in the two generations following independence tended to accentuate existing evils and to establish a process which became even more exaggerated during the Díaz period and ultimately a major component of the Revolution of 1910.

In industrial development Mexico fared somewhat better, though not nearly so well as the optimists foresaw; Francisco R. Calderón says that in 1867:

> Matías Romero, following the custom of the age which considered Mexico as a potential emporium of every description, declared to

> Congress that the manufacturing industry had a brilliant future. . . . The prognostications contrasted with hard reality. A national industry hardly existed, in spite of the projects for industrialization favored by our governments since independence.

The judgment is perhaps too harsh. Certainly Western European and United States industrial development far surpassed that of Mexico, but just as certainly a rudimentary groundwork was laid for eventual industrial development. The greatest change took place in the textile industry, and much of it came as a result of foreign investment.

The independence movement left the textile industry, none of it mechanized but employing some 60,000 workers, in complete ruins. As encouragement to a revitalization of the industry, the government allowed duty-free machinery importation and forbade the importation of yarns and cloth which would compete with the national product. The protectionist policy did recreate in part the vanished industry, but Mexican spindles and looms produced inferior and expensive goods which did not meet demands. With capital so scarce that the prospective mill owners could not buy modern European machinery, the government made its first essay into financial support for industrial development; in 1830 it established a lending bank with an initial capital of a million *pesos*. Although not specifically designed to support only textile development—its first loans financed other activities—the bank devoted nearly 70 per cent of its total resources to aiding the cotton textile industry. The bank itself may be considered a failure, since it ceased to exist in 1842 and collected only a portion of the loans advanced, but its financial stimulus did much to create a mechanized textile industry. By 1845, 52 totally mechanized spinning mills, operating nearly 115,000 spindles and converting 25,000 bales of cotton into yarn every year, employed about 5000 workers. In addition, mechanized weaving mills employing about 4000 workers on 2000 looms turned out roughly half the yard-goods produced. The total investment in the mechanization process has been estimated at close to 12 million *pesos,* of which about half came from Mexican capital and the remainder from foreign sources. After 1845 some changes took place, but in general the industry continued at approximately this level for the next twenty-five years.

Textile mechanization brought improved conditions, but at a cost. The new mills were much better than the colonial *obrajes* in terms of working conditions and in wages, but they were far from ideal even in the middle of the nineteenth century. The average operator worked twelve hours, and some labored sixteen. Women and children now did most of the work in both spinning and weaving in the mechanized plants, receiving a daily wage of from 20 to 40 cents at a time when a family of four needed 2 *pesos* a day to meet ordinary living expenses. Mechanization brought a reduction of about 30 per cent in the cost of coarse cloth, but even this cost was remarkably high compared to other countries. Furthermore the ardent protectionist policy under which the mills came to be built at times seriously hindered production. As a means of protecting spinning and weaving, the government put yarns and some textiles on the prohibited list, and to encourage the cotton. But as the mechanization process continued and the demands for cotton became greater, the Mexican growers failed to produce sufficient fiber for the mills. On numerous occasions shortages of raw materials forced the mills to suspend work, and some mill owners as a consequence went bankrupt.

Even with added production coming from the mechanized industry and in spite of the importation of raw cotton after 1846, the nation could not produce sufficient textiles for her own use. Legal importation, at a duty of 50 per cent *ad valorem* and up, generally equaled domestic production, but the high duties encouraged what appeared to be a natural proclivity for smuggling; in spite of some ingenious techniques employed by the government to limit illicit traffic, the contrabandists proved equal to the task, bringing into the country an estimated one-third of all the textiles involved in retail trade.

Aside from textiles, Mexican manufacturing industries showed little advance over that of the colonial period. A number of paper mills in the Mexico City environs produced a poor quality of wrapping paper, but in spite of government encouragement the industry failed to gain headway; paper importation continued to be heavy. Distillers, brewers, and vintners found haven behind the high tariff walls; the protection did stimulate heavy production of alcoholic beverages for national consumption, but it also led one disgruntled gourmet to remark acidly that "the overabundance of patriotism has served to substitute . . . pulque for French and Spanish wines." A wide variety of other products came from small plants in nearly every section of the country: oils, soaps, pottery, and an inferior grade of shoes headed the list. But most of this so-called industrial production came from artisanry rather than industrialization. The total annual value of manufactured products is impossible to estimate. In 1868 R. García, using inflated estimates made by two predecessors and adding a bit of exaggeration for good measure, computed the total to be well over 100 million *pesos,* but the probabilities are that a figure half that total would come closer to actuality. By way of contrast, the United States with a population of a little more than four times that of Mexico manufactured products worth over three billion.

Mexican industrial development had to contend with a multitude of discouraging factors, among which the lack of transport must be high on the list. The cost of transporting cotton-mill machinery from Veracruz to the environs of Mexico City equaled the original cost of the equipment in England. Transport costs of raw cotton, much of it unginned, from the costal regions to Guadalajara added so much to the raw material costs that the textile industry there faltered. Transport costs made it economically unfeasible to send the finished products to distant markets, and limited the market to such a degree that economies of scale could not be introduced. Everywhere the Mexican turned he found his industrial opportunities limited by the dearth of transport facilities.

But poor transport, important though it might have been, was merely one hindrance—and symptomatic of deeper economic weaknesses. In spite of advertisement of the marvelous potential of Mexico with its magnificent raw materials, the hard truth is that Mexico lacked too many of the essentials for rapid economic development. A disastrous shortage of fuel prevented wide use of steam power; mines used the wood and charcoal locally available and begged for more, the nation lacked easily exploitable coal mines, the age of fuel oil had not arrived, and water remained the sole important—and very limited—

source of power. Furthermore, the unavailability of resources in terms of metals and skills prevented the elaboration of complex machinery within the country; all machinery of any industrial use came from foreign countries at high cost.

But the greatest impediment probably lay in Mexican mentality rather than Mexican geography. The affluent Mexican as a general rule did not invest his money in industrial or commercial enterprises; the absence of banking facilities bears mute testimony to this fact. Furthermore, wasteful and inefficient national governments which regularly spent almost as much on the military as they collected in taxes contended with equally rapacious state governments for sources of funds. The national government, as a fiscal measure, therefore imposed outlandishly high customs duties in spite of an expressed free trade philosophy, and then also collected a galaxy of internal taxes which tended to discourage the movement of goods. State officials in their turn, enamored of the myth of Mexican wealth and always hungering for additional revenues which all too frequently went into their own pockets, continued the outmoded Spanish *alcabala* and invented some new tax horrors of their own. A combination of these taxes in Jalisco in the 'sixties amounted to a quarter of the market value of the goods sold, and in some states the proportion ran as high as a third. Perhaps even worse than the high taxes, most of which could be passed on to the consumer, was the uncertainty of fiscal and other economic policy which changed with the swiftness and the frequency of tenure in office. Given these conditions and the rudimentary education (5-10 per cent literacy) which prevented the development of a skilled work force, the wonder is not that so little industrial development took place, but that so much did.

With the country in a shambles during most of the period, with agriculture producing for the local communities rather than a national market, with industrial production moving but still negligible, and with internal commerce restricted by fiscal policy and poor roads, foreign commerce suffered as well. Not until many decades after independence did foreign trade equal that of the late colonial period. As was true during the colonial period, total commerce with foreign nations reflected the status of the mining industry, for the bulk of exports continued to be precious metals and the proportions changed but little during the first fifty years of the national period; in 1842 gold and silver accounted for 92 per cent, and in 1872, 86 per cent. Total importation depended upon exports as reinforced by borrowing, and as mineral production increased so did trade; after the Maximilian aberration total annual foreign trade for the first time consistently surpassed that of the late colonial years. Veracruz continued to be the major port, handling between 50 and 75 per cent of the legal trade, but new ports—Tampico, Guaymas, San Blas, Mazatlán—became increasingly important. Acapulco, the only legal port on the Pacific Coast prior to independence, lost almost all of its trade to the newer ports on that ocean.

England, taking advantage of an excellent merchant marine and a suave diplomacy, quickly moved into the forefront in Mexican trade and retained her dominant position until 1880. The United States, getting off to a bad start with the officious Poinsett and continuing it with the inept Anthony Butler, gradually improved her position in spite of the long rivalry over Texas which culminated in the 1846-48 Mexican War. By 1870, these two nations dominated the trade, accounting between them for 65 or 70 per cent of the total. France, Germany, and Spain (mostly with Cuba, but far down the list) followed in that order. Throughout the period Mexico exported more to the United States than she imported from that nation, but bought from England more than she sold to her. In one major respect the foreign trade pattern varied little from that of the Spanish period: wearing apparel continued to lead the import list, and precious metals the export.

As a consequence of the general doldrums which plagued the economy during this half-century, and the heritage from Spain which characterized the mass of the population as an inferior breed, the Mexican laborer fared poorly. His wage varied widely depending upon place, time, and activity; it reflected to some degree the cost of living and the demand, but it was always so low that it scarcely sufficed to support even a small family. Real wages remained relatively constant. In 1825 a farm laborer at day wages worked a week to buy enough cheap cloth to make his wife a dress; in 1841 the textile worker expended four or five days for the same purchase. In 1855, the miner in Zacatecas labored four days for a sack of corn, and in 1868, the loom operator in the mechanized textile mills near Mexico City spent five twelve-hour days earning enough to buy the same quantity. Even in Veracruz, which suffered from a chronic labor shortage as a result of the high yellow fever mortality rate, only the most skilled worker could command a wage sufficient to maintain a family of four. Under these conditions all members of a family sought a source of income; children worked alongside the parents in rural areas, and in some textile mills and mines, or they found work in the cities as menials. But in spite of the low wages, or perhaps because of them, vast numbers could not or would not find work; the same *léperos* who infested the colonial cities now graced the national urban centers. Fanny Calderón came into close contact with this seamy social segment soon after arriving in Mexico City, when she went to Mass at the Cathedral early one holiday morning:

> We met but few carriages there, an occasional gentleman on horseback, and a few solitary-looking people resting on the stone benches, also plenty of beggars. . . . Not a soul was in the sacred precincts this morning but miserable *leperos* in rags and blankets, mingled with women in ragged *rebosos*. . . . The floor is so dirty that one kneels with a feeling of horror, and an inward determination to effect as speedy a change of garments afterwards as possible. . . . Whilst I am writing this a horrible lepero [*sic*], with great leering eyes, is looking at me through the window, and performing the most extraordinary series of groans. . . . There come more of them!

Carl Sartorius, who lived in Mexico many years, described the *léperos* with less drama; of the central plaza in any town he says:

> The noble profession of loungers and idlers is here finely represented; the *léperos* or *lazzaroni* of the cities are driven hither by instinct, because opportunity most readily offers itself of procuring something without great exertion, whether it be by relieving someone's pocket, or the more honorable method of doing some errand.

Brantz Mayer, less accustomed than Sartorius and less shocked than Mme. Calderón, but more outraged than either, described them thus:

> I have rarely seen such miserable suburbs; they are filled with hovels built of sun-dried bricks, often worn with the weather to the shape of holes in the mud, while on their earthen floors crawl, cook, live and multiply the wretched-looking population of *léperos*. . . . There, on the canals, around the markets and the pulque shops, the Indians and these miserable outcasts hang all day long; feeding on fragments, quarrelling, drinking, stealing and lying drunk about the pavements, with their children crying with hunger about them. At night they slink off to their lairs, to sleep off the effects of liquor, and to awake to another day of misery and crime. Is it wonderful, in a city with an immense proportion of its inhabitants of such a class, (hopeless in the present and the future) that there are murderers and robbers?

And, Mayer could have added, what more could one expect when pulque, calorie for calorie, sold for less than corn?

Such economic conditions were directly related to the social values held by the dominant group in Mexico. With the mass of the population hungry, ill-clothed, and illiterate, and with few public institutions concerned with its improvement, with class cleavages as sharp in 1850 as in 1750, and with little concern on the part of the political and social leaders for its implications, with, in short, an apparently stultified and static society and little evidence of any real change in the offing, small wonder it is that both the economy and the society suffered.

But in spite of the intent of the dominant group in the final paroxysm of independence, neither the class structure nor the social institutions could remain indefinitely unchanged. By 1870 Mexico was far from being an idyllic society by contemporary European standards, but the ideas common to much of the Western World—and implanted by Morelos—could not be barred from the country. The groundwork for great social change was laid. In the struggle for change the Church occupied a central position, not because it caused the conditions or that it necessarily resisted change, but because it was symptomatic and symbolic. It impinged on every aspect of Mexican life. Even Lucas

Alamán, a brilliant and sophisticated statesman and financier, held that complete fealty to Catholicism and complete respect for the priesthood were the most important attributes of a good workman. The definition of the proper role of the Church became the critical issue; the history of Mexico from 1821 to 1872 could be written in terms of the search for that definition.

The movement for independence created a curious ambivalence toward the Church on the part of the mass of the people. Many of the most active proponents of independence in the early days, and many of those (in addition to Hidalgo and Morelos) whose heads decorated public buildings and scaffolds, were men of the cloth. Some of the greatest military leaders, including Antonio Torres from Guanajuato and Morelos's right-hand man Mariano Matamoros, went from pulpit to battlefield. In fact, says Hubert Howe Bancroft,

> The revolution, having been begun by an ecclesiastic, had from its incipiency many members of the clergy, both secular and regular, among its leaders; and it may be said that at this time the war was kept up almost wholly by them. There was hardly a battle in which priests were not found as leading officers.

Every military unit had its chaplain, and every man fighting for independence did so in the firm belief that he fought as much for God as for country. In Mexico City and in other urban centers an unkown number of clergymen acted as agents and publicists for the revolutionists. In far away Spain, Miguel Ramos Arizpe, "Priest of Bourbon" from Coahuila, took such a liberal stand in behalf of constitutional government, public education, universal suffrage, freedom of thought, and social justice that he spent six years in prison. The man fighting for independence in 1815, be he intellectual or common laborer, could well believe that the clergy supported independence and social change.

But with few exceptions the episcopate, until 1820, condemned the military movement for independence. Even Bishop-elect Abad y Queipo, well-known for his sharp tongue and pen in behalf of social improvement—and himself the subject of inquisitorial wrath—condemned the independence movement in his usual caustic terms. He did so not because of the implications for social change, but because philosophically he supported monarchy and abhorred war. The Bishop of Guadalajara organized a battalion to combat the revolutionists, the Bishop of Puebla constantly fulminated against those fighting for independence, and the Bishop of Chiapas pronounced anathema against all who fought the king. And yet, parish priests frequently led militia units in the outlying districts.

The average Mexican, particularly those fighting for independence, became terribly confused during those awful years. Who spoke for the Church? The parish priest who led him in battle, who heard his confession before battle, and who gave him spiritual and material comfort in times of danger, or the far-away body which excommunicated that priest? Who spoke for the Church? The six priests shot by royalist forces near Durango in a mass execution in July 1812, or the hierarchical officials who stripped them of their clerical protection? Who spoke for the Church? Vicente Guerrero who fought for independence but who signed a manifesto guaranteeing Catholicism as the sole religion, or Calleja who also guaranteed the status enjoyed by Catholicism even while he butchered Guerrero's followers? Did the Bishop of Oaxaca speak for the Church when he applauded a free press in 1815, or did the Metropolitan Chapter when it condemned a free press as the work of the devil? Did Ramos Arizpe represent the Church when he supported public education as the foundation of civilization, or did the Archbishop of Mexico when he condemned public education as contrary to the laws of God? Regardless of the answers to these questions, the hierarchy as a body condemned the revolution, and the hierarchy had the power of position—and of money.

Long before independence, with the spread of the Enlightenment and rationalism, the clergy came under attack in most Catholic countries; in order to defend itself against these attacks the Mexican episcopate insisted that any attempt to change the existing status of the Church or Church properties constituted an attack on the religion itself. One pamphleteer expressed this position well, even though some of his statements failed of accuracy:

> We are agreed then that when the sectarians preach the secularization of the source of sovereignty, that of the family, through civil marriage, when they deny the necessity of Christian baptism, when they attempt to secure possession of education, when they separate Christians from the sacraments and religious practices, when they change the appearance of towns by . . . secularizing charity, profaning Christian festivals, introducing death without sacraments, through civil burial and cemeteries, when they despoil the Church, weave restrictions against the Holy See, elaborate constitutions and laws, open lay schools . . . we say: they do nothing less than fight without quarter the reign of Christianity on earth.

Men of the stamp of Guerrero, Victoria, Gómez Farías—and even the clerics Ramos Arizpe and Mora—could scarcely stomach the pretensions among the higher clergy that such things as civil registration of marriages, births, and deaths, or the opening of public schools constituted an attack on either Christianity or Catholicism. These men had seen the abrupt switch performed by the upper clergy over the question of independence. They had heard, with sour humor no doubt, that the upper clergy in Mexico City in 1820 had found Morelos's 1813 declaration of independence to be a good Catholic document after all. They had witnessed the hypocritical ease with which the bishops of Puebla, Guadalajara, and Chiapas had moved from bitter enmity to ardent support of independence. And they became convinced that special interest, not patriotism or religious fealty, moved most members of the episcopate.

In this atmosphere of mounting tensions and anticlericalism the clergy itself served its own ends ill. Church discipline was notoriously lax in the villages, and many of the local priests were abominably trained in either theology or humanism. Too many clergymen, secular and regular alike, could be seen strolling about at night with attentive young ladies hanging on their arms, or could be found living with a "housekeeper" and a flock of "nephews." Too many had commercial interests from which they reaped private gain, and too many used the confessional to extract information which they used for non-religious purposes. The majority of the clergy may have been hard-working, sincere, devoted, and models of morality—the debate on this question still rages—but many were not, and they gave an odor to the whole.

But, to the sensitive and the serious, other Church conditions constituted an even greater affront. The vast majority of the clergy, secular or regular, stayed in the great urban centers and left the outlying districts devoid of clerical ministrations; one contemporary charged that at least a quarter of all the parishes had no priest assigned at any given time and that another quarter was served by temporary ministers. Furthermore, those priests who did, through a sense of responsibility or ill-luck, minister to the needs of the rural parishes received a remuneration approximating that of a rural day laborer, while the upper clergy lived in sybaritic splendor. Many of those who saw the opulence of the cathedral decorations and the filth of the cathedral floors began to wonder, as did those who saw the poverty-stricken pay five months' income for a baptism, or a wedding, or a burial in consecrated ground. Those who listened to clerics condemn public lay education as blasphemous, but who found that only one in twenty could read, became disenchanted with the clerical position regarding education. Nor could many men appreciate the Church's insistence on retaining control of charitable work, in view of the thousands (an estimated 30,000 in Mexico City alone—about one-fifth of the population) of obviously needy and undernourished men, women, and children roaming the streets and the countryside. To add injury to insult, the Church reputedly held a vast amount of urban and rural property, sometimes estimated as being over one-half the real property in the nation. Church income was estimated to be well over 100 million *pesos* annually, five times that of the government. In any case it was frequently assumed, correctly or incorrectly, that the Church in Mexico commanded greater economic resources and greater annual income than did the state. And then, to top it all, the Church and all persons connected with it enjoyed a special legal status, with a law of its own and subject only to that law. A priest who stole from his parishioners, who raped or murdered, or committed other acts generally considered as crimes against the common order, could not be brought to the bar of justice by state officials unless Church officials withdrew the special protection he was entitled to. Priests *were* guilty of these crimes as a matter of record admitted by Church officials—not many, but some—but they, unlike those fighting for independence before 1820 and captured, were always punished by the Church within the Church. They were never surrendered to the civil authorities for trial. To men of the mentality of Valentín Gómez Farías special rights, or *fueros*, which made the Church a state within a state squared not at all with the temper and the needs of the time. The Church as a religious institution, meeting a spiritual need, had to be purified, they thought. As it existed it impeded progress, and to purify it the state had to remove from its jurisdiction all those things not purely spiritual.

But the hierarchy had its arguments, too. The anticlericals, members of the episcopate insisted, vastly over-emphasized the Church's wealth and seemed to have forgotten that the wealth it had achieved came from its great concern for humanity and progress. The profitable urban and rural properties owned by the Church came not from its own acquisitiveness but from the service it had rendered as a non-interest-charging service institution to vast numbers of property owners in financial difficulty. Some properties had been willed to the Church by pious men whose last wish was to serve God by bequeathing their worldly possessions to God's servants. Church officials admitted, as did Abad y Queipo, that sometimes poorly trained or even evil men found their way into the priesthood, but these were exceptions and were ultimately weeded from the ranks. And clerics guilty of crimes, said the Church spokesmen, were properly punished by the Church: what greater punishment than everlasting penance for a God-fearing man? The state, according to the clerical argument, could have no jurisdiction over the Church. Man owed his first duty to God, for whose service man was created and whose agent on earth was the Church, and then he owed a duty to his family, the manifestation of God's will and the very center of man's mortal existence. Only after these duties had been fulfilled did a man owe anything to the state, for in contrast to the divine institutions of Church and family the profane state was a creation of the mind of man. Marriage, the Church held, was a holy sacrament and not a civil contract; the very concept of civil marriage was anathema, a sacrilege. And so the arguments ran, with each claim made by the hierarchy based upon a theological precept.

In one great sphere the Church had failed miserably. The vast majority of the Mexicans considered themselves Catholic. Born of Catholic parents, baptized in a Catholic ceremony, confirmed as a member of the Catholic Church, married to a Catholic by a Catholic priest, the Mexican knew nought of other religious sects. According to the teachings most Mexicans received, particularly in the less urbanized sections, only Catholics could claim Christianity, all non-Christians professed Judaism, and every Jew bore the mark of the devil in the form of a tail. But with all his conviction of being a Catholic, the Mexican understood his religion poorly if at all, he failed to fulfill his religious obligations except on rare occasions, and he certainly could not follow the sophisticated theological reasonings of the hierarchy. The Church had not in fact made of the average Mexican a good Catholic; it had made him merely a surface practitioner of a religious rote, deeply imbued with a form of religiosity but not neccessarily loyal to the Church as the hierarchy defined both loyalty and Church. In the end, the average man's support or non-support of the clerical position was a measure of his trust or distrust of his parish priest.

But the contending forces were not merely the members of the clergy on the one hand and all the powers of the state on the other; such a contest would have been unequal and shortly terminated. The clerical position had powerful support from many potent men, all of whom had strong reasons for putting their weight on the side of the Church. Some, like Alamán, did so for reasons of deep conviction, because they *could* follow the theological arguments and agreed with them. Some, like Antonio López de Santa Anna, did so for reasons of politics, because at the moment it appeared politically expedient to seek hierarchical support. Others, like Anastasio Bustamante, did so because the special privileges enjoyed by his class, the military, would be jeopardized if the Church lost hers. But the vast majority of those who came to be classed as pro-clericals did so because they suffered from a kind of chilling orthodoxy. In the main the leaders of the clerical position were men who found society as it then existed good; they enjoyed the fruits of this world and the expectations of the next, and they could find no reason for changing. The Church was a part of that unchanging scene. If it were undermined, the scene would no longer be unchanging, and their own fortunes, their own positions would rot away. They fought for a way of life. And they fought bitterly, sometimes even heroically, sometimes viciously, using every power, technique, and trick available. They assessed the situation correctly, of course, for the anticlericals played a dangerous game; once change has begun, no man can foretell where it goes. They fought for the right reasons, but unfortunately for the wrong cause. The life they found so good gave little to the vast majority of the Mexicans; it gave these masses neither material goods nor honor nor dignity, and above all it gave them no hope for this world and little for the next. It gave a few people power and ease and opportunity for intellectual growth, but it retained the rest in the thralldom of abject poverty and ignorance. These men, leading great numbers of the ignorant who believed in them, fought for an anomaly that the passage of time, if nothing else, would doom as surely as the hierarchy doomed Morelos.

A social problem of such intensity, over which men fought with such tenacity, inevitably became a center of bitter political controversy. The groups which controlled the national government could control government policy and determine the course of events. This contention over political control produced the conditions which fostered frequent and violent changes in government. It created the fifty-six different governments between 1821 and 1861, bringing a change in executive control every thirty-seven weeks, on the average. It made it impossible for any president to complete his elected term after 1828, and it helped create the fiscal situation which drove Mexico deeper and deeper into debt. It made each successive act more violent than the last, each leader less willing to compromise and more unreasonable in his demands. It led the anticlericals to the intellectually unsupportable extreme of prohibiting convents, and the pro-clericals to the seditious extreme of supporting foreign invasion. It also paved the way for every kind of political and military opportunist to work his way into a position of power where he could milk the public treasury. And in the end the Church and pro-clericals lost the fight. By 1872 the Church as a social institution had lost its independence and most of its properties. It had been divested of its *fueros* and had become an object of hatred and suspicion, rather than of veneration. But the Church leaders had learned little, and Mexico was destined to suffer another anticlerical convulsion before the civil power and the ecclesiastical authority agreed upon their respective roles.

The first government after 1821 showed a mild anticlericalism, for it levied a forced loan on the ecclesiastical corporations of the four major cities and confiscated some minor Church properties in 1822. The following year the government, now in the hands of the republicans who had overthrown Iturbide's empire, sold for its own profit the properties which had belonged to the prohibited Jesuits and the abolished Inquisition. In 1828, the government confiscated a few more properties and gave other evidence of anticlericalism and political liberalism. In 1829, a revolution placed Vincente Guerrero in office, and in the same year another revolution forced him out of office. At this point the Church hierarchy made its first major mistake in tactics. Guerrero, a staunch Catholic who had supported the proposition that only Catholicism should be allowed in Mexico, was nevertheless a political and social liberal; as a hero of the independence movement he enjoyed wide popular support. Anastasio Bustamante, who overthrew Guerrero and who occupied the opposite end of the political spectrum, used a dirty little trick to have Guerrero captured and shot in early 1831—and the hierarchy not only gave strong support to the Bustamante government but basked in the light of that administration and took strong steps to stamp out "heretical" ideas. From the clergy, which had been loud in its condemnation of certain of Guerrero's policies, came not one word of protest against his executioners. It thus appeared, justly or unjustly, that the Church had connived at the hero's death; as a consequence the latent and mild anticlericalism became patent and strong, and when a new military movement put the now-designated "liberals" back in office in 1833, they were quick to cut away at the Church's power.

First, a decree prohibited any priest from using the pulpit to discuss any political or other non-religious topic. Next, the government secularized the entire educational system, closed the University of Mexico, and subjected all other institutions of higher learning to the administration of a government bureau. In effect, unfortunately, these decrees meant the closing of the Church schools at a time when the government could make no adequate provisions for substitutes; the Church schools may have been ineffectual and inadequate, but they constituted the whole of the educational system save for a few municipal schools. Abolition of Church control over education, of course, was interpreted by the hierarchy as a body blow at the entire Church structure; the fact that a priest helped draft the legislation did not alter the situation. A few days later Congress passed a law which made the collection of tithes purely an ecclesiastical matter in which the government would have no part; the government traditionally had collected the tithes, retained one-ninth for its own, and turned the rest over to the Church. The hierarchy raised a storm of objection over the change, since with good reason the religious authorities believed that volunteer tithing would not bring in the customary million *pesos* a year to Church coffers. Warming to the task and apparently carried away with unrealistic reforming zeal, the legislature in quick succession gave to any member of a monastic order the legal right to forswear his vows and re-enter the profane world, removed the patronage from the hierarchy and vested it in the state, and secularized a great deal more Church property.

These reforms, if they may be called such, created a storm of opposition and encouraged some high Church officials to make statements which bordered on sedition. The violence of Church reaction brought a strong counteraction from the government, which exiled one bishop and temporarily removed others from their positions. But the anticlericals had gone too far too fast and had given the clericals too much propaganda ammunition; they lost public sympathy and soon lost control by a *coup d'état* to a pro-clerical administration which rescinded most of the enactments. The new government's policy brought to Antonio López de Santa Anna a hierarchical encomium: "A thousand blessings on this man, who has returned to God." For the next twenty years the government remained in the hands of those who generally propitiated the Church rather than fought with it over a division of jurisdiction, but the relationships were not always smooth. Internal and external disorders put a heavy strain on the national treasury, and government agents frequently and pointedly requested clerical fiscal aid—more often than not in vain. By this time a generally accepted working understanding had been established between the Church and those other groups in the society who feared any significant social or political change. The Church bowed to the army and insisted that military *fueros* be respected, in return for which the army generally gave support to the clerical position. The Church supported the provisions of the constitutions of 1836 and 1843, both of which included high property and income qualifications for holding office and thereby assured public control by the well-to-do, in return for which the government reaffirmed the Church *fueros*. And Church, government, and army opposed a free press.

The anticlericals in the meantime bided their time, began revolutions, and accused the Church as an institution and the clergy as individuals of all manner of acts against the public weal. Occasionally they were put in a position where they could vent their spleen. For three months early in 1847, Valentín Gómez Farías acted as president; in order to prosecute the war against the United States he demanded from the Church a loan of 15 million *pesos*. The archbishop flatly refused to make the loan on the plea of no funds, and Gómez Farías found his position untenable; he gave up the office. The Church won this round, but the anticlericals could say with good reason that the Church had proved to be unpatriotic since it had refused to aid the desperate effort to repel the invaders.

As the position of the Church seemed to become firmer under consecutive governments which supported its pretensions, and as it grew in wealth, its spokesmen became all the more arrogant. When, for example, a liberal politician pointed out that the priests charged a fee of 20 *pesos* to perform a wedding service for a workman who earned only 50 *pesos* a year, an official Church publication rejoined with the snide observation that the Church and only the Church had the authority to establish the fees, that the 20-*pesos* fee was justified, that no man should marry until he had saved enough for the service, and that if the workman had to borrow money at hard rates in order to pay, the fault was the borrower's and not the priest's. In other questions of a social or economic nature the hierarchy demonstrated the same highhandedness. When questioned concerning its wealth, variously estimated as between 300 million and a billion *pesos,* Church spokesmen countered with the observation that the wealth of the Church was of no public concern, that the money was needed to give dignity and prestige to the institution and to its priests, and that the money was well used. When charged that the money was not well used for economic development, and that greater economic benefit would come from the secularization of Church properties, churchmen replied that a dissipation of Church property would wreck the economy inasmuch as all agricultural, commercial, and industrial activity was maintained only through the use of Church funds. And yet, a survey of schools in Mexico City in 1851 disclosed, the clergy supported only two schools with a total enrollment of less than 500 students.

Small wonder, then, that when the anticlericals finally did regain control after the Revolution of Ayutla in 1854, they took drastic action. To the liberal the Church was the greatest stumbling block to any kind of progress, political, social, or economic. Correctly or incorrectly they believed—and with a passion—the Church to have fought republicanism and fostered monarchy, to have toadied and ministered to the privileged classes while it exploited the humble, to have robbed the poor to uphold the rich, and to have connived and fought to keep all but a few in abysmal ignorance. The archbishop, as one traveler phrased it, "carried in his hands the treasures of heaven and in his money bags the material that moves the world," but he used both to preserve stultification rather than encourage progress. Miguel Lerdo de Tejada and Benito Juárez dominated, intellectually, the new government which seized control, and Juan Alvarez had led most of the troops who won the battles against the older regime; that Juárez and Alvarez were both pure Indian indicated that social change was occurring regardless of conservative desires.

The liberal government moved into Mexico City in late 1855. It approached the problem of the Church with less haste and better planning, but with more thoroughness, than that of 1833. Within two years a series of decrees and a new constitution attempted to destroy the Church's temporal power by forcing it to sell all its real property not used for strictly religious purposes, by seriously impairing the exercise of the *fueros,* by establishing a civil registry for births, deaths, marriages, and religious vows, by removing the cemeteries from Church control, and by requiring the clergy to perform the various sacraments even when the citizen could not pay the fees. Perhaps more important than these positive acts was one failure to act: the Constitution of 1857 remained mute on the question of Catholicism as the protected cult and thus opened the way for the inroads of religious toleration.

Neither the clergy nor the pro-clerical accepted these acts without a struggle. Even before the constitutional convention met, but after the passage of some of the anticlerical laws, revolts began in various parts of the country; in each of these armed outbreaks the clergy played a prominent role. One rebellious movement centered in Puebla was so clearly supported, financially and intellectually, by the bishop there that the government exiled him and confiscated some Church property in his see to pay the costs of suppressing the insurrection. After the convention completed the new constitution, that body required every public official to swear allegiance to it; the clergy replied by refusing to administer the sacraments to any man who took such an oath unless he abjured it, or to any individual who acquired ownership of any property which had belonged to the Church. But clerical objection did not limit itself to those provisions dealing specifically with the Church; the Bishop of Michoacán listed freedom of speech, freedom of the press, freedom of assembly, the right to vote and popular sovereignty, all included in the constitution, as being contrary to the laws of God and Church. A few lonely clerical voices spoke in favor of the constitution, but the uproar of the opposition drowned them out.

The hierarchy asked for, and received, papal support; Pius IX minced no words:

> For the purpose of more easily corrupting manners and propagating the detestable malady of indifferentism and tearing souls away from our Most Holy Religion, it [the constitution] allows the free exercise of all cults and admits the right of pronouncing in public every kind of

> thought and opinion. . . . We raise our Pontifical voice in apostolic liberty . . . to condemn, to reprove, and to declare null and void the said decrees and everything else that the civil authority has done in scorn of ecclesiastical authority.

Urged on by papal wrath and episcopal nudging, a great segment of the populace roared its disapproval. The result was inevitable: a new revolution.

The three-year War of the Reform, beginning in late 1857, pushed Juárez into a position of leadership which he continued to hold until his death fifteen years later. During it the malice, the hatreds, the fears, and the frustrations of the contending parties sought surcease in wanton destruction. Juárez's party shot priests and lay brothers, gutted churches, and burned sacred images; pro-clerical generals, particularly the Indian Leonardo Márquez, executed prisoners, confiscated liberal wealth, and destroyed liberal properties. Driven to desperation by open clerical fiscal and moral support to the rebellion, Juárez decreed in 1859 even harsher anticlerical measures: the outright confiscation of all real Church property, the immediate suppression of all monasteries and a prohibition against novitiates in convents, the abolition of tithes, and a stipulation that all marriages be civil contracts rather than religious sacraments. Finally the exhausting war came to an end when Juárez's troops marched into Mexico City on January 1, 1861. The clerical forces had been defeated, but they were not beaten; they continued to harass the government in myriad ways. In one final desperate move they invited the French to aid in the establishment of an empire with Maximilian at the head; this phase lasted until 1867 when, as the last act of a vicious and beastly war, Juárez attempted to wash Mexico clean with the blood of Maximilian and his closest advisors.

The Church-state struggle was now presumably at an end, and the principles for which Morelos stood had won. All the paraphernalia supporting the retention of a highly stratified society, of special privilege, had been theoretically swept aside along with all the legal blocks to free investigation and a free society. The unrelenting struggle of over forty years' duration eliminated, the Juaristas thought, the Spanish colonial social system. But they were wrong.

The forty years' turmoil may have undermined to some extent the traditional class structure, but it also helped create a social evil. The viciousness of much of the warfare, coupled with a dollop of colonial inheritance and a simplistic conviction that independence meant license, made of Mexico a violent land, its people as undisciplined and as unpredictable as its volcanoes. The bandits who infested the highways and interrupted commerce were only a small part of

> The bands of robbers [which] were counted by the dozens, and their deeds, real or imagined, would fill volumes; but it is certain that the people felt that they were everywhere and that they would never disappear.

A San Luis Potosí newspaper in 1868 remarked that

> There is not a center of population in the country, no matter how small, which does not complain of the multitude of robbers who infest the roads.

But this multitude of violent men did not limit their activities to highway robbery; in groups of from five to a hundred they raided villages, attacked *haciendas,* kidnapped men, women, and children. In 1869 a Pachuca editor insisted that

> every day some remedy is more urgent; every day the ill becomes more dangerous; the society lives in a constant state of alarm. . . . Now the people talk about an *hacendado* whose body was found in the woods, then of a merchant whose whereabouts is unknown to his family; now of a rich property owner who ransomed his liberty with gold, but left his health where he left his money.

A Guadalajara journal estimated in 1868 that from 800 to 1000 men terrorized the immediate environs of that city, and five years later the first of four daily issues of a new newspaper reported, in succession, an attack on a small town, the sacking of an *hacienda* nearby, the robbery and burning of an *hacienda* with its nearby mill, and finally the experiences of a group of Sunday strollers near San Pedro Tlaquepaque:

> It was about five in the afternoon; the sun's rays, red as fire, bathed the treetops, when the strollers spied a band of from twenty-five to

> thirty men which soon came up to them. The women commended themselves to heaven . . . the children cried . . . the men disposed themselves to be sacrificed without a struggle. The robbers fell on them like wolves on their prey; a moment later, the women were perfect Eves and the men complete Adams.

Crimes of violence were not limited to the countryside; every city had its share of daring robberies and daily murders. The prison of the Acordada in Mexico City served not only as a jail for the living but as a repository for the unidentified dead; a visiting foreigner described it:

> In the front of one of its wings a low-barred window is constantly open, and within, on an inclined plane, are laid the bodies found daily within the limits of the city. It is almost impossible to take your morning walk to the adjoining fields, without seeing one, and frequently two corpses, stretched bleeding on the stones. These are the victims of some sudden quarrel, or unknown murder during the night.

Deliberate crimes of violence—murder for profit, robbery, kidnapping—are common to any country at any time, and a high incidence could be expected in Mexico in view of the economic conditions and the long military campagins. But violent action not deliberately planned, nor for personal profit, was characteristic and not limited to any particular social class. The economically destitute were probably more prone to such action, but members of the highest strata in the society frequently resorted to force to settle petty differences of opinion; even the august halls of the constitutional convention in 1857 witnessed at least one bit of pistol-play. Physical action, not logic, was often the arbiter, and public officials took the view that such actions were mere social gaucheries and not crimes against society.

In other respects the society which emerged from the excruciating experience of the previous half-century differed little from that at the beginning. Education had made some faltering progress in both method and number of students, but in spite of a large percentage increase, the school situation presented a picture of utter misery; in 1844 less than 5 per cent of school-age children attended any school, in 1857 about 12, and in 1874, after herculean efforts, about 16. Roughly half of these attended free schools, and the vast majority lived in the major cities. Education had scarcely made a dent despite the liberal emphasis on free public instruction. At the same time social distinctions between the various classes remained just as wide even though some bridges had been formed. Said one European with respect to the Mexican population:

> According to Mexican terminology, they are divided into two kinds, the reasonable and the unreasonable (*gente de razon y gente sin razon*), and although these two species are to be found in all quarters of the globe, and in every climate, the latter predominating, the Spaniard has his own ideas on the subject, and considers the men of his peculiar race alone endowed with reason, the red-skins being denied it.

Attitudes die hard, as the present struggle for Negro rights in the United States so amply demonstrates, and the mere fact that principles of equality now appeared in the public documents did not mean that the creole had suddenly taken the Indian and the *mestizo* into his heart. The forty years of struggle had established the principles of equality, of voting rights, of public education, of social mobility, and all that maze of abstractions which allows a man to move freely from poverty to affluence, from pariah to honored member of society as his capacity warrants; but it would be more than forty years more before those abstractions became realities.

Chapter 8 • The Age of Porfirio Díaz

The white race is the most active, the most intelligent, in a word the most civilized, and has been for ages and is presently the leader of progress and of human knowledge in all branches of science.

E. M. DE LOS RIOS, 1889

The Northamerican, the foreigner, has prospered in Mexico, but not its own sons.

REGIS PLANCHET, 1906

The Mexican social, economic, and political leadership came out of the long series of wars with a curious optimism, as though all the major issues had been settled and the only job at hand was to create a viable nation which could take its rightful place in world affairs. And in this optimism later ages could find some justification. A minor rebellion in 1872 upset the nation for a moment, a successful *putsch* in 1876 brought Porfirio Díaz to the presidency in the wake of brief but sharp fighting. Little niggling military movements of one kind or another disturbed the country for a time—that of 1879 was famous—but the dominant characteristic of the next forty-odd years was, comparatively speaking, blissful peace. Even banditry disappeared under a combination of hammer blows by government forces and the attraction of government hand-outs. Furthermore, the nation not only succeeded in getting out from under the crushing foreign and domestic debt, but developed a credit rating as favorable as any nation in the world by 1900; the treasury consistently showed a surplus.

Briefly stated, the prevailing attitude differed little from that of the colonial period, and even those who came from the ranks of *mestizos* and Indians became infected with the virus: Mexico had untold wealth, the land produced marvelously, and the great mass of the people, particularly the Indians, in their worthlessness held up progress. The mass of the population, according to most official doctrine after about 1880, could not and would not work efficiently, they were dirty and vicious and lazy, they had to be taught obedience, they would not save money because they were drunkards, and whatever wage they received was probably more than their productivity deserved. The only salvation for Mexico lay in attracting Catholic European immigrants whose industry and intelligence would transform the land. An examination of certain aspects of social and economic policy will demonstrate the depth of the conviction and its consequences.

Every responsible leader in Mexican public life at one time or another expressed his concern with the appalling mortality statistics. In 1893, 439 of every thousand live-born children died before reaching the age of one; in the state of Aguacalientes the figure reached the unbelievable height of nearly 800, and even in Mexico City the number was a frightful 323, as compared to London's 114 and Boston's 120. The national death rate exhibited the same incredible situation; it never sank below 33 per thousand each year, in some states it reached the dizzy height of 60, and the lowest ever achieved in Mexico City (43) almost tripled that of the United States for the same year. Life expectancy, quite naturally in view of these data, was abominably low. In 1895 life expectancy in Mexico City was little more than half that of the average of the major European cities and considerably less than half that of Paris or London. Most areas in Mexico had a higher expectancy than did the capital city, but the national average in 1910 barely passed 30, while in the United States it had reached 50. Worst of all, the statistics in virtually every realm of national health indicated a deteriorating condition during the last decade of the period, while in almost every European country, including Spain and Italy, conditions improved.

With a great stirring and much oration, congress after congress and convention after convention went into the question of public health, explaining the reasons for the conditions and seeking to find ways to improve them. All commentators agreed that lack of sanitation, poor diet, poor housing, and related factors were responsible. One perceptive doctor pointed out that filthy bodies and clothes could be expected among the poorer classes when

> soap would cost about 25 per cent of their income; and a greater proportion when we speak of women and children who earn only 15 or even 10 cents a day. There are still in all our major cities, streets filled with naked children, thin, tobacco colored, with enormous bellies and as timid as the savages of Polynesia.

The 1910 census classified 50 per cent of all Mexican houses as *chozas,* virtually unfit for human habitation, but Matías Romero insisted that even these substandard habitations in the countryside were preferable to the crowded urban conditions, with sometimes as many as 20 people occupying a single room. A survey of Mexico City in 1900 showed that 16 per cent of its people (15,000 families) had no home; they slept where they could when they could.

Doctors and public health men talked, Church officials consulted, editors commented, government officials conducted surveys and occasionally introduced laws, but when it was all over their activities had been so ineffectual as to be puerile: drainage of Lake Texcoco (which took nearly twenty years to complete instead of the projected three), controls over the sale of pulque, a stab at vaccination for smallpox, and some unenforced public sanitation laws. Those men concerned with the expenditure of money and the establishment of policy, however, took heart in the fact that the heaviest mortality rates were found in those areas of indigenous concentration in the central part of the nation, and that the lowest rates came from the northern border states and the coast, where the Indian population constituted an insignificant proportion of the total. Since "everyone knew" that the nation could expect "nothing, absolutely nothing," from the Indian population, according to one newspaper, it seemed useless to attempt a solution of the health problem. Most of the "elite" recognized the correlation between lack of education, low wages, unsatisfactory housing, disease and mortality rates, and poverty, but this class assumed poverty to be the controlling constant, and poverty to be a function of the nature of the mass. The poverty-stricken Mexican was poor because he wanted to be poor, because he had neither the intelligence nor the ambition to escape from the condition.

Telésforo García, among whose many properties included a small estate of nearly two million acres in Chihuahua, expressed this Mexican interpretation of Social Darwinism well. He first justified night work in cotton mills on the ground that such work kept the laborers out of the *pulquerías,* and then went on to prove, to his own satisfaction, that at the prevailing wage any worthwhile mill-worker could save enough in ten years to retire. He then concluded that if the workers were chronically short of money it was their own fault. García's computations include some curious facets, since they were based upon a monthly wage of 160 *pesos* and assumed a possible savings of 1000 *pesos* a year, while a 1900 survey of eleven textile mills in Veracruz indicated an average daily wage of something less than a *peso,* and other data indicated an average daily cost of living of about a *peso* per person. But to men of the mentality of García any talk of attempting to solve the health problem through improved living conditions, improved wages, and mass education was pure heresy.

This same antediluvian view could be found respecting other aspects of the society as well. Nine of every twenty children born in Mexico came from unions illegal under Mexican law, and in Mexico City the rate of illegitimacy reached the scandalous proportion of two in every three. Some came from marriages performed by the Church but not by the civil government, which made them illegitimate; some came from casual liaisons and concubinage; but most came from common-law unions which a combination of high clerical fees, official red-tape, and poverty dictated. They were, in essence, the product of a correctable social and economic situation, but the government generally took the view that by nature people of the "lower" class indulged in promiscuity and that the condition could be rectified only by encouraging the European to inundate the Indian and *mestizo* populations.

Since it was an article of faith among the elite that immigration was necessary, the government seriously undertook to attract the foreigner to Mexico. The Díaz period was contemporaneous with one of the greatest population movements in the history of the world; during those thirty-five years millions of Europeans surged out of their native lands in an ever-increasing flood, seeking opportunities wherever they might be. For most European emigrants the United States was their target; in 1882 nearly 1800 a day arrived at the east coast ports, and in 1907, the peak of the movement, the number arriving daily almost doubled that figure. The Mexican official, still believing in the incredible wealth of his nation, thought he could divert a major portion of the migrant flow to his own country and in the process not only improve Mexico's economy but also mitigate the dangers coming from the north. Immigration to Mexico, said one pompous official,

> would add to the population, thus increasing its number; their greater physical, intellectual and moral vigor would initiate the process of enrichment and, with time as they mixed with the autochthonous population, they would improve the population qualitatively.

And, according to a number of surveys made by the government, Mexico suffered a serious labor shortage, particularly in the richest agricultural regions. In Morelos, the *hacendados* complained, the labor shortage resulted from "indolence, vagrancy, and a complete lack of attachment to work" on the part of the population. Landowners insisted that potential rural workers left the countryside for the urban centers, where they swelled the number of poverty-stricken and added nothing to the national economy. Their solution, had they been allowed their way, was simple: a return to the forced labor practices of the colonial period which the Constitution of 1857 outlawed. But at the same time they wished to encourage immigration, since "a hundred thousand [immigrants] would be worth five hundred thousand Indians." One Mexican so denigrated his own countrymen that he stated categorically, in 1907, that the 5 million Argentines were "worth more" than all the 14 million inhabiting Mexico. But the *hacendados* cried not alone; urban employers made invidious comparisons between the Mexican and the foreigner. Matías Romero calculated that the U.S. worker on the average could produce four times as much as the Mexican, and in some kinds of work as much as ten. One economist, using a scale of 100 as the productive capacity of the English worker, placed the Mexican Indian at 25 as compared to the 50 to 80 of the Hottentots and the 40 to 70 of the Zulus; how he arrived at these figures for the African indigenous population he failed to stipulate.

Whether the Mexican worker was in fact so inferior to the non-Mexican is impossible to ascertain. Those who busied themselves making the accusations expressed conclusions arrived at by osmosis rather than analysis, and apparently never took into consideration the incredible differences in technology. The Oaxaca Valley farm laborer, following a pair of oxen dragging a wooden plow, could scarcely be compared to the U.S. midwestern farmer using a gang of six horses pulling a three-shared steel moldboard sulky plow, nor could the Mexican reaper with his sickle and cradle be compared to the neighboring country worker riding a McCormick reaper or a steam-powered combine. The U.S. farmer discovered during this period that his total production costs could be cut by 50 to 80 per cent through the utilization of the machine, but the Mexican *hacendado* could not see his way clear to purchase the equipment. He found it more comforting to blame his own economic retardation on the working population, and believed that the importation of European labor would solve all his problems.

Immigration to Mexico never reached the proportions so ardently desired by the government. Official policy gave many advantages to the foreigner; he could come freely, he could become a citizen easily, he could occupy national lands at a low price, and, under certain circumstances, he could import material needed for his work without paying the heavy customs duties. Furthermore, the foreigner in Mexico, whether resident alien or mere traveler, found many doors opened to him which were closed to the nationals; even the president made himself available for interviews with casual tourists. Occasionally a foreigner who became particularly obnoxious would be asked to leave the country, but in such cases the government always took pains to make it clear that the act contained no hint of xenophobia and that foreigners in general were doubly welcome. As a consequence of this fawning attitude foreigners did indeed come to Mexico; Matías Romero in 1890, reporting to the Chamber of Deputies, expressed his satisfaction "on seeing foreigners as owners of high finance, of credit institutions, of the electric power plants, of the telegraphs, of the railroads and all those things which signify the culture and the progress of Mexico." Sometimes a member of the establishment would become somewhat concerned with foreign influence; José T. de Cuellar sourly predicted that foreigners would acquire

> the merchant marine, the railroads, the industries, the mines, the commerce, and even the national territories.

Official policy continued to put emphasis on the value of foreign, rather than native, influence. The foreigners responded to the preferential treatment; in 1896 they paraded through the streets of Mexico City as a manifestation of their gratitude, and in 1899 Telésforo García led a delegation of the wealthiest to call upon Díaz and urge him to remain as president for the term beginning in 1900. Grateful though they might be, the foreigners in fact came only to gain a momentary economic advantage; the European laborer and farmer failed to see the attractions which the Mexican government so earnestly pushed, and he stayed clear of that country. The low wage scales, urban and rural, could not compare with those of Canada or the United States, or even Argentina or Brazil, and the immigrant sought those countries by preference. In 1895 the census takers counted a few over 48,000 foreigners living in Mexico; by 1900 the number had increased to a mere 58,000, and at the end of the period to about 116,000.

Not only did the immigrants constitute an insignificant part of the total population, but from the Mexican point of view they did not come from the most desirable countries. Citizens of the United States, to whom many Mexicans objected violently, headed the list, with the Spanish, Chinese, and British following in that order; immigration from other countries was negligible. One-fifth of the new residents could neither read nor write, only one-tenth devoted their energies to agriculture, and probably 50 per cent could not speak Spanish and had no intention of learning. A goodly portion, particularly from the United States, were not immigrants at all in the proper sense of the word; they were footloose adventurers with neither trade nor money, taking advantage of the favorable climate of official opinion to make an easy living. According to one newspaper, these mendicants filled the air of the Alameda park with their whining supplications, in broken Spanish, for a few *centavos;* the same paper feared that Mexico City was "becoming the human cesspool of the United States."

Immigration, then, tended to be divided into three great sections. One group consisted of the Chinese brought in as contract farm laborers to Sonora and Sinaloa; most of them soon abandoned farm day labor and either obtained small tracts of land on their own account or moved to the cities where they became small merchants, particularly in foodstuffs. By the end of the period this group had dispersed throughout northern Mexico but tended to congregate in or near cities such as Hermosillo, Torréon, or Chihuahua. Their presence, and their inability or unwillingness to assimilate, later created a serious social problem as they became the victims of persistent and often violent persecution. The second group, probably close to a majority, consisted of single men whose prime object in going to Mexico was to escape work, not to find it; they offered, and gave, nothing to Mexican economic or social development. The third group, far removed from the first two, were men to whom Mexico appeared as a fertile field for economic exploitation, a nation from which could be extracted sufficient wealth to allow comfortable retirement in the homeland. By and large this group contributed materially to economic development, but in a very real sense it never became Mexican. The government's dream of attracting to Mexico a vast stream of European migrants whose energies would make the land bloom and whose greater capacities would invigorate the Mexican population turned out to be just that: a dream unattainable. Mexico's immigration policy, in the words of a modern Mexican author, "failed completely."

It did more than merely fail of reaching its goals; it set in motion the development of a xenophobia which generated a nationalism that reached alarming, and at times ridiculous, proportions after 1910. The patent favoritism displayed by the government toward anything foreign irritated an ever-growing number of young men who felt themselves frozen out of many economic endeavors. Official pandering to foreign economic and social appetites provoked young Mexicans whose own economic interests suffered as a result. The incessant din of denigration cut to the quick men sensitive of their Mexican birth. By 1910 many Mexicans felt that Cuellar's dire predictions—that Mexico would become the creature of the foreigner—had come true, and when these men seized control of the government they wrote into the new Constitution and into law a rampant economic nationalism.

The utter contempt, and at times fear, which the elite demonstrated for the mass of the population fostered actions little short of criminal against those on the lower rungs of the social and economic scale, and since seven of every ten Mexicans lived in rural regions the agrarians suffered most. The opening wedge against the small landowner, particularly the Indian, appeared in 1883 in the form of legislation for the survey of national lands. These national unoccupied lands, the *terrenos baldíos,* constituted an unknown quantity, and certainly the government needed an accurate survey to determine the extent of its holdings. But the legislation for the survey opened enormous possibilities for all manner of shady operations. According to the law, any organization could obtain from the government a contract for surveying; as payment, the surveyors could select one-third of the land surveyed. The other two-thirds would remain with the government, which, under the same law, could sell the lands at a fixed price to companies or individuals in blocks no greater than about 6000 acres. Both purchasers and surveying companies were required, under the law, to maintain as "colonists" at least one person for each 500 acres of the land obtained. Within nine years various companies surveyed almost 100 million acres, of which over 30 million acres went to the surveyors and another 40 million to private individuals and companies. As his part for the surveying, added to by purchases of obvious illegality, one individual obtained nearly 12 million acres in Baja California and other northern states. Another received over 3.5 million acres, and still others from one to three million.

But even this government largess did not satisfy some of those hungry for big estates; in 1894 they sponsored a change in the surveying legislation which relieved the new landholders of the responsibility for maintaining the "colonists," and struck out the clause limiting the amount of land which could be bought by one individual. One of the legislators, who himself had acquired in Baja California nearly 3 million acres (an area only slightly smaller than Connecticut), argued that the limit imposed by the earlier legislation should be removed because it was ineffectual—that landowners could get around the law through fraud. His arguments were persuasive; the Chamber of Deputies dispensed with the regular rules of procedure and gave unanimous approval, and a short time later the Senate followed suit. The way was now cleared for the final assault. By the end of the Díaz period the government had divested itself of an area roughly equal to that of California, or equal to the combined totals of Ohio, Indiana, Illinois, and half of Kentucky; the land alienated constituted nearly one-fifth of the total land area of Mexico. In return the government received a bungling surveying job which left as many titles in doubt as it clarified; it also collected about 9 million *pesos*—slightly more than three and a half cents per acre. To be sure, most of the lands acquired were in the extreme north and the far south, where the nature of the terrain and climate made land values low, but in 1908 the average value of the lands in the ten states most heavily affected by the surveying laws was estimated to be about 2 dollars an acre.

The extent to which fraud and force permeated the surveying practices can never be known because local judges tended to throw out of court all cases questioning the validity of surveying companies' decisions concerning "vacant lands." If we judge by the number of protests coming from communities and small landholders, the surveyors intruded on lands long held by others. From Jalisco, Durango, Guanajuato, and a dozen other states came a clamor that surveying companies dispossessed legitimate landowners; the charges began almost as soon as the first law became active and lasted until the outbreak of the Revolution of 1910. Even men in high government positions succumbed to the temptation to obtain good lands by the simple expedient of declaring them vacant; Minister of Fomento Olegario Molina, in 1909, acquired over 5000 acres of land bordering his *hacienda* in Yucatán even though the land was occupied and worked by both community and private holders. The law provided that lands which had been occupied by Indians and "poor" workers for at least ten years, or for at least a year before the first law went into effect, could not be declared vacant, even though those occupying the land had no valid title. But in all cases the burden of proof lay not with the surveyors but with the man who occupied the land, and if the surveyor declared the title to be invalid, or the occupation to have been less than the minimum, it remained for the dispossessed to take his case to court. The costly judicial process, and the notorious favoritism shown by the judges, frequently stimulated recourse to direct action rather than law, but power was on the side of the surveyor or the "denouncer." Only in the case of the Mayos and the Yaquis of the northwest did force give a breathing spell; but even here the government ultimately won.

The surveying legislation opened the way for many abuses, but in the major centers of population concentration—the central region including Morelos, Mexico, Puebla, and the contiguous states—the activities of the surveyors had little effect. Here the lands had long been clearly occupied, and, even though some greedy men attempted to make a case for *tierras baldías,* it was generally conceded that these states had no vacant lands. This condition did not exempt the Indian communities and small landowners from a loss of property, however, for the great latifundists used the prevailing temper to encroach on adjoining properties. José Ives Limantour, one of Mexico's outstanding statesmen during the Díaz regime, was accused of taking lands belonging to others; the governor of Veracruz aided his friends in absorbing the lands of a number of villages; and 65 villages in Puebla claimed that the neighboring *hacendados* had despoiled them of their lands. In Morelos by 1910 the great sugar plantations were dotted with the ruins of abandoned villages, the huts rotting among the growing cane. The villagers of Yautepec in that state went to court to protect their lands from a neighboring *hacendado,* only to find themselves the objects of heavy fines imposed by the judge for daring to question the integrity of the great landowner. Emiliano Zapata, who became the scourge of the landed elite after 1910, was one of those who lost. A Kickapoo chieftain of Coahuila, it is said, called on Díaz to protest the loss of village lands to adjoining *haciendas.* Taking his seat next to the president on a bench, the earnest Indian pleaded his case with increasing vehemence, pressing against the dictator with such force that he gradually pushed Díaz completely off the seat and caused him to tumble to the floor. Thus, said the Kickapoo to the startled Díaz and his advisors, did the *hacendados* deprive the Indians of their legitimate lands. The records are filled with cases involving claims by small landowners and by communities that their lands were being taken from them, sometimes by brute force, sometimes by depriving them of a water supply, sometimes by taking advantage of legal quirks, sometimes by fraud and sometimes by threats. Most government spokesmen, of course, insisted that the *hacendados* were more sinned against than sinning, and pointed to the great number of additional private holdings registered in 1910 over those of 1877 as evidence of the general improvement of land-tenure patterns. Emilio Rabasa contended during the Díaz period, as he continued to assert in publications after the Revolution began, that the Indian population continually took over *hacienda* properties for their own use and that the only land problem which Mexico had was one of preventing the landless from illegally seizing property belonging to others.

While some men were gobbling up huge tracts of land through the surveying laws and others by encroachment, the Indian communities were beset by other laws and practices. The Constitution of 1857 had stipulated, as a means of encouraging private ownership and the development of a sturdy peasant class, that lands held in common by villages be distributed in fee simple among the villagers. Between that date and 1900 both the national government and most state governments passed laws aimed at effectuating the distribution; the general result was chaos rather than equitable distribution. Some villages sold even the village streets and parks and plazas either because the elders misunderstood the law or because they could profit personally. Other village officials sold all the lands, illegally, to nearby *haciendas,* and still others distributed the common lands among the residents but failed to register the new titles and therefore left the lands open to denunciations. Other new landowners, ignorant of the meaning of the paper giving title to the land, sold the titles for a pittance and therefore legally lost their lands. Some villages, on the advice of not always honest attorneys, formed corporations and issued stocks which gave the individuals rights to work the land, but too often the stockholder had no clear idea of the meaning of his share. Most Indian villages resisted as best they could the pressure to distribute the land, and many villages in the central states which had owned common lands in 1850 still owned them in 1910, but they were under tremendous pressure to complete the distribution. One bitter critic of the entire process insisted that the breaking up of village lands had served merely to benefit a few government officials and a handful of others who took advantage of the confusion to enrich themselves.

To sum up the results of porfirian land policy poses some difficulties, largely because of poor definitions in the census reports and because of the often exaggerated charges and counter-charges. But some tendencies were perfectly clear, and they presaged serious difficulties for the future. In the central states, with the heaviest population, the great *haciendas* and the communal villages existed side by side in bitter conflict, with the vast majority of the agrarians being landless and held in debt peonage on the *haciendas;* one estimate, probably exaggerated but certainly indicative, placed the percentage of landless peasants at 90 in Mexico, Morelos, and parts of the adjoining states. In the far northern states the communal village scarcely existed, but here the percentage of debt peonage was significantly lower. In all of Mexico only 57,000 titles of individual land holdings existed in 1910, representing slightly less then 2 per cent of the total population in a nation in which the great majority were agrarians. Most of these private properties fell into the undefined category of *rancho* of indeterminate size, but generally observed to have been small holdings giving little more than subsistence to a man and his family; two-thirds of these private holdings were acquired after 1867.

At the opposite extreme were the truly great *haciendas*. One in

Coahuila, before being divided up among members of the family or sold to foreigners late in the Díaz period, covered an area greater than the state of Oaxaca. One railroad line in the state of Hidalgo traversed over 80 miles of land belonging to one family. One estate in Durango occupied more than a million acres, and one in Zacatecas nearly two. One *hacienda* in the state of Mexico owned over 500 square miles of land. Three *haciendas* in Colima claimed ownership to about a third of all the land in the state, and four *haciendas* in the larger state of Michoacán owned one-fourth of all the property. According to one report, thirty-two families in Morelos owned virtually all the land in that heavily populated agricultural state. The average size of the Coahuila *hacienda* was roughly 20 square miles, that of Tlaxcala and Puebla a little less than 10, and those in Yucatán slightly smaller; the national average fell at about 11.5 square miles, or about 7,500 acres. But the extent of the individual *hacienda* tells only part of the story, for many families owned various *haciendas,* either in the same state or scattered around the country. Luis Terrazas in Chihuahua, for example, owned a series of *haciendas* totaling nearly 5 million acres, and the combined acreage of the Martínez del Río family in Durango and Chihuahua passed 4 million.

The fantastic concentration of land caused sufficient irritation on its own merits, but the manner in which the land was used—or not used—aroused deeper animosity. Most of the big *haciendas,* even those with magnificent extensions of arable land, left a large portion of the soil to lie fallow year after year, the *hacendados* refusing to cultivate it themselves or to allow others to do so on a rental basis. As a general rule the *haciendas,* with some notable exceptions to be sure, continued the same primitive agricultural technology which their owners had inherited from their forebears. Rare indeed was the great landowner who experimented with new varieties of basic crops, or used commercial fertilizers, or invested in the bewildering variety of new farm machines sweeping across the United States. The *hacendado* did indeed change his farming pattern in a most conspicuous fashion, one which accrued to his own financial benefit but which exaggerated the deep malaise attacking the Mexican countryside: as interior transportation facilities improved with railroad construction, and thus opened foreign markets, the agriculturalist tended more and more to produce export crops. The change put the nation's submerged classes on the ragged edge of starvation for the first time since the middle of the colonial period.

In every major category of food supply for the mass of the population, the Díaz period showed a decline in production in spite of the 50 per cent increase in population. Corn, the mainstay of the vast majority, fell from a high of about 2.5 million tons in 1877 to less than 2 million in 1910; on a per capita basis the decline was an almost disastrous 50 per cent. In 1810, when the revolution for independence began, total corn production gave the average Mexican two pounds of corn a day; a hundred years later, at the end of the Díaz regime, he had scarce fourteen ounces. Bean production in 1892 fell to about 40 per cent of that of 1877, rose slightly during the next decade, and then declined by 1910 to a figure of about 75 per cent of that of thirty years earlier; on a per capita basis, bean production at the end of the Díaz period was about one-fourth of that at the beginning. Peppers, the third great staple of the Mexican poor, maintained a relatively even production (except in years of unusual drought) throughout the period, but the per capita consumption fell in proportion to the population increase. Even wheat, consumed primarily by the upper classes, declined to such an extent that in 1910 imports constituted nearly a third of the total consumption. The total of all comestibles, in fact, fell off during this period; for her own population, the nation produced in 1910 about 85 per cent of the tonnage she had produced in 1877. Imports of foodstuffs, though considerable and increasing toward the end of the period, failed to compensate for the fall in domestic production. The conclusion is inescapable. The vast mass of the population ate less of the basic agricultural products in 1910 than they had in 1877.

Inasmuch as many of the kingdom-size *haciendas* devoted their major energies to pastoral activities (Terrazas in Chihuahua was reputed to graze more than half a million head of cattle and a quarter million sheep), one would expect a significant increase in the consumption of beef and other animal products. But such was not the case. Per capita consumption of milk and cheese remained roughly the same, and very low in comparison to the United States or the Western European countries. The number of cattle, sheep, and goats slaughtered for the domestic market did indeed increase, but not as rapidly as the population. In 1877 the annual average of beef consumption was about 30 pounds, supplemented by 4 pounds of meat from sheep and goats; in 1910 beef consumption had fallen to 26 pounds while mutton and its ally had risen to 5. The low level of butchering did not reflect meat-market prices, which rose by 50 per cent in the last two decades.

One set of comestible items did increase faster than the population; the four alcoholic beverages coming from the maguey plant (*tlachique*, pulque, mescal, and tequila in that order of quality and price) as a group more than doubled while the cheapest of the group quadrupled. Some *hacienda* owners, catering to the increased demand for the drinks, made major investments in plantations and processing plants. It would appear, in fact, as though the only realm of major investment for the production of comestibles for the domestic market came in the production of alcohol.

The nature of the relationship between the increase in alcoholic consumption and the decline of other comestibles may be debated, but the shops in Mexico City reflect the prevailing conditions. In 1864 the capital had 51 *cantinas*, but at the turn of the century the city denizens could take libations from any one of 1300 bars; at any given moment it would have been possible to crowd about one-fifth of the total population into its drinking parlors. In contrast, 34 bakeries furnished the entire city with its bread. For every three milch cows in the environs of the city, the capital supported two shops selling alcoholic beverages. One journalist in 1895 calculated—without making clear the source of his data—that on the national average the Mexican spent nearly 30 per cent more per year for alcohol than did the Dutch in spite of the vast difference in average income, that the Mexican consumed 30 per cent more than the French, and that among the alcoholics the death rate was nearly three times as high as that in England. At about the same time a doctor who devoted his time to demography as well as medicine gave the death rate due to alcoholism as six times that of France. Over-consumption of alcohol may have created social problems, but it made a booming business for those farmers who specialized in its production.

In spite of the absolute decline in domestic comestible production, Mexican agriculture in general flourished; increased production of industrial raw materials more than compensated for the loss in comestibles. In 1877, 86 per cent of all agricultural production found its way to Mexican tables; by 1910 the proportion had declined to about sixty. In those years the percentage going to Mexican plants processing non-food items increased from 10 to 18, and the proportion shipped out of the country changed from four to twenty. Using 1877 as an index year of 100, domestic comestible production in 1910 stood at roughly 87, but the combination of raw material for domestic consumption and materials for export had risen to about 126. Among the exports figured an increased proportion of comestible items; garbanzos, beans, sugar, coffee, beef, and other such items, none of great importance in itself, constituted 10 per cent of the total exports of the nation even though the per capita consumption of comestibles declined. In short, relative to the population, Mexico in 1910 produced less food and exported more.

The major concentration of agricultural effort for the domestic processing plants and for the export market revolved around the production of non-comestibles. The increasing demand for sisal fiber in the world market brought a frenzy of activity throughout the nation, but it was only in Yucatán that the henequen plantations dominated the countryside. Sisal production demonstrated many of the worst features of the Díaz economic and social system. The enormous wealth which could be amassed from the world henequen market, as an incident to the development of the corn binder, stimulated wide-scale planting on the peninsula; the craze for the profitable fiber virtually destroyed the cattle industry there, and as a result the region suffered from a chronic shortage of meat during the second half of the period. High profits from the fiber demanded extensive acreage, which in turn pushed the Yucatecan *hacendado* to encroach on his neighbors; one authority has estimated that the producers illegally dispossessed between 60 and 70 Mayan villages of nearly a third of a million acres of land. The brutality of the dispossessions further alienated the already hostile indigenes and gave incentive to a chronic state of rebellion. The military campaigns caused a great number of Indians to flee, creating an acute labor shortage which was intensified by the crude and dangerous machines built to separate the fibers from the leaves. The labor shortage in turn gave rise to the vicious system of "contract labor," a euphemism for what most contemporaries described as a veiled form of bondage in which the employer accepted none of the responsibilities usually associated with the institution of slavery. By 1910 the situation was little short of scandalous, but the peninsula was far from the center of government, accessible only by boat from Veracruz, and could therefore be conveniently ignored by the governing elite.

Yucatán was in no way unique except in degree. The drive for export products, and the items which these could bring in exchange, characterized all of Mexican agriculture; so did extensive land use and human exploitation. The general attitude led one Mexican newspaperman, with great irony, to propose a new creed as a substitute for the time-honored expression of Christian faith; he may have had the henequen growers in Yucatán in mind when he wrote:

> I believe in the Almighty golden ounce, creator of all good and of all evil, in the bank note, his only son, our Lord, who was conceived by the work and grace of the spirit of necessity, who descended to Earth and saved from anguish those unhappy poor who were awaiting his saintly advent, and who ascended into the skies and is seated at the right hand of the Almighty ounce. From that position he will descend again to give succor to the poor and to the rich. I believe in the small bill, in the ancient peseta, in the communion of speculators, in the pardon of all the sins of the counting-house, and in everlasting negotiation.
>
> Amen.

Mexican agriculture, geared to a slowly developing industrialization and to an export market which the world monetary situation made doubly profitable, helped produce a facade of brilliance. The great *haciendas* gave an aura of wealth and gracious living; the landowners determined economic policy, set the standards of social intercourse, graced the exclusive Jockey Club, entertained foreign emissaries, and talked learnedly on every subject from the Greek classics to the philosophy of Auguste Comte. Virtually every major figure in the political or intellectual world—or at least every figure not frowned upon by the ruling elite—counted himself a landowner: Pablo Martínez del Río, Enrique Creel, Bernardo Reyes, Ramón Corral, Olegario Molina, José Ives Limantour, and Rosendo Pineda were among those active in the intellectual or political world. But with all this apparent brilliance, agriculture had little vitality. Total agricultural production, according to the calculations of Luis Cossío Silva, increased only a bit more than 21 per cent between 1877 and 1907; during those same years the population increased nearly 40 per cent.

Pastoral activities paralleled agriculture in many ways, even though the growth rate well exceeded that of the population. Cossío Silva summed up the attitude of the cattlemen; they raised their cattle, he said, in an

> extensive and uncared for manner, characterized by the use of few hands. The owners, curiously enough, esteemed them more for their apparent value—size of land holding and number of head—than for their real return.

The actual number of cattle increased about 75 per cent to a total of something over 11 million, but slaughter increased only by about 37 per cent. At the same time, a larger proportion of cattle sold reached the export market; in 1877 such sales represented scarcely 1 per cent of the total, but by 1897 a quarter of all cattle sold were destined for foreigners. In the last ten years the proportion declined but continued to be high as compared to the earlier years. As was the case with agriculture in general, the people of Mexico saw little additional benefit accruing from the pastoral growth.

In another way the experiences of cattle growing equated well with agriculture. In spite of sporadic attempts by a few individuals to import blooded cattle (an annual average of 13,000 in the last five years), "a fondness for routine or for the easy solution" prevented any real improvement of the herds. By 1910 an estimated 94 per cent continued to be scrawny range animals producing neither milk nor meat in quantity; the average animal slaughtered for the domestic beef market produced only a little more than 300 pounds of meat as compared to the 600 or 700 pounds coming from the Argentine animal. In spite of an enormous world demand for good meat, and despite the establishment of packing houses in Uruapan, Monterrey, and Veracruz, the stringy Mexican beef could not compete on the world market; meat exports continued to be negligible.

The number of sheep declined between 1877 and 1910, and the pastoral pattern changed to some degree. At the beginning of the period a major portion of the nearly 6 million sheep was in the hands of independent herdsmen, many of them Indian, who paid the landowners a small fee for the privilege of running the flocks. The animals were maintained primarily for the wool they produced, with most of the wool being used locally by artisans working in small shops; the woolen goods so produced scarcely entered into the national market economy. Sheep-raising, as a consequence, was widespread throughout the country and furnished more than enough wool for domestic consumption; exports of fleeces grew rapidly until in 1891 the maximum of about 1500 tons was reached. But three factors combined to change the pattern: the weight and quality of the fleeces, the changing pattern of land tenure, and the growth of a significant mechanized textile industry. Poorly tended and poorly fed sheep, as well as poorly bred sheep, produce a coarse fiber which is uneven in its thickness and elasticity. Toward the end of the century sheep-breeding and -raising in other parts of the world, particularly in the United States and Australia, eliminated Mexican raw wool from the export market; U.S. and Australian sheep produced fleeces three or four times as heavy and of much better quality. At roughly the same time the domestic mechanized textile industry began to expand, and the inferior Mexican wool could not be handled by the European-built machines designed to process the better wools.

The mills then began to import both raw and combed wool to meet domestic demands; the annual imports reached an average of about

1000 tons in the late years of the nineteenth and the early years of the twentieth century. The artisans in their small establishments, using inferior domestic wool, could not compete with the better products coming from the mills at a cheaper price, nor could they compete with the increasingly popular cotton goods. As a consequence total wool production decreased from nearly 5000 tons in 1878 to slightly more than 3000 in 1910.

To add to the sheepman's miseries, the great drive for the alienation of national lands and the increasing concentration of landownership left less land available for him to herd his flocks. With the decline of the wool market, sheep then became more profitable as a source of meat than as a source of wool; this in turn tended to concentrate the sheep close to urban centers where a greater market could be tapped. The ten years following 1891, for example, saw a decline in Zacatecas from over 2 million to less than half that amount, in Veracruz from nearly half a million to about 45,000, and in Oaxaca from over a quarter million to some 60,000. By 1910, the total number of sheep had declined to something less than 4 million, but a much higher proportion of the total reached the mutton market, with the result that the total meat produced increased by about 25 per cent. But, as was the case with cattle, the slaughtered animals tended to be small, producing only about a third of the meat which an Argentine, Australian, or Canadian animal rendered, and to be two or three times as old as slaughtered animals in other countries. The combination meant inefficient meat production.

Goat-herding differed materially from the development of sheep-raising. Exportation of goat skins which grew in both relative and absolute terms, came to be a matter of some economic significance in the late years. The great expanses of semi-arid land in the north which could frequently be used more advantageously for the raising of goats than of cattle or sheep, the high prices the skins brought on the international market, and the greater proportional value of the skin over the meat as compared to both sheep and cattle combined to stimulate major production for the export market. In the thirty years after Díaz came to the presidency the number of goats more than trebled to reach a total of nearly 7 million, the annual slaughter nearly trebled to reach a mark of a million and a quarter, and the proportion of hides reaching foreign markets increased from 73 to 98. Meat of the slaughtered animals of course increased, but meat production constituted a by-product of little value because of its quality; nevertheless, goat-raising was highly profitable for those who entered the traffic on an extensive scale.

The changes in Mexican agriculture during the period of the Díaz regime were made possible, or even dictated, by the most clearly seen change in economic facilities; the railroad came to the nation at last. Following the period of relative calm after the final defeat of the Maximilian imperial endeavor, a little flurry of railroad building resulted in the construction of a line from Veracruz to Mexico City and a few short feeder lines, the total amounting to about 400 miles. During the four-year period of the first Díaz administration, 1876-80, the government laid the real base for rail development, but not until after some major decisions had been made.

Two great problems confronted the government regarding rail construction, one fiscal and one psychological. Despite the friendly mien of the United States during the French intervention, most Mexicans were highly suspicious of U.S. motives and intentions toward them. The Mexican War still rankled, and the attempt on the part of the Washington government to wrest from Díaz a number of concessions as the price for recognition irritated the Mexico City officials beyond measure. Mexican officialdom, consequently, had its heart set on building rail lines with a basic east-west orientation, connecting the two oceans in such a manner that the interior parts would be interconnected and with access to both the Atlantic and the Pacific. Most officials, including a majority of the Congress, looked with almost paranoic fear on any rail construction which would tie the Mexican heartland to the United States. Not only did they fear the military potential of such lines; the Mexico-Veracruz line, financed and built by the English, had taught them that heavy foreign investment in rail construction brought with it an enormous influence by the investor. A generalized and mild xenophobia, therefore, became particularized against rail investors from the United States.

At the same time, while rail construction needed heavy investments, experience had shown that the potential Mexican investor preferred to use his funds in other ways. In a long and acrimonious debate in the Mexican Congress in 1878, one deputy thought he knew why the Mexican did not invest in railroads. It was not a lack of patriotism, he said, as he cited the heroism of all classes against foreign invaders; nor was it the absence of available money, since he could name a group of five men who could organize a corporation with 20 million dollars in capital. Neither did it come from an absence of entrepreneurial interest, for where money is to be made men will invest. But, he said:

> The sole reason, the true reason, the crux of the matter, that which must always be confronted when dealing with this class of enterprise, *is the interest rate*. In England and in Holland the maximum rate is 3% annually; in Mexico any capitalist can lay his out at 12%. The average return on a railway investment is 6%. Given these three figures, the following consequence is inevitable: the capitalist there who earns three is almost certain to want to earn six; but he who here earns twelve will never lower it to this six. Then if this is the reason why the Mexican capitalists do not put money in these enterprises, we are reduced to the conclusion that the money must come from abroad; and if we must always have the susceptibilities which have been stressed on this occasion, we must renounce from this point forward any hope of railroads.

Whether the legislator was right regarding the reason for the failure of Mexicans to invest—and on this there is grave doubt, since the cattleman certainly did not earn an annual return of 12 per cent on his investment—the experiences of the time gave validity to his conclusions. Since individuals did not come forth with the money necessary to build the roads, the national government experimented with two other methods, neither of which proved of real value.

The federal government itself, at the urging of Mariano Téllez Pizarro, and under the direction of Minister of Fomento Vicente Riva Palacio, decided to build some roads on its own. According to the plan, the national government was to pay the direct costs of construction and equipment, operate the road on its own behalf for a year, and then either sell or rent the road to private individuals at a cost well below the actual outlay. In this manner, so the theory ran, the state itself would give the necessary stimulus to construction but would not become involved too heavily in railroading. The original intent was to begin by the construction of a series of feeder lines to the Mexico-Veracruz road, thus connecting to the port and to the capital a number of communities which had been on the old highway but were now left isolated. The first, and only, section actually contracted for and constructed was the short 32-mile stretch connecting Tehuacán and Esperanza on the main line. Ordered in August 1877, the narrow gauge, mule-powered line opened two years and four months later, the government opting from the beginning to allow Téllez Pizarro to operate the line on a rental basis. Even though the costs of construction were modest and the work was completed within the expected time limit, the administration abandoned any further direct building.

In the meantime, Riva Palacio experimented with another system of stimulating construction; the national government gave concessions to the states to construct roads. The terms differed in detail but followed a pattern. In each case the national government guaranteed a subsidy, ranging between 6000 and 13,000 *pesos* a mile, and the state in turn offered additional subsidies to groups of individuals who would carry out the actual work. In each case Mexico City stipulated the terms and rates of construction; failure to comply with the terms would mean cancellation of the concession. Further, in each case the government specified the rates which could be charged for various classes of goods and passengers, but also forgave various taxes as a means of reducing costs. The states became enthusiastic over the idea. Guanajuato received the first concession in late 1877 to construct a line from Celaya to León, passing through Salamanca, Irapuato, Silao, and Guanajuato. Nineteen other states followed suit in obtaining concessions for 27 different short lines, and it appeared as though some significant building might ensue. But the results proved to be disappointing. Of 28 concessions, the national government cancelled eight for failure to act and allowed another twelve to continue in force even though the states undertook no actual construction. On eight of the concessions some work was performed, but by the time Díaz left office in 1880 the total mileage added through this program was a modest 140, about half of which was accounted for by the states of Morelos and Guanajuato. The concessionaires used various gauges, some of the lines were completely isolated, and much of the construction was abominable. On the Mexico-Cuautla line, for example, the first train dumped about 300 men in a ravine when a bridge collapsed, and subsequent trains were subject to "continuous derailings." State construction was hardly the answer for major rail development.

Even before the state program had proved to be less than wildly successful, the national government finally decided that the nation must depend upon foreign money and foreign concessionaires. As early as mid-1877 a group of U.S. financiers petitioned for a concession to build a road connecting Guaymas with Nogales, Arizona, but the Mexican Congress refused to approve this concession or any others similar to it for another three years. In the face of Mexican financial and political realities, however, the Congress finally succumbed and gave the administration almost blanket authority to grant concessions for the construction of lines tying in with the rapidly developing system on the United States side of the border. Díaz granted three major concessions, all roughly equivalent, in late 1880 for the construction of lines by U.S. companies. In each case the national government voted generous subsidies, required the companies to construct lines traversing the country east-west before completing the north-south lines, set the maximum rates which could be charged, established a rate of construction, allowed the introduction of railroad materials duty free, and required the companies to make their peace with the state governments before proceeding with construction. These three contracts signed between September 8 and 14, 1880, established the groundwork for the "great push" in railroading during the following four years.

Of the three major companies the Central, with a multitude of concessions which when consolidated committed the company to build a road from Mexico City to El Paso, Texas, with an east-west line connecting Tampico with some point on the Pacific, proved to be the most efficient in its building program; the 15,000-*peso*-a-mile subsidy helped. Starting at both ends of the Mexico-El Paso line even before the government actually signed the concessions, Central engineers pushed construction at a rate almost unbelievable to the Mexicans and far in advance of the contractual provisions. The concession stipulated completion of the connection with El Paso in a minimum of ten years, but on March 8, 1884, forty months to the day of signing the contract, construction workers drove the last spike near Fresnillo; two weeks later the first international train departed from Mexico City, bound for Chicago, to traverse the 1231 miles of the Central line. But the Central failed, in fact, to conform to the contract. The original concession demanded completion of the line between the Pacific and the Gulf prior to the completion of the line to the north; construction actually began at San Blas on the Pacific and Tampico on the Gulf, but these were token efforts, since the company constructed only 25 of the roughly 600 miles of line necessary to connect the two oceans. When Díaz went into exile in 1911, the two ports were still unconnected.

In its great rush to complete the line connecting central Mexico with the United States, the Mexican Central was competing with another concessionaire; the Mexican National also obtained a series of concessions to connect the capital with the United States and to construct lines connecting the Gulf and the Pacific. The National, even though it maintained a fabulous rate of construction by previous standards in Mexico and stayed well ahead of its contractual schedule, fell far behind the Central. Forced to suspend construction for a short time in 1883 because the Mexican government failed to deliver its subsidy on time and because it was unable to find funds in depression-stricken United States, the National did not complete either its north-south or east-west connections by the time the Central drove its final spike at Fresnillo. But by the time Díaz again came to office in late 1884, the National had built over 700 miles and had opened the line between Saltillo and Laredo.

The third major concession committed the Sonora Railroad Company to connect Guaymas with Nogales in the northwest, and to build a line to the east to intersect the Central. Following the pattern established by the two larger companies, the Sonora completed the Guaymas-Nogales route but failed to drive to the east.

A number of other concessionaires moved onto the railroad scene. Stimulated by the frenzied building of the three major lines, and financed by both Mexican and foreign funds, some old and some new companies began driving lines in all parts of the country. No one company could claim any great victory in construction, but the combination added another 700 miles to the more than 2000 miles laid by the big three. The total was indeed impressive. Starting with less than 700 miles of track in 1880, Mexican railroads operated nearly 3600 at the end of 1884. Four lines connected ports of entry on the United States border (Nogales, El Paso, Eagle Pass, and Laredo) with parts of the interior, giving access for these regions to all parts of the United States. No east-west line connected the Pacific with the Gulf, but construction had begun at Manzanillo, San Blas, and across the Isthmus of Tehuantepec. A major railroad network, nearly two-fifths of which was narrow gauge and some of which used animal power to be sure, was in the making.

For the next twenty-five years construction continued, sometimes at a fabulous rate and sometimes at a limping pace, depending upon the availability of capital and the fortunes of competitive enterprise. From a high of over 1000 miles in 1887, which surpassed even the enormous growth of 1883, to a low of 13 miles in 1895, the construction rate fluctuated wildly. But the lines pushed in every direction. Building at an average rate of well over 300 miles a year, the roads by 1910 operated over 12,000 miles of line, of which well over three-fourths was standard gauge. Most of the major cities and productive areas were interconnected, the Tehuantepec line traversed the Isthmus, one line led to Guatemala, and seven U.S. ports of entry tied onto lines leading into the Mexican interior.

Furthermore, a series of consolidations allowed for efficiency of operation and for the interconnections of previously separately owned lines. And then, in the final days of the Díaz period, the government sponsored the creation of a new company, the National Railways of Mexico, which absorbed about 60 per cent of the existing lines; the government itself became the major stockholder of the new company, with central offices in Mexico City and with a purely Mexican charter. The Díaz regime (including the González interregnum) could be pardoned for boasting of its great success in the railroad field.

But all was not roses in Mexican railroading. Serious questions could be raised concerning the fiscal validity of the manner in which the government gained control of the National Railways, since the stocks it held paid no dividends and the price it paid exceeded the probable value. Toribio Esquivel Obregón went so far as to charge that the government could have obtained outright ownership of the lines and the rolling stock at a cost far below that paid for the non-dividend-paying stock alone. Furthermore, the enormous debt undertaken by the government in bringing about the consolidation and control left the nation in sorry financial shape once the income from the lines failed to meet the obligations of the debt service. Even more critical, perhaps, was the helter-skelter manner in which the companies laid out main lines and constructed branches. In spite of the Mexican government's early hopes that the railroads would connect the east and west coasts prior to connecting the interior of the nation with the United States, the lines actually served better as a pipeline from the Mexican interior to U.S. markets than they did as a stimulus to interior marketing and economic development. A shipment of goods from Mazatlán destined for Durango 100 miles away would have been forced to make 1000-mile trip via Nogales, El Paso, and Torreón; small wonder that few men interchanged goods between the two cities. By the same token, any goods produced in the northwest had to traverse roughly the same route to reach a market in Mexico City; the northwest, including the Sonora mining communities, was more intimately connected, by transport and communications, to the United States than to Mexico City. Of the west coast ports only Manzanillo, with its rail line running through Colima and Guadalajara and thence to the Mesa Central, could serve as a port for the interior without involving killing costs. And the Yucatán Peninsula remained isolated from the remainder of the country except by ship. On the other hand, the economy of the country or of the region hardly

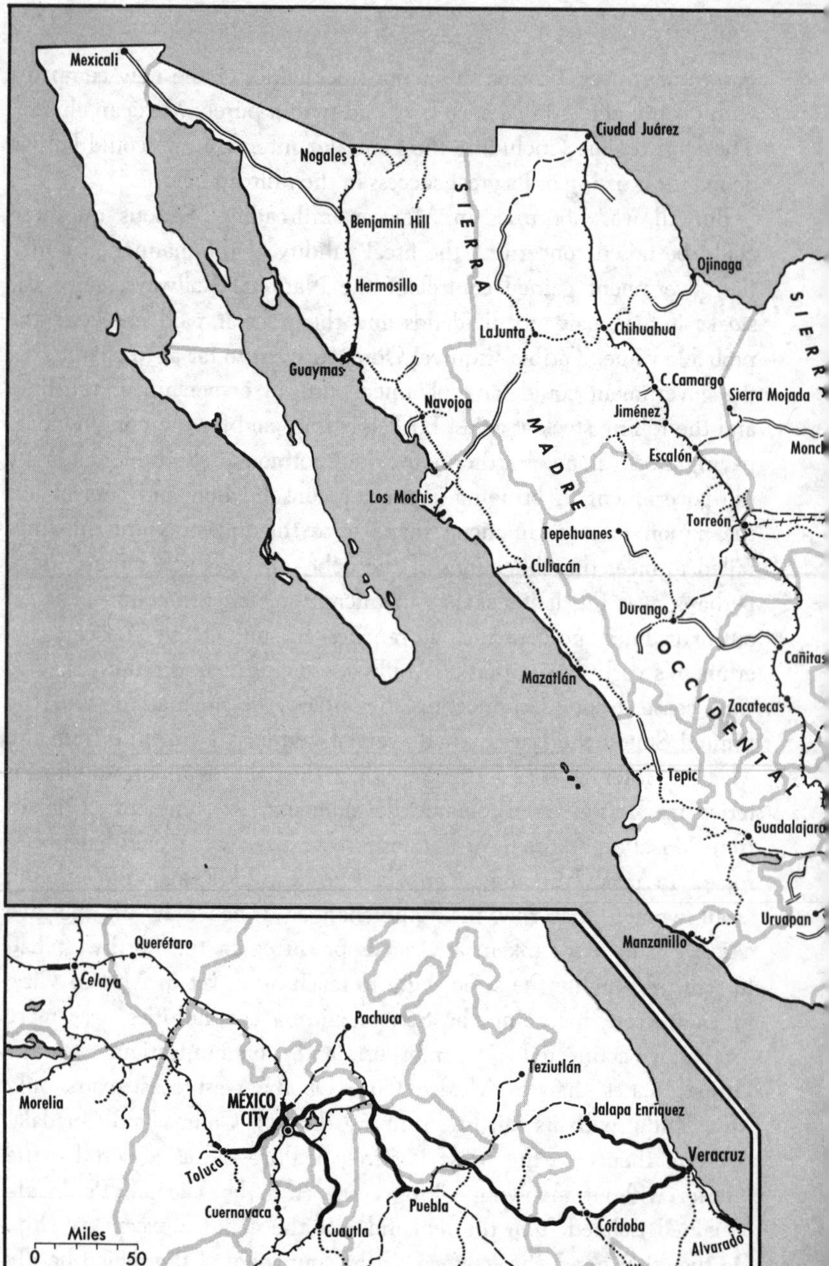

Mexicali
Nogales
Benjamin Hill
Hermosillo
Guaymas
Navojoa
Los Mochis
Ciudad Juárez
Ojinaga
Chihuahua
LaJunta
C. Camargo
Sierra Mojada
Jiménez
Escalón
Torreón
Tepehuanes
Culiacán
Durango
Mazatlán
Cañitas
Zacatecas
Tepic
Guadalajara
Uruapan
Manzanillo
SIERRA
MADRE
OCCIDENTAL
SIERRA
Querétaro
Celaya
Pachuca
Morelia
Teziutlán
Jalapa Enriquez
MÉXICO CITY
Toluca
Veracruz
Cuernavaca
Puebla
Córdoba
Cuautla
Alvarado
Miles
0
50

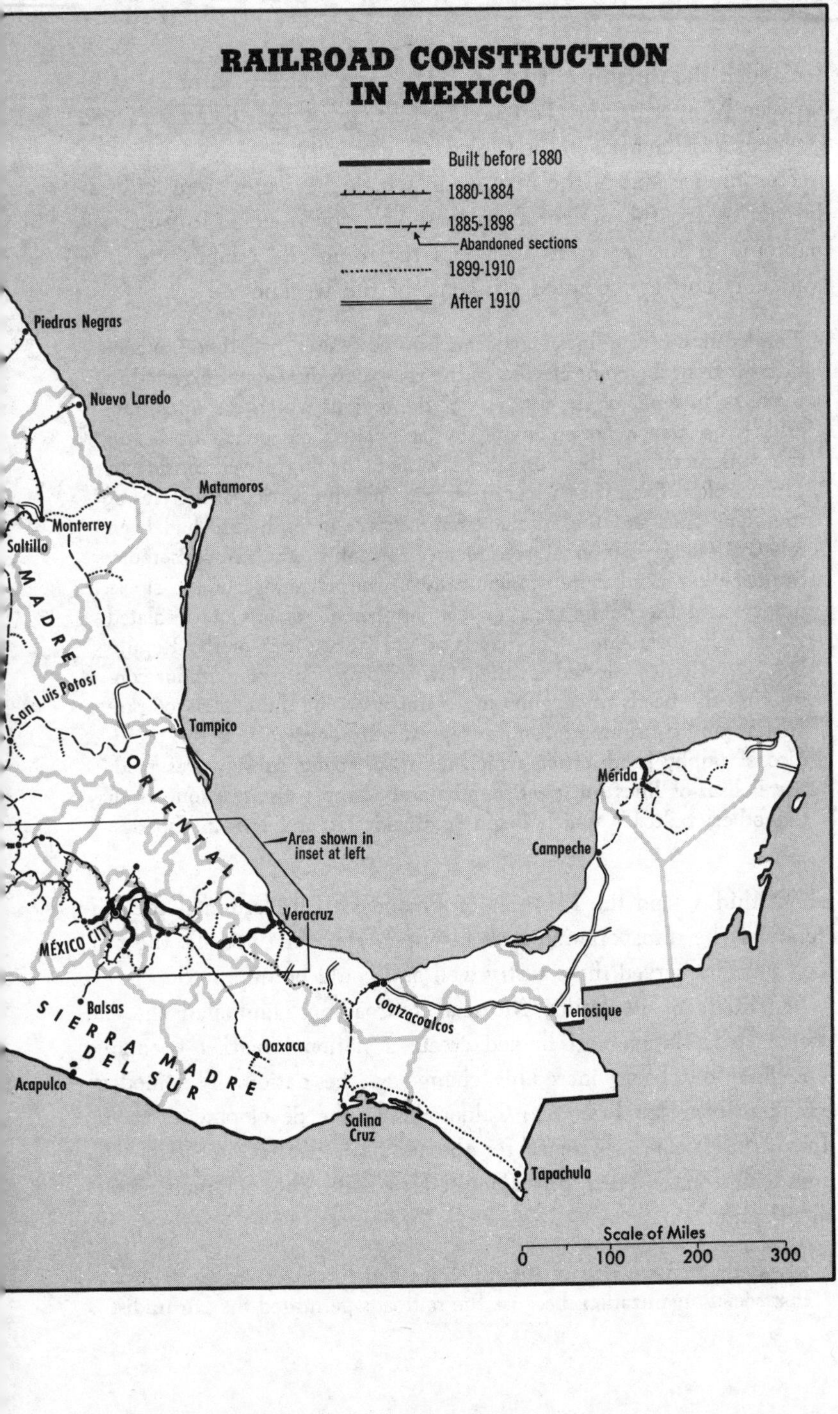
RAILROAD CONSTRUCTION IN MEXICO
Built before 1880
1880-1884
1885-1898
Abandoned sections
1899-1910
After 1910
Piedras Negras
Nuevo Laredo
Matamoros
Monterrey
Saltillo
MADRE
San Luis Potosí
Tampico
ORIENTAL
Mérida
Area shown in inset at left
Campeche
Veracruz
MÉXICO CITY
Balsas
Coatzacoalcos
Tenosique
SIERRA MADRE DEL SUR
Oaxaca
Acapulco
Salina Cruz
Tapachula
Scale of Miles
0
100
200
300

demanded the three parallel lines, in a band scarcely 40 miles wide, between Monterrey and Torreón, or the two between Salamanca and Querétaro, or the maze in the Mexico City vicinity.

The implications of the manner in which the routes were laid out did not escape the notice of many in the government. In 1908 Limantour, in his report to Congress regarding the establishment of National Railways, pointed out some of the weaknesses:

> The location of the lines leaves much to be desired, whether one considers it from the point of view of the return on the capital invested in them, or in terms of the interests of the regions which the lines traverse. Every day we resent more the lack of wisdom in having begun the construction of the trunk lines without having a well-considered general plan. Even if as a matter of principle the particular motives of the companies and the special circumstances of each case had been relegated to a position of secondary importance, the railroads today could be exploited more economically to the advantage of the stockholders and the public, and a great number of regions now isolated would have been united by bands of steel to the rest of the Republic. . . . Routes selected for their low construction costs without considering the needs of neighboring countries or of the centers of production and consumption; lines exaggeratedly developed to the prejudice of public funds, from which a per kilometer subsidy was paid; parallelism of lines for great lengths and at short distances one from the other; railroads which begin in the desert and end in the desert; . . .

These things, said the Minister of Finance, all undermined the efficiency of the transportation system, but in spite of these ills the railroad network served the country well and could be improved.

Regardless of its faults, Mexican railroading eliminated the old pockets of isolation and helped create a national market economy. The lines did bring incredible change to the nation. The modern economic historian Francisco Calderón sees the developments of the lines as a crucial experience for the nation, since, even though the lines could have been better located to serve the dominant social organization,

> it was the construction of the rail lines which accelerated the fall of that social organization, because the railroads permitted the latifundist

> to enter into an exchange economy with more lucrative products which took the place of those of popular consumption, with the result that the rural masses saw their real income reduced while the wealth flowed to the small number of big landowners.

The development of adequate lines of transportation affected not only the latifundist's pattern of production, but that of the fabricator as well; by the end of the Díaz period the nation appeared to be on the verge of developing an industrial economy. Rail lines facilitated the shipment of the varieties of raw materials necessary for industry, and allowed wide distribution of manufactured goods. In 1877 a textile mill owner in the vicinity of Mexico City paid about 61 dollars to ship a ton of cheap cotton goods to Querétaro, but in 1910 he paid only a little more than 3. The expanded market possibilities stimulated the concentration of capital in industrial enterprises, which in turn tended toward urbanization with its greater demand for goods produced by others. But other conditions also favored industrial development. The national government, in 1896, was at last able to enforce a provision of the 1857 Constitution forbidding interior custom houses; the *alcabala* finally came to an unmourned end and commerce found itself "free of an old oppression." The national government continued to maintain high custom duties as both a fiscal and a protective mechanism, thus giving an additional stimulus to industry geared for the national population. Furthermore, the weakening of the communal groups and other more or less self-sufficient communities destroyed in good part the auto-productivity of a large segment of the population, thus creating demand for manufactured goods. On top of all these, the gradual decline of the *peso,* pegged to silver, in the international market not only encouraged foreign investment but also served as an additional protective device against foreign competition.

The combination of factors most markedly influenced the textile industry, which grew enormously, but it also affected other segments of the economy as well. One contemporary claimed that city workers provided themselves with "articles of food, of clothing and of housing all, or the greater part, products of the country." The per capita purchase of industry-made cloth increased by a quarter in the decade of greatest prosperity, and the per capita consumption of refined sugar (in contradistinction to the earlier more popular loaf sugar) grew by 50 per cent. Nationally produced items of the cheaper categories of food, drink and clothing, and of some chemicals, metals, and cement, tended to displace the foreign product. In the case of cheap cottons, the share of the market for imports declined from 32 per cent in 1889 to 3 in 1911.

But the consuming habits changed, if they changed at all, in the opposite direction among the upper classes. Along with the denigration of their own nationals' ability to work or produce, and the great emphasis on creating a favorable climate for foreign investment, members of the upper class took on most of the trappings of the Europeans and the North Americans. One writer lamented the aping of foreign ways so apparent among the wealthy; he noted, with some acerbity, that

> the owners of our spinning and weaving mills do not wear the shirting [*manta*] or the cashmeres which their factories produce; they generally dress themselves in European textiles, they use European or American hats, they lay out money for European or American carriages, they decorate their houses with European art objects, and prefer, in short, everything foreign over the national; even the painting, the literature and the music with which they satisfy their desires and divert their leisure time have to carry the foreign seal.

The extent of true industrialization during the Díaz period depends upon definition. The physical volume of manufactured goods doubled, and the proportion of the export goods which had been in part processed, particularly among the metals, increased significantly. The hand spindle and loom which the artisan used to convert raw cotton to textiles all but disappeared; in 1878 over 35,000 bales of cotton found their way to the hand looms, but after 1900 a bare 6000 were so used. Paper mills furnished Mexicans with their own paper; the steel mill in Monterrey produced pig-iron, steel ingots, bars, beams, plates, and rails; and in 1910 Mexican cement plants furnished builders with nearly three times as much cement as that which had been used ten years previously. From Mexican factories came hats, shoes, tiles, glassware, soaps, furniture, cigarettes, beer, flour, and a great variety of other items. These developments, plus the fact that over two-thirds of the total new investment in industrial processes came from Mexican capital, gave the nation good reason to believe that it had achieved an important degree of industrialization.

A closer look shows the industrialization to have been more apparent than real. The textile industry specialized in cheap goods and could not tap the market for the finer materials; total textile importations roughly equaled the national product in value. The paper industry could not meet the needs for the finer papers; the value of imported paper surpassed by two times Mexican exports of manufactured goods of all descriptions. Imports of beams, plates, rails, and other metal materials for construction in the declining years of the period roughly trebled domestic production, and the cement industry could supply the nation with only half its needs. The other items of manufacture could not meet domestic needs; soap, for example, came in increasing quantities from foreign sources in spite of the national industry. But a more telling index of the real lack of industrialization can be found in the utilization of the labor force. The proportion of the working population devoted to "manufacturing" prior to 1895 cannot be ascertained, but the three censuses of 1895, 1900, and 1910 show a slight decrease in the proportion of the labor force in manufacturing and a gradual increase in agriculture. By 1910 those in manufacturing constituted slightly less than 11 per cent of the labor force, while those in agriculture made up more than 64. Furthermore the last decade, one of mild economic crisis in part brought on by conditions in the United States, witnessed such a declining rate of manufacturing growth that the per capita production remained static; after 1907 many items, including textiles, declined not only proportionately but absolutely.

And industrialization, such as it was, came at a high cost. One of the great benefits to be derived from industrialization, so marked in the United States and in the Western European countries in the last decades of the nineteenth century, was the reduction of prices, as mechanized factories poured forth their goods in quantities. In Mexico the net effect of the interplay of economic forces was the reverse. A slight decline in the price of some items of consumption produced nationally was more than offset by an increase in others and by a marked increase in the prices of most imported items. Wages in some sectors did indeed increase faster than costs of goods, but real wages in 1910 were markedly less than in 1877. Real wages, in fact, reached their highest point in 1897, then declined by about 15 per cent to the end of the regime. At the end of the Díaz regime the great mass of the population, despite the outward appearances of prosperity which the government paraded in the great centennial celebration in 1910, spent as many hours to earn a length of cloth, or a ration of corn, or a few peppers, as did their forebears four generations earlier. In fact, according to one analyst of the textile industry in the late years of the period,

> The lowest classes of the society, who literally live from day to day, . . . could divert none or almost none of their daily earnings to the purchase of *mantas* or other textiles, since it was necessary for them to sacrifice all to the imperious demands of eating.

An index of the utter destitution afflicting the great mass of the society can be found in the miserably low average annual expenditure for textiles of all the cheaper grades: 3 *pesos* a year.

The low real wages of society in general cannot be made the responsibility of the new industrial class in Mexico, but the working conditions can. Textile mill owners found that for many tasks a child could perform as well as an adult, and at considerably less daily wage. According to the British consul in the waning years of the nineteenth century, one-eighth of all textile workers were children, and Fernando Rosenzweig estimates that the same proportion existed for many other light industries. When a British traveler stated that in some mills the children were so small that they had to stand on boxes to reach the spindles, an industry mouthpiece refuted the statement by saying that "the majority employ children above the age of ten only." At whatever age, above ten or below, the industrial worker labored long at his task. Most laborers began their day at six in the morning, rested and ate during two 45-minute breaks, and completed their day's task at eight in the evening after twelve and a half hours of actual labor. Some mills, however, forced their laborers to remain at their tasks until nine or ten at night. For these twelve to fifteen hours work, a laborer received a wage ranging between 11 cents for an unskilled woman or child and 75 cents for a highly skilled metal caster. But all too frequently the wage earner did not in fact receive the money which his contract stipulated; most factory owners found ways to discount the salaries. The calendar set aside sixteen days as religious holidays in 1906, for example, and on these days the industrial concerns were closed; the worker received no wage for days he did not work, but this did not prevent the managers from holding out a part of the daily wage to pay the costs of "entertainment" during the holidays. Most factories maintained company stores and paid at least a portion of the wage in chits good only at those stores, where the prices generally stood higher than those in other establishments. Sometimes the wages were paid completely in chits, or in soap, or in other items of kind, or (after 1905) in nickel coin which was discounted at the company stores. Furthermore, every worker was held responsible for the care of his tools or his machine; any "carelessness" which caused "damage"—and the management defined the two terms —resulted in a docking of wages. In the textile industry the owners forced the workers to pay for any length of cloth coming through spotted or imperfectly woven; the workers complained that even when they paid for such damaged goods they did not receive them. The proportional wage loss as a result of a combination of these practices cannot be determined, but if we believe the frequent complaints of laborers and their friends it amounted to as much as 20 to 30 per cent.

Law, practice, and official attitude prevented the laborer from taking any effective action to improve his working condition, even to protecting himself against the verbal assaults of "brutal agents or excessively ambitious or cruel owners." Criminal syndicalist laws forbade effective labor organization; state and national government officials kept a close watch on labor agitators and maintained a close censorship of the press; and the owners discharged and blackballed individual laborers who objected too strenously and too often to specific practices. When the textile workers in Apizaco went on strike in 1898, the army forced them to return to their tasks and punished those who refused to follow orders. In 1906 the mill workers in the Puebla region demanded a series of reforms including a shorter working day, an increase in wages, compensation for injuries sustained while at work, some form of pension, and a cessation of the entire system of wage discounts and chit payments. The association of mill owners agreed only to limit the working day to twelve and a half hours and to "recommend" better personal treatment within the confines of the factory; beyond that they would not go, and Porfirio Díaz, who was asked to act as mediator, agreed with the owners' contentions. When the workers went on strike in January 1907, violence flared, and the national government came to the owners' rescue. Federal troops broke the strike and quelled the rioting, but only after shooting down hundreds of strikers. "Labor," a pompous government spokesman had said a few years earlier, "is subjected by an ineluctable phenomenon to the law of supply and demand." The government, according to the dominant theory in official circles, could not intervene in the relationship between management and labor—except, of course, when labor made the demand and seemed strong enough to win; labor was then subjected by an ineluctable phenomenon to the power supplied by the military.

In general, labor disorders were rare and no George Gallup took polls to determine the extent of labor dissatisfaction. The textile strike in 1907 and an earlier miners' strike in Cananea created sensations not only because of the brutality with which the strikes were suppressed, but because they seemed to presage a new development which would upset the economic and the social systems. In spite of a new emphasis in Mexican economy toward industrial change, the entrepreneur brought to his position a bit of cultural baggage which included the *patrón* mentality of the *hacendados:* the laborer was an essential ingredient in productivity, but the owner knew what was best for his worker and, in his infinite wisdom and kindness, distributed his beneficence to his peons. The worker could request, he could beg, he could supplicate with his hat in his hand—but he could not demand, for a demand would imply an equality which the upper class vehemently denied. To those few voices raised in protest, the dominant group could always point, with great satisfaction, to the economic development which had taken place under Díaz's tutelage.

One of the indices to which the official referred consistently in justifying economic policy was the growth of foreign trade. And indeed the increase was phenomenal, being about nine times as great in 1910 as in 1877 and increasing by four times in the last twenty years. In only two years of the thirty-three did exports fall below the previous year, but in each case the year following the slump registered a big jump. Imports were more erratic but showed a steady growth roughly paralleling exports. Perhaps more indicative of the changed economy was the changed status of the major export and import items. For the first time in history Mexican exports of precious metals in 1904 constituted less than half the total in spite of a threefold increase in silver volume and a fiftyfold increase in gold. Part of the decline in precious metal export value from nearly 80 per cent to about 46 of total exports can be accounted for by the disastrous drop in the world silver market which created such political turmoil in the United States; the value of silver export fell from over 75 per cent to less than 30. But at the same time the value of gold exports increased from less than 3 per cent to nearly 18, or from less than a million *pesos* to nearly 50 million. The value of gold, in fact, in 1910 was 50 per cent more than the total value of exports in 1877. The big change, then, came in both the absolute and proportional value of exports other than precious metals. The value of other mineral exports rose from almost nothing to 37 million *pesos,* agricultural and pastoral from less than 7 to over 100 million (one-fourth of which was henequen), and manufactured products from almost nothing to nearly 4 million. This change in export patterns, of course, reflected the improved transportation facilities which allowed the movement of goods having a low bulk value.

Import patterns followed somewhat the same trends, but with less dramatic differences. Every major category increased significantly in total value, and about half of them increased proportionately. The percentage of vegetable materials including comestibles fell from almost a third to less than a fifth, the proportion of alcoholic beverages declined by one-half, while that of paper decreased by one-sixth and the general category of arms and explosives fell by one-third, in spite of the increase in both military and mining activities. Textiles declined from about one-sixth to one-eighth of the total. Animal products, minerals, chemicals, machinery, vehicles and "diverse articles" all increased in percentage, with mineral products now topping the import list and machinery occupying third place in total value. Among the mineral products of greatest importance were processed or semi-processed iron and copper to be used for construction purposes, including railways.

In spite of Mexican fears of the United States, a combination of economic, geographic, and political factors bound the southern nation more and more closely to trade with its powerful neighbor. Rapid industrial expansion in the United States and a fantastic population growth there, together with rail connections to seven land ports of entry into the U.S. and heavy U.S. investments in Mexico, all tended to divert the exports from Europe, which in 1877 took nearly 60 per cent. At the same time, British failure to recognize the Díaz regime for some years after 1876 discouraged new British investments or more trade; while exports to Britain remained static until 1882, those to the U.S. increased by about 12 per cent. From that time forward, the British, who had been the only serious competitor with the United States for Mexican goods, ceased to make a contest of it. In 1877 the U.S. took 42 per cent of the Mexican goods and Great Britain 35; by 1901 the northern neighbor absorbed 82 per cent and Great Britain a meager 6. The British recovered a bit in the last ten years of the period, but in 1910 the figures read 76 to 12 in favor of the U.S. France in 1877 occupied third place as a customer with over 18 per cent, but by 1910 she had increased her purchases only slightly, and therefore her proportion fell to 3 per cent of the total. The remaining exports went to a number of countries, of which Germany was the most important.

Export statistics tell a story of economic frustration for the Mexicans. Many officials dreamed of a time when the remaining countries of Latin America, presumably bound to Mexico by linguistic and cultural affinity as well as by fear of the United States, would look to the northern Latin nation as a supplier of needed goods. But only in rare years did the other American nations buy any significant amounts; in 1877 these nations purchased slightly more than 1 per cent of the total, and in 1910 they accounted for a little less than 1.5 per cent. The entire export pattern attests to the lack of any real industrialization. Minerals, much of it in the form of ores and all of it coming from extraction rather than fabrication, still made up three-fifths of all exports; and the bulk of the agricultural and pastoral exports were unprocessed. Manufactured items, on the other hand, were of little greater consequence at the end of the period than they had been at the beginning. In 1910 the value of untanned goat skins exported roughly equaled that of manufactured items of all kinds reaching foreign markets.

The United States did not dominate the import market to as great an extent as it did the export, although it did sell more to Mexico throughout the period than the rest of the world combined. This pre-eminence is explained not in terms of any great longing on the part of the Mexicans for products manufactured in the United States, but by the simple fact that the heaviest purchasers of machinery, vehicles, chemicals, and mineral products were companies operating under U.S. management with U.S. financing, some of them tied in with firms in the United States producing the goods purchased. By the end of the period the U.S. furnished 55 per cent of the goods bought abroad, a figure not significantly different from the average of the last twenty-five years of the epoch. Occasionally, as during the depression of 1893-96, the proportion fell well below that mark and in one year it exceeded 66, but in normal years it ranged between 50 and 60. Great Britain and Germany vied for second place, with England holding a slight edge in most years, and France ran a consistent and sometimes a competitive third. Ironically enough, the nation purchased almost as much from the rest of Latin America as it sold there, and bought more from South America than it marketed in those countries. One final observation on foreign trade; in every year save one for which comparable statistics are available, the nation had a highly favorable balance of trade.

The enormous increase in foreign trade brought about a change in the relative importance of the old ports of entry and created new ones. Veracruz, which had always occupied first place and in 1877 handled nearly two-thirds of all goods entering or leaving, still held the lead in imports, but her export handling had so declined that Tampico took first position in total trade in the late years; the Tamaulipas port, after the completion of the railroads, was a much more convenient point for dispatching the goods from the north and the heartland. The land ports of entry such as Ciudad Juárez and Laredo drained some goods from the Gulf ports, but the combination of latter ports continued to dominate total trade; in 1910 the group handled well over 60 per cent of the mass. The cities along the international boundary with the United States registered slightly more than 30, the Pacific ports a little over 5, and the two cities on the Guatemalan border about three-tenths of 1 per cent.

Until 1905 the Mexican *peso* was pegged to silver rather than to gold, with the silver content equivalent to that of the old U.S. dollar and the colonial *peso*. As long as silver maintained its price in the international market, the U.S. dollar and the Mexican *peso* were exchanged equally, and much of the exported silver in the form of the *peso* found its way into Africa, parts of Asia, and much of Latin America where it circulated under the name of "piaster." After 1867 the Mexican gold producer could coin his metal freely, at a rate of 16.50-1 with silver, and for a few years the ratio was actual as well as legal, with no serious consequences for the nation's economy. But in 1871 silver began to fall on the international market. The decline brought reactions from many countries, including the demonetization of silver in Germany and the removal of the silver dollar from the coinage list in the United States—the famous "Crime of '73." The result was an accelerating decline in the price of silver and a fall in the value of the Mexican *peso*. By 1877 the *peso* was worth only 91 cents in New York, ten years later it had fallen to 79, and finally reached its low point of about 40 in 1903. The declining price of silver adversely affected Mexico because of the importance of silver production in its export economy, but the fall did give the Mexican industrialist an advantage as long as the *peso* remained on a silver rather than a gold basis; the silver *peso* acted as a built-in protection device against foreign competition. But in the first years of the twentieth century the fluctuations in the silver market began to cause serious disturbances in the Mexican banking world, and in turn undermined the general economy. The government therefore decided to change to the gold standard; in this decision the Minister of Finance José Ives Limantour received strong encouragement from an international commission dominated by the gold-standard countries.

The legislation putting the nation on the gold standard, at a *peso* value of one-half that of the U.S. dollar, went into effect in March 1905. The shift entailed a major reorganization of the fiscal, and therefore the economic, structure. Wages and prices determined by the silver standard had to be translated into a gold standard, and as a consequence the change had an impact on every inhabitant of the country. The new situation encouraged many of the banks to enter into wild speculative schemes; it stimulated an enormous increase in paper money which most citizens viewed with suspicion; it brought a decline in real wages for day laborers; and in general it created conditions which one eminent authority on Mexican banking perceives to have been a major factor in the success of the revolution against Díaz. Various reforms to counteract the evils failed to achieve their ends, and by 1910 the entire financial structure, apparently sound, had been seriously weakened. So critical was the situation, indeed, that Limantour made a special trip to Europe to negotiate new loans and to refund the national debt at the very moment that the political situation posed serious internal problems; the negotiations had not been completed when the revolution began.

In the light of the above data for the Díaz period, it is extremely difficult to come to any hard conclusions regarding Mexican economic development and stability at the end of the regime. Most of the indicators point to an astonishing strengthening of the economy. Public finances, which had been a scandal in prior regimes, were brought to order, and the debt was regularly serviced. By 1895 the treasury, for the first time in Mexico's experience as a nation, showed a *bona fide* surplus and, with few exceptions, the treasury surplus continued until Díaz's fall. Government income from normal tax sources, which averaged about 15 million *pesos* in the years before 1876, grew to well over 100 million in the late years; even taking into account the smaller value of the *peso* on the international market, the increase of revenues was impressive and indicated a stronger economy and greater efficiency at the government level. Mexico's international credit reputation was so sound that government bonds sold at a premium, at interest rates comparable to the most stable governments in the world, indicating a great confidence among investors. Furthermore, the stable political conditions and the promise of great profits stimulated direct foreign investments on an unprecedented scale; exactly how much money flowed to Mexico in this form cannot be determined with any exactitude, but a U.S. consul in 1911 estimated that total foreign investment ran to about 2 billion *pesos*, of which more than half came from the United States. Foreign trade, industrial production, agricultural production, mining output, lines of communication and transportation—all these aspects of economic growth registered enormous change, and certainly justified the satisfaction with which Díaz and his advisors contemplated their work.

And yet the economy indicated more subtle evidence of great weakness. Real wages declined, one estimate placing those of 1910 at one-fourth of that of 1810. Even taking a more conservative estimate of one half the latter amount, the startling fact remains that the average Mexican laborer worked fifteen times as many hours to buy a sack of wheat flour, twelve times as long for corn, and nineteen times for cheap textiles as did his counterpart in the United States. To make matters worse, the direction of the real wage "was toward death by hunger," according to Francisco Bulnes. In addition, and closely tied to the real wage, the economy simply did not produce sufficient food for the population either through domestic production or importation. Furthermore the railroads, now largely owned by the government but having high outstanding obligations abroad, operated at consistent losses in the waning years; the losses may well have been a function of the effects of the "bankers' panic" of 1907, but they put a severe strain on the national treasury. Heavy foreign direct investment may well have given the Mexican economy a great stimulus, and it certainly indicated great confidence, but some economists hold that Mexico labored under rather than benefited from it. One contemporary estimated that over two-thirds of *all* investment in Mexico came from foreign sources; the nation had become an economic fief of the United States, Great Britain, and France. And finally, the financial structure by 1910 showed serious weaknesses. Whether the national economy could have survived all these adverse conditions is completely conjectural, but certainly they contributed to the general dissatisfaction which produced the Revolution.

Had the society in its social institutions given to the mass of the population, or even the preponderant majority of the literate group, some sense of satisfaction, the government might have been able to weather the economic storm. But the social and economic institutions of a nation are often reflections of each other. The monopoly in the economic world has its counterpart in an educational or other institutional monopoly in the social situation; the vast differences in economic power demonstrated by declining real wages in the face of unparalleled prosperity for the elite is reflected in a social stratification which makes vertical mobility a rarity. And in Díaz's Mexico such was the case.

The Díaz period saw, on paper at least, a great increase in educational facilities. The number of primary schools more than doubled, the number of students enrolled in the government schools almost quintupled, the number of normal schools doubled, and total proportion of state and federal budgets for education more than doubled. All of these figures indicate an intensification of education at a rate faster than that of population growth. Furthermore, while the proportion of money going to education increased, the proportion going to the military declined by one-third.

But a closer examination of the data suggests that the educational picture was quite different from what the gross figures imply. In the first place, the data themselves cannot be fully trusted; official figures from the state of Chiapas indicating an average daily attendance of 100 per cent, or those of Guerrero of 93, make one wonder whether state officials submitted statistics to enlighten, or to deceive. But even accepting the figures at their face value, exaggerated though they might be, leads to some interesting conclusions. On the national average, only one of three children between the ages of six and twelve was enrolled, and the majority of these were concentrated in or near the major population centers. Average daily attendance was roughly two out of three at that level. In spite of the percentage increase in the budget for education, the statistics indicate that the total expenditure on education barely exceeded 1 *peso* per inhabitant. The number of teachers, while increasing in proportion to the general population, did not approach the proportional increase in the number of students enrolled; according to the figures, in 1910 50 per cent more teachers were giving instruction to 500 per cent more students than in 1878. The failure of the normal school graduate to enter, and stay in, the teaching profession can be perfectly understood in view of the salaries, which were roughly the same in 1910 as in 1878 even though the price structure had undergone great change; they approximated the daily wage of a household servant. Furthermore, for every *peso* expended by the national government on education, 3 went for the military and an additional 1.5 to the federal police; at the state level the ratio was 3 for education to 2 for defense of one kind or another—and this during a period of internal stability and external peace. Finally, the statistics tell us, about 80 per cent of the population above the age of ten could neither read nor write.

Commentary by contemporaries, some of it official, tells an even more doleful story. One educator in 1910 insisted that the vast majority of those few students who did enroll in school went only through the first year, and that relatively few completed the primary course of instruction; this would imply that the great majority of those who emerged as statistically literate in 1910 were not in fact functionally literate. One legislator in the last decade of the nineteenth century insisted, regardless of official statements to the contrary, that only one of four enrolled students attended class; poverty kept the other three out. "If we want obligatory instruction," he declaimed, "we must decree obligatory bread." At the turn of the century one courageous advocate of expanded public education charged that the politically powerful Ahumada and Terrazas families, in control in Chihuahua, budgeted great sums for education but pocketed most of it and left many districts totally without schools; in making the charge he expressed a view widely held concerning most of the states.

Perhaps more critical in the educational pattern than the number of students in schools and the amount of money spent on education is an attitude which may be seen in both the official figures and in public statements. Despite the dedication of some educators such as Justo Sierra, and despite both state and federal laws regarding compulsory education, the majority of the Mexican elite looked upon universal instruction with fear and suspicion. To be sure, those who held such views were somewhat reluctant to express them clearly and publicly. Like the northerner in the United States who hides his racial prejudice behind a facade of pious platitudes, the Mexican could always think of dozens of "realistic" reasons for failing to implement the philosophy of free, obligatory, universal education. But occasionally a public figure showed his real concern, as did Francisco G. Cosmes in 1880 when he urged a "practical" education for the laboring masses because it would be "less dangerous and ugly" than the kind of schooling which both state and federal law envisaged. But the attitude can be most clearly seen in the fantastic differences in per pupil expenditure for the primary grades and for the higher ranks. For the great mass of the population, even in the urban centers, any hope of an education beyond the primary level was completely illusory; in 1907 the primary schools enrolled well over a hundred students for every student in the preparatory curriculum for college. The elite reserved for itself the higher realms of education, and there it put the major financial resources, proportionately. For every pupil enrolled in the primary schools, the total expenditures in 1910 approximated 7 *pesos;* but for every student in the college preparatory schools which were not strictly private the various government agencies spent nearly 100 *pesos*. In 1910 Mexico spent more per enrolled pupil at the preparatory level than did the United States for the roughly equivalent secondary student, but only one-fifteenth the amount of her northern neighbor for each student at the primary level. This was class legislation with a vengeance. In addition, of course, the elite had access to the private schools which, because of high tuition costs, remained closed to the vast majority. The entire educational system, then, both public and private, was geared to take care of the tiny minority which controlled Mexican political and economic life.

By the end of the Díaz regime the Church, as a religious institution, and the state, as a civil institution, had learned to live in peace. Evidences of bitter anticlericalism or fanatical pro-clericalism, so characteristic of the earlier periods, can be found throughout the *porfiriato;* but by 1910 these maneuvers by the contending parties seemed to have taken on the flavor of a formal dance in which each step by one elicited a predictable response from the other, with both step and response being essentially meaningless. Occasionally, particularly in the earlier years, the old animosities flared. In 1881 Governor Evaristo Madero of Coahuila, in attempting to enforce the reform laws as he understood them, forbade the religious rites of marriage or baptism without prior registration with the civil authorities. The Church, contending that neither the law requiring civil registry of births nor the constitutional amendment stipulating marriage as a civil contract demanded *prior* registration, appealed to the courts for aid. The judges, in a decision filled with doubtful legal logic and obvious political compromise, upheld the governor's right to require prior registration for marriage but denied the validity of his demand for prior registration for baptism. A short time later a parish priest, with petty petulance and jactation, refused to officiate at a baptismal ceremony in which Governor Madero was due to take part as the child's godfather. The entire episode blew up a minor national storm, with the anticlerical press generally condemning the priest's action as illegal, immoral, and un-Christian, while the Catholic press gave strong support to the cleric on the grounds of the constitution (no man could be forced to work without his own consent), canon law (a priest could take any action which he thought wise), and "public sentiment," which had been scandalized by the governor's decrees. No commentator in the clerical press questioned the moral validity of condemning an innocent child to everlasting oblivion for the political sins of the godfather, and the hierarchy maintained a stoic silence on the issue. A few months later, however, the Bishop of Puebla published a pastoral letter urging the faithful to register prior to either weddings or baptisms, and when the governor of Guerrero, in 1887, followed Madero's lead in requiring prior registration, only a few protested mildly. By 1910 most of the bishops had urged, but not required, prior registration, and the issue had died out—in spite of the fact that in many areas, particularly the Federal District, Michoacán, and Guanajuato, conformance tended to be the exception rather than the rule.

In all questions concerning education the Church issue intruded. In 1887 and 1888 members of the national legislature engaged in a long and bitter debate over the establishment of centrally supported schools in the Federal District and the territories. Joaquín Casasús in battling for lay education, insisted that the clergy "did not want the child to learn to read, because if he read the Scriptures he would lose his faith; nor did they want him to learn science, because then he could scoff at the fables in Genesis." Others, of course, argued in an opposite vein: that lay education was atheistic, an affront to Catholic Christianity, a progenitor of iniquity, a Masonic plot. But Casasús and his view prevailed; the law as finally passed established free, lay public schools in those regions directly under the control of the national government, and forbade the employment of any minister of any faith, or of any person who had taken religious vows, as a teacher in such schools.

By the terms of the law, school attendance was obligatory for all children between the ages of six and twelve, but parents could opt to send their children to either public or private schools. State and municipal law concerning education generally conformed to the principles laid down in the national legislation, and as public education increased in quantity the proportion of children attending Catholic schools decreased alarmingly; by 1910 only one child in fifteen received his education in a school interlarded with Catholic dogma. Church officials were caught in a trap. Since they were, according to their own admission, "breathing more freely" in the friendlier atmosphere of the late porfirian era, they were extremely reluctant to make a frontal assault in an effort to bring Catholicism into the schools, nor could they hope to build enough schools, with rates of tuition low enough, to constitute serious competition for the public schools. But neither could they overlook the implications of a system devoted to lay education heavily influenced by the philosophy of positivism which, they believed, was largely responsible for the increase in "divorces, illegitimate births, infanticides, crimes of adolescents, . . . suicides of minors, . . . immorality, pornography, scandal, crime, suicides, prostitution and drunkenness." Pro-clericals therefore mounted the attack on lay education and the philosophy of positivism, rather than on the governments which supplied the money for the first and attempted to effectuate the thinking of the second. Eusebio Bustillos in 1909 flatly asserted that the children were becoming more wicked as a result of the moral laxity demonstrated in lay education, and one anonymous priest asserted that any parent who sent his child to a lay school could not be a good Catholic. The Third Catholic Congress, held in Mexico City in 1906, sanctioned a statement which said in part:

> Crime increases in proportion to the progress of lay education, as statistics show; and the general upheaval of society is the bitter and putrid fruit of the atheistic school!

But Church officials well knew that mere condemnation of lay education would produce no results, save, perhaps, a recrudescence of rabid anticlericalism. Criticism of public education, then, was complimented by an intensification of educational activity and social service. The clerical faction, to be sure, talked more than it acted, and carefully avoided any action which might be deemed a threat to the government or to the elite, but it also gave real evidence of increasing concern for the welfare of the vast majority of society. Whether these tentative steps in the first decade of the century could have developed into a strong movement within the Church, had not the devastating revolution occurred when it did, cannot be answered. The dominant patterns in the society militated against any significant change in the Church's role, but sensitive and thoughtful men saw the necessity for a shift in direction, and the great strength of the Church has always been its ability to change as conditions warrant.

Spokesmen for the Church in 1904 were able to say, with full justification, that even though the whole galaxy of restrictive Laws of Reform were still embodied in constitutional or statutory law,

> we work with less restrictions, and . . . now we can consecrate ourselves under the protection of the law and the aegis of an honorable government to the remedy of our necessities.

On the surface, Church and state had developed a working partnership for the improvement of Mexican society; but the course of the next few years demonstrated with sickening certainty that fanaticism and suspicion on both sides lay close to the surface. Whether high officials in the Church in Mexico were engaged in plotting and conniving for the return to the position of economic and political dominance which it had enjoyed in an earlier age, as a great host of anticlerical writers have asserted, or whether the Church had in fact accepted the diminution of its power, cannot now and probably will never be established with certitude. But it is clear that the clericals misread the temper of the times and made some grievous errors. The din of condemnation concerning public lay education made few friends among those dedicated to that concept, and the failure of both the Second and the Third Catholic Congresses to act on socially significant resolutions served to strengthen existing suspicions and prejudices. For example, a resolution condemning the entire system of wage discounts and chit payments, introduced to the Third Congress (1906), could not muster sufficient support for passage. All manner of valid arguments can be advanced for the failure to act, but the infuriated survivors of the 1907 textile machine-gunning in Puebla could see only that Church spokesmen had refused, when given the opportunity, to give them support in one of their legitimate demands. Similar failures on a wide variety of matters dear to the hearts of the economically disadvantaged led Ernest Galarza, over twenty years later, to make the caustic observation that all significant resolutions "died in committee, or were lulled to sleep by long prayers about social justice." The suspicious could convince themselves, easily, that the Church was engaged in outrageously cynical hypocrisy.

Furthermore, the Church appeared to be involved again in the acquisition of real property in spite of constitutional prohibition. Taking advantage of a 1901 law which gave to charitable institutions the right to own property under certain limited conditions, cleric-dominated stock companies obtained control over a great deal of real estate and led to the supposition that the Church once again, through dummy corporations and other hidden measures, dominated the economy. A few years later Luis Cabrera submitted no proof to support his assertion that the Church controlled most of the state of Durango, but a great proportion of the population believed him nonetheless; the groundwork for belief had been laid by the clerics themselves.

In September 1910, Mexico celebrated its centennial of the Grito de Dolores. Special delegations came from nearly every country in the world to help the nationals consume champagne and other delicacies—and all returned to their homelands extolling Mexico's stability, peace, and prosperity. They, along with the great majority of the regular diplomatic and consular representatives, had missed the essential temper of the Mexican society; they were unduly impressed by the splendid facade and not perspicacious enough—who could have been?—to see the fundamental weakness of the regime with its economic imbalances and its social injustices. They and the national elite dismissed the just-concluded Madero electoral campaign as of no import and would have agreed with Francisco Bulnes in his contemptuous reference to unhappy agrarians as "ragged plebeians, with their thin veneer of civilization, . . . acting like savage gluttons of human carrion." The ingredients for violent revolution remained hidden from their eyes.

Chapter 9 • The Epic Revolution

I do not ask for anything out of the ordinary; I ask only that you equalize us with the capitalists, that if you do not force a capitalist to operate his business, then that you do not attack the worker when he goes on strike, either.

NICOLÁS CANO, 1916

A revolution is not always a source of evil and tears, just as fire does not always produce devastation.

LUIS CABRERA, 1917

Madero has unleashed a tiger; let us see if he can control him.

PORFIRIO DÍAZ, 1911

Perhaps Don Porfirio, forcibly relieved of the responsibilities of the presidential office and cleansed of the self-aggrandizing sycophants who had surrounded him for years, could finally see Mexico with a clarity earlier denied him. The tiger to which Díaz referred as he boarded ship for exile was the amalgam of frustration, of injustice, of poverty, of ignorance from which the great mass of the Mexican society had been suffering for generations; the ex-dictator's statement was a doleful prediction, for neither Madero nor a host of others during the following fourteen years could control the tiger. Cabrera's apt comparison of the Epic Revolution with a fire best describes the devastating years between 1910 and 1924 which wrecked the economy, may have cost as many as two million lives, destroyed the interior lines of communication and piled an insufferable debt, foreign and domestic, upon the Mexican people. Those bitter years left deep scars which debilitated the nation for another generation, but the cauldron produced a new Mexico, free at last from most of the traditional assumptions which prevented healthy social and economic change.

Despite a new Constitution filled with provisions distinctly at variance with porfirian thought, however, the issue remained in doubt until 1924. The unsuccessful de la Huerta rebellion of late 1923, with its odd assortment of dissidents representing all points on the ideological spectrum, brought an end to an age; for even though spiteful little episodes such as the *Cristero* rebellion and the *pronunciamientos* in the 'twenties and 'thirties came from deep conviction and cost lives and money, they had little chance of success. When Plutarco Elías Calles took office on December 1, 1924, the Epic Revolution was over and a new era had begun, however inauspiciously. The mass of the population probably had less to eat than they had two decades earlier, their educational opportunities had improved not at all, and they had no greater political rights. In almost every sense their condition was dismal. But the Epic Revolution had laid an institutional and intellectual base which has made the Mexican Revolution one of the most significant social movements in modern times.

The overwhelming characteristic of this revolutionary era was utter chaos. During the entire fourteen-year span the only period of real peace during which the government could devote its energies and its finances to the solution of the nation's desperate plight came in the three-year interregnum immediately prior to the abortive de la Huerta insurrection. Throughout the other eleven years rebellious movements, some niggling and some momentous, cut into the country's economic and social growth. Sometimes the fighting involved real issues of social and economic thought, while at other times men professing the same creed fought one another bitterly as other men holding philosophical views poles apart fought side by side. Many "rebellions" or "insurrections" served merely as a front used by leaders to indulge in pillage against the "enemies" of progress; a claim of revolutionary status generally served as security against eventual prosecution by the government. At no time during these critical years did any revolutionist of status make a clear statement of well-defined aims within an internally consistent ideology; the closest statement approximating such a philosophy appears in the Constitution of 1917, hammered out after two months of bitter haggling and nasty recriminations by a small group of men representing a small minority of the literate populace but expressing the inchoate aspirations of the great mass.

The opening gun in the Mexican Revolution came in late November 1910, when Francisco Madero crossed the border near Ciudad Porfirio Díaz (presently, and earlier, Piedras Negras). After a slow start, the insurrection gained headway in the following spring and forced Díaz's resignation in late May. A man of moderation and of limited intellectual endowments, Madero was no ardent revolutionary; his basic philosophy was probably best summed up in one oft-misquoted sentence delivered to a group of workmen in Puebla during the 1910 presidential election: "The Mexican does not want bread; he wants liberty to earn bread." No radical and a reluctant revolutionist, Madero accomplished little in his short sixteen months in office, except perhaps to create an ambient in which the need for social and economic change could be discussed frankly and openly. But his moderation appeared as shocking radicalism to those who had profited from the Díaz regime, and as arch reaction to those demanding instant change; as a consequence his period in office was punctuated with minor rebellions which kept the country upset even though they did not seriously disturb economic activity. The *porfiristas* finally had their way; a *coup d'état* engineered by Victoriano Huerta removed Madero from office in late February 1913, and brought to an end the stumbling and tentative steps toward social change.

Huerta, whom U.S. Ambassador Henry Lane Wilson labeled as "a man of iron mold, of absolute courage, who knows what he wants and how to get it, and . . . is not . . . overly particular as to methods," hoped to stamp out every vestige of Madero "radicalism," but in his crude methods he overstepped his bounds: he gave his blessings to the assassination of Madero, the president's brother Gustavo, Vice President José María Pino Suárez, Chihuahua Governor Abraham González, and a few lesser lights. A little more than two weeks after the *coup d'état* a new revolutionary movement began in the north and soon spread to all parts of the country. Venustiano Carranza, ably seconded by Alvaro Obregón, Plutarco Elías Calles, Francisco Villa, and a host of others who detested the thought of a return to *porfirismo,* soundly defeated Victoriano Huerta. Emiliano Zapata fought against Huerta in the south, but he always made it clear that his was a separate movement, unconnected with that under Carranza's leadership. By August 1914, the victors took over the government, but by late November they began to fight among themselves, even though there were no discernible ideological differences between the major contending groups; both sides (the "Conventionists" and the "Constitutionalists") had, among their leaders, men representing almost every point from moderate liberal to quasi-socialist. By mid-1915 the Carranza faction, the Constitutionalists, had shown their mastery over Villa and the Conventionists, but Villa in the north and Zapata in the south continued their military rebellions until 1920 and 1919, respectively. Carranza, a moderate, emerged as president, but the more reform-minded members of the victorious armies drubbed him in the 1916 constitutional convention, and the Constitution of 1917 as it finally emerged contained many provisions to which Carranza objected and which he refused to enforce in the final three years of his presidency. In 1920 Carranza, fearful of the potential radicalism written into the Constitution and determined to limit its application, attempted to doctor the presidential election of that year, but a new revolution forced him to flee to his death in May. The reform-actionists, with Obregón and Calles in control, were firmly in the saddle, but the government still had to contend with the fruitless de la Huerta rebellion of December 1923, with its sprinkling of the politically ambitious, the philosophically conservative, and the out-and-out reformist. When the rebellion collapsed after four months, a semblance of peace and order returned; the military struggle, the Epic Revolution, was over.

And what had it cost in lives? In those confused and chaotic times no one noted the deaths which could be directly or indirectly attributed to the long military struggle; even the thousands of battle reports purportedly giving accurate details of minor skirmishes and major battles were more often than not written to minimize the reporter's losses and maximize the enemy's. The fighting was vicious and bloody, though, and the battles resulted in phenomenally heavy losses of life; given the poor medical facilities the seriously wounded seldom survived. Those not succumbing on the battle field or dying in the field hospitals frequently fell before firing squads; field commanders, as their reports to superiors attest, routinely ordered prisoners executed. Not all officers saw the extermination of six or seven thousand men, as Felipe Angeles did at Zacatecas in 1914, "from the artistic point of view, as the success of a well-performed task, as the master work completed," but few had any qualms at all.

Those doing the fighting probably suffered mortality rates not higher than the civilian populations in the areas swept by raging armies. Men bent on the enemies' destruction did not always conform to the niceties of "civilized" warfare, but even had they done so the nature of the contest almost guaranteed that death from malnutrition, exposure, and disease would take an appalling toll from fleeing innocents. And then, as a kind of gloomy climax to the whole macabre affair, tens of thousands of Mexicans—in numbers too great to count, in floods too heavy to contain—escaped to the haven of the U.S. border states. Many, but not all, of these ultimately returned.

We have no firm data upon which to construct an accurate image of human losses, but the five censuses between 1895 and 1930 give a base for a gross estimate, even though the figures are admittedly questionable. From the first three censuses and the last an approximation of a growth-rate curve may be constructed, and on such a curve the population of 1921 should have fallen between 17 and 16 million—but the census of that year counted slightly less than 14.5 million. How much of this difference can be accounted for in a declining birth rate, how much credited to emigration which later flowed in the opposite direction, how much to statistical inaccuracies and how much to military-connected deaths can only be guessed at, but one thing is fairly clear: in 1921 the nation had nearly three-quarters of a million fewer inhabitants than in 1910. There are no data to suggest even faintly that a drastic decline in live births accounted for this retrogression. On the contrary, all the censuses from 1921 onward indicate a high rate of live birth and survival during the 1910-21 period, and therefore suggest that from all causes the nation lost about two million citizens.

One of the major elements in the ferocity of the Revolution was a deep and passionate desire for land on the part of those whose very subsistence depended upon agriculture in one form or another. Madero made some inadequate moves to make land available to those who pined for it, and his failure to achieve anything of note constituted one of the bases for the restlessness which so undermined his administration. In some areas agrarians began occupying land without benefit of law, but it was only in the region dominated by Emiliano Zapata that the great landowners really suffered. After the beginning of the Constitutionalist movement under Carranza the peasants repeated the pattern established by their forebears a hundred years earlier; they seized land, drove off cattle (the military, too, of course sequestered cattle), burned *hacienda* buildings, destroyed sugar mills, and generally brought desolation to the countryside. Throughout the decade the nation suffered a drastic shortage of agricultural products, partly because the landowners could not work the land, partly because uninvited occupants produced only enough for themselves, partly because of destroyed transportation facilities, and partly because the armies in campaign—as all such armies are—were extraordinarily wasteful. In the major urban centers, particularly Mexico City, prices skyrocketed to fantastic levels, the natural increases engendered by shortages accelerated into a formidable inflationary spiral through the lavish printing of paper money by government and rebels alike. Agriculture suffered drastically, but its fate was as nothing compared to the northern cattle industry. Not only did every marauding band operating under a military flag requisition cattle for its own use, but meat on the hoof served as one of the few movable assets which could be used to acquire arms and ammunition north of the border. The enterprising military procurement officer, regardless of whom he represented, could always find a ready buyer, no questions asked, in Texas, New Mexico, or Arizona. As late as 1921, H. N. Branch reported that "even at best, it will be many years before the Mexican ranges are restocked to capacity and the effects of the revolution wiped out."

The economic desolation of the countryside, and the consequent malaise agriculturally, can be glimpsed but not completely analyzed from the inadequate and questionable statistics available for the period. In 1918, when one phase of the Revolution was almost over and another phase not yet begun, when active military campaigns were sporadic and confined to Morelos and Chihuahua, the estimated production of most agricultural products and all comestibles save chick-peas showed a marked decline from the average of the late porfirian years. Corn, that great and necessary staple of the populace, had fallen to a point well below the 2-million-ton mark—a total production not significantly greater than that in the late eighteenth century and far less than the earlier period on a per capita basis. And this year was probably one of those of greatest productivity during the period of the Epic Revolution; both before and after, marching armies rent the countryside. In 1924 the Mexican poorer classes had less corn to grind, and fewer tortillas to go around, than at any time during the two centuries past. The same dismal picture appears with beans, which fell to a total only a little above 100,000 tons: 65 per cent of the average production from 1906-10, and barely 51 per cent of the production in 1878. Sugar fell to about 65 per cent of the pre-revolutionary period, but in view of the nature of sugar culture and the heavy investments necessary, the decline was surprisingly small. Among the comestibles only garbanzos, or chickpeas, showed a small increase, the result primarily of the peace and stability which prevailed after 1913 in the northwestern states producing most of this. But the average Mexican benefited little from the increase; almost three-quarters of the total production ended on European tables.

Consular reports to the U.S. Department of State from 1914 onward give a doleful picture of food shortages and malnutrition; with few exceptions the consular officials in all parts of Mexico recorded a gradually deteriorating situation until 1918, and then a renewed degeneration after 1921. A few examples, exaggerated to be sure, of the desperate plight should suffice to give a flavor of the whole. Piedras

Negras in early 1916 reported starvation conditions and food riots. Both Mexico City and Veracruz in the same year saw unsuccessful governmental attempts to fix prices and force hoarded cereals on the public market. Durango, in late 1916, insisted that the mass of the poor—always a majority—suffered from starvation and lack of clothing, with an average of about a hundred dying every day. The Bajío, traditionally the richest agricultural region, witnessed crop failures in 1917, with widespread semi-starvation, as did the Laguna district. A lengthy report from Mexico City in the same year analyzed the "corn famine" throughout the country, while Guadalajara witnessed a corn crop of about 40 per cent normal and a bean crop even less. Aguascalientes in late 1917 reported a 10-per cent increase in the price of corn, and a 20-per cent rise in sugar prices, in one week; at prevailing wages, unskilled workers earned about a pound of corn a day. In early 1918 Guadalajara reported that in one year the price of corn and beans had trebled and flour had doubled. Good weather and relative peace brought increased crops in 1918 and 1919, but by late 1920 the bells of disaster began tolling anew; the words "economic crisis," "disaster," "desolation," "bad," "worsening," and "depression" sprinkle the pages of the economic reports. These were, indeed, hard years for the Mexican mass, whose plight could not be materially improved through importations because of the demands posed by the European war.

But at least one aspect of agricultural production improved, largely because of that war in Europe: henequen production doubled over the pre-revolutionary average. Yucatán, the principal producer, did not suffer as much from the devastating military campaigns as did central Mexico, and both the United States and the European Allies avidly sought the fiber. These conditions, plus a rigid control exercised over production and sale by a special commission created in 1915, stimulated not only an enormous increase in productivity but an even greater increase in income. On several occasions the Carranza government depended almost wholly on subsidies from Yucatán to maintain even a semblance of financial stability. With the end of the European war, coincidental with mismanagement by the commission, the industry fell on evil days in the early 'twenties, but by the end of the Obregón administration, productivity and profits had again climbed to near record-breaking levels.

Even with all the heartbreaking decline in agricultural production and the miseries created by destroyed transportation systems, receipts to the government by 1918 had increased by roughly 50 per cent, and by 1921 to about 170 per cent. Only a small portion, if any, of the growth was the result of government policy; most of it came from an enormous increase in oil production and a price rise of most metals demanded by the war and by developing U.S. industry. At the end of the Díaz period the Mexican oil industry was still in its infancy, dominated by U.S. and British interests. To the oil operators the military campaigns were a nuisance, but little more; through threats, cajolery, and bribery they managed to get full protection for their wells and equipment, and production climbed steadily. In 1910 the combined companies produced 3.6 million barrels, in 1912 they reached 16.6, in 1917 they poured out 55.3, and in 1921 they grew to 193.4, making Mexico the world's third largest petroleum producer, with nearly a quarter of total production. Quarrels between the oil companies and the government over the application of the new constitutional provisions and the system of taxation, coupled with wanton extractive practices, brought a steady decline after the 1921 high point, but the income from oil served as the mainstay of government finance to the end of Obregón's tenure.

Despite the mutuality of interests and dependence, the government and the oil companies quarreled almost incessantly, with each accusing the other of shoddy principles and shady practices. The oil companies, knowing full well that any oil stoppage would cause serious fiscal embarrassment to the government, depended upon bluff, threats, and diplomatic pressures to attain their ends, which amounted, in spite of a constant harping on liberty, freedom, justice, and other abstractions dear to U.S. hearts, to uncontrolled and highly profitable —even wasteful—exploitation of the incredibly productive Mexican fields. The government had weapons of its own. The oil companies little suspected that the Obregón government, in particular, knew almost as much about the profitability of the oil operations as did the companies themselves. Obregón maintained an extraordinarily effective spy service, which not only obtained access to the most secret reports made by company executives and analysts but also supplied the Mexican government with reports on the oil situation drafted by U.S. military intelligence officers operating from Fort Sam Houston. When in 1921 the U.S. oil companies, objecting to new and higher taxes, threatened to suspend operations and did indeed interrupt their shipments for about two months, Obregón refused to knuckle under. The companies claimed the taxes to be confiscatory, but the Mexican president *knew,* on the basis of an analysis by an oil economist whose report an Obregón agent read and digested, that the companies could operate profitably under the new tax schedule.

The Obregón government won the tax round in 1921, but by using United States recognition as the lever and the U.S. Department of State as the agent, the oil companies forced the Mexican government to concede some legal points in 1923. Unfortunately for both the companies and for the Mexican nation, the 1923 agreements served only as a temporary truce and brought no abatement of the mutual animosities and suspicions. The quarrel subsided only after two decades of bickering which culminated in the expropriation of the major foreign oil companies' properties. The real issue between foreigner and government over the oil question arose from the Constitution of 1917, the provisions and implications of which will be considered in another connection.

As could be expected, and as had happened a hundred years earlier during the struggle for independence, the mining industry suffered enormously, sometimes catastrophically, from the military phases of the Revolution. Gold, which reached its highest production figure ever in 1910, fell until in its 1915 nadir total production amounted to only a little above 20 per cent of the 1910 zenith. Silver fell not quite as dramatically, but its 1914 low point amounted to a mere 35 per cent of the pre-revolutionary high. Copper fell by about 65 per cent from its 1909 figure, coal by roughly 75 per cent from the 1910 high, and both zinc and lead fell to less than 5 per cent of their highest previous totals. Part of the decline came from seizures by the various contending forces, and part from somewhat capricious tax levies, but the lack of labor and transportation served as the major debilitating force; by 1915, at the height of Villa's great struggle with Carranza, the entire industry was in desperate straits, and the government was receiving scant income from an activity which had served as its mainstay in earlier times. But the broadening European war and a lessening of military activity in Mexico brought about a resurgence in both productivity and value after 1916. By 1920 silver mining had reached a level of production not significantly less than that of 1910, but, with the price almost doubling in the intervening years and the government imposing heavier taxes, income to the treasury increased enormously. The other metals, save gold, followed roughly the same pattern; before the end of the Carranza regime zinc and copper surpassed pre-revolutionary production at high prices, while lead failed to reach earlier tonnage but produced greater value.

The Mexican government may have reaped great advantages from the renewed production and the increased prices, but the laborer gained little, despite a great many pious statements regarding the working man's welfare. Most Mexican mining companies, basically owned and controlled by foreigners, were a part of an international complex of mining interests little concerned with the physical well-being of the Mexican miner. As a consequence thousands of men were thrown out of work and hundreds died from disease complicated by malnutrition in Guanajuato when the U.S. owners closed the mines for reasons having little, if anything, to do with Mexican conditions. And in spite of the higher prices commanded by the mineral products along with the higher food prices in 1920, no significant increase in wages can be found. Marvin Bernstein, after extensive research and analysis, has given a rough calculation of the wage structure in Guanajuato in 1908; a comparison of his findings with the report of H. N. Branch in 1920 points up the situation:

	BERNSTEIN, 1908 *pesos per day*	BRANCH, 1920 *pesos per day*
Skilled workers	3.00	2.50
Semi-skilled	1.00 to 2.00	1.50 to 2.25
Unskilled	0.50 to 0.75	0.75 to 1.00

Since a minimum daily food cost for a family of three at the prevailing costs in 1920 has been calculated at approximately a *peso* and a half, it becomes clear that the Guanajuato miner in 1920 scarcely benefited from the general mining prosperity.

But mining health began to fail rapidly in 1920 as an incident of the worldwide post-war depression. Silver prices fell from a high of $1.11 per ounce in 1919 to $0.90 in September 1920, and then collapsed to $0.65 in December of that year. Zinc declined as disastrously in price, copper fell only slightly less in proportion, and lead prices fell to such a low that only the most concentrated ores were mined. The Mexican government, confronted with vast unemployment among the mine workers as mines curtailed their activities or closed down entirely, attempted by a variety of tax measures to rescue the foundering industry. In essence the new measures, the first of which went into effect in June 1920, permitted the extraction of silver tax-free from late 1920 to September 1921, and the extraction of lead and copper without payment of taxes until March 1923. In addition, the government temporarily abandoned the import duties on mining equipment and material for most of the year 1921. But tax forgiveness had almost no effect on the total output. In spite of the many government concessions, production of lead, copper, and zinc fell off to a point roughly equivalent to the lowest figure during the revolutionary period. World stockpiles in these metals, not Mexican taxes, determined the tempo of productivity.

The mining slump had a corrosive effect on miners' welfare and on government income. The miner suddenly deprived of an income when virtually all the mines in Zacatecas ceased operations in early 1921, for example, may have been embittered toward the foreign mine owner—but his condition forced him to accept a cut in wages when the mines reopened. By 1922, when general depletions of stockpiled metals in various parts of the world encouraged a revival of the Mexican industry, the miner was in no wise better off than he had been under the Díaz period. In the meantime, reduced taxes and lessened production deprived the national government of an excellent source of income; government revenues from mining operations in

1921 was less than a third of the amount the previous year, and in 1922 it was only slightly more than half of the 1919-20 average.

Although neither the Mexicans nor the mining officials knew it, the post-revolutionary recession in the mining industry brought the long era to a close, for the primacy of the three most important metals was ending. Never again would gold production reach the heights of the pre-revolutionary period, and in only a few exceptional years would silver and copper produce as well as they had prior to 1920. In this post-revolutionary period the entire mining industry began an imperceptible shift, which grew in magnitude, away from the more dramatic minerals toward a galaxy of more commonplace but ultimately more valuable metals. Zinc and lead replaced silver and copper, and even the lowly sulphur came to be a challenger to the more exalted silver—and far surpassed gold—as producers of income. The trilogy of gold-silver-copper, which had dominated mining statistics during the porfirian period, was far from dead. For another twenty years the first two maintained a steady level of production, with minor annual variations, not significantly different from the earlier period; copper has retained its productive pattern to the present, with greater year-to-year fluctuations. But while these minerals remained static, others grew in importance until they far surpassed them. The three dominant metals, which had accounted for about 90 per cent of mining value until the final lustrum of the Díaz period, fell to less than 50 per cent within a generation and to about a third by 1960. The Epic Revolution marked a change in Mexican mining from a romance to a business.

The long revolutionary period, topped off with the sterile de la Huerta rebellion, brought utter havoc to Mexican public finances and increased the indebtedness, both foreign and domestic, to incredible heights. From the beginning the various governments had affirmed an intention to accept financial responsibility for losses sustained by foreigners as a consequence of revolutionary activities, and these obligations, piled on top of the unpaid interest and capital of pre-revolutionary foreign debts, made previous external debts seem puny in comparison. In 1922 the government admitted, in negotiating for a

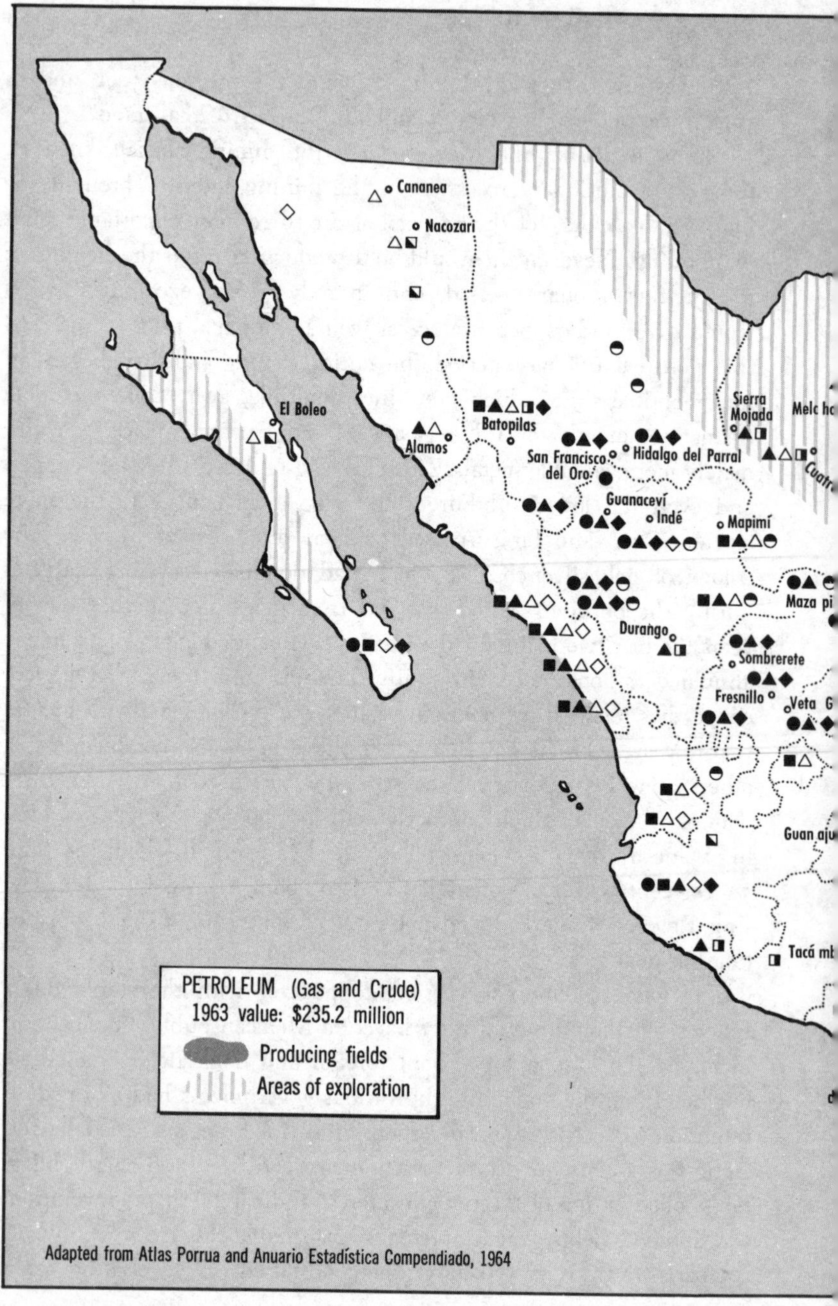

Cananea
Nacozari
El Boleo
Alamos
Batopilas
San Francisco del Oro
Hidalgo del Parral
Sierra Mojada
Guanaceví
Indé
Mapimí
Durango
Sombrerete
Fresnillo
PETROLEUM (Gas and Crude)
1963 value: $235.2 million
Producing fields
Areas of exploration
Adapted from Atlas Porrua and Anuario Estadística Compendiado, 1964

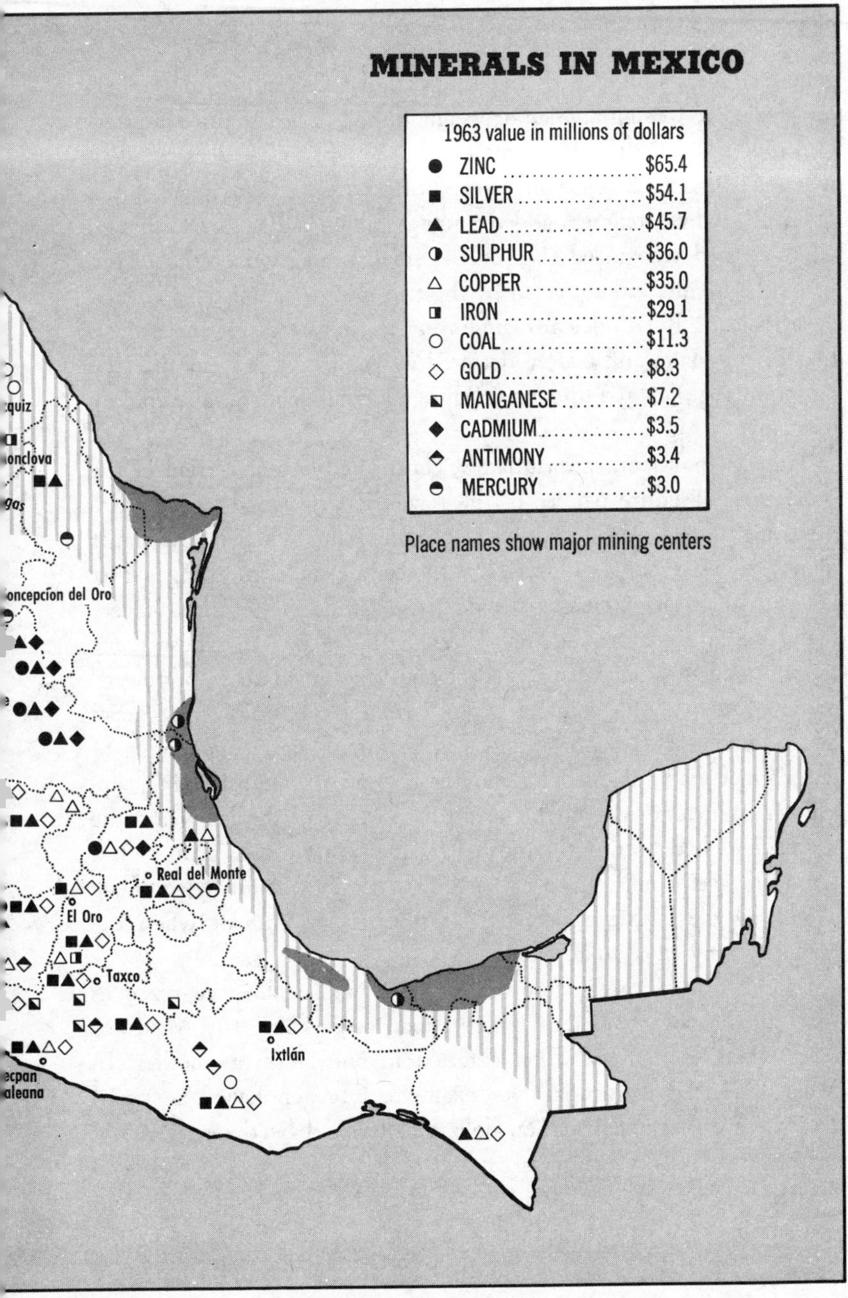
MINERALS IN MEXICO
1963 value in millions of dollars
ZINC $65.4
SILVER $54.1
LEAD $45.7
SULPHUR $36.0
COPPER $35.0
IRON $29.1
COAL $11.3
GOLD $8.3
MANGANESE $7.2
CADMIUM $3.5
ANTIMONY $3.4
MERCURY $3.0
Place names show major mining centers
Real del Monte
El Oro
Taxco
Ixtlán

general understanding with the International Committee of Bankers on Mexico, to foreign bonded debts amounting to nearly three-quarters of a billion dollars; this sum amounted to almost three times the debt when Madero took office in 1911. Furthermore, claims against the government by foreigners added another billion dollars, even though all concerned recognized that only a small proportion of the claims would be finally authenticated by the two mixed commissions created to adjudicate. But under any circumstances, regardless of the proportion of the claims ultimately declared as valid, it was clear that the nation in 1924 labored under a crushing external debt and a stumbling economy.

The external debt, unfortunately, constituted only a portion of the problem. The entire pattern of the revolutionary period had contributed mightily to fiscal chaos and economic ruin. Each of the paper money issues, though presumably superceding and cancelling earlier issues, had in fact increased the domestic public indebtedness. Every major military commander, regardless of the faction in whose name he appeared to be operating, had at one time or another "borrowed" money (often at the point of a gun) from local banks, commercial houses, private citizens, or religious institutions. Many commanders of lesser grade had subsisted for months on end by requisitioning supplies from anyone who might have them. Many of the loans and the requisitions had been authenticated by the military men only with a scrawled receipt on a scrap of paper, but they constituted legitimate claims by the Mexican people against their government when the major fighting came to an end.

By the side of these more or less legitimate debts, recognized as such by the government in theory, stood other claims by Mexicans from whom money had been extorted in one guise or another. In Mexico City in early 1915, for example, Obregón levied a special "tax" of a quarter of a million dollars to be paid by the religious of the city, and a further special impost on all business in the Federal District. As was the case with respect to the "loans," the transient governments gave to their field commanders great discretion in the matter of special taxes to be imposed for the purpose of supporting the army or carrying out needed social services. Many Mexicans—and foreigners—complained that the fluidity of the military situation and the everlasting money-hunger of the military commanders meant, in effect, paying the same tax over and over again. These claims, even more amorphous than those arising from requisitions, formed a part of the public debt only as the government recognized their validity, and their "validity" frequently depended upon friends-at-court rather than abstract justice. On top of all these domestic debts were the arrears in pay owing to an army of civil servants and military men, the sum of which at any given time depended upon the state of the treasury but averaged about 15 per cent of the national budget.

But even with this mass of indebtedness, the government after 1917 took on additional obligations to pay an undetermined amount for land to be distributed to villages under the new agrarian reform program. By the end of the Obregón period the government had barely begun land distribution and therefore had added little to the public debt, but the groundwork had been laid for an enormous increase in the money which the national government was pledged to pay to its citizens.

By 1924, after nearly fifteen years of warfare and "revolution," the panorama of material conditions was indeed dreary. Compared to the pre-revolutionary period, the vast majority of the Mexicans probably ate less well, had fewer schools to attend and fewer job opportunities. The internal transportation and communication systems, although somewhat recovered from the earlier devastation and fully functioning, suffered from a drastic shortage of equipment and were kept operating through jury-rig repairs which made the prompt arrival of either goods or messages highly problematical. The entire economy lacked that viability which seemed to characterize the late Díaz period; the oil industry, which in 1924 produced 130 million barrels and presented the government with 55 million *pesos* in taxes (more than half the total Díaz budget of 1910), was an economic bright spot, but the major issues between companies and government presaged a drastic decline. To be sure, central government revenues trebled over the late Díaz years, but the vast increase in public indebtedness vitiated the advantages which might have accrued. Furthermore, the Revolution had left a legacy of military men who gobbled up from 70 per cent in 1918 to 1924's 40 per cent of the total expenditures and sometimes as much as 80 per cent of total normal revenues. Any man who saw in Obregón's Mexico a bright and rosy future, as many Mexicans as well as foreigners did, was truly infused with optimism.

The conviction that Mexico stood on the threshold of great progressive development came not from actual changes which had taken place in the mode of living but from remarkable changes which had come in the manner of thinking. The Revolution produced a new breed of public figure, almost fanatically proud to be Mexican and determined to drive that nation into the modern world. They were not all honest or even honorable. The immediate post-revolutionary period probably was the most financially corrupt in Mexican history. A society in which a general could call on the national treasury to pay a one-night gambling loss of 40,000 dollars, or in which a labor leader could come to rival Diamond Jim Brady in mode of dress, certainly represented a degeneration from the financial incorruptibility of the major figures in the Díaz period. In spite of great pronouncements from government officials regarding public morality, the fact is that virtually every public figure—and his friends and family—reaped an enormous financial harvest from his revolutionary affiliation. Nor were all those who achieved a position of leadership constant in their revolutionary zeal. Luis Morones, who fought bitterly and tenaciously for the rights of laborers in the early revolutionary years, became considerably less fervid as he grew fat and satisfied. Plutarco Elías Calles, second to none in his passionate nationalism and in his search for social justice from 1910 to 1928, ultimately lost his enthusiasm and began to question the entire reform program. José Vasconcelos, who perceived himself to be the outstanding intellectual leader of revolutionary Mexico, grew so embittered that he came to denounce later policies as a perversion of the true revolution. But as each of these, and many more, fell by the wayside in frustration and disillusion, another took his place and demonstrated for a time that constancy to ideals which every successful experiment in social change must have.

And those who did labor to make the revolt into a revolution had sufficient guidelines in the Constitution of 1917.

At the time it was drafted, few constitutions in the world offered a more nearly cohesive blueprint for social change and political development than did that which came from two months of bitter recriminations and violent wrangling at Querétaro. Whether the new charter reflected the majority will or majority desire is a subject which can be debated to the end of time, but that the method of selecting the delegates denied representation to a significant proportion of the population, possibly a majority, is quite clear. By decrees on September 14 and 19, 1916, Carranza established a system for "electing" delegates and stipulated the time and place for the opening session. On the face of it, the second decree appeared to establish a modicum of democracy in the selection process: each state and territory was to elect, on October 22, one delegate and one alternate for each 70,000 inhabitants as recorded in the census of 1910. But in fact the election was something of a sham, especially in two respects. The government forces did not control all the territory in the nation, for both Villa and Zapata still had armies at their command and controlled areas of at least one-tenth of both land and people. Villa may have been fleeing from the American General Pershing, and Carranza insisted that he did have effective control over Villa country, but the sovereignty exercised by the First Chief scarcely went beyond the railroads and cities. Furthermore, even in those areas effectively pacified a combination of local political jealousies and a growing economic crisis effectively destroyed an intelligent selection of candidates. As a consequence, many districts had only one candidate for the post of delegate, 24 districts held no election, and a goodly number sent two delegates who clamored for admission. One delegate had a grand total of 23 votes.

Any vestige of a truly representative constituent assembly disappeared, in addition, with the publication of the September 14 decree, which prohibited candidacy to any man who had "aided with arms or served public office under the governments or factions hostile to the constitutionalist cause." The decree not only eliminated from consideration anyone who had ever carried a gun supporting Huerta (even those who momentarily joined Huerta to defend Mexico against an expected major invasion after the U.S. occupied Veracruz) or had continued in the civil service during the Huerta administration, but also all those who had given aid to either Zapata or Villa after November 1914. The decree probably excluded well over half those who had taken an active part in public affairs since 1910; the supreme irony is that even Francisco Madero's brothers were thus denied the right to help draft the constitution. The delegates who in late November began to arrive in Querétaro far removed from the political tensions of Mexico City, were consequently good orthodox Constitutionalists who had supported Carranza in every turn of the road. The First Chief therefore looked forward to a *pro forma* approval of his changes in the Constitution of 1857. Since the *carrancista* draft presented to the constituent assembly contained so few changes of a significant nature over the earlier constitution, one may wonder legitimately why he was interested in a new constitution at all. In all probability it was another demonstration of the phenomenal Carranza egoism.

Any illusions Carranza might have held regarding his complete domination of the constituent congress should have been dispelled even before the formal opening. For ten days prior to the opening session at which a new constitution itself was to be discussed, the delegates concerned themselves with the task of examining and either authenticating or rejecting credentials. It was in this process that the first lines were clearly drawn between the moderate and the "radical" wings, between those anxious to follow Carranza's lead and those who rejected it. Within a week the acrimonious quarrel over credentials, during which insulting personal attacks gave a distinctive flavor to the debates, separated the strong Carranza supporters from those who tended to coalesce around Obregón. By December 1, when Carranza made his formal presentation to the assembly, the cleavage was manifest; the only question in doubt was which group could command a majority. But even that query was soon answered to Carranza's discomfiture. On December 5 Luis Manuel Rojas, a strong *carrancista*, proposed the names of five men for the crucial Committee on the

Constitution; three of the five reflected his thinking on constitutional—and social—issues. A strong, almost violent, reaction from the floor forced Rojas to withdraw his nominations, and the following day the convention proceeded to elect five *obregonistas* to the committee. The committee itself then elected from its membership Francisco Mújica as chairman. The radicals held the whip handle, and they never relinquished it, in spite of persistent efforts by the Carranza clique to gain the upper hand. To Carranza's great credit, he made no overt attempt to dominate the proceedings.

The quarrel over credentials and committee membership demonstrated a fundamental ideological split rather than a mere bickering over personal power; the issue in question was not *who,* but *what.* Carranza and those who surrounded him as civilian advisors—Félix Palavicini, José Natividad Macías, Alfonso Cravioto, Gerzayn Ugarte, Rojas—were all imbued with a sense of decency and humanism which led them to reject the basic tenets upon which the Díaz regime was based. In this sense they were truly revolutionary, and on these points they differed not one whit from the Obregón group. But their perception of the state was somewhat Jeffersonian; government was neuter, playing no positive role in the development of the society other than that of furnishing needed instruction and protection. Institutions, they believed, grew slowly and ultimately conformed to society's needs. Intensely nationalistic and dedicated to growth and to change, they nevertheless rejected forced change through governmental imposition. Anticlericals all, and some even violently so, they were nonetheless reluctant to subject the Church to excessive restrictions.

The contending faction which Obregón supported, and which Francisco Mújica, Esteban B. Calderón, Enrique Colunga, Enrique Recio, and Luis G. Monzón best represented in the constituent assembly, differed only slightly from the *carrancistas* in their view of the ultimate Mexican society. The two factions fought over methods, not aims. The radical group saw the government as an active force—perhaps *the* active force—in instituting the social and economic changes which all members of the assembly accepted as necessary for the eventual good of the nation. Mújica believed it necessary to destroy certain entrenched elements in the society, and then to rebuild on the ruins. He and his group, no more anticlerical than the *carrancistas* but less constrained by philosophical niceties, were determined to encircle the clergy with a web of restrictions which would eliminate the Church as a dominant force in Mexican life. Among the hundred-odd men who composed the left, only a few ever demonstrated a strain of anti-Catholicism, and even fewer indulged in anti-religious feeling, but they all saw the clergy—particularly the foreign priests—as potent instruments in the preservation of institutions and concepts which reflected a sick society. Only through the destruction of clerical power, they held, could the reconstruction process begin; the government, the agent of the state, must take the lead not only in the destruction but in the rebuilding.

On December 1, 1916, Carranza appeared before the assembly to inaugurate its labors formally and to present a proposed draft of a new constitution. The draft, largely the work of José N. Macías, followed the Constitution of 1857 in basic philosophy and in major provisions with remarkable tenacity. A bit here and there regarding property ownership and citizenship underscored a seething nationalism, a few provisions demonstrated an increased concern for the rights of the individual, and a number of articles dealing with the governmental process served to broaden the base of political participation. But it was, in general, a negative document; it emphasized what the state could not do rather than what it must do. Even in the area of land reform, so obviously necessary to meet the demands of a major portion of the population, the draft constitution remained almost silent. Macías had included one innocuous statement as a part of an article which dealt with the nature of property:

> The town ejidos, whether retained after the Law of Disentailment, restored or newly established, according to law, will be enjoyed in common by the inhabitants of the towns until such time as they are divided according to laws to be enacted.

Carranza certainly recognized the drastic need for some form of changed tenure system, and nothing in the draft constitution would have prohibited a wide-ranging reform program, but he just as certainly perceived the function of government to be one which would *allow* the acquisition of land rather than one which would *force* redistribution. In his long discourse on the need for changes in the Constitution of 1857 (the speech lasted nearly two hours), Carranza spent less than a minute on land reform; his only mention:

> Article 27 of the Constitution of 1857 provides for the occupation of private property without the consent of the owners but with prior indemnization, if public utility demands it. This power is, in the judgment of my government, sufficient for the acquisition of lands and their distribution . . . among the people who wish to dedicate themselves to agricultural labors, and thus to establish small holdings which should be developed as public necessity demands them.

In his December 1 appearance before the assembly, Carranza justified the need for constitutional changes and presented to the president a copy of the draft constitution, but the members of the constituent congress had no opportunity to study the document until December 6, when one of the secretaries read it aloud in its entirety and distributed copies to the delegates. In the course of the following six weeks the assembly accepted without major revision the vast majority of the 132 articles proposed by Carranza; most of them appeared in the final Constitution in the exact form that they were presented in the draft. But the Constitution of 1917, nevertheless, bore little resemblance to the earlier constitution; it had a different emphasis and a different philosophy. It was not what historian Herbert I. Priestley perceived it to be when he wrote in 1921 that the document was imbued with "extreme communistic theories" and sought to "create a state socialism where property rights . . . are subverted," but it did undercut traditional institutions and give to the government a role far beyond that written into other contemporary charters. The keys to the Constitution, and to later Mexican developments, are to be found in the four articles dealing with education, property rights, the rights of labor, and religion.

After the formal reading of the draft the assembly suspended its ordinary sessions for five days in order to give the various committees time to study the proposals, and when the assembly next met on December 11 the Commission on the Constitution, under Mújica's chairmanship, set off the first bomb. Carranza's article 3 stated:

> There is to be full liberty of instruction, but that given in official educational institutions will be secular, and the instruction imparted by these institutions will be free at both the upper and lower primary levels.

The article reflected constitutional and legal provisions then in force. Under its provisions religious groups or lay individuals could establish schools at any level without government supervision; in short, the Church could continue its educational program unmolested and could, if the hierarchy so chose, intensify a campaign against attendance at "godless and atheistic" public schools.

Such a provision may have satisfied Félix F. Palavicini, convinced as he was that religious schools, Catholic or Protestant, could not compete with good public schools. But Mújica, who declared himself to be an "enemy of the clergy, which I consider to be the most doleful and perverse enemy of the nation," demanded that the clergy be eliminated entirely from primary education. In passionate phrases he addressed the assembly:

> What ideas can the clergy bring to the soul of our Mexican mass, and to the soul of the children of the middle class or the wealthy? Nothing but the most absurd ideas, the greatest odium for democratic institutions, the deepest hatred for those principles of equity, equality and fraternity nurtured by that greatest of apostles, by the greatest democrat known in ancient times, who was called Jesus Christ.

Mújica's committee therefore brought in a substitute article 3; by its provisions

> There will be freedom of instruction, but instruction given in the official establishments of instruction will be secular, as will be the upper or lower primary instruction given in private schools. No religious corporation, minister of any cult or any person belonging to a similar association may establish or direct schools of primary instruction,

> nor give instruction in any college [*colegio*]. Private primary schools may be established only subject to the supervision of the Government. Primary instruction will be obligatory for all Mexicans, and in official establishments it will be free.

Here the issue was drawn, and all members of the assembly knew full well that the outcome of this issue would determine the ultimate orientation of the new Constitution. For a solid week the debate raged, with Mújica and his cohorts pressing home points and denouncing the clergy as perverters of Christianity and destroyers of human values. The contending faction fought a delaying action hour after hour and day after day. Speakers opposing the Mújica proposals equaled Mújica in their criticism of the clergy, but they insisted that such restrictions on clerical freedom undermined the very foundation of liberty and democracy. They used every parliamentary trick available to them, and they launched bitter personal attacks on the intelligence and experiences of their opponents, but they could not prevail; on December 16, after a continuous six-hour session, the assembly accepted the new proposals—with a few minor changes—by a vote of 99 to 58.

Article 3 set the tone of all succeeding events. By its provisions the Church was deprived of what it considered one of its most precious rights, the opportunity to impart Catholic instruction during those first six critical years of a child's educational life. It must be made clear that neither this article nor any other in the Constitution prevented the clergy from giving instruction in Catholic dogma, outside of regular school hours, but the article nevertheless destroyed a traditional view concerning the function of the Church. It was, logically, a basic attack on individual liberty and certainly limited the freedom of choice. It put the emphasis on the well-being of the social organism even at the sacrifice of individual rights; the other crucial articles fell into the same general category, each was the subject of the same kind of debate, and each was passed by roughly the same margin.

Article 27 in the draft proposal contained a definition of private property, a prohibition against Church ownership of real estate except for religious purposes, and general statements regarding the kinds of corporations which could own property. It was the 1857 article 27 with a few minor modifications; in its totality it consisted of approximately 400 words. But article 27 as it came from Mújica's committee, and as it was finally passed, was a lengthy disquisition on the nature and function of private and public property; the most lengthy of all the articles in the Constitution, it consisted of nearly 2500 words—more than half the total number of words appearing in the original Constitution of the United States. It was at one and the same time an article which destroyed and an article which built, an article which prohibited and an article which demanded. It required the destruction of the *latifundia* and the redistribution of land among the populace. It eliminated any monopoly, actual or potential, over water and mineral resources and in so doing laid the base for state-controlled irrigation, power, and extractive industries. At one stroke it voided all the concessions granted by earlier governments for the exploitation of natural resources and in doing so brought howls of anguish from foreign investors and indignant denunciations from foreign governments. It was, in a word, the very heart of the Constitution and a perfect expression of the actionists' philosophy of nationalism and function of government.

Article 27 was a strange and powerful synthesis of the traditional and the revolutionary. Traditional Spanish law had reserved for the crown inalienable ownership of certain subsoil deposits, notably the precious minerals; the new constitutional provision extended the principle to include all natural resources, save growing plant life and certain limited quantities of water. The right of eminent domain had long been an accepted principle not only in the Spanish world but in Western countries in general, and the various Mexican constitutions had traditionally included some statement concerning the right of the government to expropriate private property for reasons of public utility. The new article simply extended the definition of "public utility" far beyond the bounds usually recognized in what the U.S. citizen calls "condemnation" proceedings. Community holdings had been a part of the Mexican pattern of land tenure since long before the arrival of the Spaniards; Mújica's article not only provided for the reinstitution of the pattern which had been interrupted since 1856 but required the destruction of the large *haciendas.* Traditionally both Spanish and early Mexican law imposed restrictions on foreign ownership of certain kinds of property; article 27 of 1917 not only broadened the scope of such prohibitions by banning foreign ownership of land or waters along the frontiers but wrote into the Constitution the Calvo Clause which defined aliens' rights. And, finally, the 1857 prohibition of Church ownership of real estate was extended to include all buildings, which now became the property of the nation.

The revised article 27 gave great discretion to the state governments in defining public utility beyond that stipulated in the article itself, and charged the states with the responsibility of setting a maximum size for landholding. But neither state nor national government, under the article, had any discretion whatsoever in setting the amount or determining the method for payment to the owners of expropriated land. Lands taken for public utility were to be paid for by a special issue of agrarian bonds to mature in a maximum of twenty years at a maximum interest rate of 5 per cent; furthermore, the price to be paid was set at the declared tax value plus 10 per cent. Both state and national legislatures were required to enact, during the first session to be held after the promulgation of the new constitution, the laws necessary to put the article into effect. Under the article land reform, of which community landholding was a part, became not merely possible but mandatory.

Carranza himself may have seethed with resentment over this frontal attack so in conflict with his own philosophy, but he made no public protest or comment then or later. He had too much pride, too much *don de mando.* The constituent assembly was his congress, picked according to his specifications and limited to his supporters. Outside the assembly halls it was generally assumed, even by presumably competent diplomatic representatives from the United States, that Carranza controlled the deliberations and the outcome; Carranza in his egoism would scarcely wish to dispel the illusion. The self-styled First Chief and soon-to-be constitutional president apparently decided, during the course of the constitutional convention, to fall back on the colonial viceregal prescript of *Obedezco pero no cumplo*: he would accept the new document without demur, but he would take little action in effectuating it.

The draft constitution contained no special provisions regarding social welfare or the rights of labor; any rights which the laborer might have to organize into syndicates, to negotiate with employers, or to strike were contained in general provisions regarding the rights of citizens. The draft simply failed to recognize labor as a distinct class in the social organism and therefore established neither perquisites nor prohibitions, though it did give Congress the power to legislate on questions of "mining, commerce, credit institutions, and labor." Carranza thought this power sufficient to establish minimum wages and maximum hours. In view of the wooing to which labor had been subjected by Carranza agents in 1915, and the negotiations with labor leaders which had produced the enormously important Red Battalions in the struggle against Villa, Carranza's failure to recognize the specialized problems of the laboring man came as a distinct disappointment. But it should have come as no surprise, since only four months prior to the opening of the convention he had not only broken a railroad strike with armed force but had also blasted labor groups for their arrogance in demanding "the right to impose such conditions as they may deem convenient to their interests."

But the radical majority in the assembly was in no mood to leave to future chance the enactment of labor laws which might or might not be beneficial to labor, and so they wrote into the Constitution a mandate to the national and state legislatures. Labor legislation, according to article 123, was required to be enacted by state and national governments, but all such legislation had to conform to a set of specific guidelines. Minimum wages were to depend upon the nature of the regional economy, but in any case to represent a sufficient income to a head of family to "satisfy the normal needs of life. . . , his education and his lawful pleasures." Eight hours of day work, and seven at night, were to be the maximum for adults, while children under the age of 16 were to be limited to six hours. Double time was to be paid for overtime, and the amount of overtime was closely circumscribed. All employers were required to pay equal wages for equal work, regardless of sex or nationality, and to make provision for adequate housing, medical, and educational facilities for the laborers and their families. Compensation for accidents or job-affiliated disease was prescribed, while payment in anything save legal tender was proscribed. Workers could strike and employers lock out, but certain conditions had to be set before either was legal. A board of arbitration and conciliation, consisting of representatives of labor, management, and government, was to be established to settle labor disputes. These provisions, plus a number of others concerning the right to organize, conditions of employment, safety features, sanitary requirements, discharges, and employee indebtedness to employers, gave to Mexican workmen those guarantees for which they had been agitating, and many more besides. Article 123 put the laborer in Mexico on a legal par with any worker in the world; he could now claim as a matter of constitutional right those things which the German, British, and U.S. laborers were demanding in negotiation.

As the constitution-makers neared the completion of their task, they faced the problem of clarifying in detail the position of the Church and the clergy in Mexican society. A general air of virulent anticlericalism had already pervaded the earlier deliberations. In addition to article 3 prohibiting clerical intervention into primary education and a portion of article 27 divesting religious organizatons of all real property, the Constitution forbade monastic orders in article 5 and obligated children to attend secular schools in article 31. Carranza's draft included an article which simply restated existing constitutional and legal provisions regarding religious institutions. This proposal would have reserved to the national government the exclusive right to legislate in the field of Church-state relations, would have prohibited the government from either establishing or forbidding any religion, and would have continued marriage as a civil contract. But this rather simple formula fell far short of satisfying the assembly radicals; they wanted something much more powerful.

Article 130, which the majority hoped would be the *coup de grâce* to clerical power, reflected both the fear and the contempt with which the constitution-makers viewed the clergy; many of the provisions gave clear evidence that the writers recognized that their work would be objectionable to the majority of the public. By the provisions of the article the existing legislation was verified, and additional restrictions, some unreasonable, were imposed. All churches were denied juridical personalities, all ministers of religions were to be considered as members of a profession subject to laws governing professions, no foreigner could exercise the functions of a minister, and no minister could ever criticize any government policy, act or official, nor could any minister vote, hold office, or engage in a political gathering. The states were authorized to designate the number of ministers who could perform religious services. No studies undertaken in seminaries could ever be used for credit toward professional training in any public institution, no religious services could be conducted outside the confines of a building designated for religious worship, and no such building could be used for any assembly of a political nature. No periodical publication of a religious nature, even "by general tendencies," could comment in any way on the political scene, nor could any political party be in any way associated or identified with religion. No minister could inherit any real property except from close blood relatives. And, finally, no person charged with the infraction of any of the provisions could claim the right to trial by jury.

The Constitution contained no word which could be interpreted as anti-religious; on the contrary, article 24 guaranteed to every Mexican the right "to embrace the religion of his choice and to practice all ceremonies . . . of his creed . . . ," and article 130 itself prevented the state from prohibiting any religion. The radical majority insisted, vehemently, on freedom of conscience. And yet, from the standpoint of religious freedom, most of the restrictions bordered on the ridiculous. In terms of logic, of abstract principles of justice or freedom, these violent anticlericals could find no justification for their extreme position. They based their actions upon history—sometimes accurate and sometimes garbled—and upon a long trail of hypocrisy and double-dealing on the part of the clergy. At the very moment that the article was being debated, for example, the clergy in Puebla were flaunting long-established laws against Church ownership of real property. Mújica and his friends knew that their work in the convention undercut fundamental liberties, but they were also convinced that only through the circumscription of one set of liberties could a much broader freedom be achieved ultimately for the Mexican people. But the restrictions themselves were mild in comparison to some of those for which the more extreme members of the assembly fought. The delegation from Yucatán, for example, hoped to prohibit oral confession, to prohibit the ownership of any real property by any member of the clergy under any circumstances, and to limit the priesthood to men over the age of 50. Even after article 130 had been approved by a majority of the assembly, one persistent anticlerical introduced an amendment which would have required marriage for all ministers of any faith.

As the news dribbled out of Querétaro concerning the nature of the Constitution as it was being drafted, those Mexicans and foreigners whose interests were jeopardized became understandably upset. The immediate enactment and enforcement of enabling legislation consistent with the spirit of the four crucial acts would, of course, have been enormously disrupting to the social and economic patterns upon which the vested interests fed. Articles 3 and 130 would probably have caused less disruption, in and of themselves, than the others, but by May 1, 1917, when the new Constitution went into effect, neither the proclericals nor the anticlericals could see anything in a rational light. Rigid enforcement of the anticlerical provisions would have meant not only closing or materially altering about one-fifth of the nation's schools, but also bitter quarrels in all parts of Mexico over supervision of the Church buildings, the registration of ministers, and all other aspects of clerical freedom. But rigid enforcement of articles 27 and 123 would have meant a complete re-ordering of the entire economic structure. These provisions put in doubt the validity of virtually every title and concession to major land or subsoil holdings, and presaged interminable haggling over labor conditions and contracts. Small wonder that every mining company, oil concern, landholder, banker, and merchant viewed the future with apprehension, or that the foreigners among these groups appealed to their governments.

But so far as it can be determined on the basis of available data, the promulgation of the Constitution of 1917 had little immediate detrimental effect on the economy, principally because the critical articles remained unenforced. Carranza himself showed no great eagerness to enact enabling legislation, and the states generally demonstrated even greater reluctance. Even though article 27 had given a mandate for immediate legislation for land distribution and the creation of agrarian bonds, two years elapsed before any state faced the problem, three years elapsed before the national government authorized the issuance of agrarian bonds, and five years passed before national law defined a "community" for the purpose of obtaining land. By the end of Carranza's tenure, land distribution was still a thought rather than an act; less than one-tenth of 1 per cent of the land had changed hands, and much of this droplet actually consisted of lands which agrarians had forcibly occupied prior to 1917. But even this pitiful show under article 27 exceeded that of article 123. State legislatures dillied while the national congress dallied, and the combined result was a welter of conflicting laws which gave neither philosophical comfort nor material advantage to the laboring men. The Constitution of 1917 was fourteen years old before a national labor code, putting into law the principles of 1917, saw the light of day.

Even though the major provisions of the Constitution remained unenforced in 1924, every major political figure had sworn fealty to the basic concepts, and the government had steadfastly upheld their validity in the face of strong pressure by other nations. The Constitution may not have been effectuated, but it was the law of the land; during the following decade and a half successive governments put into effect all the revolutionary provisions.

Chapter 10 • At Last

The agrarian revolution and the industrial revolution in Mexico are . . . twin aspects of the same phenomenon. The agrarian revolution had and continues to have as its object the destruction of the enslaving and feudalistic system under which the country lived, so that capitalism could be established. The industrial revolution has as its final end the installation of the capitalistic regimen.

MANUEL GERMÁN PARRA, 1954

When Gustavo Díaz Ordaz took the oath of office as president of Mexico on December 1, 1964, he could look back over the past forty years with pride and satisfaction, and he could look forward with hope and confidence. Since the consolidation of the Revolution with Calles's election in 1924, the nation had grown in stability and maturity and in economic well-being. Except for a bit of restiveness over the election of 1940, and a "rebellion" led by Saturnino Cedillo in 1938 which amounted to nothing, the country had been remarkably peaceful since 1929—and all this without strong dictatorial control or a show of military force. After 1929 military spending steadily declined. In that year the military took one-third of federal expenditures, five years later one-fifth, and in 1950 one-fourteenth. In 1964 total military expenditures accounted for about one-thirtieth of the national budget, and a major portion of the military budget went into road construction and other items of social capital. Peace and stability came as a result of a general consensus, within a gradually developing democratic framework. Private armies, a Mexican characteristic even during the *pax porfiriana,* disappeared, as the central administration became truly national and the economy became so integrated that the fortunes of one region depended upon the events in another.

Throughout the nineteenth century and well into the twentieth, political instability, which in turn had its maleficent effects on economic development and social change, was fostered by the lack of any effective institutional system under which widely divergent economic and social sectors could participate politically. Díaz's insistence on his own re-election in 1910 lighted the fuse which produced the Revolution, and Carranza's attempt to elect a puppet-successor in 1920 brought on the military movement which destroyed him. Obregón, who engineered a constitutional amendment which enervated that document's proscription against re-election, fell to an assassin's bullet before he could resume office a second time.

Out of the political crisis which sprang from Obregón's death came the beginnings of an institutional development which, though of doubtful theoretical democratic validity, has served as a magnificent instrument for peaceful executive change and of mass political participation. Anxious to retain his own dominant position, Plutarco Elías Calles took the lead in 1929 by organizing the National Revolutionary Party (PNR), which ostensibly represented all segments of Mexican society but in fact consisted of Calles's supporters who blindly did his bidding. But later presidents—Cárdenas in 1938 and Avila Camacho in 1946—changed the name and broadened the base to such a degree that the resulting Partido Revolucionario Institucional (PRI) probably represents the interests and aspirations of the great majority of Mexicans. This institution—for it is something more than a political party—has been primarily responsible for the peaceful transfer of executive authority regularly every six years since 1934 and has made a reality of the hoary "No-Reelection" maxim so much a part of previous political paroxysms. At worst PRI has allowed social and economic change; at best it has been responsible for it.

And enormous change has come about. Critics of the Revolution insist that the frightful chaos of the 1910-20 period delayed rather than stimulated change, and that the revolutionary practices introduced an element of moral degeneration which weakened the Mexican nation. Whether the Revolution in fact created the remarkable economic development which took place after 1950 may be debated. The evidence suggests a strong affirmative answer, but neither logic nor evidence prevails against an argument based upon "what might have been." And so those who either have a romantic view of the porfirian period, or who agree through conviction with the basic tenets of that era, give no credit to the Revolution for any beneficent changes which occurred. But it is feckless to contend that the Revolution weakened the Mexican nation. Díaz's Mexico was not a nation; it was some 15 million people surrounded by national borders, with a government which exercised a modicum of national sovereignty. The Revolution, if it did nothing else, produced a nation of people with a national sense, a nation whose art, architecture, and every mode of thought are distinct.

The fundamental changes came slowly, and they came hard. The two decades after Obregón were years of tensions, of unreasonableness, of international quarrels and domestic crises. During those years many men, foreigners and nationals alike, suffered enormous economic and spiritual loss, while the great mass of the population remained, materially, in conditions worse than those for which the Díaz regime has been so bitterly castigated. The average peon ate measurably less in 1936 than in 1896, and the low real wage paid to him in 1910 would have looked magnificent in 1934. But during those years of deprivation a vast array of institutional changes were in the making, all intimately related and designed, hopefully, to serve as a base for future benefits. No single facet of the reform program—land redistribution, Church-state relations, education, economic nationalism, industrial encouragement, petroleum nationalization—makes much sense when isolated. Only in juxtaposition with other policies and programs, as the various elements impinged one on another, do the various aspects become logically or socially justifiable. The combination of measures touched every Mexican, regardless of social status or economic condition, from the wealthy to the poverty-stricken, from the urban creole to the isolated Lacandón or Huichol indigene. Not all were affected in the same manner, or at the same time, and not all benefited immediately or even ultimately. Each reacted as he saw the process aiding or harming him, and many reacted passionately.

Predictably, the Church became the storm-center. Initially, the enforcement of the anticlerical constitutional provisions depended almost wholly upon the zeal of local officials. Carranza objected philosophically to the harshness of most of the stipulations and took action only when forced to do so, and until 1926 both Obregón and Calles were too involved in touchy international and political problems to undertake a rigid enforcement of principles to which possibly a large portion of the public would object violently. In the first bloom of enthusiasm in 1917 some of the state administrations engaged in a spate of pointed anticlericalism, but most of the actions were more irritating than fundamental. Yucatán exiled seventeen clerics; five states (Campeche, Coahuila, Jalisco, Sonora, and Tabasco) limited the number of priests and required registration of them; some of the states confiscated Church property; Durango razed a number of churches in the name of beautification; and most of the states by decree forbade foreign ministers to perform religious services. But only rarely did the states attempt full enforcement of their own laws, and only in Jalisco did a major quarrel develop, one that would be a harbinger of a national explosion that was to rock the nation a few years later.

Jalisco in 1917 was traditionally conservative and clerical; with roughly 8 per cent of the national population, the state had almost 20 per cent of the priests, proportionately twice as many as Mexico City itself. The archibishop was a young, fiery member of a distinguished Guadalajara family; even before the Constitution was written, he was often in hot water with the civil government, and it was he who precipitated the fight. When the Constitution was promulgated on February 5, 1917, nearly half the Mexican episcopate lived in exile in San Antonio, Texas. There, probably at the urging and certainly with the help of some U.S. churchmen, fourteen bishops and archbishops drafted and signed a bitter "Protest" excoriating the Constitution's anticlericalism. For about five months copies of the document circulated in Mexico, but the civil authorities ignored its existence until July 8, when it was read, on the orders of the archibishop then in hiding, in the cathedral and seven other Guadalajara churches. The reading stimulated massive public demonstrations against the government. Civil authorities could overlook the document's private circulation, but they could scarcely turn their heads when the "Protest" became an official pronouncement of the Guadalajara clergy. Nor could they look with equanimity on a hierarchical exposition of policy which said that

> we will disavow any act or statement, even though it emanates from persons in our dioceses who might be invested with ecclesiastical authority, if it is contrary to our declarations and protests.

Both words and tone called on the faithful to reject the Constitution by thought and deed, and by extension to refuse to abide by either law or Constitution. By reading the protest in the churches, the Guadalajara clergy challenged the government to act, and the results should have been foreseen. The governor closed the cathedral and the seven other churches, arrested the priests who had read the offending document, and jailed the leaders of the public demonstrations; the "Protest," he said, amounted to sedition. While rumors circulated that the archbishop would be executed on the spot were he found, that dignitary remained in hiding; on one occasion, at least, he masqueraded as a mule drover. For the next few months the archbishop and the police played an aimless game of hide-and-seek (police inefficiency was so obvious that one wonders whether it were deliberate) while passions cooled. In October the closed churches were allowed to resume services, though neither side had budged from its original position. Ten months later a decree limiting the number of priests to roughly one-third of those then in the state, and requiring registration as a prior condition for officiating in any service, brought on a new crisis. Rather than conform to the decree, the priests simply refused to carry on their ministerial duties, and one church after another closed its doors to the public. By late 1918 all Jalisco churches were effectively closed for religious services, and the faithful were on the point of rebellion. The clerical strike proved effective; in early February 1919, a new governor struck the offending decree from the record, and the churches reopened. Clerical success in combatting civil regulation proved to be unfortunate, for the episcopate generally assumed that they had discovered a powerful weapon to bring the government to heel. Dependence on this weapon in 1926 brought momentary disaster to the Church and to the government.

Despite the Jalisco quarrel, and a number of others less serious which resulted in exile for members of the hierarchy, state and national policy put little emphasis on legal anticlericalism. Catholic schools continued to function, foreign priests performed religious rites, priests wore their distinctive garb in public and officiated at open-air ceremonies, and clergymen regularly criticized government acts. As far as the vast majority of priests were concerned, the Constitution of 1917 simply did not exist. But tensions were building and patience wearing thin; with such a vast gulf separating the contending groups on matters of principle, the situation could not continue indefinitely. In early 1926 the issue was finally squarely joined, and before it was settled thousands of lives had been lost.

It is impossible to determine who must bear the responsibility for the carnage that followed. The clericals charged that Calles planned a campaign of rigid enforcement for the spring of 1926, and this they were attempting to forestall. The president, on the other hand, insisted that his government, "totally absorbed . . . in the tremendous administrative problems and the resolution of serious matters affecting the development of Mexico," had not realized that "bad Mexican and foreign clergy" were fomenting rebellion. Regardless of motivation, the opening gun came from the clergy when on February 5, 1926, a Mexico City newspaper published a statement attributed to Archbishop José Mora y del Río; the prelate, one of the signers of the 1917 "Protest," was quoted as having said:

> The protest which the Mexican prelates lodged against the Constitution of 1917 regarding those articles opposing liberty and religious dogmas is firmly maintained. It has not been modified; it is strengthened because it is derived from the doctrine of the Church. . . . The Episcopate, the Clergy and all Catholics disavow and combat Articles 3, 5, 27 and 130 of the present Constitution.

The government responded by exiling foreign priests, by closing Catholic schools, and by encouraging the states to limit the number of priests who could officiate; by mid-summer every state had not only set the number of clerics who could perform religious services, but had stipulated the conditions under which they could do so. Members of the episcopacy reacted by issuing additional public criticisms, one of which extended the "reprobation and anathema to each and every one of the precepts" in the Constitution which might violate "divine or natural rights." When the national government decreed a new code for the Federal District and territories to go into effect on August 1, Catholic laymen, with the blessing of the hierarchy, instituted a boycott to force withdrawal of the offending law. But in late July it became obvious that Calles would not retreat from his position. The episcopate, harking back to the Jalisco victory seven years earlier, then decided that the Church could force moderation by a simple refusal to perform religious services. Spokesmen for the clergy announced that after July 31 all religious services–including marriages, baptisms, and burials–would be suspended until such time as the civil authorities allowed the priests to perform their religious functions unmolested. On Thursday, August 1, for the first time in over four hundred years, no Church bells rang, no masses were said, no Catholic religious rites of any kind were performed. But the churches remained open, occupied and maintained by civil officials. The Mexican still had the solace of his church and his religious artifacts, and the great mass of the population seemed to be able to satisfy their spiritual needs without the intervention of the priesthood–a shocking surprise to the clergy.

But some, including an unknown number of priests, reacted violently. By October guerrilla bands had organized in many sections. Government military commanders reported that priests led some of the rebellious groups, but clerical spokesmen always maintained that the priests acted as chaplains, not fighting men. Members of the hierarchy never gave public approval to the resort to arms, but the government interpreted the episcopate's failure to condemn the uprisings as tacit consent. As the months passed the fighting became more savage, particularly in Jalisco and Michoacán where the rebels went into battle shouting *"Viva Cristo Rey"* ("Long Live Christ the King"), and in keeping with Mexican tradition both rebels and government forces committed acts of vicious cruelty. The rebels burned schools and public buildings, assassinated teachers and public officials, executed labor leaders who supported the government, executed prisoners, and generally wreaked havoc where they could. The government executed prisoners, hanged some priests, took hostages, drove entire villages from their lands, and in a thousand ways mistreated men identified as sympathetic to the rebel cause. Some government commanders used the situation as a means of enriching themselves. The commander in Jalisco sold arms and ammunition to the rebels, confiscated for his personal profit crops from peasant and *hacendado* alike, and deliberately kept the profitable insurrection alive. Other military chieftains had less success in becoming millionaires, but not for want of trying.

The final atrocity which drove the government to precipitate action against the clergy, and did much to condemn the Cristero movement both at home and abroad, came on April 20, 1927, when about 400 men shouting *"Viva Cristo Rey"* attacked a Guadalajara-Mexico City passenger train. Not content with derailing the train and firing into the wrecked cars, the attackers poured kerosene on the remains and set fire to the whole, burning to death those trapped inside; the death toll of men, women, and children, all civilians, reached well over a hundred. When survivors reported that three priests, in clerical garb, actively directed the assault, the government took the not unwarranted position that Church officials should be held responsible for the outrage. Calles therefore ordered the expulsion of those bishops and archbishops who remained in Mexico, and by late April the nation had neither Catholic services nor hierarchy.

By the summer of 1927 the rebellion, never a serious threat to the government, lost its charge in all areas save portions of Jalisco and Michoacán. In those two sections the rapacity of the federal commanders rather than the fanaticism of the peasants kept it alive; some evidence suggests that the major factor in driving the Jalisco peasants to arms initially was rooted in hatred for the local military officials, and that the religious issue was distinctly secondary. A gradual change in the severity of punishment meted out to captured rebels and a generally more conciliatory attitude during Portes Gil's year as president weaned the peasants away from the movement, and the insurrection slowly died out. But the lessening of fighting did not solve the religious question, for the churches remained closed and the hierarchy exiled. Unfortunately, clerics and government officials alike were victims of a passionate distrust which made any meeting of the minds almost impossible, but both groups realized the utter futility of attempting to maintain conditions as they were. Since the great mass protest which the clergy had visualized failed to materialize, the Church found itself in a ridiculous position. The government, on the other hand, was confronted with the embarrassing reality of having been party responsible, at the very least, for a situation in which a heavily Catholic nation had no Catholic Church services. Furthermore, priests did perform illegal religious services surreptitiously in private homes, and every attempt by officials to prevent the practice exposed the government to charges of religious persecution. Leaders of both groups knew that some compromise had to be reached, but they could devise no formula which would even lead to discussion.

Under these circumstances, U.S. Ambassador Dwight Morrow decided that regardless of diplomatic protocol he had a right and a responsibility to meddle in Mexican domestic affairs. Moving with extraordinary caution in this delicate situation, Morrow arranged a meeting between Calles and Father John J. Burke of the United States in April 1928, at San Juan de Ulúa in Veracruz harbor. From this meeting came a tentative suggestion as to the manner of settlement, which was followed by a meeting between Calles and Archbishop Leopoldo Ruiz y Flores of Michoacán, one of the signers of the 1917 "Protest" and the chosen representative of the exiled prelates in San Antonio. The archibishop and the president agreed to a mode of settlement on May 17, but the prelate felt it necessary to consult with the Vatican before he could commit the Mexican hierarchy; the secrecy with which all the negotiations had been surrounded could not be preserved indefinitely, however, and before Ruiz y Flores reached Rome word of the impending settlement reached the newspapers.

Public discussion of the subject seriously jeopardized the venture's success; León Toral's assassination of president-elect Obregón on July 17 killed it. Not again until April 1929 was the domestic situation in Mexico conducive to a resumption of negotiations, and again Morrow acted as intermediary between Church and state. Months passed before government officials and churchmen, in great secrecy, reached an agreement. But finally on June 21, 1929, the Vatican approved the compromise, and on Sunday, June 30, Catholic services resumed, after a suspension of two years and eleven months.

But the compromise settled nothing; the much-heralded agreement left the contending parties in roughly the same position they had occupied before. Portes Gil assured the faithful that the government did not intend to "destroy the integrity of the Catholic Church, . . . nor to intervene in any way with its spiritual functions." Furthermore, he said, the Church was perfectly free to give religious instruction within the churches, and any citizen could petition for a repeal of the offending laws and constitutional provisions. These two "concessions" by the government were not concessions at all; these positions were clearly stated, explicitly or implicitly, in the Constitution. But Portes Gil did make one concession: only those priests designated as being responsible for the churches needed to register, and the Church itself could designate those so responsible. Thus the three years of bitter struggle resulted in a stalemate.

The Church-state issue was far from solved. During the next few years official and unofficial attacks on the Church grew in number and intensity, the most severe coming as a result of clerical objection to a new educational policy. But at least some of the persecution—for the actions of 1931-36 must be so labeled—came from purely political considerations, reflecting a bitter fight among the revolutionaries for power; anticlericalism could be used effectively as a rallying point for ambitious politicians. Many actions of national and state officials smacked of anti-Catholicism rather than mere anticlericalism, even though no responsible official ever publicly railed against the Church itself.

The new wave began in the state of Veracruz in 1931. Following a series of incidents which included the bombing of the cathedral, an attempt to assassinate the anticlerical governor, and the shooting of two priests by a police officer within the confines of a church, the state government decreed that the "maximum number of ministers for each faith, in this state, will be one for each hundred thousand inhabitants." The decree meant, effectively, that of the nearly two hundred priests then officiating at churches in the state, only thirteen could continue to do so. Violence in Veracruz spread to other states in late 1931, at the very time that Church officials were planning a mammoth celebration of the four-hundredth anniversary of the appearance of the Virgin of Guadalupe. The celebration at the Shrine irritated the most intransigent anticlericals, for they saw in it a deliberate affront to the existing laws, and both state and federal governments reacted. The Jalisco government exiled the Archbishop of Guadalajara, the national government limited the number of priests in the Federal District to twenty-five, and many states severely limited clerical activities. In the course of 1932, eight states cut the number of priests to a ridiculously low level, seized Church buildings for public non-religious use, changed place names with religious connotations to those of secular heroes, and in general so harassed both clergy and communicants that religious practices became difficult and dangerous.

The wave continued to grow in the following two years. By 1934 thirteen of the states had closed most churches on one pretext or another ("sanitary laws" were a favorite gambit), in some states no religious services of any kind were tolerated, and in a few not a single priest remained. State and federal law combined limited the number of priests to about 10 per cent of those functioning in 1925, but since some states required the priests to be married or imposed other restrictions, effectively Mexico had about 5 per cent of the priests who had earlier been performing religious services. The ultimate in insanity was reached when the national government early in 1935 prohibited the use of the mails for any material of a religious nature.

Under this series of attacks the clergy in general reacted with remarkable moderation. Apostolic Delegate Leopoldo Ruiz y Flores counseled patience in a number of statements in 1931 and 1932, and in each specifically denounced the use of force by those objecting to government policies. But even his patience wore thin, and in 1934 he issued a vigorous protest against what he considered the tyrannical acts by both national and state governments. As the persecution mounted and as "socialistic education" began to permeate the countryside in 1935 and 1936, individual priests took it upon themselves to defend their faith by inciting their ignorant parishioners to acts of violence. One of these acts ultimately led to a general amelioration of the situation.

Lázaro Cárdenas, who came to the presidency on December 1, 1934, showed signs early in his administration that he was unsympathetic to rampant Catholic persecution, but during his first year in office his contest with Calles for political power prevented any radical change in central government policy. By early 1936 he felt strong enough to challenge some of Calles's concepts, even though the *Jefe Máximo* was still a potent political threat. While on one of his frequent tours of the country, the president received word that a clash between some teachers and some devoted pro-clericals in a nearby Jalisco village had resulted in a number of deaths. Cárdenas went to the village, made a personal investigation which convinced him that the priest had instigated the trouble, and ordered the cleric to leave the state within forty-eight hours. Within a few days other teachers in the region came to request protection from fanatical villagers; Cárdenas took the opportunity to enunciate a policy which he hoped would put the functions of the Church and the state into proper perspective:

> To break down the resistance of fanatics egged on by the enemies of the Revolution, the people in the communities must be organized. . . . But this Government has no intention of falling into the error of previous administrations. The duty of a revolutionary administration like the present consists in doing all that may be necessary to carry out the program of the Revolution, the fundamental aspects of which are social and economic in character. . . . It is no concern of the Government to undertake anti-religious campaigns. . . . Hereafter, there must be no anti-religious propaganda in the classroom. All our attention must be concentrated upon the great cause of social reform.

Almost immediately the new policy could be seen in official publications; the violent attacks on the Church and the priesthood disappeared from the pages of government organs to be replaced by essays dealing with the proper role of religion as an ethical complex. State governments modified the restrictive legislation, and gradually more priests returned to their religious functions. In 1938 the Archbishop of Mexico not only issued mollifying statements, but urged strong support from all Mexicans to the government during the crisis over the oil expropriations. Slowly, between 1938 and 1940, the country returned to the religious practices of the past, without persecution and without molestation; by the latter year army officers in uniform went to Mass for the first time in many years, and in the following year the national government authorized new church construction. The crisis had come to an end, and with it the "Church-state problem" subsided into nothingness.

After 1941 the Church and the state lived with each other with a minimum of friction. Most of the constitutional and statutory provisions to which the clergy objected with such bitterness remained and were generally respected. The government officially retained ownership of all churches; the clergy could not appear in public in distinctive garb; the Church officially maintained no primary schools; and the ban on open-air religious services continued. On those rare occasions when some churchman openly and obviously acted contrary to the restrictions, public opinion expressed though the newspapers, not official action, came to the defense of constitution and law. But with all this, and perhaps because of it, the Catholic Church as a religious institution grew stronger than it had ever before been in the history of Mexico, colonial or national. In the understanding of his religion, and in the acceptance of his religious obligations, the Mexican finally came to maturity.

Central to the Church-state struggle in the most critical years was the question of education. To the revolutionary reformer the most important issue facing the Mexican nation was the creation of a new process of thought, a new value system which would allow every individual to make his maximum contribution to himself and to society. No true development could come, the reformer held, as long as the elite minority showed contempt for the majority, and this contempt could be destroyed only through an educational process which gave the individual something more than the rudiments of literacy. Correctly or incorrectly, the revolutionary viewed the clergy as the major stumbling block to this process, for history had convinced him that the Church was the ally of the entrenched elite, of the *hacendados,* and all others who stood for a continuation of a dreary social system which denied the essential equality of man. He held the village priest responsible for the superstitious traditionalism which pervaded the mass of society, and which prevented the acceptance of new thought or new processes. One student at the National School for Agriculture at Chapingo reported that his priest had warned the villagers not to abandon their wooden plows, for soil through which steel had passed would grow no crop. Another priest, according to rumor, forbade his Baja California parishioners to dig a well, for the digging would free terrible demons which would ruin the crops and devour the people. The priests, anticlericals insisted, interpreted every natural phenomenon as a manifestation of divine munificence or wrath, and so taught the simple peasant or artisan that he had no control whatsoever over his own earthly destiny; by this technique, the critics said, the Church maintained iron control over the populace. Though these charges can scarcely be made seriously against the Church as an institution, in fact many priests—some in their own ignorance and some for selfish reasons—were guilty of such practices. Priests in Oaxaca in 1925 pointed to a plague of locusts as divine retribution for land seizures by the villagers. Priests in Jalisco warned peasants that crops planted on lands granted the villages by the government would die, and priests everywhere were more prone to send their sick parishioners on pilgrimages than to a doctor.

Regardless of who was responsible for the ignorance and the poverty, the superstition and the traditionalism, these attitudes were deeply ingrained in the fabric of the society with which the educational reformer had to work. He concluded that he could do little with the older generation, but he subscribed wholeheartedly to the belief that "the children of Mexico belong to the Revolution." It was through the child that the reformer hoped to bring about change, and in order to do so he had to give to the child a freedom from all superstitions and misconceptions of the past. It was this conviction which drove him to eliminate the Church from the entire educational process and which led him ultimately to the development of "socialistic education."

Admittedly enormous problems faced the educators. In 1924 only a quarter of those over the age of ten could read and write, no more than one-fifth of the school-age children attended class on any given day, few schools existed in the rural districts, and the country could count only about 25,000 teachers—most of whom had only a secondary education themselves. Furthermore, the economic conditions of the vast majority of the population made the income from all family members crucial to survival; the average Mexican father might have been intrigued with the idea of a literate son, but he could scarcely afford the added expense and the loss of the income involved in sending his child to school. Faced with such a situation, educators frequently made decisions on whim; schools opened one year fell into disrepair the next, programs begun with great fanfare dribbled away into nothing, and money allocated for one school district ended in another—or in some official's pocket. But even in those bleak days of international tension, of the Cristero rebellion, and of political crisis, the school system made some headway. By 1930, 51 per cent of those between the ages of ten and fourteen could read and write (how well the data do not tell us), 42 per cent of those between the ages of six and ten were enrolled in school, the number of rural schools had trebled, and nearly 14 per cent of the national budget was allocated to education.

During the next few years, despite the depression which hit Mexico as well as other nations, the struggle for quantity education continued to be of prime importance. When Cárdenas took office in late 1934, the number of rural schools had almost doubled over 1930 and the total number of primary schools had increased by more than 40 per cent; but as a result of the economic crisis the total number of enrollees in the primary grades had declined. Central government expenditures for education, and the total expended by national, state, and municipal governments, declined slightly between 1930 and 1934, but even in the latter year the federal educational appropriation more than quadrupled the greatest amount ever spent by Díaz in one year. Even so, progress was tortuously slow. The majority of school-age children still failed to enroll in spite of the constitutional provision for compulsory education, and of those who did enroll only a bare majority completed the academic year successfully. Worse yet, in the eyes of men like Narciso Bassols, education failed miserably to change fundamental attitudes. Babies had grown to young manhood since the drafting of the Constitution, but there had been little change other than a small increase in the proportion of the population who could stumble through simple prose.

The answer, some thought, was a new approach in education, and so "socialized education" became a part of the Six-Year Plan which outlined the goals for the Cárdenas administration. According to the revised constitutional article 3, adopted by Congress on October 10, 1934:

> The education imparted by the state shall be socialistic and, in addition to excluding all religious doctrine, shall combat fanaticism and prejudices by organizing its instruction and activities in a way that shall permit the creation in youth of an exact and rational concept of the universe and of social life.
>
> Only the State—Federation, States, Municipalities—shall impart primary, secondary and normal education.

Alongside the constitutional change came a new definition of the rights and duties of both child and teacher. According to official doctrine, the child had a right to come from healthy parents and to enjoy health himself; he had a right to develop normally both physically and mentally; he had a right to rise to a cultural level of which he was intellectually capable; and he had a right to become a free mind and to discover for himself the excitement of learning. Furthermore, he had a right to good schools, to hygienic surroundings, to good teachers of high character and vocational excellence, to healthful recreation and exercise, and to the companionship of members of his own and the opposite sex.

> The boys have a right to be educated with the girls, and the girls with the boys, because . . . the man does not live in a world exclusively

> masculine, or the woman in one exclusively feminine. Care will be taken that they do not lose the essential characteristics of their sex.

The child had a right, in short, to grow up in a healthful world and to develop his own intellect and personality so that he could make his maximum contribution to himself and to his society, as free as possible from superstitions and misconceptions.

Nothing in this basic concept should have caused grave concern, other than perhaps the emphasis on the child as a social animal rather than as an individual; it was little more, in fact, than John Dewey's "Education is not preparation for life; it is life," which a contemporary generation of prospective teachers in the United States committed to memory. But the proclivities of some Ministry of Education officials to talk in Marxist clichés offended some, much talk about "sex education" shocked others, and the total exclusion of Church or clergy raised a storm of protest which helped bring on the 1934-36 crisis between the Church and the state.

The new creed, which rejected in theory the old-style rote classroom instruction that measured teaching effectiveness in terms of the din of repetition, aroused a crusading zeal among many young men and women who went out from the major cities to staff the new schools. Cárdenas struck a strongly responsive chord when he said, during his campaign for the presidency in 1934:

> The revolutionary teacher must be a social leader, an advisor, an orientor. He must not only teach how to read and write, but he must also show the proletariat the manner of living together better, of creating a more human and just existence.

The teacher, who in Mexico had always been looked upon as roughly equivalent in social value to a domestic servant, now achieved a crucial role in society; official dogma held the school "to be the determining factor in the new economic and social order" and the child to be "an agent of social transformation."

The national government reflected the new mood of determination in its budgets in succeeding years; the 1935 allocation exceeded that of

1934 by 42 per cent, and in 1937 it increased to 77, accounting for more than 18 per cent of the total national budget. Since the most critical area was at the primary level, the greatest emphasis was put on primary rural schools. By 1940 the number of rural teachers and of students enrolled had doubled over the 1930 figure. But the way of the rural teacher was hard. The system demanded supermen, with sophistication in political philosophy, in economics, in health, in agronomy, and in any other thing which the local community might need or demand. As the agent of the government he not only was expected to be versed in agrarian and labor law, but to encourage the proletariat to demand its rights. Ignorant parents sometimes resisted passively, but too often violently—the number of teachers killed or maltreated as "agents of the devil" ran into the hundreds. And for running the risks, battling parents, and living in isolated villages, the teacher received approximately a dollar a day.

Even worse, the teacher seemed to be involved in a losing cause. Despite the emphasis put on education by the national government, centralization of educational authority in Mexico City brought a corresponding loss of interest at the local level, particularly with regard to financing, and the school men could not keep up with the population. Between 1930 and 1940 the percentage of illiteracy dropped, but the number of illiterates increased by 300,000; the nation simply did not have sufficient teachers or schools to serve all the educational needs, even had the parents wanted to send their children to school. A survey in 1942 showed a dismal situation. In the rural schools, over 65 per cent of the students enrolled were in the first year, and over 95 per cent were in the first three years; a third-grade education may give a student the rudiments of literacy, but it scarcely gives him the breadth of vision and the social consciousness envisaged in the doctrine of "socialistic education." In the urban schools the situation was somewhat better, for 26 per cent went beyond third grade. The "agents of social transformation" may have been presented a bill of rights in 1934, but in 1940 it was still on paper.

Under these circumstances new President Manuel Avila Camacho put education on a slightly different tack. Without abandoning the primary aims (on the contrary, strenuous efforts were continued), the new administration took some of the sting out of article 3 and made it more palatable to the Church and to those offended by the word "socialistic." The new article still prohibited the Church or the clergy from taking part in primary, secondary, or normal education, but the phraseology was not quite as insulting. The most important portions read:

> The education that the State—Federation, States, municipalities—imparts shall tend to develop harmoniously all the faculties of the human being and shall develop in him a love of the Fatherland and a consciousness of international solidarity, independence and justice. Freedom of belief . . . shall be maintained by complete freedom from any religious doctrine and, based on the results of scientific progress, shall struggle against ignorance and its effects, servitudes, fanaticisms and prejudices.

The article then emphasized that education would be oriented toward the development of democracy, nationalism ("without hostility or exclusivism"), and human co-operation. Furthermore, since the Six-Year Plan with its emphasis on primary education had not transformed the society, Avila Camacho inaugurated an "each one teach one" campaign to increase literacy among the adults. The total effect remains in doubt but, according to the census, literacy of those over six years of age had climbed from 41 per cent in 1940 to 55 per cent in 1950. Viewing the statistics from a different angle, we can see that for every hundred persons added to the population over six years of age, 108 learned to read and write.

The census of 1950, nevertheless, showed some glaring weaknesses in the educational process. Of the 19,000 rural primary schools, only 5 per cent offered classes through the sixth year; about half consisted of the first three grades only. Of the slightly more than 6 million children in the 6 to 14 age bracket, only 50 per cent enrolled in school, only 37 per cent attended class regularly, and only 33 per cent did sufficient work to earn a promotion to the next grade. In that year, 1.4 million rural children enrolled in primary schools; 57 per cent were in the first year, 91 per cent were in the first three years, and only one-half of 1 per cent in the sixth year. In this respect conditions had changed little in the past ten years. Urban schools presented a slightly more encouraging picture, but even here less than 8 per cent of total primary enrollment was in the sixth year.

The situation in the secondary schools, of course, was even more disheartening. The nation could count on only 455 secondary schools in which only 63,000 students were enrolled and in which a mere 9,000 completed the third year. A nation of nearly 26 million that could produce only 9,000 students ready to enter a preparatory curriculum still had far to go, even though proportionately the number of students in secondary schools had doubled since the pre-revolutionary period. The government, now in the hands of President Miguel Alemán, was fully aware of the critical needs in education. The Federation allocated 18 per cent of its budget for educational purposes, with a heavy proportion of it being devoted to the construction of new schools—including over a hundred secondary—and the repair of old ones. In that one year the government spent more money on school construction than the Díaz administration expended for the entire educational system during its last ten years in power.

The long concern over literacy and education finally began to pay dividends after 1950. At the end of that decade over 60 per cent of the population could read and write, and by 1966 some estimates on literacy ran as high as 75 per cent. Estimates for 1964 placed over three-fourths of the 6 to 14 age group in school, with an increasing proportion completing the primary grades and entering secondary or pre-vocational schools. Between 1950 and 1964 nearly a thousand new secondary schools opened, with enrollments increasing from 63,000 to nearly half a million. In 1966 President Díaz Ordaz announced that during his first two years in office secondary school enrollments had increased by 50,000 each year, and that by the end of his administration (1970) the secondary system would have enough classrooms to service all students who completed the primary grades. In the fourteen years after 1950, too, nearly 13,000 new primary schools, 9000 of them in rural areas, had been constructed and staffed by an additional 70,000 teachers coming from the 120 new normal schools and the 68 already in existence. Teachers at all levels reflected the change in both educational level and in salaries. Two-thirds of the primary teachers had at least a normal school education, and the average salary equaled that of a skilled industrial laborer.

More telling than these impressive statistics, and perhaps responsible for them, has been a clearly discerned change in attitude within the generation after Cárdenas. Cárdenas had accepted "To educate is to redeem" as his fundamental tenet, and, even though little redemption could be detected by the end of his administration, his drive for education and civic responsibility had long-range effects which could not be determined at the time. The children to whom Cárdenas directed his attention had by the mid-1960's grown to maturity, with children of their own, and their demand for education had become startlingly intense. Education, said the national government, was a necessary attribute to patriotism, and the citizenry accepted it as such. Education, which among the peasantry and proletariat in 1936 was considered to be something quite unnecessary to existence, was now an essential, the key to the future, for which parents and children alike were willing to make a temporary sacrifice. With an improved and extended educational system, the aspirations of the Mexican young climbed—perhaps to unrealistic levels. The ambitious twelve-year-old son of a rural mechanic in 1936 could look forward only to being a better mechanic than his father and dream of being an engineer. Three decades later, a boy in the same position *believed* that he could become an engineer, and the fact that in 1964 nearly half a million students attended over 1400 schools beyond the secondary level gave him reason to think that a professional education was within his grasp. The fact, too, that nearly seven times as many men earned engineering decrees, and nearly six times as many earned professional titles in all fields, served to give him a firm base of reality for his ambition.

Nevertheless, even in the 1960's the ultimate aim of Mexican education was far from being realized. Well over half of all the secondary schools were private with high tuition costs rather than being public and free, and reputedly education in the public schools was inferior. Too great a proportion of those who began school dropped out after two or three years, and too few completed the education necessary for full intellectual development. The system still produced too few highly qualified men in specialized fields; proportionately, for example, the United States produced nearly six times as many engineers. But all data after 1950 indicated an accelerating pace, and a comparison between the Mexico of 1924 and Mexico forty years later showed a phenomenal educational growth.

Of all the aspects of social and economic change ushered in by the Mexican Revolution, agrarian reform took top priority and created the greatest dissension. Article 27 of the Constitution reflected the demands of the vast majority of Mexicans for a drastic change in the tenure system, but any change giving the peasantry legal access to land would mean the eviction of those who already had title. The peasant himself thought of "land reform" only in the sense of tenure, a system which would allow him the opportunity to work the land as he saw fit and to enjoy the fruits of his labor; but the intellectual agrarian reformer saw something much more fundamental in "land reform" than a mere redistribution of the land itself. He accepted, as an article of faith, land reform as the basis for all other social and economic change. He was convinced that redistribution of land would, ultimately, increase productivity, since much idle land would be cultivated, but much more importantly he believed that land ownership or usufruct would give to the peasant a sense of dignity, of responsibility. Community-owned lands would serve as a practical school of local democratic and representative government, and the entire process of marketing the product would make the peasant more aware of the outside world. Only through this process, the reformer held, could that vast submerged 80 or 90 per cent of the population become national and Mexican, and thereby make their contribution to the society as a whole. Within this scheme of thought, increased agricultural production was secondary.

But even before the Revolution food had reached a critical level, and many thoughtful men were convinced that any widescale tampering with the existing tenure system would bring a decline in agricultural goods reaching the market which would, in turn, drive prices—and tempers—up. Furthermore, any significant change in the tenure system could come only as the result of force. Article 27 included a provision for voluntary subdividing and sale by landowners, but since the experiences during the Madero administration had shown clearly that this technique was not dependable, the article also included a method for forcing the owner to divest himself of his land. The revolutionary years certainly weakened the *hacendado* class, but they had not destroyed its power completely, and any frontal attack on the entire group could have resulted in catastrophe for the Revolution itself.

Although a majority of those vitally concerned with land reform favored, in theory, a system of small individual landholdings, the bitter experiences in the latter part of the nineteenth century demonstrated the folly of giving land in fee simple to ignorant and naïve peasants. If the government were to assume a heavy debt in order to give the peasantry access to the land, most planners agreed, the government then must accept the responsibility for establishing a system which would prevent exploitation and ultimate loss of land. The major emphasis, in land distribution, then, revolved around the reinvigoration of the *ejido,* or communal landholding system, which had been outlawed by the Constitution of 1857 as retrograde. But the re-establishment of the *ejido* as the dominant pattern for agrarian reform posed some serious problems, the most crucial of which was to define a "community" eligible for land, only a minority of the rural population lived in groups which had already been designated as political entities. Nearly two decades passed before the legal intricacies of definition, of usufruct, and of protection were put into a satisfactory form. As finally established, almost any bona fide peasant had legal access to land; the lands belonging to the communities (the *ejidos*) could not be alienated except under rigidly controlled circumstances; and every member of a community had a right to the usufruct of a portion of the community lands as long as he made the land productive. The *ejido* became the center of agrarian reform, but the reform program also stimulated an increase in the number of private holdings, which doubled between 1930 and 1960.

Venustiano Carranza, the first Mexican president after the adoption of the Constitution, demonstrated a marked reluctance to take any bold steps in the field of agrarian reform; he had no great faith in the ability of the untutored peasant to boost agricultural production. In spite of the general clamor for land, and even though Zapata remained in rebellion over the land question until his death in 1919, Carranza gave only 200,000 hectares of land to the communities—and much of this was in fact little more than a legalization of conditions which had existed for a number of years. Obregón, more daring, more ruthless, and more committed than his predecessor, stepped up the program of redistribution to such a point that it began to have some significance. Under the able direction of Minister of Agriculture Antonio Villarreal, the National Agrarian Commission supervised the distribution of approximately one and three-quarter million hectares of land to nearly a thousand villages consisting of over 100,000 heads of family.

The Obregón administration distributed land, but it did not increase agricultural production. The 1925 corn crop of slightly under 2 million tons was not only less than the average pre-revolutionary output but was about the same as that of 1918, when both Villa and Zapata were still engaged in military operations; other important food crops fared about the same. One obvious weakness of agrarian reform (a weakness generally recognized) was that the new possessors of the land lacked experience, seeds, and tools. The *ejidatario* had no financial resources of his own with which to buy those things he needed and certainly could not depend upon the limited and conservative banking institutions to advance him the money. President Calles, Obregón's successor, took the first tentative steps to remedy the situation through the establishment of a government banking institution especially designed to aid the *ejidatarios*. But from the beginning the new bank was something more than a mere credit institution; it did indeed lend money, but it also advised the peasants on farming techniques, acted as the agent for the sale of produce, and in general served as an overseer for the *ejidal* program. Ideally, the bank assured the *ejidatario* a steady income, a fair price, and improved agricultural technology; and in some cases the ideal was met. Too often, nonetheless, the regional managers or their agents took advantage of a magnificent opportunity for self-enrichment; in many cases the bank simply took the place of the departed *hacendado*, exploiting the peasantry even more ruthlessly. One of the major criticisms of the *ejidal* program was that the peasant had traded a human and responsible patron for an inhuman and mechanistic institution.

Calles was not content, in his early years, merely with the establishment of the *ejidal* bank; he showed more enthusiasm for land distribution and peasant education than did Obregón. In his first two years he distributed about the same amount of land as Obregón had in his four, and by 1930 (he was no longer legal president, but actual dictator) the reform program under his tutelage had established an impressive record. Including the beneficiaries from earlier administrations, over 4000 villages consisting of about 2 million people had received more than 8 million hectares of land. Less than 2 of the 8 million consisted of arable land; over 12 million hectares of crop land remained in private hands. But despite the activities of the *ejidal* bank and the educational groups and all the other agencies involved in agrarian reform, agricultural production continued to slide downward. According to the first official agricultural census taken in 1930, corn production was disastrously low; the million and a third tons harvested that year was the lowest in over a hundred years and only slightly more than the late colonial average; on a per capita base the yield was the lowest ever recorded in Mexico. The bean crop of 83,000 tons was less than half that of 1910 and even below that of 1918. Most other agricultural statistics told the same doleful story.

The reform-minded tried to explain away the decline in terms of statistical errors: the peasants ate more and reported less, and consequently a significant proportion of the actual production never entered statistical columns. Or they stressed the social values of agrarian reform, glossing over the decline in production. But the dismal fact remained that land reform in terms of effective land use in 1930 was a colossal failure; the *ejidatario* was not even using the land given him. *Ejidatarios* planted only 51 per cent of the crop land in their possession, while private owners planted 57 per cent. Of the lands planted, the *ejidatarios* harvested only 72 per cent and the private owners 81.

One of the major arguments earlier used to justify agararian reform was that the private owner was making inefficient use of his land and that the peasantry, if given the opportunity, would use every available scrap. But 1930 government statistics would no longer support that contention, and if the statistics erred at all they favored the *ejidatarios*. Under these circumstances the opponents of land reform found justification for condemning the *ejidal* program in its entirety and for insisting that it was not "reform" but retrogression. To that point land redistribution had been costly to the national government; not only was the nation saddled with an enormous debt in the form of agrarian bonds to pay for the expropriated territories, but the proceedings had created serious problems with countries whose nationals were adversely affected. All in all, it appeared to Calles and his closest advisors that land distribution must come to a halt; consequently the tempo of the program slowed almost to a standstill.

When Lázaro Cárdenas took the oath of office in December 1934, he came with a burning desire to hurry the Revolution along in all directions. During the pre-electoral campaign he had crisscrossed the country, listening as much as he talked, and to him the concepts embodied in the Constitution were as full of vitality in 1934 as they had been in 1916. He was fully aware of the agricultural statistics, but he was confident that the humble people of Mexico, given time and the proper stimulation, would justify his faith in them. He knew of Calles's disillusionment, but he nevertheless said:

> If I am elected president, there will be no one who can stop me until the peasant has received the best lands and the State has given him all financial, moral and material aid possible.

He came to office dedicated to give more land, not less, and the agricultural situation had improved enough to give him a glimmer of encouragement. Productivity of most agricultural items was up from the 1930 figure, although still below the pre-revolutionary mark. More importantly, the *ejidos* produced almost half the corn, a third of the beans, and a fifth of the wheat; in 1934 the communal villages harvested almost a quarter of all the agricultural commodities even though they controlled only a fifth of the arable land.

During his six years in office Cárdenas spent almost as much time traveling as he did in his office, and on every trip he cut through official red tape, granted land on the spot to villagers who crowded around him, ordered wells to be dug and dams to be constructed, and did everything he could to encourage the peasantry. He created administrative chaos, but he distributed land. In his first three years he doubled the number of heads of family with land to work and the amount of land available to the *ejidatarios*. By the end of his term he had expropriated and distributed over 17 million hectares to nearly 8000 new villages in which over two million people lived. As a result of his efforts and those of his predecessors, by 1941 nearly 15,000 villages accounting for a quarter of the total population enjoyed the use of slightly less than half the crop land and about one-fifth the total land. Twenty-five years earlier almost none of these people had land they could call their own.

Data on productivity indicated that Cárdenas's faith was fully justified. *Ejidal* productivity was generally less than that of privately owned land, but average agricultural production during the three-year period 1939-41 was higher than it had been at any time since the beginning of the Revolution. Total production of food products, including fruits, registered the greatest gains, increasing by one-third over the 1930-34 average and comparing favorably with the last years of the *porfiriato*. Corn production was roughly the same as the last porfirian years, but wheat, rice, tomatoes, chickpeas, sugar cane, and a number of other items showed substantial increases. Critics of agrarian reform, of course, could justifiably contend that per capita production had declined, and then could conclude that the entire program had been a failure. They could also point to significant differentials, in favor of non-*ejidal* tenure, in the per acre production of virtually every crop. In every category the larger private holdings outstripped the *ejidos*, and even the 5-hectare-and-less category produced better than the *ejidos* in all crops save wheat, beans, and bananas. On the other hand, statistical and impressionistic data both indicated that the peasants were enjoying a better standard of living in 1940 than in 1910. Mortality rates in 1940 had declined enormously since 1910 (general from 33.3 to 23.2; infant from 323.1 to 125.7), and life expectancy had accord-

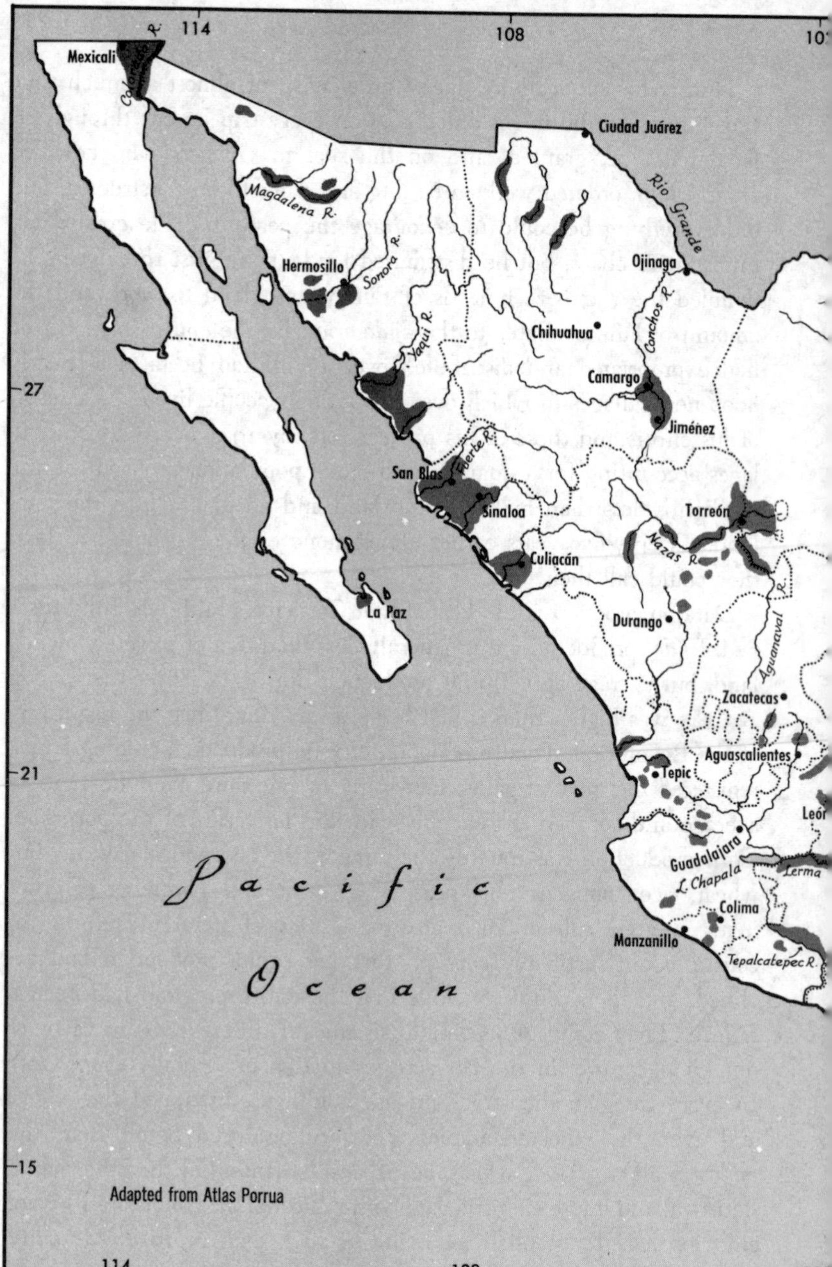
114
108
10
Mexicali
Colorado R.
Magdalena R.
Hermosillo
Sonora R.
Yaqui R.
Ciudad Juárez
Rio Grande
Ojinaga
Conchos R.
Chihuahua
Camargo
Jiménez
Fuerte R.
San Blas
Sinaloa
Culiacán
La Paz
Torreón
Nazas R.
Aguanaval R.
Durango
Zacatecas
Aguascalientes
Tepic
León
Guadalajara
L. Chapala
Lerma
Colima
Manzanillo
Tepalcatepec R.
27
21
15
Pacific
Ocean
Adapted from Atlas Porrua
114
108
102

MAJOR IRRIGATION WORKS
(Does not include wells)
Scale of Miles
0
100
200
300
96
90
27
21
15
Piedras Negras
Nuevo Laredo
Salado R.
Rio Grande
Matamoros
Monterrey
C. Victoria
Tampico
Gulf of Mexico
Panuco R.
Querétaro
Pachuca
MÉXICO CITY
Toluca
Tlaxcala
Puebla
Cuernavaca
Jalapa
Veracruz
Córdoba
Papaloapan R.
Coatzacoalcos
Frontera
Villahermosa
Balsas R.
Chilpancingo
Oaxaca
Salina Cruz
Tuxtla Gutiérrez
Grijalva R.
Progreso
Mérida
Campeche

ingly increased by approximately 50 per cent. On the great collective *ejidos,* such as those in the Laguna district, the peasantry enjoyed all manner of social services which had earlier been limited to the larger urban areas. The *hacendado* may have complained that the reform program was a failure, but the peasantry could not be so convinced.

After Cárdenas, the reform program concentrated less on land distribution and more on land utilization. To be sure, by 1960 an additional 4000 villages had received land and an additional 16 million hectares had been distributed, but by that year the total number of *ejidatarios* had declined slightly, even though the *ejidal* population had increased by 50 per cent; the smaller number of *ejidatarios,* partially a function of a growing urbanization, of course gave each remaining *ejidatario* a greater portion of land. More importantly, the total amount of crop land for the entire nation had almost doubled through conservation practices, of which reclamation and irrigation were aspects. In 1960 the *ejidos* alone harvested almost as many hectares of land as did the private holders in 1930, and private holders harvested more than the *ejidos.* Furthermore, by 1960 Mexican agriculture had become more mechanized. In 1930 the tractor was almost unknown on Mexican land; by 1960 the nation could claim one tractor for each 250 hectares of arable land, and by 1966 some estimates placed the total number of tractors as double that of 1960. Commercial fertilizers, used nowhere in Mexico except on an experimental basis in 1930, had grown so common by 1960 that one acre of every six planted had been treated. And, finally as indicative of changing agricultural patterns, by 1960 hybrid corn began to make its appearance in significant amounts. In that year a third of a million hectares of land—5 per cent of the total planted to corn—was planted with hybrids; the average yield was five times that of common corn.

Improved techniques, the extension of the credit system, better marketing devices, and the change in agricultural attitudes began to show in increased production by 1950. Corn, at long last, surpassed prerevolutionary production, wheat almost doubled, beans increased by 20 per cent, coffee by 50 per cent, and vegetables in general by amounts over 50 per cent. But cotton and sugar cane jumped to nearly five times the 1900-1910 average. After 1950 production increased at an accelerated pace; production figures for a number of crops indicate the trend:

CROP	1950	1960 (in thousands of metric tons)	1964
Corn	3,122	5,606	8,454
Wheat	590	1,135	2,134
Beans	250	661	891
Peppers, green and dried	53	78	132
Sugar cane	9,418	19,541	21,837
Coffee	62	98	145
Rice	187	205	274
Potatoes	134	294	425
Tomatoes	355	388	481
Lemons	70	99	122
Oranges	554	766	859
Cotton	260	470	566

The trend, according to some preliminary estimates, continued into 1966. Some statisticians predicted a 10-million-ton corn crop as well as significant increases in all other agricultural goods.

All data indicate clearly that Mexican agriculture between 1924 and 1960 improved enormously. Even with the rapid growth in population, which increased almost two and a half times during that span of years, per capita production of every major item of food increased and, in spite of inflation, the real wages of the rural worker grew. The question nevertheless remains, and will always remain, whether the agrarian reform program aided in this improvement, or hindered it. In 1960, 43 per cent of the crop land belonged to *ejidos,* but they produced only 40 per cent of the total crop value, they had only one-fifth the total number of tractors, and they realized only 39 per cent of the total amount of cash for crop sales. It is quite clear that the *ejidos* are less productive than privately owned land on either a per acre or per capita basis, and that the private owners fare better in terms of living standards. A great proportion of *ejidatarios* seek work off the *ejidos,* and over two-fifths earn more than half their annual income from other sources. These and other data can be used to argue that a system of private ownership could have given greater agricultural production. But the

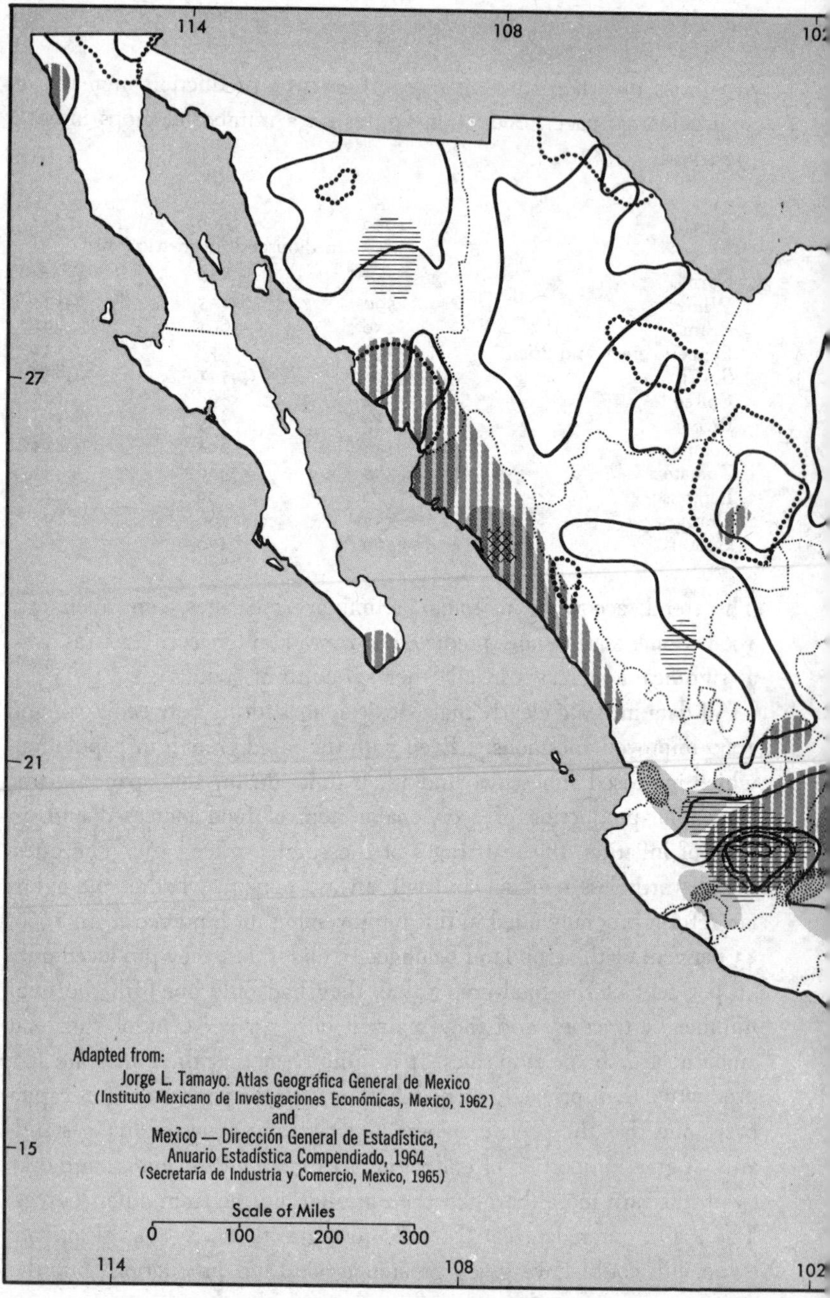
114
108
102
27
21
15
Adapted from:
Jorge L. Tamayo. Atlas Geográfica General de Mexico
(Instituto Mexicano de Investigaciones Económicas, Mexico, 1962)
and
Mexico — Dirección General de Estadística,
Anuario Estadística Compendiado, 1964
(Secretaría de Industria y Comercio, Mexico, 1965)
Scale of Miles
0
100
200
300
114
108
102

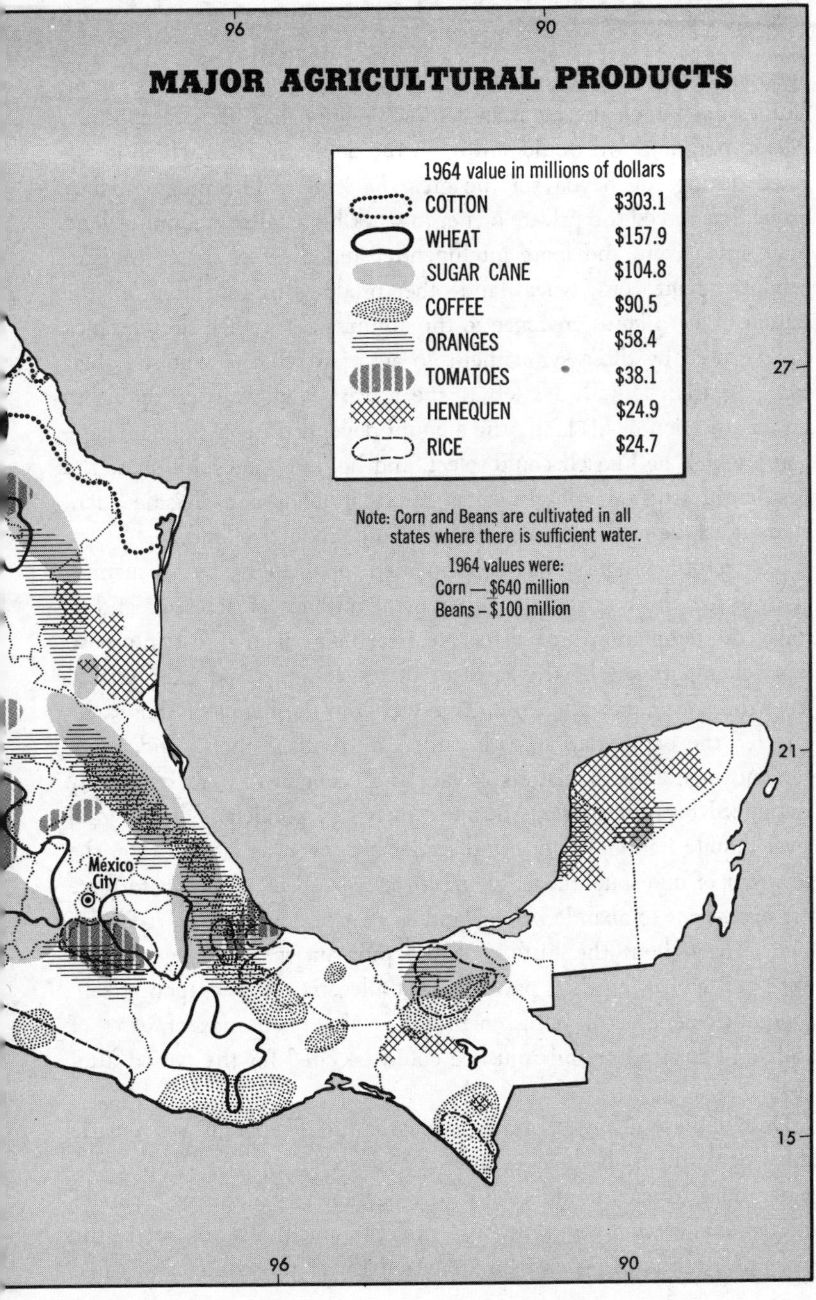
96
90
MAJOR AGRICULTURAL PRODUCTS
1964 value in millions of dollars
COTTON $303.1
WHEAT $157.9
SUGAR CANE $104.8
COFFEE $90.5
ORANGES $58.4
TOMATOES $38.1
HENEQUEN $24.9
RICE $24.7
Note: Corn and Beans are cultivated in all states where there is sufficient water.
1964 values were:
Corn — $640 million
Beans – $100 million
27
21
15
México City
96
90

agrarian reformers can argue that without a fundamental change in attitudes, for which the agrarian reform program has been responsible, Mexican agriculture would still be in the doldrums from which it suffered during the heyday of the great *haciendas*. The program, they argue, has forced the private owner to work his smaller amount of land more intensively and more intelligently, and the fact that the *ejidos* produced more corn, wheat, and other products in 1960 than all the nation in 1910 lends credence to the argument. Another circumstance can be used by those sympathetic to agrarian reform to bolster their case. Agrarian law always left to the private landowner an option to retain a portion of his land (the amount depended upon the land category) which he himself could select, and he quite naturally chose the best land for his own. The process of expropriation and division, then, guaranteed the private owners slightly more productive land.

The reform program was accompanied, predictably, by all manner of injustice and corruption; with tens of millions of acres of land at stake, the temptation proved too great for many men thrust into positions of importance by the accident of revolution. Land expropriated from the *hacendado* often found its way into the hands of those who directed the expropriation, rather than into village plots. *Ejidatarios*, generally ignorant in matters of law and economics, were frequently victimized by unscrupulous business men and politicians at the local level despite national policy and leadership; even as late as 1966 the governor of one state allegedly employed a band of *pistoleros* to force the *ejidatarios* to abandon their land so that he might claim it for his own. Throughout the history of the program many village leaders were guilty of using their power of plot allocation as a weapon of self-aggrandizement or of punishment for rivals. Thousands of cases of graft and corruption and injustice could be cited for the period after 1915.

Despite these seamy attributes, the agricultural program was remarkably successful in both its economic and social aspects. Within two generations Mexico produced a sturdy peasantry, which was a part of the national economy and responsive to economic pressures, to take the place of a horde of peons who knew naught of the nation and cared less. Land considered worthless for agriculture in 1910 produced bountiful crops in 1960, and men considered worthless during the Díaz regime were an integral and proud part of the national system by mid-century. Peons grown to maturity within the shackles of a Díaz *hacienda* saw their sons become national political and economic leaders.

The agrarian reform program touched the quick not only of the Mexican *hacendados* but of many foreigners as well. Neither the Constitution nor subsequent law made any distinction between lands owned by foreigners and those by nationals, and the foreigners adversely affected by the program clamored for relief from their home governments. The protection of foreign "rights" in Mexico caused serious diplomatic problems, among other things preventing United States recognition of the Obregón regime for nearly three years, but the violent protests by foreign individuals and governments had little effect on agrarian reform; the Mexican leaders determined to solve Mexico's problems within a Mexican context regardless of outside objections.

The Mexican Revolution breathed nationalism; a fierce national pride and a pathological xenophobia pervaded the thinking of almost every revolutionary leader after Madero. The foreigner, who had enjoyed enormous benefits under Díaz, suddenly became an object of suspicion, an intrusive force whose activities must be controlled and whose maleficent influence must be destroyed. The attitude was written into the Constitution in numerous ways, and every government for the following thirty years was embroiled in one or more quarrels with foreign governments over the question of foreign rights within the country. And indeed the foreigner did constitute a threat. Every aspect of the revolutionary program impinged upon foreign interests: foreigners owned lands subject to expropriation; foreigners owned subsoil deposits nationalized by article 27; foreigners worked mines whose employees were given benefits under article 123; foreigners owned concerns required by the Constitution and later law to build schools; and foreign clerics performed religious functions and operated schools forbidden by articles 3 and 130. The foreigner, in fact, owned Mexico prior to the Revolution. According to estimates made in 1914, both

United States and French investors owned more of Mexico than did the Mexicans, and the combined total of foreign holdings more than trebled that of the nationals. Under these circumstances and under the best of conditions, any wide-ranging reform program would inevitably undercut foreign interests. But the conditions were not the best. Neither the national government nor the foreign investor—direct or portfolio—approached the subject rationally. With some notable exceptions, the foreigner found every action by the government which touched his interests, even legitimate taxation, somehow discriminatory. The government eyed every action by a foreign concern as exploitative. The fact that occasionally the government did discriminate and the foreigner exploit gave each a justification for his views.

Although most foreign enterprises were affected, the major area of contention was oil, almost wholly dominated by international combines whose Mexican interests constituted only a part of their whole operation. Coming into the country in the late Díaz years, the oilmen obtained title to enormous stretches of exceedingly valuable deposits which they managed to work almost unhindered even during the most hectic days of the military movements; by the time the new constitution went into effect Mexico's 40-million-barrel annual production made her one of the world's major producers, with her share of world production steadily growing. Under article 27 all subsoil deposits became the nation's property; the oil companies contended that title granted prior to the Constitution could not be vacated by fiat and that therefore their holdings were inviolable. Staging a bitter fight in the courts and wild exploitation in the field, the oil companies were producing by 1921 at a rate of almost 200 million barrels a year; in that year Mexico produced nearly one-fourth of the world's supply. For the next fifteen years the government and the major oil companies waged a constant struggle in and out of courts with varying degrees of intensity. And while the quarrel went on, production declined steadily until it reached a low point of about 33 million barrels in 1932.

At issue during the conflict were fundamentally different points of view. The companies contended that under the terms of the original concessions to them they had a perfect right to manage their own business in their own way; not only did they have a legal right to the oil under the land they owned or leased, they contended, but any major revision of the regulatory code constituted a discriminatory act which amounted to confiscation. The government countered by citing court cases in the United States which held that landowners did not "own" the oil until they had captured it, and by insisting that as a sovereign nation Mexico had perfect authority by political theory and by practice to impose constitutional restrictions. Furthermore, Mexico maintained, no act by the government with respect to oil discriminated inasmuch as all subsoil exploiters, whether Mexican or foreign, or those concerned with metals, were subject to the same general policies.

The companies argued that the cards were stacked against them, by constitution and law, in any disagreement between company officials and labor leaders, since the arbitration boards included government officials who always sided with labor. The government answered that its representatives had no preconceived notions but judged each case individually on its merits; if these members of the labor boards upheld the workers' view it was because justice demanded it. The companies insisted that they paid the best wages in the country, and any demand for higher wages was unreasonable. The government replied by admitting that the companies paid better wages than most Mexican concerns, but pointed out that the practice of paying United States citizens at a higher rate contravened that portion of article 123 which demanded the "same compensation . . . be paid for the same work, without regard to sex or nationality." The government charged that the companies refused to place Mexicans in supervisory or administrative positions and thus not only discriminated against the nationals but also maintained a barrier behind which they could retain the secrets of their unscrupulous and illegal acts. The companies countered by claiming that the Mexicans had neither the training nor the native aptitude for highly technical work, and that any attempt to use Mexicans in responsible positions would create chaos.

The companies then argued that the enormous sums which they invested in developmental work fully justified the modest profits which they gained; they had taken the risks and they should be allowed to reap the harvest. The government claimed that the "enormous sums" were a figment of the oil companies' imagination, that the investment had been moderate, and that the tax structure before 1920 had been such that all investments had long since been paid for; one government official contended that Royal Dutch-Shell had paid a minute total of 50,000 dollars in taxes on a production of nearly 40 million barrels prior to 1917. At various times the oil companies claimed that the taxes were unrealistic and unusually burdensome; every time the government revised the tax structure or raised the rate the companies objected to the action as discriminatory and confiscatory. Mexico countered by pointing out that the tax per barrel produced in the United States vastly exceeded the Mexican taxes. Far from being confiscatory, the Mexicans maintained, the tax system allowed the companies to make a fantastic profit, much of which was hidden by the companies through the use of a number of questionable accounting devices.

And finally the companies charged that Mexico's labor policies, the tax structure, the concession system, and the production regulations enmeshed the operations in a web of restrictions which precluded efficient operation. The government completely denied these allegations. Mexican spokesmen maintained that the decline in production after 1921 came from a combination of field exhaustion and a lack of new investment; the companies, they charged, came to Mexico to skim the cream off the top only. And the cream had indeed been thick. One oil well sustained an average of a million barrels a month for five years, another the same average for eight years, and one an average of nearly 800,000 a month for ten years. At prevailing prices before the drastic price decline in 1921, these three wells alone produced a daily gross income of over 300,000 dollars. In January 1921, the combined 367 producing wells yielded a gross income of over a million and a half dollars a day; furthermore, on the average the Mexican well produced over 300 times as much per day as the well in the United States.

This fantastic production may have been excellent for the companies, but it was disastrous to Mexico. Wells allowed to flow unchecked were, according to Mexican officials, ultimately wasteful; too rapid a flow of oil allowed salt water to creep in and to leave pockets of oil which could not be economically exploited. But every effort on the part of the government to institute good conservation practices was frustrated by the companies in flagrant violation of the law. The government had other complaints as well. Mexican property holders came to government offices in a steady stream demanding justice: the oil companies had cheated them of their land, the foreigners were encroaching on their properties, the oilmen were not paying the royalties due them, oil company "white guards" were terrorizing the area. How many of these accusations had substance can never be known, but thousands of documents in Mexican archives give mute testimony that the citizens did complain, and that they convinced government officials.

But individuals were not alone in receiving ill-treatment from the big companies. In a hundred little ways the major concerns put the squeeze on the small producers, frequently forcing them into bankruptcy and then gobbling them up. The small independent producers, some foreign and some Mexican, found it difficult to transport the oil to the coast, or to find a tanker which would take their oil, or to obtain equipment. They accused the major concerns of stealing their oil by off-set drillings, of hiring "bandits" to shoot up their tanks or set fire to wells or prevent their employees from working. Furthermore, the companies were notorious in their efforts—often successful—to bribe government inspectors and other officials; such an attempt during the 'twenties to buy Cárdenas is reputed to have been a key factor in the development of the future president's well-recognized animosity toward the oil concerns. In short, the government contended, the foreign oil companies in general refused to obey laws, objected bitterly to legitimate regulation and taxes, ran roughshod over the nationals, and used every unethical means available to continue their destructive exploitation. It was the foreigner, not the Mexican, who benefited from Mexico's oil. Petroleum products flowing from Mexican refineries cost more in Mexico City than in Chicago; a great natural asset to economic development was in the process of being exhausted with no benefit to the nation itself.

The struggle between the Mexican government and the oil companies revolved around a fundamental inability to communicate. Every protest and contention put forward by the oil companies reflected a deep laissez-faire philosophy perfectly consistent with pre-revolutionary concepts but completely at odds with a basic tenet of revolutionary governments. Oilmen's arguments also contained a strong hint of Social Darwinism and "racial" arrogance which the Mexican authorities rejected. The oil companies, in short, still wanted to live by porfirian precepts and had neither the desire nor the intention to accept the Mexican revolutionary pattern of thought and action. By the time the companies and the Mexicans had their last great confrontation, the mutual suspicions and animosities had grown to such a point that no peaceful solution could be reached; the companies had become convinced that confiscation was Mexico's ultimate aim, and the Mexicans had become convinced that the oil companies, in their ruthless exploitation, would never conform to law.

Cárdenas's decree of expropriation, signed on March 18, 1938, brought an end to one long phase of the struggle between oil companies and government, and ushered in a shorter, and more acrimonious, debate. The final step by which Mexico ultimately freed herself from the constant bickering with the international oil concerns came as a result of a long labor dispute beginning in 1936 when the workers demanded wage increases, positions in management, and a wide variety of fringe benefits which the companies considered utterly ridiculous. The union and the companies went through the entire process demanded by the law in labor disputes, including a decision by an arbitration board and a case before the Mexican Supreme Court, but the final ruling upheld most of the union's original demands. The companies steadfastly insisted that complying with labor's demands would not only be economically ruinous but would constitute a surrender of the management to the employees; this they could not and would not do. Threatened with a complete paralysis of the oil industry, which employed thousands of Mexicans and furnished the needed fuel and lubricants for industry and commerce, Cárdenas reluctantly signed the decree of expropriation by which the Mexican nation became the owner of most of the industry. The companies appealed to the Mexican Supreme Court and to their home governments; the Supreme Court upheld Cárdenas's action on December 2, 1939, while the British and United States governments put pressure on Mexico for a satisfactory settlement.

The companies, of course, denied the validity of the entire expropriation process. They claimed that the hearings before the arbitration board and the Supreme Court had been farcical, deliberately designed to be nothing more than a grand act to give a legal façade to an illegal act; in this contention the British government agreed, accusing Mexico of a denial of justice in such haughty and peremptory terms that Cárdenas broke diplomatic relations. Even assuming that Mexico had the right under international law to expropriate, the companies contended, Mexican and international law demanded an immediate payment in cash for the properties; a failure to do so constituted confiscation, not expropriation. But Mexico was obviously in no position to make an immediate cash payment. She simply did not have sufficient money in the treasury, and any attempt to get the money through a special bond issue would have been patently foolish in view of the depressed economy. Even had the treasury been overflowing, though, no payment could be made until some agreement had been reached regarding the value of the properties—on this issue the companies and the government were as far apart as ever. The companies, consistent to the end, claimed ownership of all the oil still underground, while the government, equally consistent, contended that only the oil actually captured belonged to the companies; the companies' contention led to a value of about a billion dollars, while the Mexicans gave a value of about one-tenth that amount, and it was the resolution of this difference which consumed time, fostered an ugly xenophobia, and begat all manner of questionable activities on both sides. The companies, hoping to create a financial crisis in Mexico which would force the return of the holdings, used their international power in an attempt to cripple the industry now in the hands of the Mexican government. They refused to allow tankers carrying their own oil to touch Mexican oil, and they met those few independent tankers carrying Mexican oil to European ports with liens accusing Mexico of selling "stolen" oil. Not only did the companies refuse to handle Mexican oil; they refused to sell the chemical necessary for the refining process and threatened oil equipment companies who hoped to sell material to Mexico with a boycott. And while they were clamping down on Mexican oil in every conceivable fashion, the companies engaged in a campaign of propagandistic invective which depicted the Mexicans as conniving thieves too lazy and too incompetent to work for themselves but, like jackals, ever willing to rob others of the fruits of intensive labor. The entire campaign was designed to create financial chaos in Mexico and a public feeling in the United States which would bring on intervention.

Mexico, on the other hand, painted the oil companies—and by implication the governments and people of both Great Britain and the United States—as imperialistic exploiters whose only ambition was to drain Mexico of her wealth and to enslave her people. With great drama and fanfare Cárdenas spoke to exuberant crowds about the Economic Independence Day, and began the erection of a monument to the memorable occasion. With great passion he declaimed that the nation would "honor her foreign debt," and asked for public donations. All classes, including Church dignitaries, responded by contributing money, jewelry, pigs, chickens, and anything of value available; as a propaganda technique it was a stroke of genius, but as a fund-raising device it amounted to nothing, since the total collection constituted less than 1 per cent of the final settlement.

With the dispute reaching a point of white heat and no progress in 1939, the outbreak of war in Europe encouraged a more rational and sensible attitude on both sides; Mexico suddenly found herself in the same ideological camp as the British and wholeheartedly agreeing with the United States on the Nazi threat to world peace and institutions. In this atmosphere, and with a change in administrations in Mexico, the United States and Mexican governments in late 1941 worked out a settlement agreeable to the two governments regarding the amount and method of payment for U.S. properties expropriated; the companies had no alternative but to accept, albeit with ill grace. The British, with a greater stake and busy with the war, tarried a few years in making the settlement but finally signed a convention in 1947. In round figures, the United States companies received 32.5 million dollars plus interest, while the British obtained 82 million and interest; the final payment to the U.S. companies came in 1949 and that to the British in 1962.

While the negotiations went on, Mexican technicians proved that one of the foreign oil companies' basic assumptions was as false as those of the Spaniards at an earlier time. Throughout the period from 1917 to 1938, the companies contended that the Mexicans could not become technically competent to accept positions of responsibility in the oil industry; firm in this belief they confidently looked for a total collapse of the industry once it came under national management. Probably to the surprise of the companies, and certainly to their discomfiture, the Mexicans not only kept the industry operating but increased production; in view of the fact that no Mexican occupied a position of any responsibility in the industry prior to March 18, 1938, the feat was indeed remarkable. Save or a slight dip in 1942-43, production steadily increased for the next two and a half decades. By 1950 total output more than doubled that of the 1932 low point when foreign companies dominated the industry, and by 1963 the amount had almost doubled again, with a production of approximately 125 million barrels. The Mexicans proved themselves fully competent to seek and tap their own oil, without the guiding hand of foreign technicians.

Even more important than the production of crude petroleum was the shift of consumption patterns. Until 1938 the major share of petroleum and its derivatives, in both crude and refined forms, found an outlet in foreign rather than domestic markets. Given the incredible productivity of the wells and the low wages paid national workers, the Mexicans contended that the products on the domestic market were outrageously high; the high prices, they charged, effectively prevented industrial development or transport modernization. The new government oil agency, Petroleos Mexicanos or Pemex, set about to rectify the situation by a deliberate policy of price-setting which encouraged domestic use. Between expropriation and 1951, domestic consumption almost tripled; by that date nearly a third of all production was converted into gasoline in Mexican refineries. During the next decade and a half the process continued; by 1965 the quantity of Mexican refined gasoline used within the nation roughly approximated total crude production at the time of Cárdenas's famous decree. Within a generation after expropriation, petroleum had become an important adjunct of economic development within the nation, intimately related to the improved standard of living and to social change. The disgruntled spokesmen for the major oil companies still insisted, of course, that the government-owned oil industry was inefficient and that the industry in private hands could have met Mexico's needs with less cost and more speed. As is the case with agrarian reform, such an assertion is predicated on an assumption that those who controlled the industry prior to 1938 would have been willing to convert their operations into one primarily aimed at the domestic market. What might have been is always conjectural; what *was* may be ascertained with some degree of accuracy, and nothing in the history of private oil development in Mexico prior to 1938 suggests a willingness to change a pattern of operations.

The rampant nationalism and anti-United States feeling so exaggerated during the height of the oil controversy spilled over into other aspects of Mexican life and gave a distorted picture of some of the revolutionary aims. In violent contrast to porfirian practice of denigrating things Mexican and adulating things foreign, the principal spokesmen for Mexico rejected all things foreign except those absolutely essential to the economy and to the society. In some states the craze went to the interesting extreme of prohibiting the use of foreign words or phrases in advertising; *l'amour* perforce became *el amor* on billboards extolling the excitements of French perfumes. Most Mexicans contemptuously dismissed any expression of respect for foreign institutions or products as *malinchismo* (from Malinche, Cortez's native mistress) or *pocho* (colloquially "discolored," therefore dirty or unpatriotic) and loudly proclaimed that Mexico needed neither foreign technology nor foreign money to develop its economy. This constant harping on the dangers of foreign penetration, particularly until after

World War II, gave an impression abroad that Mexican revolutionary policy was dedicated to the extirpation of all foreign investment and, by extension, all private enterprise. Expropriation of foreign-owned land, expropriation of the oil industry, an ill-fated and temporary surrender of railroad operation to the employees (reminiscent of Franklin Roosevelt's attempt to use the Air Force to deliver air mail), and widespread oil company propaganda gave currency to the myth—for myth it was.

Mexico, in fact, attempted neither to extirpate private enterprise nor to evict foreign investment. A distinguished Mexican economist writing in the middle 'fifties insisted that the fundamental aim of government policy was the "installation of the capitalistic system in the length and breadth of the land," and an examination of the business climate upholds his view. The government did, nevertheless, intervene directly into the economic process and after 1920 did acquire possession of some of the most critical enterprises. In addition to oil and land (the "state" legally owns *ejidal* lands) the state obtained control of railroads, fertilizer plants, electrical power, and agricultural storage facilities. Petroleum, railroads, and electrical power were considered so crucial to economic development that they could not be left to the vagaries of private control and possibly destructive monopolies; they became, then, a part of the permanent patrimony of the nation itself. Fertilizer plants built and operated by the government, on the other hand, served as temporary expedients to stimulate both the production and the use of a chemical crucial to increased agricultural production. Herein lies the key to government activity in the economic field. Faced with an underdeveloped and unintegrated economy, the government officials after the Revolution—and particularly after 1930—used any available expedient consistent with national sovereignty to nudge the economy in a healthy direction. The government had no "plan"; it was completely pragmatic. In the absence of private concerns dedicated to the production of hybrid seeds, fertilizers, insecticides, and the like, the government itself undertook the task until such time as private companies could operate at a profit. In view of the dearth of private investment capital, and the reluctance of those with money to engage in new activities which the economy needed but which entailed great risk, the government established a lending agency on which hopeful entrepreneurs could call. As economic conditions changed, the lending policies changed in order to stimulate needed development. By 1961, for example, the economic potential in industrial development was being hindered by the lack of funds for the importation of industrial machinery, and therefore in that year a new category of loans, specifically for this purpose, became available. In the three-year span, 1961-64, the agency loaned nearly a quarter of a billion dollars to companies who wished to import industrial machinery of various kinds.

While the government encouraged domestic investment, it also belied the accusation that it was forcing foreign investment from the country. In spite of a very real fear of foreign influence coupled with a sizzling nationalism, Mexico in fact made no attempt to curtail either existing or new foreign investment as such. The issue between the foreigner and the government, if there was one, revolved not around the magnitude nor the nature of the investment, but touched on the nature of the control to be exercised. Mexico took the position that direct investments in the Mexican economy had to conform to Mexican law and Mexican usage, whatever they might be and however they might change, and generally assumed that special concessions made to the foreigner ultimately produced more ill than good. In the eyes of Mexican officialdom, businesses operating on an investment from abroad were Mexican businesses, not foreign, and were constrained in the same way they would be if all funds were domestic. At the height of the conflict between Mexico and the foreign direct investor, prior to World War II, the United States or British investor generally disagreed violently with the Mexican contention and in so doing took a strangely inconsistent position. The British company operating in the United States—Royal Dutch-Shell, for example—never questioned the right of the United States government to treat that company in exactly the same fashion as it would any domestic company; however, the same company in Mexico not only resented that government's attempt to regulate but argued that as a foreign company it had rights which could not be abridged. The attitude was the product of the history of investment in economically underdeveloped and politically unstable countries, where the major concentrations of capital were put into the transportation and extractive industries. Not only in Mexico but in other countries as well the foreigner had become the spoiled darling of the investment world; he had demanded so many special concessions, and had received them, that he had come to expect them as a matter of right. But the Mexican governments following the Revolution denied both the right of the foreigner to special concessions and the validity of special concessions to anyone except under rigidly controlled conditions. Mexican pride forbade an open plea for foreign investment to stimulate economic growth, and Mexican suspicion demanded close examination of funds coming from abroad, but foreign investments tended to be much more diversified, and the investment in each enterprise smaller.

United States direct investment in Mexico in 1946, for example, totalled slightly more than half a billion dollars spread over nearly 200 different enterprises; the average investment in each fell at about 2.75 million dollars. In the following ten years, nearly a quarter billion additional dollars came in from the U.S., but more than 400 different enterprises benefitted; the average investment per enterprise topped half a million only slightly. The trend continued in the following decade.

By 1965 Mexico had become one of the favorite spots for U.S. investors, whose direct holdings amounted to more than a billion dollars and accounted for 2.6 per cent of all U.S. direct investments outside the country. One-eighth of all U.S. direct investment money in Latin America was in Mexico in 1965. More interesting perhaps, as indicative of Mexican policy and economic development, nearly two-thirds of all U.S. direct investments in the country were in manufacturing in contrast with the general tendency to invest in the Latin American extractive industries. And U.S. direct investments, of course, were only a part of the total foreign investment in the Mexican economy.

A combination of foreign investment and Mexican encouragement —including money—had a remarkable effect on industrial development after World War II, and particularly after 1950. The older industries—textiles, leather goods, and the like—bloomed under the impact of new money and a generally improved economy, but much more important were the multitude of new industries pouring their products onto the market. By 1960 chemical plants, food-processing plants, tire and tube factories, paper mills, synthetic fabric producers, automobile assembly plants, and a galaxy of other light industrial concerns took an increasingly larger share of the labor force; in that year nearly 20 per cent of the economically active found work in the industrial complex, as compared to about 10 per cent twenty years earlier. Industries relating to automotive transportation demonstrate most clearly the pattern of development. The industrial census of 1945 listed three concerns involved in assembling automotive vehicles of all kinds, employing fewer than 500 persons; the same census gave no separate listing for tire and tube factories. By 1964, thirteen assembly plants employing 12,000 men produced 100,000 automobiles, trucks, and buses; in the same year five tire factories employing 5000 men produced nearly 2 million truck and automobile tires, a million bicycle tires, and more than a million and a half tubes. But these 1964 data only begin to tell the story in the automotive field. Preliminary figures for 1965 indicated a 10-per cent increase over the previous year, while new facilities under construction in 1965 and 1966 presaged a production in certain makes and models of automobiles which would not only satisfy Mexico's domestic needs but also make that nation an automotive exporter.

Increased agricultural and industrial production after 1939 brought an enormous increase in national income and a shift in the contribution of the various sectors to the economy. In 1965 the net domestic product measured five and half times greater, in constant dollars, than in 1939; the major portion of the growth came after 1955, with some years showing an astounding growth rate of 10 per cent gross and 7 per cent net. Electric power, upon which so much of the industrial process depended, far outstripped all other sectors in rate of growth, having a value in 1965 of over fourteen times as great as that of 1939. In the later year electric power, in fact, contributed almost as much value to the national product as did mining, the total value of which increased only slightly after 1939. Agriculture and its allies of stock-raising, forestry, and fishing, increased by roughly four times and therefore declined slightly in its share, in 1965 contributing almost one-fifth of the gross product. Manufacturing, which between 1939 and 1950 grew at about the same rate as the remainder of the economy and therefore changed little in its share of the domestic product, began a surge after 1955. During the following ten years manufacturing more than doubled—in one year it increased 14 per cent—and came within one-half of 1 per cent of being the greatest contributor to the gross domestic product; only commerce, with 25.9 per cent exceeded it.

For the first time in the history of Mexico, after 1940 a sustained and healthy economic growth outran population increase. Between 1940 and 1965 the population doubled, while the total of goods and services more than quintupled and agriculture quadrupled; the economic growth was somewhat tempered by inflation, but in general wages and salaries increased more rapidly than the cost of living, particularly after 1960. At prevailing average monthly income and yearly average retail prices in Mexico City in 1964, any skilled or semi-skilled worker could support a family of five through his own labor. A skilled cigarette-worker could give his family a balanced diet including meat or fish, fresh vegetables, fresh fruits, sweets, and cereal grains on less than a quarter of his income; including rent, one movie a week for each member of the family, cigarettes and beer for himself, and sufficient inexpensive clothing to meet the minimal needs of his family, his weekly essential expenditures ate up only three-fifths or two-thirds of his income. The remainder he could use to purchase luxuries or to put in savings. The steel or iron worker fared less well, but his income did meet the minimal requirement of article 123 of the Constitution of 1917 with its demand that income should "satisfy the normal needs of life," including "lawful pleasures." Those workers in the Federal District who received the minimum wages found it necessary to scrimp and scrounge in order to furnish the minimal needs for their families, but for the first time in the history of the country an unskilled worker could earn sufficient income to support a family and thus leave the children free to attend school.

Many pockets of real poverty—grinding poverty—still remained in

1960. Nearly a million peasants, outside of the *ejidal* system, worked plots of land too small to give sustenance to a family; the majority of them lived at a bare subsistence level and enjoyed few of the advantages accruing from the burgeoning economy. But even many of those who earned an income above the subsistence level lived in conditions far from ideal, reflecting none of the prosperity which the economic data indicate. One-half the population lived in housing averaging five persons to the room. Only one of every three Mexicans had access to running water within the building in which he lived, and only one of four dwelling places included a bathroom with running water. Two of every three families depended upon wood or charcoal for cooking and heating but, curiously enough, one of every three families owned a radio or television or both. These data give statistical support to a frequently observed phenomenon—Mexican economic gains have been funneled into a small segment of the population, with the vast majority benefiting only slightly from the impressive gains registered after 1950.

But one facet of social change after the Revolution clearly benefited the total population, regardless of class or income level—the nation's health improved enormously. In 1910 more than 300 of every thousand live-born children died before reaching the age of one; by 1940 that incredible figure had fallen to 125, by 1950 to 96, and by 1964 to 66. In 1964 infant mortality still compared unfavorably with the rate of approximately 24 in the United States, but it compared favorably with the rates in other countries in Latin America. The general mortality rate, which at slightly above 33 in 1910 was well over twice that of the United States, declined to 23 by 1940, to about 17 in 1950, and to a respectable 10.3 in 1964 compared to the 9.4 in the United States. This vast decline in death rates, coupled with a marked increase in marriage and birth rates, was responsible for an annual population increase of 3 to 4 per cent in the decade after 1950.

Viewed from any angle, the social and economic change evident in Mexico during the quarter century after 1940 was remarkable. During that twenty-five year span the population more than doubled, but productivity increased more rapidly than the population and demonstrated an accelerating rate in the last lustrum. Only Costa Rica among the Latin American republics, at the end of the period, spent a larger share of its national budget on education, and only three countries of Latin America maintained a better ratio of doctors to the population. In 1964, Mexican universities graduated as many medical doctors, proportionately, as the U.S. Only Argentina, Chile, and Uruguay—all traditionally literate and prosperous—circulated more newspapers on a per capita base, and no Latin American nation printed more papers daily. The number of movie houses and the admission prices allowed the Mexicans to attend more cinema productions than the nationals of any other Western Hemisphere country save the United States. Only El Salvador and Costa Rica maintained proportionately fewer men in their armed service; Argentina's army was nearly four times the size of Mexico's proportionately, Brazil's was nearly two times, and Chile's more than two times. In most agricultural crops production after 1950 increased much more rapidly than in the world in general, and outstripped all other Western Hemisphere nations; the rate of increase in all grains nearly doubled the world rate and was half again as great as Latin America in general; the rate of beans more than doubled the hemisphere rate, as did sugar. Mexico became the third largest coffee producer in Latin America, the second in tobacco, and the third in raw milk. Among the Latin American nations, only Brazil increased manufacturing at a faster rate; the Mexican rate was twice that of Argentina, and greater than that of either the United States or Canada.

Despite these impressive data, Mexico by the mid-1960's had not yet arrived in the Promised Land. The nation still suffered from millions of illiterates, inadequate housing, and a mean real income which most Western Europeans would perceive to be near destitution. Whether the nation can ever become "prosperous" in the sense of Swedish or German prosperity, or ever achieve a standard of living roughly equivalent to that of the United States, still remains in serious doubt in view of the limited natural resources with which she has to work. But at long last the leaders of the Mexican nation had come to realize that the greatest natural resource available to any society is its people, who with proper training and stimuli can do wondrous things. With that recognition the battle was half won, and it was this realization which gave President Díaz Ordaz the confidence with which he assumed office in 1964.

Political Chronology

1325 Struggles with neighbors force Aztecs to leave mainland and settle on island in Lake Texcoco.

1427 Alliance among Tenochtitlán, Texcoco, and Tlacopán (Tacuba) allows Aztecs to expand power.

1440-87 Aztec power and control over other peoples greatly expanded under Moctezuma I.

1492 The "Reconquest" in Spain completed; by decree the Jews are expelled from Castille; Columbus discovers America.

1502 Moslems in Spain forced to convert or leave; Columbus, on his fourth and last voyage, hears of Mayan Empire, but does not follow the lead; Moctezuma II becomes emperor of Tenochtitlán.

1503 The Casa de Contratación established in Sevilla to control trade with the new Spanish territories.

1512 Conference at Burgos results in a series of laws regarding the treatment of American indigenous population.

1516 Charles I, the first Hapsburg, becomes king of Castille and of Aragon.

1517 Francisco Hernández de Córdoba explores coast of Yucatán.

1518 Juan de Grijalva, sailing under orders from Diego de Velázquez in Cuba, covers the coast of the mainland from the island of Cozumel to Pánuco (Tampico) and reports great wealth and civilization.

1519 Charles I of Spain elected Emperor, as Charles V, of the Holy Roman Empire; Hernando Cortez sailing under orders from Velázquez, lands in Tabasco, takes Malinche as his mistress, lands near Veracruz and breaks with Velázquez, begins conquest and enters Tenochtitlán late in the year.

1520 Cortez retreats from Tenochtitlán with heavy losses in "La Noche Triste" (June 30). Charles V orders end to the granting of *encomiendas*.

1521 Tenochtitlán reduced and razed; Cuatémoc captured; Cortez grants *encomiendas* to his principal captains.

1521-42 Central Mexico effectively conquered and occupied.

1523 Pedro de Gante establishes a school for Indian boys.

1526 The "fleet system" of sailing between Spain and the colonies inaugurated to cut losses to pirates and privateers.

1527 First *Audiencia* established in Mexico; first bishopric established, with Bishop Juan de Zumárraga arriving following year.

1535 First colonial viceroy, Antonio de Mendoza, appointed for New Spain.

1537 First printing press arrives in New Spain; first guild, of silversmiths, founded.

1540-80 Most of present Mexico explored and partially settled; silk industry flourishing in Puebla region.

1542 The "New Laws," prohibiting Indian slavery and limiting the *encomiendas*, promulgated by Charles V, but not enforced in New Spain.

1545 Epidemic in Central Mexico costs about 800,000 Indian lives.

1546 Major silver strike at Zacatecas; by 1600, most of major silver mining areas discovered.

1548 *Audiencia* of Nueva Galicia (Guadalajara) established.

1550-64 Luis de Velasco second viceroy of New Spain.

1551 Tribute payment in labor prohibited; charter granted for the establishment of the University of Mexico.

1553 University of Mexico opens with first class.

1555 Charles V abdicates, succeeded by Philip II. *Patio* process of silver beneficiating perfected by Fray Bartolomé Medina at Real del Monte.

1559 Crown extends monopoly on mercury to colonies, to control mining.

1571 Office of the Inquisition established in Mexico City.
1575 *Alcabala* or transaction tax first collected, at 2 per cent.
1576 Epidemic, probably typhus, costs about two million lives.
1590-95 Luis de Velasco, son, viceroy.
1598 Philip III becomes King of Spain.
1598-1605 Indians "congregated" into larger villages in central Mexico.
1600 By this time debt peonage has become common.
1607-11 Luis de Velasco, son, viceroy for second term.
1609 Reform of laws regarding *encomiendas* and *repartimiento*.
1624-25 Quarrel between Viceroy Marqués de Gelves and Archbishop Juan Pérez de la Serna leads to rioting in Mexico City, resulting in burning of viceregal palace and heavy loss of life. An important element was hatred between *criollo* and *peninsular*.
1636 *Alcabala* raised to 6 per cent.
1650 Low point of Indian population reached, about one million.
1692 Crop failures and food shortages stimulate a great *tumulto* in Mexico City, resulting in heavy damage and loss of life.
1700 Philip V, first of the Bourbons, becomes king of Spain; the Bourbons introduced many new techniques of government.
1759 Charles III, greatest of the Bourbon kings, ascends throne and inaugurates a period of reform.
1764 Royal tobacco factory, a monopoly, established in Mexico.
1765 José de Gálvez *visita* begins, culminating in many administrative and fiscal changes.
1767 Jesuits expelled from all Spanish dominions. Reduction of cost of mercury to stimulate mine production.
1768 School of Medicine founded.
1770 As part of commercial reform, direct trade allowed between Yucatán and Spain.
1778 End of Sevilla monopoly on trade; last Spanish "fleet" arrives in Veracruz. Further reduction of mercury price. From this date forward both commercial activity and mining production increase significantly, bringing a period of apparent prosperity.
1779 Smallpox epidemic in Mexico City costs an estimated 20 per cent of population.
1779-80 Crop failures and epidemics in Bajío bring heavy loss of life.
1783 New mining code, to stimulate mining.
1788 Botanical Gardens for scientific study laid out near Mexico City.

1790 Intendancy system established, bringing changes in administrative structure; enormous growth in trade begins.

1791 School of Mines established.

1793 First attempt at a census, incomplete.

1800-10 Silver mining reaches highest point for colonial period.

1808 Napoleon occupies Madrid, selects brother Joseph as king, stimulating guerrilla activities by Spaniards. In Mexico, fearful of government falling into creole hands, *peninsulares* by *coup d'état* remove corrupt and inefficient Viceroy Iturrigaray and impose aged Pedro de Garibay.

1809 Attempt by creoles for independence easily quashed.

1810 French control all of Spanish mainland, loyal government fleeing to island near Cádiz. Francisco Xavier de Venegas appointed viceroy. Hidalgo begins movement for independence.

1811 Hidalgo and other leaders captured and executed.

1811-15 Period of Morelos leadership for independence, culminating in his capture and execution.

1813 Félix Calleja, tough and efficient, appointed viceroy.

1814 Ferdinand VII re-installed on Spanish throne as constitutional monarch.

1815 Ferdinand VII seizes absolute power, abrogating constitution.

1815-20 Independence movement degenerates into sporadic guerrilla activity, with Vicente Guerrero most important leader.

1816 More moderate viceroy, Juan de Apodaca, appointed.

1820 Revolution in Spain led by Rafael de Riego re-installs constitutional monarchy; in Mexico, conservative elements choose Agustín de Iturbide to maneuver for independence.

1821 Plan de Iguala and independence for Mexico; New Viceroy Juan O'Donojú signs Treaty of Córdoba recognizing independence, but not accepted by Spanish government as valid.

1821-22 Provisional government under Iturbide.

1822 Iturbide becomes Emperor Agustín I. Mexico recognized by United States.

1823 Iturbide forced to abdicate, and provisional government formed. French intervention in Spain restores Ferdinand VII to absolute power. Stephen F. Austin grant in Texas confirmed, opening region to colonization from the United States.

1824 Federal republican government established under new constitution modeled on that of United States, with Guadalupe Victoria as president. First foreign loan, from England, negotiated.

1827 Rebellion by Nicolás Bravo, suppressed by Guerrero.

1828 Corrupt presidential election and reprisals by ultra-conservative Anastasio Bustamante lead to rebellion, at the end of which Guerrero declared president (early 1829).

1829 Spanish invade Tampico, but yellow fever among troops forces capitulation to Santa Anna, who becomes a hero. Guerrero decrees abolition of slavery as a means of discouraging immigration to Texas.

1830 Rebellion by Anastasio Bustamante drives Guerrero from presidency; Bustamante assumes dictatorial powers; further immigration to Texas prohibited, but decree not enforced.

1831 Guerrero captured through a ruse, executed with obvious approval of clergy.

1832 Santa Anna rebellion drives Bustamante from Mexico City; Santa Anna "elected" president, with Valentín Gómez Farías as vice president.

1832-34 With Santa Anna absent much of the time, government under Gómez Farías enacts many reform and anticlerical laws.

1834 Santa Anna dismisses congress, repeals by decree the reform legislation, governs as centralistic dictator.

1835 On the grounds that the federalistic constitution had been violated, Texas begins rebellion.

1836 Texas declares independence, Santa Anna captures Alamo in San Antonio and kills all defenders; Sam Houston defeats Santa Anna at San Jacinto, forces recognition of Texas independence from Santa Anna. Santa Anna "perpetually" exiled, and new centralistic constitution promulgated.

1837 Anastasio Bustamante becomes president, Santa Anna allowed to return to Mexico. First railroad concession let.

1838 French "Pastry War" invasion of Veracruz; Santa Anna emerges a great hero, having lost a leg.

1840 Liberal rebellion against Bustamante government fails; railroad concession cancelled for lack of work done.

1841 Conservative rebellion against Bustamante successful, Santa Anna assumes control as dictator.

1842 Santa Anna retires to his *hacienda,* leaving government to Nicolás Bravo; congress dissolved, Committee of Notables convened to draft new centralistic constitution. New rail concession let.

1843 New constitution, giving president dictatorial powers, promulgated, and Santa Anna chosen president.

1844 New revolution forces Santa Anna into exile again.

1845 Texas admitted as a state in the United States, over bitter Mexican objections which cause breach in diplomatic relations. General Mariano Paredes overthrows government in Mexico.

1846 Beginning of Mexican War. Paredes overthrown, Gómez Farías becomes acting president, Santa Anna returns with connivance of the United States, and becomes president.

1848 Treaty of Guadalupe Hidalgo closes Mexican War. Santa Anna again exiled, and liberal General José Joaquín Herrera becomes president.

1851 As a result of the first honest election since 1824, Mariano Arista becomes president, and Herrera surrenders power to him peacefully.

1853 A combination of conservative and clerical forces overthrows Arista and invites Santa Anna to return. For the next year, Santa Anna's government takes on all the trappings of an absolute monarchy, partly financed by the sale of the Mesilla Valley (the Gadsden Purchase) to the United States.

1854-55 Liberal Revolution of Ayutla sends Santa Anna into fourth exile. Juan Alvarez becomes acting president, but late in 1855 resigns in favor of Ignacio Comonfort.

1855 First road connecting Gulf and Pacific coasts completed. The nation could also boast of having fifteen miles of railroad.

1856-57 Under the leadership of Comonfort, Miguel Lerdo de Tejada, and Benito Juárez, a number of anticlerical laws and a new constitution drafted. Numerous small rebellions resulted, and Félix Zuloaga seized Mexico City in late 1857.

1858-61 The War of the Reform, a bitter struggle pitting liberal against conservative-clerical. Juárez, claiming presidency by constitutional succession, directs liberal forces from Veracruz. Anticlerical decrees from Juárez more stringent. Seizure of foreign money by both sides presages international difficulties.

1861 After defeat of conservatives, Juárez returns to Mexico City to an empty treasury and governmental chaos. Tripartite agreement for intervention signed by England, France, and Spain. Spanish troops land at Veracruz.

1862-67 Period of French intervention.

1862 Defeat of French at Puebla, May 5, gives national holiday.

1863 Juárez forced to abandon Mexico City; French in control.

1864 Archduke Maximilian of Austria arrives in Mexico as emperor.

1867 Faced by defeats in Mexico, harried in Europe, and under pressure from the United States, French withdraw forces from Mexico. Maximilian's Mexican armies defeated; Maximilian captured and shot.

1867-76 Period of the "Restored Republic" under Juárez and then Sebastián Lerdo de Tejada. Strong anticlerical laws passed. A few minor rebellions, but generally peace with some economic restoration, including railroad building

1872 Rebellion of La Noria, led by Porfirio Díaz, suppressed. Juárez dies; Lerdo elected president. Santa Anna allowed to return.

1876 Díaz-led rebellion of Tuxtepec overthrows Lerdo; Díaz, on platform of "No-Reelection," elected to presidency.

1876-1911 Period of the *porfiriato,* or Díaz dictatorship.

1879 Minor rebellion in Veracruz suppressed with great brutality; this the last rebellion for nearly 25 years.

1880 Favorable concessions given to U.S. railroad company introduce the great railroad boom. Manuel González elected president.

1883 First land survey law, setting in motion the eventual heavy concentration of landholding.

1884 Mining code reformed, giving landowners the ownership of subsoil hydrocarbons and easing other regulations. Díaz reelected.

1887 Revised mining laws make foreign investment in mines more attractive.

1888 Constitution changed to allow Díaz to succeed himself, and he is reelected.

1892 Díaz again reelected.

1894 New land survey law makes landholding concentration and Indian despoliation easier.

1896 Interior customs houses, which collected the *alcabala,* finally abolished. Díaz reelected.

1898 Strike of textile workers at Apizaco broken by army, but with no loss of life.

1900 Díaz reelected.

1904 Constitution changed to allow a six-year term for the president, and the creation of the office of vice president. Díaz and Ramón Corral elected. Francisco I. Madero, a young Coahuila *hacendado,* begins political career in opposition to Díaz.

1905 Economic and international fiscal conditions force Mexico to change monetary system, creating internal economic problems.

1906 Strike and riots at the Cananea copper mines suppressed with loss of life. Partido Liberal, led by Ricardo Flores Magón, formed in exile.

1907 Bloody repression of textile strike in Rio Blanco.

1908 Madero publishes his *La sucesión presidencial en 1910,* and becomes a national political opposition figure.

1910-24 The period of the Epic Revolution.

1910 Government forces harry political opponents and finally arrest Madero. Financial difficulties force Secretary of Treasury Limantour to go to Europe to refinance international debt. Revolution against Díaz begins late in year.

1911 Díaz overthrown and, after a provisional government, Madero is elected president. Emiliano Zapata, who had helped overthrow Díaz, rebels, demanding quick reforms. General Bernardo Reyes rebels but is quickly quashed.

1912 Many minor rebellions, most important of which are those of Pascual Orozco and Félix Díaz, suppressed.

1913 Madero overthrown by *coup d'état* led by Félix Díaz and Victoriano Huerta, then assassinated. Huerta seizes control, while Venustiano Carranza begins Constitutionalist Revolution in the north, supported by Francisco Villa and Alvaro Obregón. United States refuses to recognize Huerta.

1914 U.S. forces occupy Veracruz. Huerta defeated and forced to flee to exile. Provisional government under Carranza, but Villa begins fight against him while Obregón supports Carranza.

1915 Villa defeated, but continues to fight and raid for next five years. Carranza government recognized by the United States.

1916 Pershing's Punitive Expedition chases Villa in vain, causes bitterness between United States and Mexico.

1917 New constitution, featuring stringent anticlericalism and rampant nationalism, promulgated. Hydrocarbons declared to belong to the nation. Carranza becomes constitutional president.

1919 United States threatens intervention as outcome of the kidnapping of a U.S. consular agent. Zapata ambushed and killed.

1920 As a result of his attempt to impose successor, Carranza is overthrown and killed. Villa "retires." Adolfo de la Huerta becomes provisional president, holds election in which Obregón elected.

1923 United States recognizes Obregón government. Villa assassinated under curious circumstances. De la Huerta rebels, but soon suppressed.

1924 The election of Plutarco Elías Calles and the peaceful transfer of office bring the Epic Revolution to an end.

1926 Conflict between government and Church hierarchy results in the Cristero rebellion.

1927 Constitution amended to allow Obregón's election, and to extend term to six years.

1928 Obregón reelected, but assassinated before taking office. Special convention selects Emilio Portes Gil as provisional president to hold election.

1929 Cristero rebellion suppressed and agreement between government and clergy reopens churches. National Revolutionary Party (PRN) formed by Calles; Pascual Ortiz Rubio elected but Calles remains as recognized "boss."

1931 A new wave of clerical persecution begins, with a radical reduction of the number of priests allowed to officiate.

1932 Ortiz Rubio resigns "for reasons of ill health," and Abelardo Rodríguez chosen to complete the term.

1934 Lázaro Cárdenas elected to carry out a new "Six Year Plan" of reform and economic progress.

1936 Calles, who attempted to interfere with the government, deported. Cárdenas brings an end to violent religious persecution.

1938 Cárdenas decrees expropriation of properties of major oil companies. Saturnino Cedillo, the last of the old-style *caudillos,* rebels unsuccessfully and is killed in battle. The PRN is reorganized, becomes the "official party" under the name of the Mexican Revolutionary Party (PRM).

1940 Manuel Avila Camacho elected president, and Juan Andreu

Almazán, the unsuccessful opponent, threatens to rebel but does not.

1942 Mexico joins Allies in war declaration against Axis.

1946 The PRM reorganized to give wider representation, becomes the Party of Revolutionary Institutions (PRI). Miguel Alemán elected, emphasizes industrialization.

1947 Final payment made by Mexico to U.S. oil companies for expropriations.

1950 By this date literacy had climbed to over 50 per cent for the first time in Mexican history, and per capita agricultural production reached the pre-revolutionary level.

1952 Adolfo Ruiz Cortines, the first true civilian candidate to be elected since Madero, takes office. Women's suffrage extended to national level.

1958 Adolfo López Mateos, another civilian, elected president.

1960 After this date, agricultural production increases at an accelerated rate.

1962 Final payment made to British for expropriated oil properties.

1964 Gustavo Díaz Ordaz elected president.

A Selective Guide to the Literature on Mexico

The literature on Mexico, covering nearly a thousand years of development, is vast and sometimes exciting. Selecting from that mountain of books a representative sample, which will give a flavor of both what has happened and what men have said about the events, poses a difficult task; the following essay on the available literature, for the casual reader and for the specialist as well, refers to material which the author considers to have peculiar merit, oftentimes because the writer there expresses a viewpoint diametrically opposed to that presented in the present work. The first of the following sections deals with books in English, generally easily available in university and public libraries, a combination of which will give a good understanding of Mexican history. The second section includes materials dealing with geography, and the third lists a minute proportion of the great many excellent works on pre-Hispanic cultures. The fourth section concerns the colonial period, the fifth the movement for independence, and the sixth the pre-revolutionary national period. The seventh section, which includes more titles than any other, concerns the incredibly complex and important developments after 1910. The last section mentions a few bibliographical aids and includes a number of generalized works which cover the sweep of Mexican history.

I. SELECTED STUDIES IN ENGLISH

The best single volume, in spite of its many weaknesses, covering the entire history of Mexico is Henry B. Parkes, *A History of Mexico* (Boston, 1938, 1950, 1960), which replaced the older and duller H. I. Priestley, *The Mexican Nation: A History* (New York, 1923). Hubert Howe Bancroft's six-volume *A History of Mexico* (San Francisco, 1886-88) is coming back into repute after having been the butt of scholarly jokes for many years; the quality of each section depends upon the care with which Bancroft's numerous aides did their work. Wilfrid H. Callcott's two works, *Church and State in Mexico, 1822-1857* (Durham, 1926) and *Liberalism in Mexico, 1857-1929* (Stanford, 1931), give a general coverage despite their deceptive titles; Callcott leaves the reader in no doubt concerning his point of view. Howard Cline's two books, *The United States and Mexico* (Cambridge, Mass., 1953; New York, 1963) and *Mexico: Revolution to Evolution* (New York, 1962), give an excellent but not particularly original overview of the period after 1910; they have the additional advantage of being easily available in paperback. Ernest Gruening, *Mexico and Its Heritage* (New York and London, 1928), is old but still intriguing for its wealth of information (some inaccurate) and its passionate denunciation of all those groups who, in Gruening's terms, opposed progress. Lesley Byrd Simpson, *Many Mexicos* (New York, 1941 and later editions), is a series of vignettes rather than a long narrative, but it is delightfully written and based on sound scholarship. Hudson Strode's *Timeless Mexico* (New York, 1944) is of the same type, but inferior to Simpson. For a balanced but sadly out-of-date presentation of the Church-State problem, John Lloyd Mecham, *Church and State in Latin America* (Chapel Hill, 1934), will suffice.

Some remarkably perceptive and delightfully written books on the pre-Hispanic populations are readily available. Ignacio Bernal, *Mexico before Cortez: Art, History and Legend* (New York, 1963); Miguel León-Portilla, *The Broken Spears: The Aztec Account of the Conquest of Mexico* (Boston, 1962); George C. Vaillant, *The Aztecs of Mexico* (Garden City, New York, 1941); Paul Westheim, *The Art of Ancient*

Mexico (Garden City, New York, 1965); and Eric Wolf, *Sons of the Shaking Earth* (Chicago, 1959) all are excellent in scholarship and presentation; each was either originally published as a paperback or has been marketed in a paperback edition. Frances Gillmor, *The King Danced in the Marketplace* (Tucson, 1964), is a marvelously presented quasi-biography of Moctezuma I, and Jacques Soustelle, *The Daily Life of the Aztecs on the Eve of the Spanish Conquest* (London, 1961; also in French, 1955), is exciting reading. Laurette Sejourne, *Burning Water: Thought and Religion in Ancient Mexico* (New York, 1956); Helen Augur, *Zapotec* (Garden City, New York, 1954); and Thomas Gann and J. E. Thompson, *History of the Maya from the Earliest Times to the Present Day* (New York, 1931) are all excellent. Charles Gibson, *The Aztecs under Spanish Rule, 1519-1810: A History of the Indians of the Valley of Mexico* (Stanford, 1964), is the outstanding book, both in scholarship and literary style, yet written on colonial New Spain.

William H. Prescott, *History of the Conquest of Mexico* (first published 1843, numerous editions since), is still the best book on the conquest itself, and Bernal Díaz del Castillo, *Historia verdadera de la conquista de la Nueva España* (numerous editions, under varying titles, some in English, also in paperback), is an intriguing account written years later by one of Cortez's lieutenants. Thomas Gage, *The English American his Travail by Sea and Land: or, A New Survey of the West Indies* (London, 1648 and many later editions, under varying titles), gives a bitterly jaundiced view of the Spanish and their practices. Francis Borgia Steck, *Motolinía's History of the Indians of New Spain* (Washington, 1951), gives an annotated version of the great Franciscan's sixteenth-century study, and Herbert E. Bolton's *The Padre on Horseback* (San Francisco, 1932), is a beautifully written and sensitive distillation of the same author's long biography of Father Eusebio Kino, published four years later. Irving Leonard, *Baroque Times in Old Mexico: Seventeenth Century Persons, Places and Practices* (Ann Arbor, 1959), is a first-rate and beautifully written study of the period. Alexander von Humboldt, *Political Essay on the Kingdom of New Spain* (4 vols., London, 1811; reprinted New York,

1966), is a little heavy for an evening's easy reading, but it is highly rewarding despite the poor translation, which made Humboldt furious.

Wilfrid H. Callcott, *Santa Anna: The Story of an Enigma Who Was Once Mexico* (Norman, 1936), Ralph Roeder, *Juárez and His Mexico: A Biographical History* (2 vols., New York, 1947), and Carleton Beals, *Porfirio Díaz, Dictator of Mexico* (Philadelphia, 1932), overlap one another and together give a continuous history of most of the nineteenth century; of the group, Roeder is the best combination of scholarship and style. Frances Calderón de la Barca, *Life in Mexico* (Boston, 1843; many later editions), is the extraordinarily perceptive remarks of the Scottish-born wife of the first Spanish minister to Mexico; and Fanny Chalmers Gooch, *Face to Face with the Mexicans* (New York, 1887; a new edition, Carbondale, 1966), gives another lady's less important views on Díaz's Mexico. Charles C. Cumberland, *Mexican Revolution: Genesis under Madero* (Austin, 1952), and Stanley R. Ross, *Francisco I. Madero: Apostle of Democracy* (New York, 1955), cover the fall of the Díaz dictatorship with remarkable agreement on sources and interpretation. Robert Quirk, *The Mexican Revolution, 1914-1915* (Bloomington, 1960), covers that enormously complex period with excellent style and sound interpretation. Tomme Clark Call, *The Mexican Venture: From Political to Industrial Revolution in Mexico* (New York, 1953), J. H. Plenn, *Mexico Marches* (Indianapolis, 1939), Virginia Prewett, *Reportage on Mexico* (New York, 1941), Ramon E. Ruiz, *Mexico: The Challenge of Poverty and Illiteracy* (San Marino, 1963), Frank Tannenbaum, *Peace by Revolution* (New York, 1933), and *Mexico: The Struggle for Peace and Bread* (New York, 1950) together cover the period since 1920 in a rather sympathetic vein, while Graham Greene, *Another Mexico* (New York, 1939) and Frank L. Kluckhohn, *The Mexican Challenge* (New York, 1939), let their disgust with anticlericalism and expropriation, respectively, interfere with objective reporting. Both William C. Townsend, *Lazaro Cardenas, Mexican Democrat* (Ann Arbor, 1952), and Nathaniel and Sylvia Weyl, *The Reconquest of Mexico: The Years of Lazaro Cardenas* (New York, 1939), adulate the Mexican president.

Eyler Simpson, *The Ejido: Mexico's Way Out* (Chapel Hill, 1937), and Nathan L. Whetten, *Rural Mexico* (Chicago, 1948), examine with great thoroughness the agrarian reform program; Whetten is a bit more pessimistic than Simpson. Clarence O. Senior, *Land Reform and Democracy* (Gainesville, 1958), is the epitome of optimism in this study of land reform in the Laguna district. James Morton Callahan, *American Foreign Policy in Mexican Relations* (New York, 1932), Frederick S. Dunn, *The Diplomatic Protection of Americans in Mexico* (New York, 1933), and Edgar Turlington, *Mexico and Her Foreign Creditors* (New York, 1930), cover various aspects of Mexican international relations with great scholarly competence and considerable dullness. Of a different order are Otis A. Singletary, *The Mexican War* (Chicago, 1960; also in paperback), Clarence C. Clendenen, *The United States and Pancho Villa: A Study in Unconventional Diplomacy* (Ithaca, 1961), Sheldon B. Liss, *A Century of Disagreement: The Chamizal Conflict, 1864-1964* (Washington, 1965), and Robert Quirk, *An Affair of Honor: Woodrow Wilson and the Occupation of Veracruz* (Lexington, 1962; paperback, New York, 1964); in each the fine scholarship is complemented by a sprightly style. H. S. Person, *Mexican Oil* (New York, 1942), is a remarkably perceptive and objective examination of the issues which led to the 1938 expropriations; his analysis must have been a great disappointment to those who were urging strong retaliatory actions by the United States. Marvin Bernstein, *The Mexican Mining Industry, 1890-1950* (Albany, 1965), is an excellent and lengthy study of the multitudinous problems facing the industry, and William E. Cole, *Steel and Economic Growth in Mexico* (Austin, 1967), is a fine but poorly-written examination of the steel industry.

Finally, three books dealing with contemporary Mexican mores are invaluable. Octavio Paz, *The Labyrinth of Solitude* (New York, 1962; first published Mexico, 1959), and Samuel Ramos, *Profile of Man and Culture in Mexico* (Austin, 1962; first published Mexico, 1934, in Spanish), are both outstanding attempts by distinguished Mexicans to analyse their own society. Oscar Lewis, *The Children of Sanchez: Autobiography of a Mexican Family* (New York, 1961), is a fascinating book but leaves the erroneous impression that all Mexicans suffer from serious psychoses.

II. GEOGRAPHY

Undoubtedly, the most valuable work on Mexican geography is Jorge L. Tamayo's four-volume *Geografía general de México* (Mexico, 1949; revised edition, 1962). Much of the text has been converted into an excellent series of maps and charts in his *Atlas geográfica general de México* (Mexico, 1962); the visual representations of complex statistical data are outstanding. A less comprehensive study is the one-volume Jorge Vivó, *Geografía de México* (Mexico, 1948; many later editions); the information is excellent, but the style tends to be as exciting as a statistical table. Julio Riquelme Inda, *Monografías geográficas sintéticas* (Mexico, 1946), has less information but a better style; the book is primarily concerned with the economic circumstances of towns of over 2,000 population as listed in the 1940 census. The numerous works of Antonio García Cubás in the last half of the nineteenth century are all excellent, particularly considering the dearth of data with which he had to work. His *Memoria para servir la carta general de la república mexicana* (Mexico, 1861) consists primarily of a listing of all the places shown on the newly-issued map, with a population estimate for each town. His *The Republic of Mexico in 1876* (Mexico, 1876) is much more comprehensive and, in part, a propaganda tool for foreign consumption. The *Cuadro geográfico, estadístico é histórico de los Estados Unidos Mexicanos* (Mexico, 1884), which García Cubás compiled and issued as an official publication of the government, is an invaluable though not always accurate work. A partial listing of the many special geographic studies may be found in Charles C. Cumberland, *The United States-Mexican Border: A Selective Guide to the Literature of the Region* (Ithaca, 1960), and the most important geological studies may be found in Marvin Bernstein, *The Mexican Mining Industry,* discussed above. But the indispensable guide to geographic literature is Angel Bassols Batalla, *Bibliográfía geográfica de México* (Mexico, 1955).

III. PRE-HISPANIC SOCIETIES

In addition to the references mentioned in the first section dealing with the pre-Hispanic civilizations, literature on the Mexican-Indian populations is extensive, though sometimes highly technical. The Mexican Instituto Nacional de Antropología é Historia has been publishing a series of highly specialized works dealing with the findings through excavations; the titles of most of these, except the most recent, may be found in Ignacio Bernal, *Bibliografía de arquelogía y etnografía: Mesoamérica y norte de México* (Mexico, 1962). Aside from the information gleaned from archeology, the best sources for ancient Indian life comes from the accounts left in the sixteenth and seventeenth centuries by the Spaniards. Toribio de Motolinía, *Historia de los Indios de Nueva España* (various editions), made the first determined attempt to make a record of the earlier society as related to him by the Nahua people among whom he worked. Juan de Torquemada, *Monarquía indiana* (first published in Madrid, 1613-1615; most recent publication in Mexico, 1943-1944, 3 vols.), compiled massive and painstaking data—in part, to be sure, to forestall the civil authorities from moving in on clerical indigene control. Diego de Landa did his work and made his report in the second half of the sixteenth century, but he was long dead when Brasseur de Bourbourg finally published it as *Relation des choses de Yucatan* in 1864. Since then it has appeared in numerous editions, in both Spanish and English; the latest from Mexico in 1959. Both Gerónimo de Mendieta, *Historia eclesiástica indiana,* and Diego Durán, *Historia de las indias de Nueva España y islas de Tierra Firme,* suffered the same fate as Landa; written in the late sixteenth century, they were both published in the nineteenth. The most recent edition of Mendieta is from Mexico, 1945, in 4 volumes, and that of Durán is in English under the title of *The Aztecs: The History of the Indies of New Spain* (New York, 1964). The first volume of Durán was first published, under the editorship of José Fernández Ramírez, in 1867; before he could complete his work the Maximilian Empire fell, and Fernández Ramírez thought it best to go into exile, with the result that the second volume waited until 1880 for publication. Two sixteenth century descendants of both the conquered and the conquerors made their contributions to the knowledge of their native ancestors. Fernando de Alva Ixtlilxochitl, *Historia Chichimeca* (most conveniently found as Volume II of Alfredo Chavero, *Obras históricas de Fernando de Alva Ixtlilxochitl*, Mexico, 1952), must be used with some care since, as one wistful critic put it, it were better had he written less extensively and more accurately. Fernando Alvarado Tezozomoc finished his much shorter but more accurate *Crónica Mexicayotl* in 1609, but he wrote it, unfortunately, in Nahuatl. Working from photographic copies of the original manuscript, scholars at the National University have recently (1949) published it in the original and in Spanish translation, paragraph by paragraph. Arthur J. O. Anderson and Charles D. Dibble have partially reproduced and completely translated the *Florentine Codex* (Santa Fe, 1950-1955, in 13 parts) which Bernardino de Sahagún had compiled in the sixteenth century.

Among the twentieth-century works not previously mentioned, the best in English are Thomas Gann, *Mexico, from the Earliest Times to the Conquest* (London, 1936), Frans Blom, *The Conquest of Yucatan* (Boston, 1936), John Eric Thompson, *Mexico Before Cortez* (New York, 1933), and Edgar L. Hewett, *Ancient Life in Mexico and Central America* (Indianapolis, 1936), written in a most zestful style. Barbro Dahlgren de Jordan's very recent *La Mixteca: su cultura é historia prehispánicas* (Mexico, 1966) is the only serious attempt at a full-scale examination of that important group of expert artisans. Woodrow Borah and Sherburne F. Cook have caused an uproar in scholarly circles by computing *The Aboriginal Population of Central Mexico on the Eve of the Spanish Conquest* (Berkeley, 1963; *Ibero-Americana 45*) to have been well over twenty million; critics object, but they have not been able to refute.

IV. THE COLONIAL PERIOD

Much of the history of the colonial period may be found in biographical studies ranging chronologically from a rash of Cortez biographies

—from excellent to indifferent—to James M. Manfredini, *The Political Role of the Court of Revillagigedo, Viceroy of New Spain: 1789-1794* (New Brunswick, 1949). Between these extremes are Arthur S. Aiton's excellent *Antonio de Mendoza: First Viceroy of New Spain* (Durham, 1927), Herbert I. Priestley, *José de Gálvez, Visitor-General of New Spain, 1765-1771* (Berkeley, 1916), and Bernard Bobb, *The Viceregency of Antonio María de Bucareli in New Spain, 1771-1779* (Austin, 1962). Alongside these biographies of major political figures are three of major religious figures. Richard E. Greenleaf, *Zumárraga and the Mexican Inquisition* (Washington, 1961), places that great man, chiefly remembered as the destroyer of priceless Aztec structures and codices, into proper perspective. Herbert E. Bolton, *Rim of Christendom: A Biography of Eusebio Francisco Kino, Pacific Coast Pioneer* (New York, 1936), treats that dedicated Jesuit scholar and missionary with tenderness and with the sound scholarship which his subject deserved. Lillian Estelle Fisher, *Champion of Reform: Manuel Abad y Queipo* (New York, 1955), sympathetically scrutinizes the career of a clerical firebrand, but she somehow manages to make dull reading of a fabulous subject. A number of biographies of lesser figures have appeared; the best is probably John Lloyd Mecham, *Francisco de Ibarra and Nueva Vizcaya* (Durham, 1927). Added to these biographies are the many editions, in both Spanish and English translation, of Cortez's letters to his sovereign, and the delightful account of a young Italian who passed through Mexico briefly on a trip around the world in the late seventeenth century; Gemelli Carreri, *Viaje a la Nueva España: México a fines del siglo XVII* (2 vols., Mexico, 1955), was first published in Italy in 1700.

The basic elements of the administrative system in colonial Mexico are synthesized as a part of the painstakingly accurate but unexciting books by Lillian E. Fisher, *Viceregal Administration in the Spanish American Colonies* (Berkeley, 1929) and *The Intendant System in Spanish America* (Berkeley, 1926). Juan de Solórzano y Pereira, *Política Indiana* (Madrid, 1647, a translation from the Latin published 1629-1639), the *Recopilación de las leyes de los reynos de las indias* (most convenient of many editions, 3 vols., Madrid, 1943) and Joseph

Antonio Villa-Señor y Sánchez, *Teatro Americano* (most convenient, Mexico, 1952) are crucial for a study of the administrative and legal structure, although the last tends to be more descriptive of the countryside than of the administration. Much data, including material on the multitudinous frustrations facing the viceroys, may be gleaned from *Instrucciones que los virreyes de Nueva España dejaron a sus sucesores* (2 vols., Mexico, 1867-73), from Fabián de Fonseca and Carlos de Urrutia, *Historia general de la real hacienda* (6 vols., Mexico, 1845-53) which was a thorough study undertaken by order of Viceroy Revillagigedo for his and his successors' edification, and from Bernardo de Gálvez, *Instructions for Governing the Interior Provinces of New Spain* (Berkeley, 1951).

The manner in which the colonial system worked, rather than how it was designed to work, may be found in part through two of Lesley Byrd Simpson's uniformly excellent works; the titles explain the subjects: *Exploitation of Land in Central Mexico in the Sixeteenth Century* (Berkeley, 1952) and *The Encomienda in New Spain: Forced Native Labor in the Spanish Colonies, 1492-1550* (Berkeley, 1929). The same author has also given us an excellent series of shorter works under the general title of *Studies in the Administration of the Indians in New Spain*, published as parts of *Ibero-Americana;* the specific titles are *The Laws of Burgos of 1512, The Civil Congregation, The Repartimiento System of Native Labor in New Spain and Guatemala,* and *The Emancipation of the Indian Slaves and the Resettlement of the Freedmen, 1548-1555.* Silvio A. Zavala, *Fuentes para la historia del trabajo en Nueva España* (8 vols., Mexico, 1939-1945), gives an enormous amount of raw data with which to work. Charles Gibson, *Tlaxcala in the Sixteenth Century* (New Haven, 1952), is characterized by the easy style and the exacting scholarship which mark all his work. Woodrow Borah has contributed a great deal of information on the sixteenth century; his *The Population of Central Mexico in 1548; an Analysis of the Suma de Visitas de Pueblos* (Berkeley, 1960) is a companion-piece to his two works in collaboration with Sherburne F. Cook: *The Indian Population of Central Mexico: 1531-1610* (Berkeley, 1960) and the already-cited work on pre-Conquest population.

The three taken together give a startling picture of population decline. Borah's *New Spain's Century of Depression* (Berkeley, 1951) should be used in conjunction with the Borah and Cook *Price Trends of Some Basic Commodities in Central Mexico, 1531-1570* (Berkeley, 1958). All the Borah material mentioned here was published in the Ibero-Americana series. The information to be elicited from the foregoing works shows a steady decline in native fortunes, which should have produced serious unrest. Luis González Obregón attempted to prove the existence of the unrest in his *Rebeliones indígenas y precursores de la independencia mexicana en los siglos XVI, XVII, XVIII* (2 vols., Mexico, 1906-08, revised 1952), but he was hard put to find anything worthy of the name "rebellion" after the Mixton War.

Some particular aspects of the colonial economy, and consequently the Spanish thought process, have been examined by U. S. scholars. The best of the lot is Clement Motten's delightful and thoughtful *Mexican Silver and the Enlightenment* (Philadelphia, 1950), followed closely in all-around quality by Lyle N. McAlister, *The "fuero militar" in New Spain, 1764-1800* (Gainesville, 1957); the military privileges, of course, were not an economic institution but did have important economic consequences. Walter Howe, *The Mining Guild of New Spain and Its Tribunal General, 1770-1821* (Cambridge, 1949), tends to be a bit legalistic, but it is a thorough examination. William H. Dusenberry, *The Mexican Mesta: The Administration of Ranching in Colonial Mexico* (Urbana, 1963), has much information, but the interpretation is virtually nil and the work raises almost as many questions as it answers. Fausto de Elhuyar, the mining expert sent from Spain to revivify the industry late in the colonial period, submitted a thoughtful *Memoria sobre el influjo de la minería en la agricultura, industria, población y civilización de la Nueva España* (Madrid, 1825), which should be used along with Modesto Bargalló, *La minería y la metalurgía en la América Española durante la época colonial* (Mexico, 1955). Philip Wayne Powell, *Soldiers, Indians and Silver: The Northward Advance of New Spain, 1550-1600* (Berkeley, 1952), is adequate.

Additional sidelights on the colonial period may be found in Manuel Romero de Terreros y Vincent, *Bocetas de la vida social en la Nueva España* (Mexico, 1944), Julio Jiménez Rueda, *Historia de la cultura en México: el virreinato* (Mexico, 1950), Fernando Benítez, *La vida criolla en el siglo XVI* (Mexico, 1953), and George Kubler, *Mexican Architecture in the Sixteenth Century* (2 vols., New Haven, 1948), which includes data concerning the life of the artisans. Luis González Obregón contributed *La vida de México en 1810* (Mexico, 1911). Donald B. Cooper, *Epidemic Disease in Mexico City, 1761-1813* (Austin, 1965), is an admirable study which needs to be bolstered by others dealing with earlier periods.

In addition to the studies mentioned here on the colonial period, the reader should not overlook the titles mentioned in the first and last sections of this essay.

V. INDEPENDENCE PERIOD

The literature on the movement for independence is at best sketchy and, despite some excellent individual works, unsatisfactory. Basic to an understanding of the period is Juan E. Hernández y Dávalos' undigested *Colección de documentos para la historia de la guerra de independencia* (6 vols., Mexico, 1877-1882). Among the later monographs concerning the period the best are Lillian Estelle Fisher, *The Background of the Revolution for Mexican Independence* (Boston, 1934), filled with information but dull, and John Rydjord, *Foreign Interests in the Independence of New Spain* (Durham, 1935), both enlightening and readable. Nettie Lee Benson, *Mexico and The Spanish Cortes, 1812-1822* (Austin, 1966), consists of a series of essays growing out of a graduate seminar. The essays are of different quality, but as a group they point up some of the greatest frustrations on the part of the Mexican *criollo*. Four contemporaries, three of the liberal persuasion and one of the conservative, put their minds and pens to a retrospective clarification of the issues and the events. Lucas Alamán devoted only a part of his *Historia de Méjico desde los primeros movi-*

mientos que prepararon su independencia en el año 1808, hasta la época presente (5 vols., Mexico, 1849-1852) to the independence period, and he has a somewhat jaundiced view of the Hidalgo-Morelos phase, but his information is generally accurate and his argumentation excellent. Carlos María Bustamante, who fought for years for independence and despised Iturbide, in his *Cuadro histórico de la revolución en la américa mexicana* (6 vols., 1823-1832), takes a different view from Alamán; Lorenzo de Zavala, *Ensayo histórico de las revoluciones de Méjico desde 1808 hasta 1830* (2 vols., Paris, 1831-1832) is in basic agreement with Bustamante. José María Luis Mora, *México y sus revoluciones* (various editions, the most convenient Mexico, 1950) is less factual and more interpretative than the preceding three.

Four of the principal figures of the period have been the subjects of excellent biographies. Hugh Hamill, *The Hidalgo Revolt* (Gainesville, 1966), is a biography of a movement rather than of a man; the tenor and the orientation are quite different from those presented in this book, but there is no basic disagreement. William H. Timmons, *Morelos: Priest, Soldier, Statesman* (El Paso, 1963) is a short but excellent study, the burden of which is that Morelos was not as radical as his contemporaries thought him. William F. Sprague, *Vicente Guerrero* (Chicago, 1939), is only partly concerned with the *suriano's* revolutionary career; his presentation is sympathetic. William Spence Robertson, *Iturbide of Mexico* (Durham, 1952), and Rafael Heliodoro Valle, *Iturbide, varón de Díos* (Mexico, 1944), are both a bit more laudatory than their subject warrants. Iturbide speaks for himself, not always accurately, in *Memoires autographes* (Paris, 1824) and in *Correspondencia y diario militar, 1810-1821* (3 vols., Mexico, 1930); his brilliance shows through, but his greed and his lust for power remain hidden. Hidalgo speaks for himself, through the medium of court records, in Antonio Pompa y Pompa's editing of *Procesos inquisitorial y militar seguidas a D. Miguel Hidalgo y Costilla* (Mexico, 1960); the records give a fascinating insight into Hidalgo's character.

The materials listed above may be supplemented by the relevant sections of the general works listed in section VIII of this bibliographical essay.

VI. NINETEENTH CENTURY

The Mexican situation being what it was in the early years of nationhood, many foreigners who by force of circumstance found themselves in that country recorded their observations. Among the most perceptive of these foreign accounts come from two men who, by position, were each dedicated to destroying the influence and work of the other: Henry G. Ward, adroit British Minister and consummate maneuverer, includes excellent material in his *Mexico* (2 vols., London, 1829), while Joel R. Poinsett, the gifted United States Minister whom Ward consistently outfoxed, wrote his excellent *Notes on Mexico Made in the Autumn of 1822* (Philadelphia, 1824) after a short sojourn in that country before he accepted the diplomatic post. Captain G. F. Lyon, sent to Mexico by a group of Britishers interested in Mexican mining investments, wrote a rather sprightly *Journal of a Residence and Tour in the Republic of Mexico in 1826* (2 vols., London, 1828); he visited regions seen by neither Ward nor Poinsett. Two U. S. diplomatic officers in the 1840's left their accounts. Brantz Mayer, *Mexico As It Was and As It Is* (New York, 1844) has slightly more data than does Waddy Thompson, *Recollections of Mexico* (New York, 1846); both are exceptionally interesting. Luis Manuel del Rivero, a Spaniard who came to Mexico shortly after his country recognized the newer nation, was somewhat more sympathetic in his *Méjico en 1842* (Madrid, 1844) than one would have supposed; both his observations and his style tend to be romantic. Carl Sartorius, who left Germany for Mexico soon after independence, was prevailed upon by his friends to write *Mexico: Landscapes and Popular Sketches* (London, New York and Darmstadt, 1858; recently republished as *Mexico About 1850* in Stuttgart). Lucien Biart, *La Terre Chaud: Scenes de la vie Mexicaine* (Paris, 1862) and *La Terre Tempérée: Scenes de la vie Mexicaine* (Paris, 1866), was a bit sharper in his observations than the German or Spaniard; both works have been translated and published in Mexico in recent years. At roughly the same time a U. S. citizen fleeing from the chaos of the post Civil War period kept records of his observations; recently found, Ramon E. Ruiz has published them as *An American in*

Maximilian's Mexico: The Diaries of William Marshall Anderson (San Marino, California, 1959).

Frederick A. Ober, *Travels in Mexico and Life Among the Mexicans* (Boston, 1884), William L. Purcell, *Frontier Mexico, 1875-1894* (San Antonio, 1963; these are Purcell's letters) and Julio Sesto, *El México de Porfirio Díaz* (Valencia, 1909) all tend to glow regarding their host country; Sesto, particularly, was highly pro-Díaz. A rather startling negative view is Henry H. Harper, *A Journey in Southeastern Mexico* (Boston, 1910), who concluded his short book by saying: "Verily it may best be said that this part of Mexico . . . was made for Mexicans, and so far as I am personally concerned, they are everlastingly welcome to it." Charles Flandrau's delightful *Viva Mexico* (New York, 1908, many later editions) and Hamilton Fyfe's *The Real Mexico* (New York and London, [1914?]) tend to have a somewhat jaundiced view of what they saw.

Biographical studies of nineteenth century Mexican figures leave much to be desired in both quantity and quality. Frank Cleary Hanighen, *Santa Anna: the Napoleon of the West* (New York, 1934), is inferior to the Callcott work, and Santa Anna's own *Mi historia militar y política* (edited by Genaro García, Mexico, 1905) is a marvel of jactancy and apology. Thomas E. Cotner, *The Military and Political Career of José Joaquín Herrera, 1792-1854* (Austin, 1949) and Frank A. Knapp, Jr., *The Life of Sebastián Lerdo de Tejada* (Austin, 1951) are both excellent studies of lesser lights. David Hannay, *Díaz* (London, 1917) and James Creelman, *Díaz, Master of Mexico* (New York, 1911) are both light-weight, but are far superior to the blindly eulogistic Ethel Brilliana Tweedie, *The Maker of Modern Mexico, Porfirio Díaz* (New York, 1906). Carlos Díaz Dufoo, *Limantour* (Mexico, 1922), is adequate. The great number of short biographies written by the Mexicans tend to fall into the category of polemical rather than scholarly literature.

Among the works by contemporary Mexicans who tried seriously to analyze their nation's situation soon after independence, the best (in addition to Alamán, Bustamante, Zavala and Mora cited in the previous section) is probably José María Bocanegra, *Memorias para la historia de México independiente, 1822-1846* (2 vols., Mexico, 1892-1897). Much of the thinking of both Alamán and Mora has been synthesized in two books put together by Arturo Arnaiz y Freg; they are, respectively, *Lucas Alamán, semblanzas é ideario; prólogo y selección de Arturo Arnaiz y Freg* (Mexico, 1939) and José María Luis Mora, *Ensayos, ideas y retratos; prólogo y selección de Arturo Arnaiz y Freg* (Mexico, 1941). Toward the end of the century a distinguished Mexican statesman attempted to clarify nineteenth century Mexico for the foreigners; Matías Romero, *Mexico and the United States: A Study of Subjects Affecting their Political, Commercial, and Social Relations, Made with a View to Their Promotion* (New York, 1898) is an excellent but frustrating book.

The Texas Revolution and the subsequent Mexican War brought a spate of writing, most of it polemical. Among the more interesting of these accounts available to the reader in English are Carlos E. Castañeda, (ed.), *The Mexican Side of the Texas Revolution* (Dallas, 1928), William Jay, *A Review of the Causes and Consequences of the Mexican War* (Boston, 1849), Edward D. Mansfield, *The Mexican War* (New York, 1849), Nathan C. Brooks, *A Complete History of the Mexican War: Its Causes, Conduct and Consequences* (first publishes 1849; republished Chicago, 1965), Robert Anderson, *An Artillery Officer in the Mexican War, 1846-1847* (New York, 1911), and Cadmus M. Wilcox, *History of the Mexican War* (Washington, 1892). Taken as a group they fail to answer many of the most pressing questions concerning responsibilities and issues. The best works on the questions are the old but still reliable Justin H. Smith, *The Annexation of Texas* (Corrected edition, New York, 1941), Justin H. Smith, *The War with Mexico* (2 vols., New York, 1919) and George L. Rives, *The United States and Mexico, 1821-1848* (2 vols., New York, 1913). An addendum to the results of the Mexican War is covered in Paul Neff Garber, *The Gadsden Treaty* (Philadelphia, 1923), which puts the onus on Santa Anna rather than the United States.

The Mexican War brought a series of events in train, directly or indirectly. Rufus K. Wyllys, *The French in Sonora, 1850-1854* (Berkeley, 1932), covers a facet of filibustering into the defeated nation, and Richard A. Johnson's short *The Mexican Revolution of Ayutla, 1854-1855* (Rock Island, Illinois, 1939) gives scanty treatment to an important development intimately related to the earlier defeat. *The Actas Oficiales y minutario de decretos del Congreso Extraordinario Constituyente de 1856-57* (Mexico, 1857) is the official publication of the convention which emanated from the Revolution of Ayutla, while Francisco Zarco, *Crónica del Congreso Extraordinario Constituyente, 1856-1857* (Mexico, 1957), is the daily report of that congress's actions as reported in the newspaper *El Siglo XIX* by Zarco, who was a delegate. Walter V. Scholes, *Mexican Politics during the Juárez Regime, 1855-1872* (Columbia, 1957), attempts to do too much in a short book.

Books on the French intervention and the Maximilian period are legion, but no one book covers the intricacies of the situation with complete satisfaction. The most delightful to read is Blair Niles, *Passengers to Mexico* (New York, 1943), and the most informative is Egon Caesar Corti, *Maximilian and Charlotte of Mexico* (New York and London, 1928), which includes many documents. José Fuentes Mares has two books on the period, *Juárez y la intervención* (Mexico, 1963) and *Juárez y el imperio* (Mexico, 1963). Percy F. Martin, *Maximilian in Mexico* (New York, 1914), José Luis Blasio, *Maximilian, Emperor of Mexico* (New Haven, 1934), a translation of the memoirs of Maximilian's secretary, and Jack A. Dabbs, *The French in Mexico* (The Hague, 1963) are all worth consulting. Fernando Iglesias Calderón, *El egoismo norteamericano durante la intervención francesa* (Mexico, 1905) takes the U.S. severely to task for its policy during that unfortunate period.

The indispensable work for the period from 1867 to 1910 is the great multivolume *Historia Moderna de México,* compiled under the able direction and partial authorship of Daniel Cosío Villegas and published in Mexico over a period of years starting in 1955. The first series of three thick volumes deal with the political, economic and social history of the "Restored Republic" from 1867 to 1876; the second series, using essentially the same format but also including studies on foreign relations, covers the Díaz period. A large number of individual authors took part in the writing, but as a whole the series is history at its best: the data are carefully compiled, the interpretation is clear and the writing is lucid and witty. The only objectionable feature in all the works is a tendency to put too much statistical information into the text itself and to slight the use of tables. The scholarly world owes an enormous debt of gratitude to Cosío, his aides, and the various agencies which made the writing and publication of this great series possible.

Cosío Villegas has also written some special studies on the Díaz period. His rather small *Porfirio Díaz y la revuelta de la Noria* (Mexico, 1953) is a little gem, and his *Estados Unidos contra Díaz* (Mexico, 1956; also in English translation by Nettie Lee Benson) is an excellent study of Díaz's recognition by the United States. Percy F. Martin, *Mexico in the Twentieth Century* (New York, London, 1907) and A. H. Noll, *From Empire to Republic* (Chicago, 1903), are somewhat pedestrian as well as outdated. José C. Valadés, *El porfirismo: historia de un régimen, 1876-1884* (Mexico, 1941), was an attempt to bring some semblance of balance to an interpretation of the period. Francisco Madero's *La sucesión presidencial en 1910* (San Pedro, Coahuila, 1908, and many later editions) is bad history but interesting for the circumstances of its publication. Ricardo García Granados, *Historia de México desde la restauración de la República en 1867 hasta la caída de Porfirio Díaz* (Mexico, 1923), is written from a nineteenth century liberal viewpoint. Charles F. Lummis, *The Awakening of a Nation* (New York and London, 1898), is as laudatory as John Kenneth Turner, *Barbarous Mexico* (Chicago, 1911), and Henry Baerlein, *Mexico: The Land of Unrest* (London, 1914), are condemnatory. Carlos Díaz Dufoo, *México y los capitales extranjeros* (Paris, 1918), and Jorge Espinosa de los Reyes, *Relaciones económicas entre México y los Estados Unidos 1870-1910* (Mexico, 1951), both concern themselves with the overweaning influence of the United States on the Mexican economy, and Alfred Tischendorf, *Great Britain and Mexico in the Era of Porfirio Díaz* (Durham, 1961) presents much data badly handled. Robert Danforth Gregg, *The Influence of Border Troubles on Relations between the United States and Mexico,*

1876-1910 (Baltimore, 1937) is concerned more with the formal diplomacy than with the rationale for the raids themselves. Pauline S. Relyea, *Diplomatic Relations between the United States and Mexico under Porfirio Díaz, 1876-1910* (Northampton, 1924) is standard. David M. Pletcher, *Rails, Mines and Progress: Seven American Promoters in Mexico, 1867-1911* (Ithaca, 1958), is a series of vignettes, predominantly about men who failed to profit from their ventures; as such is it a good antidote to the general picture of fabulous wealth accruing to foreign investors there. Andrés Molina Enríquez, *Los grandes problemas nacionales* (Mexico, 1909) is a hard-hitting examination of some basic ills, mostly agrarian, confronting the nation at the time; unfortunately, only a few persons read the book, and no one in a position of authority gave it any credence. And finally, Wistano Luis Orozco, *Legislación y jurisprudencia sobre terrenos baldíos* (Mexico, 1895), is a thorough examination of the laws and decisions which led to the despoliation of many small landowners.

VII. REVOLUTIONARY PERIOD

Inasmuch as events after 1910 were dramatic and oftentimes violent, an enormous amount of time and energy have been spent in "setting the record straight" by all manner of participants, observers, and many foreigners with an abiding interest in some aspect of the situation. Selecting material from this vast amount of essentially polemical literature and documentation poses a difficult problem; the following choices demonstrate, insofar as possible, the contrary sides of the various questions raised, and are interlarded with some straight reporting of varying shades of reliability.

Alfonso Taracena, *La verdadera revolución mexicana* (17 vols., México, 1960-1965) is a compilation of a series of small booklets published by Taracena over the years; it consists basically of a daily catalog of events gleaned from newspapers, documents, and the like. In spite of some serious flaws, the items are generally accurate. Jesús Romero Flores, *Anales históricos de la revolución mexicana* (5 vols., Mexico, 1939-1940), is a rather simple narrative written by a member of the

1917 Constitutional Convention of the principal events; designed for popular reading, each of the volumes is small. Emilio Portes Gil, *Quince años de política mexicana* (Mexico, 1941), is a semi-memoirs by an able ex-president. All the above authors participated in the events as revolutionaries, and their works reflect their biases, while ex-Huertista Jorge Vera Estañol showed his anti-revolutionary bias in *La revolución mexicana; orígenes y resultados* (Mexico, 1957). John W. F. Dulles, *Yesterday in Mexico: A Chronicle of the Revolution, 1919-1936* (Austin, 1961), contains an enormous amount of undigested and often unrelated material, while Betty Kirk, *Covering the Mexican Front* (Norman, 1942), is a well-written, sympathetic account of events in the years immediately prior to publication. Manuel González Ramírez collected a great deal of documentation, much of it ephemeral and often difficult to use, which he published in a number of volumes under the general heading of *Fuentes para la historia de la revolución mexicana* with subtitles generally descriptive of the nature of the documentation. Among the most interesting of the series is *Planes políticos y otros documentos* (Mexico, 1954), which begins with the 1906 plan of the Liberal Party and ends with the curious Almazán plan of 1940, which led to nothing.

The place to be rightfully occupied by Francisco Madero in the revolutionary process has been, since the beginning of his revolution, subject to serious debate. Among the most balanced books on the subject coming from his contemporaries are Roque Estrada, *La revolución y Francisco I. Madero* (Guadalajara, 1912 [?]), Manuel Bonilla, *El régimen maderista* (2nd edition, Mexico, 1962), Diego Arenas Guzmán, *La consumación del crimen* (Mexico, 1935), Francisco Urquizo, *Viva Madero* (Mexico, 1954), Alfonso Taracena, *Madero: Vida del hombre y del político* (Mexico, 1937), Luis Lara Pardo, *Madero: Esbozo político* (Mexico, 1937), and Pedro González Roa, *De Porfirio Díaz a Carranza* (Madrid, 1916). Since Madero is generally conceived to have been a pristine hero martyred through the connivance of the U.S. ambassador, he is generally kindly treated in the literature. Perhaps the most interesting book emanating from the period is Querido Moheno, *Mi actuación política después de la decena trágica* (Mexico,

1939), a fawning attempt to divest himself of any responsibility for the actions of the Huerta government; but by his own words he condemns himself as spineless and overly ambitious. Of peripheral interest to the mainstream of the Mexican Revolution, but perfectly illustrative of a major problem confronting the nation, is Lowell L. Blaisdell's excellent *The Desert Revolution: Baja California, 1911* (Madison, 1962).

Carranza has not been surrounded by the protective aura which shielded Madero, and accordingly his activities aroused violent passions. Manuel Aguirre Berlanga, who joined the revolution with Carranza against Huerta, attempted to lay ugly rumors to rest and to justify Carranza's claim to a "constitutional" revolution in his *Revolución y reforma* (Mexico, 1918), and Alfredo Breceda, another Carranza companion in arms, covered essentially the same ground in *México revolucionario, 1913-1917* (Mexico, 1920). Manuel W. González, *Con Carranza: Episodios de la revolución constitucionalista, 1913-1914* (2 vols., Monterrey, 1933-34) in retrospect supported his erstwhile chief, and Félix F. Palavicini glorified his leader in *El Primer Jefe* (Mexico, 1917 [?]). But Jorge Vera Estañol could understandably see nothing good in the revolutionary chieftain when he appealed to the U.S. public fears by publishing *Carranza and His Bolshevik Regime* (Los Angeles, 1920). The two thick volumes of over three thousand pages issued by the notorious Fall Committee as *Investigation of Mexican Affairs* (Washington, 1919-1920), pictured the Carranza regime as corrupt, inefficient, thieving, anti-U.S., and destructive. But the palm for invective must go to Thomas Edward Gibbon for his *Mexico under Carranza: A Lawyer's Indictment of the Crowning Infamy of Four Hundred Years of Misrule* (New York, 1919). An excellent source for the study of military operations in the early phases of the Carranza revolution is Juan Barragán Rodríguez, *Historia del ejército y de la revolución constitucionalista* (Mexico, 1946); Barragán was Carranza's chief of staff.

One of the most intriguing questions then, and now, is the exact role played by Ambassador Henry Lane Wilson in the Madero overthrow and assassination. Wilson, of course, disclaimed any responsibility and insisted in his *Diplomatic Days in Mexico, Belgium and Chile* (Garden City, 1927) that Madero richly deserved his fate. In this contention he has strong support from one of his aides's wife in two books. Edith O'Shaughnessy, in *A Diplomat's Wife in Mexico* (New York, 1916) and *Intimate Pages of Mexican History* (New York, 1920) wrote well but showed an appalling lack of sympathy for or understanding of the revolutionists. Cuban Minister Manuel Márquez Sterling, on the other hand, accused Henry Lane Wilson of complicity in his *Los últimos días del Presidente Madero* (Havana, 1917). Francisco Bulnes, completely out of sympathy with the anti-Díaz and anti-Huerta revolutions, laid the responsibility for what he considered a messy situation on President Woodrow Wilson in his *The Whole Truth about Mexico: President Wilson's Responsibility* (New York, 1916); in this task he was aided in a less vitriolic fashion by Manuel Calero, *The Mexican Policy of President Woodrow Wilson as It Appears to a Mexican* (New York, 1916), which was simultaneously published as *La política mexicana del Presidente Wilson* (Mexico, 1916). Josephus Daniels, *The Wilson Era: Years of Peace, 1910 1917* (Chapel Hill, 1944), and *The Wilson Era: Years of War and After* (Chapel Hill, 1946), quite naturally gives a sympathetic view of Wilsonian policy. J. N. Palomares, *La invasión yanqui en 1914* (Mexico, 1940), is passionately critical of the U.S. occupation of Veracruz, while Alberto Salinas Carranza, *La expedición punitiva* (Mexico, 1936), through documents gives a balanced view of the Pershing expedition. Viscount Edward Grey, *Twenty-five Years, 1892-1916* (New York, 1925), is somewhat caustic concerning what he considered Wilsonian simplicity in the Mexican affair. Charles Wilson Hackett, *The Mexican Revolution and the United States* (Boston, 1926), is an excellent short work based upon the limited public documents available at the time. Isidro Fabela, *Historia diplomática de la revolución mexicana, 1912-1917* (Mexico, 1958) belies its title since the coverage is from February, 1913, to April, 1914, and is primarily concerned with the United States; within these limits it is a good, but not original, synthesis in which he absolves Woodrow Wilson from evil intent but not disastrous decisions. A. H. Feller, *The Mexican*

Claims Commission, 1923-1934 (New York, 1935), covers, in a pedestrian fashion, the question of the settlement of claims growing out of the revolution.

Of all the principals in the revolutionary movement, none has been more dramatic than Francisco ("Pancho") Villa. Even during his lifetime the distinction between Villa the man and Villa the legend grew dim; since his mysterious assassination in 1923 the line has disappeared all together. Even the *Memorias de Pancho Villa* (Mexico, 1934 and later editions; also translated into English) are not his memoirs at all, but a brilliant work by Martín Luis Guzmán based upon some meager Villa papers and great deal of other documentation. Villa did not write the *Memorias,* but had he been able to do so he would have written in this vein. Federico Cervantes M., *Francisco Villa y la revolución* (Mexico, 1960), presents the Centaur of the North in a very favorable light, but Manuel W. González and Alvaro Obregón, both of whom fought against him, were contemptuous of his ability and doubtful of his sincerity in their works, respectively, *Contra Villa: Relatos de la campaña, 1914-1915* (Mexico, 1935) and *Ocho mil kilómetros en campaña: Relación de las acciones de armas efectuadas en más de veinte estados de la república durante un período de cuatro años* (Mexico, 1917). The latter work, incidentally, gives a good view of the Obregón mind at work. Nellie Campobello, *Cartucho: Relatos de la lucha en el norte de México* (Mexico, 1931), and *Apuntes sobre la vida militar de Francisco Villa* (Mexico, 1940) are both interesting but tend to perpetuate the myth. Haldeen Braddy, *Cock of the Walk* (Albuquerque, 1955), is a perfectly delightful book if read as folklore but virtually useless if read as a book that "will report the true Villa once and for all", which it purports to be. William Douglas Lansford, *Pancho Villa* (Los Angeles, 1965), is a distinct disappointment, being neither good folklore nor good history.

Emiliano Zapata is another of the half-legendary figures of the revolutionary period; many peasants in Morelos still believe that he will one day reappear even though the events surrounding his death in 1919 are perfectly clear. Gildardo Magaña, one of Zapata's officers who retained most of the Zapata archive, began the multivolume and generally excellent *Emiliano Zapata y el agrarismo en México* (5 vols., Mexico, 1951-1952), but died before completing the third volume; the work was completed under the direction of Carlos Pérez Guerrero. The only serious flaw in Magaña's work is a tendency to inflate Zapata's importance, which is perfectly understandable. Edgcumb Pinchon, *Zapata the Unconquerable* (New York, 1941), is a romanticized version of the agrarian leader's life. Harry H. Dunn, *The Crimson Jester: Zapata of Mexico* (New York, 1934), is no less factual, but considerably less sympathetic. Neither Pinchon nor Dunn truly understood Zapata's position in Mexican life.

The convention which produced the Constitution of 1917 has unfortunately escaped the attention of serious scholars even though it was one of the most dramatic and important assemblies of the 20th century. Fernando Romero García compiled and edited the *Diario de los debates del congreso constituyente* (2 vols., Mexico, 1922); it is absorbing reading. Juan de Díos Bojórquez, one of the delegates, under the pseudonym of Djed Bórquez later wrote *Crónica del constituyente* (Mexico, 1938); it is, essentially, Bojórquez's memories supplemented with long sections of the debates. The only serious effort of synthesis, unfortunately not completely successful, is Gabriel Ferrer Mendiolea, *Historia del congreso constituyente, 1916-1917* (Mexico, 1957). The debates of the less important Convention of Aguascalientes have been compiled and published by the Mexican Government as *Crónicas y debates de las sesiones de la Soberana Convención Revolucionaria* (2 vols., Mexico, 1964-1965). Quirk, cited in the first section, is still the best authority on the subject.

Once most of the fighting was over, a number of foreigners visited Mexico to give their judgments. Carleton Beals, *Mexico: An Interpretation* (New York, 1923), Hubert Herring and Herbert Weinstock, *Renascent Mexico* (New York, 1935), Emile J. Dillon, *Mexico on the Verge* (New York, 1921), John William Brown, *Modern Mexico and Its Problems* (London, 1927), and George Creel, *The People Next Door* (New York, 1926), were all optimistic in varying degrees. But Spanish novelist Vicente Blasco Ibañez reported in *Mexico in Revolution* (New York, 1920) that conditions were little short of scandalous. Looking back on the situation from the vantage point of a quarter of a century Juan Gualberto Amaya, a military leader during the revolution, in *Los gobiernos de Obregón, Calles y régimenes "peleles" derivados del callismo* (Mexico, 1947), reported that Obregón and the earlier leaders represented a "great politico-social movement" but that after 1924 Calles "prostituted the ideal."

The incredible destruction of the revolutionary years put Mexico in a precarious position regarding her fiscal and debt situations. Edwin Walter Kemmerer, *Inflation and Revolution: Mexico's Experience* (Princeton, 1940), is an excellent study of the confused monetary policy and its economic consequences. During the 'twenties Mexico, pleading financial inability, halted service on the foreign debt; Butler G. Sherwell in *Mexico's Capacity to Pay* (New York, 1929) argued, in an unconvincing fashion, that unwillingness rather than inability fostered the payment suspension. The Mexican government, through the Secretario de Hacienda y Crédito Público, *La deuda exterior de México* (Mexico, 1926), indicated the magnitude of that debt. A short time later the Secretaría de Industria, Comercio y Trabajo, *La Industria, el comercio y el trabajo durante la gestión administrativa del Señor Gral. Plutarco Elías Calles* (5 vols., Mexico, 1928) presented an unwarrantedly rosy picture of conditions.

The titanic struggle between the Church and State produced an enormous flood of literature both in Mexico and the United States. The best statement of the government's position, and the historical necessity for the position, can be found in Emilio Portes Gil, *The Conflict of the Civil Power and the Clergy* (Mexico, 1935; published in Madrid as *La labor sediciosa del clero mexicano*), a dispassionate but utter denunciation. The fact that the Mexican Ministry of Foreign Affairs published the book in English demonstrates the importance of the subject in the United States. Ernest Galarza, a national of the United States, in his *The Roman Catholic Church as a Factor in the Political and Social History of Mexico* (Sacramento, 1928), is even more bitter than Portes Gil; he puts the onus on the Church, not merely the clergy. Antonio Uroz, *La cuestión religiosa en México* (Mexico, 1926), views the clergy as a pernicious force. But the Church and the clergy had their spokesmen. Bishop Francis Clement Kelley produced two books twenty years apart. His *The Book of the Red and the Yellow; Being a Story of Blood and a Yellow Streak* (Chicago, 1915) was a vitriolic attack on the Mexican revolutionary leaders for their actions, and on the United States government for its inaction. *Blood-Drenched Altars: Mexican Study and Comment* (Milwaukee, 1935) still showed the Kelley fire. Leopoldo Lara y Torres, *Documentos para la historia de la persecución religiosa en México* (Mexico, 1954), is an excellent collection edited by the clergyman who was Bishop of Tacámbaro during one of the worst periods of persecution. Wilfrid Parsons, *Mexican Martyrdom* (New York, 1936), is more moderate than Kelley, but a clearly condemnatory account by a U.S. priest. Graham Greene, *The Lawless Roads* (London, 1950), plays on the same theme. Charles Stedman MacFarland, *Chaos in Mexico: The Conflict of the Church and State* (New York, 1935), is a Protestant minister's view of the problem. The only serious monographic attempt to put any aspect of the situation into proper perspective is Elizabeth Ann Rice, *The Diplomatic Relations between the United States and Mexico, as Affected by the Struggle for Religious Liberty* (Washington, 1959); given the author's religious affiliations, the presentation is remarkably moderate.

The outstanding Mexican authority on the agrarian question is Lucio Mendieta y Núñez; his classic *El problema agrario de México* has gone through numerous editions since it was first published in 1923. His *El sistema agrario-constitucional: Explicación é interpretación del artículo 27 de la Constitución Política de los Estados Unidos Mexicanos en sus preceptos agrarios* (Mexico, 1932 and later editions) is an excellent study. An enthusiastic account of the reform program is *Despertar Lagunero: Libro que relata la lucha y triunfo de la revolución en la camarca lagunera* (Mexico, 1937), designed to encourage other groups to demand their rights. But the heartaches suffered by those who lost lands in the reform program are well illustrated in Manuel de Castillo Negrete, *Robos judiciales* (Mexico, 1930), written by a victim of expropriation. Andrés Molina Enríquez, one of the stalwarts demanding agrarian reform before the revolution, gave his views of the post-revolutionary events in *Esbozo de la historia de los primeros diez años de la revolución agraria de México, de 1910 a 1920* (Mexico, 1932). Jesús Silva Herzog, *El agrarismo mexicano y la reforma agraria: Exposición y crítica* (Mexico, 1959) points out some of the weaknesses of the administration of the program. Helen Phipps, *Some Aspects of the Agrarian Question in Mexico* (Austin, 1925), and George M. McBride, *The Land Systems of Mexico* (New York, 1923), are both pioneering studies, excellent at the time of publication but now outdated. Frank Tannenbaum, *The Mexican Agrarian Revolution* (New York, 1929), is still valuable, particularly for the consolidation of statistical material. Koka Freier and Henrik Enfield, *People in Ejidos* (New York, 1954), gives a moderately idyllic picture of *ejidatario* happiness, while Tom Gill, *Land Hunger in Mexico* (Washington, 1951), presents a doleful picture which stresses the need for proper conservation practices.

The struggle between foreign oil interests and the Mexican government over the ownership of the subsoil brought heated charges and countercharges, in print and out. The best single exposition of the government view of the entire question which eventuated in the expropriation is Government of Mexico, *Mexico's Oil: A Compilation of Official Documents in the Conflict of Economic Order in the Petroleum Industry, with an Introduction Summarizing Its Causes and Consequences* (Mexico, 1940). An oversize volume of nearly a thousand pages, it was designed to create sympathy in the United States. In order to counteract some of the oil company propaganda, the government also published *The True Facts about the Expropriation of the Oil Companies' Properties in Mexico* (Mexico, 1940). The Mexican publications questioned the flood of adverse criticism coming from special interests in the United States. William E. McMahon, *Two Strikes and Out* (New York, 1939), and Roscoe B. Gaither, *Expropriation in Mexico: The Facts and the Law* (New York, 1940), both argue that the companies were blameless and legal in their actions, but that the Mexicans simply saw an opportunity to get something for nothing; the presentations are plausible, but erroneous. Burt M. McConnell, *Mexico at the Bar of Public Opinion* (New York, 1939), purports to be "a survey of editorial opinion of newspapers in the Western Hemisphere," but is in fact a carefully selected group of editorials in U.S. newspapers condemning the Mexican policy. Evelyn Waugh gives the orientation of his book in the title, *Robbery under Law: The Mexican Object Lesson* (London, 1939). Wendell Gordon, *The Expropriation of Foreign-Owned Property in Mexico* (Washington, 1941), is an economist's attempt to examine the entire question in perspective with objectivity.

Economic development and industrial progress after World War II attracted much thought. Sanford A. Mosk, *Industrial Revolution in Mexico* (Berkeley, 1950), argues that industrial expansion created severe problems for other sectors of the economy; Frank Tannenbaum, *Mexico: The Struggle for Peace and Bread* (New York, 1950), insists that industrialization was destroying the very essence of Mexico; but Manuel Germán Parra, *La industrialización de México* (Mexico, 1954), holds that industrialization was not only inevitable but beneficial. Combined Mexican Working Party, *The Economic Development of Mexico* (Baltimore, 1953), is the report of the International Bank of Reconstruction and Development staff working with the Mexicans. It is generally optimistic, but much of the data do not agree completely with similar data published by the Mexican government. Raymond Vernon, *The Dilemma of Mexico's Development: The Roles of the Private and Public Sectors* (Cambridge, 1963), is a thorough examination of one of the greatest problems faced by Mexico since the Revolution began. Jack Richard Powell, *The Mexican Petroleum Industry, 1938-1950* (Berkeley, 1956), found little basis for optimism, but most of his conclusions soon proved faulty. Wilbert Ellis Moore, *Industrialization and Labor: Social Aspects of Economic Development* (Ithaca, 1951), is an excellent study by a competent sociologist.

The development of organized labor, and its relationship with the government and the economy, unfortunately has been slighted by serious scholars both in and out of Mexico. Joseph H. Retinger, *Morones of Mexico: A History of the Labour Movement in that Country* (London, 1926), is a panegyric not completely justified, but in Retinger's defense it must be pointed out that Morones showed his greed only after the Englishman completed his work. Marjorie Ruth Clark, *Organized Labor in Mexico* (Chapel Hill, 1934), is excellent for the period covered. Guadalupe Rivera Marín, *El mercado de trabajo: Relaciones obrero-patronales* (Mexico, 1955), is excellent for description and data indicating the differing patterns of strikes and lockouts, but it does not explain the differences. Rosendo Salazar, *Historia de la CTM* (Mexico, 1956), is fairly good, but makes no pretense of being a study of the labor movement as such.

Mexican education in the 20th century, which created a ripple of outside interest during the Cárdenas period, has been somewhat neglected by responsible scholars. Carlos Alvear Alcevedo, *La educación y la ley* (Mexico, 1963), is a compilation of educational laws since independence but is not an examination of revolutionary education in the context of the society. George I. Sanchez, *Mexico: A Revolution by Education* (New York, 1936) is an enthusiastic and justifiably optimistic account written just as the drive for education was getting under way. Cameron Duncan Ebaugh, *The National System of Education in Mexico* (Baltimore, 1931), is a thin description, and George C. Booth, *Mexico's School-Made Society* (Stanford, 1941), is only partially satisfactory. Guillermo Bonilla y Segura, *Report on the Cultural Missions of Mexico* (Washington, 1945), is skimpy, and Marjorie C. Johnston, *Education in Mexico* (Washington, 1956), is a short and unsatisfactory treatment with an excellent bibliography.

Two books on deviant political behavior are of interest. Mario Gil, *Sinarquismo: Su origen, su esencia, su misión* (Mexico, 1944) examines a semi-fascist organization, and Karl M. Schmitt, *Communism in Mexico* (Austin, 1965), finds communism to have been inconsequential.

VIII. BIBLIOGRAPHICAL AIDS AND GENERAL WORKS

Most of the books listed heretofore contain bibliographies which refer to the special topics treated in the work; they vary in quality from useless to good. Of the bibliographies as such, one of the most useful is Juan B. Iguíniz, *Bibliografía bibliográfica mexicana* (Mexico,

1923) which lists some 600 publications containing bibliographical materials and references; excellent for the time it was published, it is of course now far out of date. Miguel Angel Peral, *Diccionario biográfico mexicano* (2 vols., Mexico, 1944), is a most convenient reference for short biographies (from a few lines to a page or more) of a great number of Mexican figures; in spite of some errors, it is generally excellent. For readers of English only, Robert A. Humphreys, *Latin American History: A Guide to the Literature in English* (London and New York, 1958), is excellent in both organization and coverage. Roberto Ramos, *Bibliografía de la historia de México* (Mexico, 1956), lists nearly five thousand titles, but it is difficult to use inasmuch as the listing is by alphabetical order of authors and includes only that which is on the title page. Joaquín García Icazbalceta, *Bibliografía mexicana del siglo XVI* (Mexico, 1954, last edition), describes the books printed in Mexico from 1539 to 1600. Brasseur de Bourbourg, *Bibliotheque mexico-guatemalienne* (Paris, 1871), is excellent for the material it covers; it was Brasseur de Bourbourg who first published Landa's *Relación* and the Mayan *Popul Vuh*. Jesús Guzmán y Raz Guzmán, *Bibligrafía de la reforma, la intervención y el imperio* (2 vols., Mexico, 1930-31), is good. Roberto Ramos, *Bibliografía de la revolución mexicana* (3 vols., 1931-1940), gives excellent coverage, but suffers from the same weakness as his more general work. Probably the outstanding bibliographical aid is Luis González, *Fuentes de la historia contemporánea de México: Libros y folletos* (3 vols., Mexico. 1961-62), which gives information concerning over 24,000 items. The organization, including the subject and author index in volume 3, is excellent and makes the series easy to use. Josefina Berroa, *México bibliográfico, 1957-1960* (Mexico, 1961), is a listing, by subject and author, of the books published in Mexico during the stated years. Angel Bassols Batalla, *Bibliografía geográfica de México* (Mexico, 1955), contains nearly five thousand entries dealing with the subject. Manuel Germán Parra and Wigberto Jiménez Moreno, two of Mexico's outstanding scholars, collaborated to produce *Bibliografía indigenista de México y Centroamérica, 1850-1950* (Mexico, 1954), containing over 6,400 entries. Ignacio Bernal, *Bibliografía de arqueología y etnografía: Meso-*

américa y norte de México (Mexico, 1962), is an excellent companion piece to the preceding book. Mexico: Secretaría de la Economía Nacional, *Bibliografía mexicana de estadística* (2 vols., Mexico, [1945 ?]) is excellent. Herbert E. Bolton, *Guide to the Materials for the History of the United States in the Principal Archives of Mexico* (Washington, 1923), is concerned primarily with the Spanish borderlands. Anita Ker, *Mexican Government Publications: A Guide to the More Important Publications of the National Government of Mexico, 1821-1936* (Washington, 1940), is an excellent description of materials often difficult to find. Charles C. Cumberland, *The United States-Mexican Border: A Selective Guide to the Literature of the Region* (Ithaca, 1960), discusses over 3,000 books, articles, and theses dealing with the area.

Among the best of the general histories of the country is Vicente Riva Palacio, *México a través de los siglos,* which has recently (1962) been reproduced as a facsimile of the original edition; copiously, and sometimes beautifully illustrated, the work is generally of high caliber. Niceto de Zamacois, *Historia de Méjico desde sus tiempos más remotos hasta nuestras días* (18 vols., Mexico, 1876-82; four additional volumes later published), has greater detail than Riva Palacio. Mariano Cuevas, *Historia de la nación mexicana* (3 vols., Mexico, 1952, 2nd edition), is a classic of conservative clerical interpretation, and Alfonso Junco, *Un siglo de México* (Madrid, 1956), consists of a series of essays written by Junco in the 1930's; in a nutshell, Junco ascribes all Mexico's ills as coming either from anti-clericalism or from the greed of the United States. Mariano Cuevas, *Historia de la iglesia en México* (4 vols., Mexico, 1921-1926), would have us believe that Church and clergy throughout Mexican history have been near-perfect, and Alberto María Carreño in two books, *México y los Estados Unidos* (Mexico, 1922) and *La diplomacia extraordinaria entre México y los Estados Unidos* (2 vols., Mexico, 1951), would have us believe that the United States has been consistently evil.

Jesús Reyes Heroles, *El liberalismo mexicano* (3 vols., Mexico, 1957-1961), is excellent in both information and interpretation. Leopoldo Zea, *Del liberalismo a la revolución en la educación mexicana* (Mexico, 1956), is a thorough and excellent study of attitudes and views in the 19th century. His *El positivismo en México* (Mexico, 1953) concerns the philosophical trend which had such influence on Mexican education in the latter part of the Díaz period. Francisco Larroyo, *Historia comparada de la educación en México* (Mexico, 1956, 4th edition), is a convenient but text-bookish history of education, which should be supplemented by Irma Wilson, *A Century of Educational Thought in Mexico* (New York, 1941). Alfonso López Aparicio, *El movimiento obrero en México: Antecedentes, desarrollo y tendencias* (Mexico, 1952), does not live up to its title.

Max Winkler's *Investments of United States Capital in Latin America* (Boston, 1928) was written at a time when the U.S. had its great economic influence in Mexico; excellent for the period in which it was written, it should now be followed by a more contemporaneous volume. Walter Flavius McCaleb, *Present and Past Banking in Mexico* (New York, 1920), and *The Public Finances of Mexico* (New York, 1921), are both criticisms of Mexican fiscal policy written by a conservative economist. Ricardo Torres Gaitán, *Política monetaria mexicana* (Mexico, 1944), is a more sympathetic treatment. Stuart Alexander MacCorkle, *American Policy of Recognition toward Mexico* (Baltimore, 1933), is an unexciting examination of that aspect of Mexican-United States relations. Carlos Basauri, *La población indígena de México: etnografía* (3 vols., Mexico, 1940), is a thorough study of all the remaining indigenous groups, with some historical treatment.

Tables

TABLE I. VITAL STATISTICS

Year	Marriage per 1,000 inhabitants	Births per 1,000 inhabitants	Gen. mortality per 1,000 inhabitants	Infant mortality per 1,000 liveborn	Natural increase per 1,000 inhabitants
1901	4.4	34.2	32.3	266.4	2.1
1903	4.3	33.4	32.6	310.1	0.8
1905	4.0	34.1	32.9	286.9	1.2
1907	4.1	32.8	33.0	310.6	−0.2
1909	3.7	34.0	32.3	294.3	1.7
1911*	n.a.	n.a.	n.a.	n.a.	n.a.
1923	3.8	32.0	24.4	222.4	7.6
1925	4.3	33.1	26.5	215.9	6.6
1927	4.8	30.5	24.0	193.0	7.0
1929	5.0	39.3	26.8	167.6	12.0
1931	5.9	43.8	25.9	137.7	18.0
1933	5.8	42.2	25.7	139.3	16.0
1935	6.6	42.3	22.6	125.7	19.0
1937	6.9	44.1	24.4	130.8	19.7
1939	6.9	44.6	23.0	122.6	21.6
1941	6.3	43.5	22.1	123.0	21.4
1943	7.6	45.5	22.4	117.2	23.1
1945	6.8	44.9	19.5	107.9	25.4
1947	6.3	46.1	16.6	96.4	29.5
1949	6.7	45.2	17.9	106.4	27.4
1951	6.8	44.6	17.3	98.8	27.3
1953	6.5	45.0	15.9	95.2	29.1
1954	7.1	46.4	13.1	80.5	33.1
1955	6.9	45.1	13.3	83.3	31.8
1956	7.1	45.2	11.7	71.0	33.5
1957	6.6	45.5	12.7	80.1	32.8
1958	6.7	42.9	12.0	80.1	30.2
1959	6.9	45.6	11.4	74.4	31.2
1960	6.6	44.6	11.2	74.2	33.4
1961	6.4	44.2	10.4	70.2	33.8
1962	6.4	44.2	10.5	69.9	33.7
1963	6.5	44.1	10.4	68.5	33.7
1964	6.8	44.8	9.9	64.5	34.9
1965	6.9	44.2	9.5	60.7	34.7

SOURCE: *Anuario Estadístico,* various years.
* Data for 1911-1922 are not available

TABLE II. POPULATION STATISTICS

YEAR	Total pop. '000's	Indigenes in '000's	European Creole & Peninsulars in '000's	Castas or Mestizos '000's	Per cent literacy[4]	Per cent rural	LABOR FORCE DISTRIBUTION, PER CENT Agric.	Extract. indus.	Industrial transport	Commercial	Other
1520[1]	25,000	25,000									
1570	4,313	4,200	63	50							
1646	1,435	1,250	125	160							
1742	3,425	2,260	565	600							
1772	4,646	2,490	784	1,372							
1793	5,450	2,700	1,050	1,700							
1803	6,225	2,900	1,095	2,230	5						
1810	6,122	3,376	1,107	1,639							
1820	6,204	3,426	1,057	1,721							
1831	6,382	3,520	1,060	1,802	5						
1840	7,016	4,000	1,000	2,016	5						
1850	8,000	4,500	1,500	2,000	6						
1861	8,212	3,203	1,560	3,449	7						
1875	9,495	3,513	1,899	4,083	9						
1880	10,448	3,970	1,985	4,493	10						
1895	12,632	4,800	2,526	5,306	14	81	64.3	.5	11.2	5.0	19.0
1900	13,607	5,021	2,700	5,886	18	80	64.3	.7	11.0	6.1	17.9
1910	15,160	5,609	2,729	7,822	20	77.7	64.4	.6	10.9	5.8	18.3
1921[2]	14,334	4,110	10,224		34	74.7	71.4	.6	10.9	5.6	11.5
1930	16,553	2,648	13,965		39	66	70.2	.9	13.4	5.3	10.2
1940	19,654	2,945	16,607		48	65	65.4	1.8	10.9	9.4	12.5
1950	25,791	2,889	23,502		56	57	58.3	1.2	11.8	8.2	20.5
1960	34,923	3,632	31,291		62	49	54.2	1.3	13.7	9.5	21.3
1965[3]	42,689				78	45	51.2	1.3	15.2	10.3	22.0

NOTES

1. Data given for years prior to 1900 should be used as gross indicators, not finite figures.
2. After 1910 the census figures make no distinction between creole and mestizo.
3. 1965 data are estimates.
4. Literacy rates are for those 10 years of age and older.

TABLE III. MINERAL PRODUCTION AFTER 1890

YEAR	GOLD	SILVER	COPPER	LEAD	ZINC	COAL	IRON ORE
	(1,000 kilograms)		(in 1,000 metric tons)				
To 1890	272.0	88,427	80.0	300.0		1,000	
1892	1.7	1,251	7.9	47.3		350	
1894	4.4	1,423	11.9	57.0	.3	300	
1896	9.5	1,524	11.3	63.0	.5	253	
1898	12.5	1,743	15.9	71.4	1.2	367	
1900	12.7	1,766	22.5	63.8	1.1	388	
1902	14.8	1,898	36.4	106.8	.7	710	3.0
1904	19.2	1,973	51.8	95.0	.8	832	23.0
1906	27.4	1,803	61.6	73.7	22.6	768	31.0
1908	32.0	2,221	38.2	127.0	15.7	866	23.6
1910	41.4	2,417	48.2	124.3	1.8	1,304	54.6
1912	32.4	2,527	57.2	105.2	1.3	982	57.8
1914	8.6	857	26.6	5.7	.7	780	n.a.
1916	11.7	926	28.4	20.0	37.0	300	20.0
1918	25.3	1,945	70.2	98.8	20.7	782	25.9
1920	22.8	2,069	49.2	82.5	15.6	716	26.0
1922	23.3	2,522	27.0	110.4	6.1	933	41.6
1924	24.6	2,844	49.1	165.1	24.7	1,227	52.4
1926	24.0	3,057	53.8	210.8	105.4	1,309	93.0
1928	21.7	3,376	65.1	236.5	161.7	1,022	80.3
1930	20.8	3,272	73.4	240.9	142.9	1,294	107.0
1932	18.2	2,156	35.2	137.3	57.3	691	27.1
1934	20.6	2,306	44.2	166.3	125.2	782	133.4
1936	23.5	2,409	29.7	215.7	150.3	1,308	146.8
1938	28.7	2,520	41.9	282.4	172.2	1,093	125.7
1940	27.5	2,570	37.6	196.3	115.0	816	132.0
1942	24.9	2,640	50.9	197.0	189.9	914	106.6
1944	15.8	2,286	41.3	185.3	219.0	904	134.6
1946	13.1	1,346	61.1	140.1	139.5	977	171.0
1948	11.4	1,789	59.1	193.4	179.0	1,057	226.5
1950	12.7	1,528	61.7	238.0	223.5	912	285.7
1952	14.3	1,566	58.5	246.0	227.4	1,317	340.2
1954	12.0	1,241	54.8	216.6	223.7	1,314	314.0
1958	10.3	1,480	65.0	201.9	224.1	1,471	581.5
1960	9.4	1,385	60.3	190.7	262.4	1,771	521.4
1962	7.4	1,282	47.1	193.3	250.7	1,893	1,353.6
1964	6.5	1,298	52.5	174.8	235.6	2,138	1,392.5

SOURCES: Marvin Bernstein, *The Mexican Mining Industry, 1890-1950* (New York: State University of New York, 1964); William E. Cole, *Steel and Economic Growth in Mexico* (Austin: University of Texas Press, 1967); *Anuario Estadístico,* various years.

TABLE IV. LAND TENURE DATA
(1 hectare equals 2.471 acres)

	1923	1930	1940	1950	1960
TOTAL LAND CENSUSED (000 HECTARES)	129,106*	131,595	128,749	145,517	169,084
TOTAL ARABLE**	n.a.	14,618	14,871	19,928	23,817
Seasonal	n.a.	11,497	11,523	16,009	18,345
Humid	n.a.	1,304	766	669	754
Irrigated		1,677	1,732	2,432	3,408
PASTURE	n.a.	66,493	56,172	67,379	79,092
WOODS	n.a.	25,856	38,115	38,836	43,679
TOTAL NUMBER HOLDINGS (000 UNITS)	624	858	1,234	1,383	1,365
5 hectares or less (000)	367	577	929	1,005	899
Over 5 hectares (000)	255	277	290	361	447
Ejidos (000 units)	1.589	4.189	14.680	17.579	18.699
TOTAL LAND (000 HECTARES)	129,106	131,595	128,749	145,517	169,084
5 hectares or less (000 hectares)	n.a.	889	1,157	1,363	1,328
Over 5 hectares (000 hectares)	n.a.	122,361	98,669	105,260	123,259
Ejidos (000 hectares)	2,021	8,345	28,923	38,894	44,497
TOTAL ARABLE LAND (000 HECTARES)**	n.a.	14,618	14,871	19,928	23,817
5 hectares or less (000 hectares)	n.a.	889	1,074	1,280	1,259
Over 5 hectares (000 hectares)	n.a.	11,788	6,752	9,858	12,219
Ejidos (000 hectares)	n.a.	1,941	7,045	8,791	10,329
EJIDOS, NUMBER UNITS	1,589	4,189	14,680	17,579	18,699
TOTAL LAND (000 HECTARES)	2,021	8,345	28,923	38,894	44,497
ARABLE (000 HECTARES)	n.a.	1,941	7,045	8,791	10,329
Seasonal	n.a.	1,628	5,581	7,155	7,995
Humid	n.a.	91	398	416	394
Irrigated	n.a.	219	1,066	1,220	1,418
MECHANIZATION					
Steel plows, private (000's)	n.a.	735	325	514	578
Steel plows, ejidos	n.a.	169	401	621	708
Tractors, units, private	n.a.	3,802	3,591	19,093	43,501
Tractors, ejidos, units	n.a.	73	958	3,618	11,036

LAND TENURE DATA (CONTINUED)

	1923	1930	1940	1950	1960
Planters, private, units	n.a.	20,679	16,519	32,473	60,436
Planters, ejidos, units	n.a.	1,736	10,020	27,428	32,156
Harrows, private, units	n.a.	n.a.	19,857	38,888	51,718
Harrows, ejidos, units	n.a.	n.a.	14,208	26,392	32,182
PRODUCTION, SELECTED ITEMS					
Corn, private (000 tons)	n.a.	1,643	1,496	2,665	3,027
Corn, ejidos (000 tons)	n.a.	348	1,493	1,863	2,679
Beans, private (000 tons)	n.a.	74	81	215	322
Beans, ejidos (000 tons)	n.a.	13	115	156	340
Sed cotton, private (000 tons)	n.a.	53#	86	314	675
Seed cotton, ejidos (000 tons)	n.a.	2#	77	202	363
Wheat, private (000 tons)	n.a.	250	189	324	800
Wheat, ejidos (000 tons)	n.a.	26	235	194	336
Oranges, private (000 tons)	n.a.	50	85	373	275
Oranges, ejidos (000 tons)	n.a.	5	21	36	93
Coffee in cherry, private (000 tons)	n.a.	40##	60	179	416
Coffee in cherry, ejidos (000 tons)	n.a.	3##	15	88	154

* Censused land only; does not include areas within urban centers, rivers, lakes, roads, etc. The increasing amounts in the various censuses reflect changing definitions and more accurate censusing. The total continental area is 196,-469,120 hectares.

** Arable land here includes orchards and agave plantations; some tables in the various agrarian censuses do not include these lands as a part of the "arable" computation.

\# Ginned or lint cotton, not exactly comparable to later years.

\## Coffee beans, not exactly comparable to later years.

SOURCES: *Primer Censo Agrícola-Ganadero, 1930; Segundo Censo Ejidal, 1940; Tercer Censo Agrícola, Ganadero y Ejidal, 1950; IV Censos Agrícola-Ganadero y Ejidal, 1960;* Frank Tannenbaum, *The Mexican Agrarian Revolution;* Eyler Simpson, *The Ejido: Mexico's Way Out;* Nathan L. Whetten, *Rural Mexico.* The production data in this table are not comparable to the data in Table VI (Agricultural Production, Selected Years), which come from the *Anuario Estadístico* for various years.

TABLE V. LAND TENURE AND USE BY STATES, 1960 PERCENTAGES

STATES	ARABLE LAND[1]	CROPLAND HELD[2]			IRRIGATED LAND HELD[2]			CROPLAND IRRIGATED		
		Ejidos	Private over 5 ha.	Private 5 ha. or less	Ejidos	Private over 5 ha.	Private 5 ha. or less	Ejidos	Private over 5 ha.	Private 5 ha. or less
Aguascalientes	32	77	22	*	56	41	3	11	27	31
Baja California	26	38	61	*	33	67	*	52	66	50
Baja California, Territory	4	12	86	2	7	91	2	31	61	70
Campeche	6	40	60	*	10	52	38	*	*	10
Chiapas	22	63	35	2	69	25	6	2	2	5
Chihuahua	5	37	62	1	27	69	4	14	22	50
Coahuila	4	50	49	*	47	53	*	39	45	50
Colima	28	58	42	*	50	49	*	9	12	25
Durango	7	38	61	*	50	49	1	23	14	22
Federal District	37	33	26	41	29	62	10	5	13	1
Guanajuato	41	48	48	4	51	47	2	19	18	10
Guerrero	22	34	62	4	45	50	5	3	2	3
Hidalgo	39	55	28	17	48	30	22	11	14	16
Jalisco	23	43	54	3	62	36	3	13	69	7
Mexico	37	55	25	21	51	31	18	16	21	15
Michoacán	31	56	39	4	77	20	3	29	11	14
Morelos	35	74	16	10	83	11	6	29	18	14
Nayarit	17	67	32	*	38	60	2	1	5	10
Nuevo León	9	32	65	3	17	79	4	10	24	25
Oaxaca	21	19	67	14	20	56	23	4	3	6
Puebla	40	47	32	21	24	61	15	8	29	11
Querétaro	28	57	36	6	41	54	5	11	23	13
Qunitana Roo	8	17	83	*						
					NO IRRIGATION					
San Luis Potosí	13	60	37	3	60	38	2	6	6	6
Sinaloa	21	52	47	1	42	58	*	26	40	10
Sonora	6	29	69	2	28	70	2	70	73	73
Tabasco	23	40	55	5	34	61	5	*	*	*
Tamaulipas	10	32	67	*	39	61	*	48	36	14
Tlaxcala	64	56	25	19	58	13	29	3	2	5
Veracruz	27	46	49	5	64	30	6	2	*	1
Yucatán	29	40	60	*	54	35	11	*	*	5
Zacatecas	14	48	50	3	50	46	4	5	5	8
All Mexico	14	44	51	5	42	55	4	14	16	11

SOURCE: *IV Censos Agrícola-Ganadero y Ejidal, 1960: Resumen General,* from which data for calculations taken.

NOTES:
1. Includes orchards and agave plantings; croplands in following computations do not include these categories.
2. Because of rounding, combinations may not total 100.

* Less than 1%.

TABLE VI. AGRICULTURAL PRODUCTION SELECTED YEARS
In 000's of Metric Tons*

Year	Corn	Wheat	Rice	Beans	Garbanzos	Potatoes	Cotton	Sugar cane	Coffee	Oranges
1800	771	130						29#		
1877	2,731	339	15	210	11	8	25	630	8	
1895	1,827	273	12	118	14	13	20	2,688	14	
1897	2,399	194	21	140		10	26			
1907	2,128	293	33	159	34	20	48	2,500	24	38
1910	1,975	350		160			60	2,500	40	
1918	1,930	284	18	107	69		79		47	
1925	1,970	251		187			43	2,873	34	
1926	2,135	281	91	199	82	43	78	3,158	40	
1928	2,173	300	83	176	64	54	60	2,947	42	
1930	1,377	312	75	83	49	46	38	3,293	39	
1932	1,973	263	72	132	44	52	22	3,405	33	
1934	1,723	298	69	124	53	59	48	2,774	37	
1936	1,597	370	86	107	43	76	86	4,341	49	
1946	2,383	340	139	139	106	124	91	7,197	57	342
1948	2,832	477	163	210	111	128	120	9,559	53	400
1950	3,122	587	187	250	84	134	260	9,419	62	555
1952	3,202	512	151	299	83	139	265	10,730	71	534
1960	5,420	1,190	328	528	114	294	470	19,542	124	766
1962	6,015	1,432	304	680	122	341	527	19,967	134	795
1964	8,454	2,134	274	892	104	425	565	21,837	145	860
1965	8,865	2,088	333	945	101	436	593	23,079	178	863

NOTE:

Sugar, refined and semi-refined.

* The data in this table are not comparable to the production data in Table IV (Land Tenure Data).

SOURCES: *Anuario Estadístico,* various years; Alexander von Humboldt, *Political Essay on the Kingdom of New Spain;* Daniel Cosío Villegas, *Historia Moderna de México;* Matías Romero, *Mexico and the United States, 1898;* Antonio García Cubás, *Cuadro Geográfico, Estadístico, Descriptivo é Histórico.*

TABLE VII. EDUCATION AFTER 1950

	1950	1962	1965
Population, 6-14 age	6,215,070	9,084,900	10,502,000[1]
In school, 6-14 age	3,026,691	6,542,073[2]	7,262,847[2]
Number of primary schools	24,075	33,860	37,703
Urban	5,065	7,930	8,889
Rural	19,010	25,930	28,814
Number of primary teachers	71,159	138,622	162,939
Urban	44,297	90,617	106,045
Rural	26,862	48,005	56,894
No. primary teachers with degree or certificate	n.a.	66,482	103,103
Number students, grades 1-3			
Urban	1,174,820	2,337,664	3,081,796
Rural	1,278,681	2,185,906	2,393,566
Number students, grades 4-6			
Urban	497,248	1,290,254	1,333,045
Rural	70,942	291,933	382,928
Number secondary schools	455	1,345	1,540[3]
Public	219	684	802[3]
Private	236	661	738[3]
Students in secondary schools	69,402	329,287	420,830[3]
Number normal schools	68	157	176[3]
Students attending normal schools	13,698	59,975	48,952[3, 4]
Number preparatory schools	98	204	215[3]
Students in preparatory schools	17,694	61,755	67,521[3]
Number of professional schools[5]	506	960	1,038[3]
Students in higher education[6]	87,890	307,702	334,229[3]
Educational and military expenditures			
% of total on education, Federal	9.1	12.4	11.0
% of total on military, Federal	7.4	3.1	4.1
% of total on education, states	18.2	28.6	27.2

SOURCES: *Anuario Estadístico*, various years.

NOTES:

1. Author's estimate, based on *Anuario Estadístico* data.
2. In primary schools only; some in the age group were in kindergarten, and some in secondary.
3. Data for 1964; 1965 data not available at this date.
4. The decline in normal school enrolments is accounted for by the larger number of students electing teaching curricula in the universities.
5. Includes vocational, commercial, professional and special.
6. Includes normal and all other professional careers.

TABLE VIII. ROADS AND AUTOMOTIVE EQUIPMENT

(Kilometers; 1 kilometer equals 0.625 miles)

YEAR	TOTAL (cumulative)	GRADED (cumulative)	GRAVEL, ALL-WEATHER (cumulative)	PAVED (cumulative)	CARS (000's)	TRUCKS (000's)
To 1928	695	209	245	241	n.a.	n.a.
1930	1,426	629	256	541	n.a.	n.a.
1932	1,814	802	367	645	n.a.	n.a.
1934	4,260	1,786	1,291	1,183	n.a.	n.a.
1936	6,304	1,891	2,406	2,007	67.2	25.7
1938	8,463	2,035	3,424	3,004	n.a.	n.a.
1940	9,929	1,643	3,505	4,781	93.6	41.9
1942	13,526	2,250	5,194	6,082	113.4	53.5
1944	16,394	2,336	6,375	7,683	111.9	57.3
1946	18,544	2,663	7,267	8,614	120.9	71.7
1948	19,927	2,590	6,775	10,562	150.3	99.8
1950	21,422	1,865	5,972	13,585	173.1	111.3
1952	23,925	2,039	5,905	15,981	257.1	154.8
1954	26,353	2,465	6,394	17,494	273.7	193.5
1956	28,616	2,432	6,770	19,414	320.4	240.1
1958	31,967	2,334	7,328	22,305	378.9	273.7
1960*	45,089	7,398	10,332	27,369	483.1	293.4
1962	53,646	9,425	14,943	29,278	548.2	327.9
1964	57,455	6,376	16,518	34,561	687.8	364.0
1965	58,278	6,817	18,438	33,023	771.1	388.7

* Beginning in 1959 neighborhood roads were included in the total.

SOURCE: Various years of the *Anuario Estadístico*.

Index